THE

Old Farmer's Almanac

CALCULATED ON A NEW AND IMPROVED PLAN FOR THE YEAR OF OUR LORD

2004

BEING LEAP YEAR AND (UNTIL JULY 4) 228TH YEAR OF AMERICAN INDEPENDENCE

Fitted for Boston and the New England states, with special corrections and calculations to answer for all the United States.

Containing, besides the large number of Astronomical Calculations and the Farmer's Calendar for every month in the year, a variety of

New, Useful, and Entertaining Matter.

Established in 1792

by Robert B. Thomas

The goal of life is living in agreement with nature.

–Zeno, Greek philosopher (335–263 B.C.)

Cover T.M. registered in U.S. Patent Office

Copyright 2003 by Yankee Publishing Incorporated
ISSN 0078-4516

Library of Congress
Card No. 56-29681

Original wood engraving by Randy Miller

Address all editorial correspondence to: THE OLD FARMER'S ALMANAC, DUBLIN, NH 03444

Contents

The Old Farmer's Almanac • 2004

Gardener's Companion Special Sample

PAGES GC1–GC32

- Plant an Heirloom
  Flower Garden
- Mum's the Word
- All About
  Houseplants

. . . and more!

(continued on page 4)

Contents

(continued from page 2)

To Patrons

Patterns, Predictions, and Percentages

Over the past 211 years, this Almanac has contained information on a variety of topics, but it is probably best known for its predictions of the weather. It's easy to understand why: Everybody is interested in the weather. (How many times have you talked about the weather today?) And many people are genuinely fascinated by (or, we admit, skeptical of) our ability to forecast the weather with reasonable accuracy. For years, you've asked us how we do it. Now we're going to tell you.

First, we don't divine the weather by counting onion layers, measuring woolly-bear bands, or tabulating the acorns that squirrels sock away—although such phenomena may well be indicators of upcoming weather.

Neither do we guess. That would be foolhardy, and *anybody* can guess.

Our methodology for predicting the weather is scientific, state of the art, and—this may come as a surprise—not a secret. Mind you, as we have claimed for years, the formula from which it derives and which was devised by the founder of this Almanac, Robert B. Thomas, in or around 1792, is a secret and is locked in a black box here in Dublin, New Hampshire, and shall not be divulged in my lifetime. But this much I can tell you: Robert B. believed that sunspots, which are magnetic storms on the surface of the Sun, in-

fluence the weather on Earth. He didn't originate the idea; it evolved after Galileo first noted sunspots in 1610.

The notion that sunspots and other solar cycles could have a direct impact on our weather was dismissed by most of the meteorological community for years. More recently, the idea has been receiving serious consideration. For example, correlations have been found between solar activity and cooling and warming periods on Earth. Similarly, scientists now recognize that the solar constant (amount of energy that the Sun puts out) isn't constant; it varies—minutely, but not insignificantly over time.

Janice Stillman
(13th Editor since 1792)

Just as important as solar science to our formula are two other scientific disciplines: climatology, the study of prevailing weather patterns, and meteorology, the study of the atmosphere. We believe that by comparing solar patterns and historical weather conditions with current solar activity, weather trends and events can be predicted.

You'll notice that our forecasts (on pages 122–139 in this edition) emphasize temperature and precipitation

The <u>affordable</u> way to keep insects from spoiling your time outdoors!

Cool Shade and UV Protection, too!

Shown with our optional Patio Lights

Factory-Direct Prices Save You Hundreds of Dollars!

Corner Zippers Offer Easy Entry

Now Enjoy Your Deck or Patio <u>BUG-FREE!</u>
... with the SunSetter Screen Room!

Forget annoying "bug zappers" and smelly citronella candles. Now get the **best protection** from flies, mosquitoes, and other insects — day or night — with a SunSetter Screen Room. Mounted on a SunSetter Awning, this great Screen Room creates a beautiful **"outdoor room"** that guards you from insects, showers, UV rays, and scorching hot sun. **(It can be as much as 20 degrees cooler under a SunSetter!)** You'll get far more use and enjoyment out of your deck or patio, because you

control the weather — and the bugs! With sizes and colors to fit every home and decor, a SunSetter Screen Room will give you years of trouble-free service. It's backed by a full **5-Year Warranty, and a 90-Day No-Risk Money-Back Guarantee of Satisfaction.** Best of all, because you buy direct, with no middleman markups, you'll <u>save</u> <u>hundreds of dollars</u> on your Screen Room. Let us send you a complete **FREE Information Kit and Video,** without any obligation.

Good Housekeeping Promises

Awning available separately... add a Screen Room anytime! Complete protection from hot sun, showers, and insects!

- ● **Low** Factory-Direct Prices
- ● **Easy Payment Plans**
- ● **No-Risk, Money-Back Home Trial**
- ● **Superb Quality, 5-Year Warranty**

© 2003 SunSetter® Products

Call Today for a **FREE** Catalog & Video:
Toll Free: 1-800-876-8060, ext. 4194

24 hours a day, 7 days a week

☑ Yes, please send me your FREE literature and video on SunSetter Screen Rooms and Retractable Awnings.

Name _____

Address _____

City _____ State ____ Zip _____

E-mail address _____

Important: Be sure to include your e-mail to learn about specials and sales!

SunSetter, Dept. 4194, 184 Charles St., Malden, MA 02148

SunSetter®
RETRACTABLE AWNINGS

Or visit us at www.screen-room.com

deviations from averages, or normals. To determine those, we use 30-year statistical averages that are prepared by government meteorological agencies and updated every ten years. The most-recent tabulations span the period from 1970 to 2000.

All these methods enable our meteorologist, Michael Steinberg, to forecast the weather in defined regions of the United States and Canada up to 18 months in advance.

Throughout the year, we monitor the forecasts, comparing the actual weather with our predictions. (Mike never updates the forecasts.) At the end of the year, we use a complex and proprietary formula to determine our accuracy rate. When all is said and done, the results are almost always *very* close to our traditional claim of 80 percent. Weather predicting is, after all, an inexact science.

Far more predictable than the weather is the success you can have in your garden if you follow the tips and advice in our sister publication, *The Old Farmer's Almanac Gardener's Companion*. Each issue is loaded with time-tested garden wisdom, ideas, and information for gardeners of all experience levels and gardens of all sizes. See for yourself! There's a special sample edition in the back of this Almanac. It's our gift to you, with best wishes for a bountiful year.   J. S., June 2003

However, it is by our works and not our words that we would be judged. These, we hope, will sustain us in the humble though proud station we have so long held in the name of

Your obedient servant,

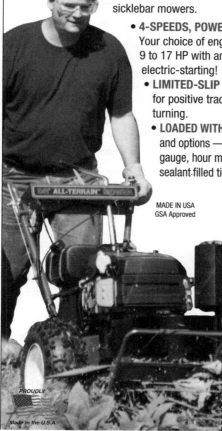

COMPILED BY CHRISTINE SCHULTZ

FORECASTS · FADS · FASHIONS · FASHIONS, AND FACTS

FASHION AND STYLE

"For years, fashion was all about copying everyone. Now it's all about customizing . . . for individual self-expression."
—Ellen Sideri, CEO, ESP Trendlab

A FACT OF LIFE

Every type of clothing will have electronic functions in ten years.

TOP THREE FASHION THEMES FOR WOMEN

■ **I Dream of Genie.** Watch for harem pants, tunics with hanging gold coins as trim and as earrings, and waists wrapped with obis and scarves in bright pinks, oranges, midnight blue, and exotic eggplant, in fabrics of silk and chiffon.

■ **Future Ancients.** Think of the Greeks and Romans: fabrics draped over one shoulder and sandals wrapped high up the calf.

■ **Scuba Girl.** The wet look, in neopreen and spongy rubberized fabrics once reserved for wet suits, is the latest in sport fashions. No longer limited to black bodysuits, we'll see rubberized floral-print minidresses, tunics, leggings, and pants. In addition, expect lots of zippers, playful faux logos, and blocks of color in fruity hues.

IN/OUT FOR WOMEN

1. Colorful customized handbags/Designer bags with clunky hardware

2. Metallic-silver and bronzed-gold fabrics/Basic black

3. Canvas and cargo pants/High-fashion denim

TOP THREE FASHION THEMES FOR MEN

■ **Retro Warrior.** This look is decidedly not uniform, running from ammunition belts that clench overcoats closed to nostalgic World War II styles of the 1940s such as Eisenhower jackets and camouflage suits.

■ **Man and Machine.** Gear and gadgets set the tone, and the look is motorcycle jackets; yellow-tinted architecture, or "statement," glasses; Teflon-enhanced fabrics; and techno garments like the Scott eVest, a windbreaker with 22 pockets for all your stuff: phone, organizer, pager, CD player—you-name-it.

■ **Extreme Sports.** Think surfing, scuba diving, tennis, and golf attire.

IN/OUT FOR MEN

1. Body-fitting T-shirts/Oversize T-shirts

2. Fabric colors in pink-tinted blues, pumpkin orange, yellowish greens/Neutral colors

3. Snug jackets with zippered seams/Boxy suitcoats

CONTINUED

You can buy this iron for $100.
Or you can have it free.

Try my amazing 8-lb. vacuum free of charge for 30 days, and my $100 Cordless Iron is your gift.

HI, I'M DAVID ORECK. I WANT YOU TO CLEAN YOUR HOME FOR A MONTH ON ME ABSOLUTELY FREE. THERE'S NOTHING TO BUY, EVEN THE SHIPPING IS FREE! My next generation Oreck XL® with the Violet Blue Dirt Search® is a giant step forward in American ingenuity. At barely 8 lbs., it takes the hard work out of house work. In fact, it has so many work-saving features you'll wonder why all vacuums aren't this thoroughly thought out. It features MicroSweep,™ which lets you pick up sand off bare floors. It adjusts to every thickness of carpet, and automatically goes from carpets to bare floors. To really clean under beds and furniture, it lays flat. Our exclusive Helping Hand® Handle eliminates stress and strain on your wrist, forearm and elbow. Thanks to its top-fill design, it won't spew a cloud of dust every time you turn it on. Plus, my Oreck XL is hypo-allergenic, trapping 99.9% of all harmful allergens as small as 1/250th the width of a human hair. And odds are you'd go through three other vacuums in the time you own one 8-lb. Oreck XL.

WITH ORECK, YOU GET A COMPLETE SYSTEM. For above-the-floor cleaning, I'll give you my $165 Super Compact Canister, with 8 attachments, absolutely free with purchase of an Oreck XL Hand held, or shoulder worn, this little dynamo is great for those hard-to-reach places, like ceilings, blinds, lampshades, and book shelves.

IF YOU DON'T LOVE MY VACUUM, DON'T KEEP IT. BUT KEEP THE $100 IRON. My Oreck Cord Free Speed Iron® is a great work saver. It cuts ironing time in half. And it's yours with no strings attached. Why do I give away gifts? It's simple. 9 out of 10 people who try an Oreck, buy an Oreck. So hurry, this offer is limited.

My 8-lb. Oreck XL˚ is hotel proven, built to last twice as long and comes with this free Super Compact Canister.

Strong Enough To Pick Up A 16-lb. Bowling Ball.™

©2003 ORECK HOLDINGS, LLC. All Rights Reserved. All word marks, logos, product configurations and registered trademarks are owned and used under the authority of Oreck Holdings, LLC.

PBH6R

Free Shipping. Try Before You Buy.

1-800-281-6420 ext. CC656

Or mail in this coupon today or visit oreck.com   CC656

☐ Yes, please call me to arrange a free 30-day trial of the Oreck XL® and send me a $100 Oreck Cord Free Speed Iron® just for trying the XL. I understand I will receive the Super Compact Canister free with purchase and that shipping (a $29.95 value) is free.

☐ Send me a free information kit on the amazing 8-lb. Oreck XL.

☐ Include details of Oreck's 12-month Interest Free Payment Plan.

Name_____

Address_____

City_____ State_____ Zip_____

Tel (____)_____ e-mail_____
    optional

ORECK
Nothing gets by an Oreck.®
Oreck Direct, LLC 100 Plantation Road, New Orleans, LA 70123

ON THE HOME FRONT

"The home is the active center.... The overall effect [is] a more playful look."

–Sharon Graubard, creative director and V.P., ESP Trendlab

CONSUMER TASTES & TRENDS • 2004

HERE A KITCHEN, THERE A KITCHEN

The latest trend in home design is the satellite kitchen (often called a morning bar) in master bedrooms, family rooms, and outdoor patios. Features include sinks, espresso machines, wine safes, refrigerators, cabinets, and countertops.

THE DEFINITIVE DISHWASHER

Who wouldn't want the Audine? Invented and patented (April 2002) by Harold DeHart in Durham, North Carolina, this is a "dining table with integral dishwasher." After eating, you open the doors of your dinner table, lift up the rack, insert your dirty dishes, close the doors, and start the wash cycle. When you are ready for your next meal, clean dishes are already handy. DeHart expects the Audine (named for "automatic dining") to be in homes within five years.

THE WHEEL-LESS WELCOME WAGON

The new neighborly "how-do-you-do" trend involves having communities connected by closed-circuit-like television channels. You move in, post your family's photo so that everyone knows you've arrived, and instantly you have information about schools, babysitters, and neighbors.

FASHIONS IN FURNISHINGS

This year, the buzzword is *eclectic*. The mix won't always match, but here's what works:

■ **Combining formal mid-1800s antiques** (Chippendale, Queen Anne) **with traditional 1950s furniture** (womb chairs) **and offbeat ethnic pieces.**

■ **Mixing rustic artisan materials** (lots of leather and handwoven fibers, old doors used as headboards for king-size beds) **with sleek modern furniture and fun fixtures** (think floor lamp shaped as a cactus).

■ **Lots more low, lounge-y furniture, and furniture that serves dual purposes** (a modular chair that folds into a daybed).

THE CANADIAN PERSPECTIVE

Canadians are also mixing it up, with 18th-century antiques keeping company with 1960s shag rugs and sleek modern furniture. Other trends include:

■ **"Blobism"** (think Karim Rashid's bubblegum blob couch)

■ **Hotel chic** (luxury fabrics and rich hues)

■ **Modern metallics** combined with dark woods (walnut, mahogany, teak)

■ **Bold 1960s colors** like hot pink and lime green

CONTINUED

TEMPUR-PEDIC CELEBRATING 10 YEARS OF EXCELLENCE · 1993-2003

Furniture components not included

Nesting.

A perfect refuge from the cares of the day.

Our incredible Weightless Comfort™ mattress must be *felt* to be believed. Not only does its uncanny VISCOELASTIC SLEEP SURFACE *react* to your bodyshape, bodyweight, <u>bodyheat</u>, it also can absorb *enormous* pressure without uncomfortably pressing back!

Tempur-Pedic's sleep technology is light years ahead of outdated inner-spring, air, and water bed standards. We've attracted countless rave press reviews and television coverage. Plus...well over 25,000 medical professionals worldwide recommend us to their patients—an enviable record of success.

The reason for Tempur-Pedic's meteoric rise in popularity is simple...

The heavy pads that cover most mattresses are necessary to keep their "insides" from poking out—or leaking out. Yet they create a "hammock" effect that can actually *cause* painful pressure points. Inside our high-tech bed, billions of micro memory cells function as molecular springs that contour precisely to your body.

Tempur-Pedic's sleep scientists used NASA's early anti-G-force research to invent TEMPUR® pressure-relieving material™ a revolutionary new kind of bedding that's the wave of the future!

Our bed utilizes *natural* principles of physics—nothing mechanical or electrical. No motors, switches, valves, air pumps, or water heaters. It can't break, leak, short-circuit, or stop working. It needs no rotating, turning, flipping.

No wonder, 3 out of 4 Tempur-Pedic owners go out of their way to recommend our Swedish Sleep System® to close friends and rela-tives. Moreover, 88% of "problem sleepers" report real improvement!

Please return the coupon, without the least obligation, for a FREE DEMONSTRATION KIT. Better yet, phone or send us a fax.

CERTIFIED SPACE TECHNOLOGY

THE <u>ONLY</u> MATTRESS
RECOGNIZED BY NASA
AND CERTIFIED BY THE
SPACE FOUNDATION ✦

Proud Sponsor of

NATIONAL SLEEP 2003 AWARENESS WEEK

**FREE SAMPLE
FREE VIDEO/FREE INFO**
Everything you need to know about the
high-tech bed that's changing the way the
world sleeps! Free Demo Kit also includes a
FREE IN-HOME TRYOUT CERTIFICATE.

*YOURS FOR
THE ASKING!*

1-888-702-8557
Call toll-free or fax 1-866-795-9367

Name

Address

City/State/Zip

Phone (optional)

✚ **TEMPUR**-PEDIC®
PRESSURE RELIEVING
SWEDISH MATTRESSES AND PILLOWS

IN THE GARDEN

"People are re-creating their outdoor garden rooms to suit the family's changing lifestyle."

–Bruce Butterfield, research director,
National Gardening Association

A FACT OF LIFE

Gardeners who don't have time to compost their own stew of organic matter are buying compost tea at garden-center vending carts called SoilSoup Kitchens.

PLANT-BY-NUMBER GARDENS

With more homeowners time-challenged to dress up their landscapes, the latest trend—garden branding—is thriving. You choose a palette of colors and prearranged plants from companies like Proven Winners or Simply Beautiful. Your garden-in-a-box comes complete with a plant-by-number design sheet to help you properly place your monochromatic garden or prairie perennials.

IN/OUT

1. **Wild anything-goes beds**/Straight brigades of bulbs

2. **Bold, monochromatic tone-on-tone colors in flowers, garden furniture, and trellises**/Pastels

3. **Tall, organic meadow grasses and plants that attract wildlife**/Traditional, chemical-rich lawns

4. **Flowering shrubs**/Boring bushes

5. **Xeriscapes, rock gardens, fishponds**/Water-needy gardens

EXOTIC SPECIMENS

The latest horticultural craze, coming out of South Florida, is giant palms (with giant prices): A 20-foot-tall Borassus palm is going for $10,000 (crane cost not included), and a 40-pound coco-de-mer seed (just one seed) is selling for $800. Take your pick from the 2,800 known palm species: enormous black-matted sugar palms, blue-leafed Bismarckians, and towering talipots—they're all hot.

GOT-TO-HAVE GARDEN ACCESSORIES

- **Antique toy sailboats** to float in backyard ponds

- **Antique lawn sprinklers** in figural shapes (cowboy with a lasso that spins around his body)

- **Garden gnomes**

- **Architectural salvage,** especially drainpipes from old buildings, and old factory and locomotive gears

- **Millstones,** original and reproduction, from old grain-grinding mills

THE CANADIAN PERSPECTIVE

In response to water shortages, the city of Vancouver is offering subsidized rain barrels to residents to catch rain for lawns and gardens. During peak summer months, each barrel is expected to save some 1,300 gallons of water.

CONTINUED

HOT COLLECTIBLES

"Kitsch is not a dirty word anymore."

–Terry Kovel, coauthor,
Kovels' Antiques & Collectibles Price List 2003

A FACT OF LIFE

Art pottery is the collectible of the century. Prices are expected to continue to rise for Roseville, Hampshire, and Weller, but Marblehead and Grueby pottery are the most desirable.

KITSCHY KEEPSAKES

Got the itch for collecting kitsch? Here are the best bets:

- ■ **Black-velvet Elvis paintings**
- ■ **Gravel art**
- ■ **Niagara Falls paperweights**
- ■ **Hawaiian tiki glasses**
- ■ **Shell-decorated picture frames**
- **Star Wars cookie jars**
- **Plastic salt and pepper shakers** in the shape of barnyard animals wearing overalls

STILL GOING

America's most collected brand of china is still Fiestaware. Discontinued Fiestaware items are almost too hot to handle: sectional relish tray, $300 to $400; turquoise onion-soup bowl, $8,800; two mixing bowl lids (yes, just the lids), a whopping $35,000.

MAKING NEWS

Reflecting on current events, experts expect that these will be big in the coming year:

- **War toys and patriotic memorabilia**
- ■ **Space collectibles** from the *Apollo* Moon-landings
- ■ **Religious objects,** especially irreverent items (such as the Jesus Christ action figure)

HIGH TIMES FOR HANDIWORK

With people suddenly realizing how long it takes to handsew a seam, women's antique piecework has become the rage. Sought-after items include handstitched samplers, embroidery, quilts, and handwoven undergarments. Prices can range from $800 to $2,800 or more.

CATCH 'EM IF YOU CAN

Experts tell us that the markets for these items are heating up:

- **Old paper beer bags** with advertising logos
- ■ **Strips of pictures** of strangers in photo booths from the past
- **Microphones** from the 1930s through the 1950s
- **Cowboy hats** worn by real cowboys
- ■ **Farm tools,** such as fencing grips, hatchets, and staple pullers
- ■ **Vintage mystery novels** by Agatha Christie, Arthur Conan Doyle, and Raymond Chandler

16

CONTINUED

ON THE FARM

"Excessive groundwater pumping presents special problems for farmers. As the water table drops, it takes substantially more energy to get the water to the surface. This increase in costs has already led to the conversion from irrigation to dry-land farming."

–Robert Glennon, author of *Water Follies: Groundwater Pumping and the Fate of America's Fresh Waters*

WHAT WILL THEY THINK OF NEXT?

■ **The Featherless Chicken.** "Naked chickens," broilers without plumage, have less body fat and so are being promoted as more healthful by advocates. Critics are squawking about animal integrity, saying that a chicken in a farmyard should not look identical to a plucked chicken in a fridge.

■ **The Tearless Onion.** Scientists are fine-tuning the onion enzyme that causes tears. The new onion won't make you weep when you cut it.

■ **The Heatless Jalapeño.** Called "Fooled You Jalapeño," this red-hot pepper looks like the real thing but is without the sting.

WHAT'S NEW IN AGRICULTURE

■ **The Almighty Alfalfa.** Now used both as livestock feed and biofuel, alfalfa will be used to produce biodegradable plastic.

■ **The Secret Life of Soybeans.** Already used in more than 350 commercial products (imitation bacon, soy milk, newspaper ink, tape), the humble bean is a miracle plant. Now soy diesel, which can fuel tractor engines without the use of sulfur as an air pollutant, may be its next big market.

■ **Mystery Oil.** For years, oat has been all about bran, but now its oil has been found to be rich in polar fats (thought to help battle cognitive decline and to lower body fat) and may soon appear in margarines, cookies, salad dressings, and frozen dinners.

■ **The Big O.** Organic farming has hit the big time. Annual worldwide markets are valued at $22 billion, with $8.8 billion spent yearly in the United States.

■ **The New Red Meat.** Watch for bison to catch on as the new healthy alternative to beef.

THE CANADIAN PERSPECTIVE

More than a third of Canada's farmers who are 55 years or older are fast moving toward retirement. Those who have small farms (grossing under $100,000 annually) are being bought out by farmers under the age of 35 who are running large farms (grossing over $250,000 annually). As a result, Statistics Canada foresees a definite trend toward industrialized farming in the next decade.

CONTINUED

Every month somebody wins!
WIN A FREE
RASCAL!®

ENTER TODAY!
You may be NEXT!

Monthly Drawings!
Up to 12 chances to win!

These lucky winners WON Free Scooters in our Monthly Sweepstakes.

Dennis Arnquist

Annie Campbell

No-Obligation and No Purchase Necessary!

Medicare or Private Insurance may provide a new Rascal at little or no cost to you. So call or return the coupon for full details.

The All-New Rascals are here...and now you can win one...FREE!

The All-New 20th Anniversary Rascals are packed with great features including a New lighting package...stylish New look...and New cushioned swivel seats for a comfortable ride.

Call the number below to be entered instantly or return the coupon. We'll enter you for up to 12 chances to win a new FREE Rascal this year! The sooner you enter the more chances you'll have to win!

ALL-NEW UltraLite Models

They fold flat for easy transport and storage!
Ask about them when you call to enter!

To enter the sweepstakes, call TODAY...TOLL FREE
1-800-662-4548 (EXT. 9680)
or return the coupon!

☑ **YES!** Enter me in the Rascal Sweepstakes, and send me a FREE Rascal Catalog, UltraLite Brochure and Medicare Insurance Information. Also include my Special Introductory Offer!

Name _____

Address _____

City _____

State _____ Zip Code _____

Phone ☐☐☐ ☐☐☐ ☐☐☐☐

Don't forget to include your phone number so we may contact you if you win!
Electric Mobility, One Mobility Plaza, Dept. 9680, Sewell, NJ 08080

FOOD FADS

"Throughout this decade, it will be packaging innovation, more than the food or beverage itself, that truly defines convenience to customers."

–Bob Messenger, publisher of the food & beverage industry's *Food Trends Newsletter*

THE NEW TAKEOUT: CUP-HOLDER CUISINE

With snacks now sold as travel-mug meals (soup in a cup, breakfast in a bowl), Americans are eating smaller portions in five or six meals a day instead of three. To satisfy cravings, around-the-clock storefront-size vending machines, called Shop 2000, are debuting around the country, offering snacks like chicken sandwiches and bottles of milk.

THE NEXT BIG CHEESE: CHOCOLATE

How sweet it is! Exotic chocolates are the new affordable luxury. Today, highbred candy bars and bonbons (Guittard, Jamieson's, Omanhene, Scharffen Berger) are sampled at chocolate-tasting events, with tasters challenged to identify 88-percent-pure cocoa-bean pedigrees from the Ivory Coast, Ghana, Ecuador, and Mexico.

MORE NEW TRENDS

- **The New Ketchup:** Salsa
- **The New Coffee:** Green tea
- **The New Bar Drink:** Old-style cocktails dressed up with newfangled garnishes (vodka martinis topped with miniature electric-blue ice pops)
- **The New Restaurant Chic:** Fondue dipping and sushi bars
- **The New Power Lunch:** Hearty barbecue or a simple sandwich

A TRULY SUPER MARKET

Grocery-store items will soon be encoded with radio-frequency identification (RFID) tags. At the checkout, the items in your automated shopping cart will instantly be tabulated and the cost deducted from your debit card—without a wait. At home, your high-tech kitchen not only will take inventory of your new groceries but will communicate with the virtual brain in your frozen pizza to ensure the correct cooking time.

FOOD AS MEDICINE

Wellness foods, called nutraceuticals, will be the hottest food category in the next five years. Powdered shark fin, vitamins, and herbs will be added to foods reputed to cure the sick, put muscles on the weak, and take pounds off the obese. Experts see no end in sight: Think mineral-enriched ice cream, omega-3-enhanced burgers, and St. John's-wort in breakfast cereal.

CONTINUED

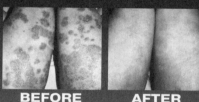

THE FUN FACTOR

"The whole superhero thing has moved from just collecting action figures to role-play."

–"The Toy Guy," Chris Byrne, on the popularity of Electronic Hulk Hands and Spider-Man's Web Blaster gloves

THE NAKED TRUTH

Don't look now, but nudist tourism is at an all-time high, with membership in the American Association for Nude Recreation having grown 20 percent over the last decade. Central Florida is the top destination, but the trend (and luxury resorts that invite it) is expanding to Atlanta and other locales. Who's doing stuff in the buff? Affluent trend-setters over 30.

FEELING SICK? GO AWAY!

The next prescription your doctor gives you may include a travel guide. Medical tourism is a way to make the most of your time off for a hospital visit by scheduling your stay in a hospital at a vacation destination and including time for taking in the sights after recuperating. Look for travel councils to join with medical centers to promote hospitals with hospitality.

SENIOR SPORTS

Seniors are participating in a wider range of physical activities (tai chi, yoga, Pilates, luge, dogsledding). Many seniors are in softball and soccer leagues, and they're having to compete with the kids for field time.

OUR MOST POPULAR PASTIMES

1. Watching TV
2. On-line computing
3. Video games

PASTIMES GAINING IN POPULARITY

■ **Turkey hunting.** With the comeback of the wild turkey—up to an estimated 5.6 million from only 30,000 in the early 1900s—it's the fastest-growing form of hunting in America.

■ **Needlepoint.** Up to 38 million women are pulling yarn these days, says the Craft Yarn Council of America.

■ **Bargain hunting.** More Americans flock to flea markets than to baseball games, concerts, or golf courses.

ULTIMATE ADVENTURE

Bungee jumping is now passé for the outdoor crowd. The latest adventure sport is canyoneering, which has come to the United States by way of Switzerland, New Zealand, and Australia. The sport involves hiking down into canyons and then swimming, climbing, and wiggling your way past any obstacles you encounter.

22

CONTINUED ON PAGE 26

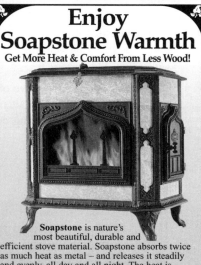

TO YOUR HEALTH

"Research scientists are on track to alter the biological rate of aging. We think it's going to happen in our lifetime."

–Jay Olshansky, epidemiology professor, University of Illinois in Chicago

A FACT OF LIFE

Beer is good for you; the silicon in it is good for bone density.

WHAT WILL THEY THINK OF NEXT?

■ **Super Soap.** Colgate-Palmolive is testing a shower gel that won't rinse off but instead will form a microbe-thin shield to protect your skin from bacteria and other foul goo.

■ **Spa Dentistry.** It's the wave of the future. Think aromatherapy; foot, neck, and hand massage; a vibrating chair; movies (via virtual-reality glasses); access to the Web on a screen wired to the ceiling; concierge services; and, oh yeah, clean teeth.

SIGNS OF THE TIMES

■ Fitness consultants who charge from $10 to $100 per month to contact clients by e-mail, phone, and wireless devices to coach them or check that they've done their workout.

■ People trading in the treadmill, stationary biking, and step aerobics for the real things—trekking, biking, and snowshoeing.

DEMOGRAPHICA

OUR NEW TACO NATION

Hispanics' buying power in the United States has increased twice as fast as that of the overall population, rising to $300 billion. With their numbers expected to reach 56.3 million residents by 2025, watch for Hispanic and particularly Mexican tastes to seep into mainstream America. Look for

■ **taco and tamale stands to become the hot-dog stands of the 21st century.**

■ **salsa rhythms and other latino beats to be the new rock and roll.**

■ **more Spanish words and phrases to find entry into our dictionaries.**

A CENTURY OF CHANGE

THAT WAS THEN . . .

The average American at the start of the 20th century was a man under age 23, who rented a house in the country with five or more people.

THIS IS NOW . . .

The average American at the start of the 21st century is a woman over age 35, who owns her own home in the city and lives alone or with one other person.

CONTINUED

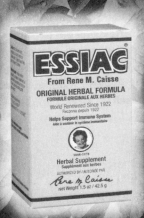

PET NEWS

"I see this in our future: old-age homes for animals."

–Marie Davis, executive director, Peggy Adams Rescue League,
West Palm Beach, Florida

A FACT OF LIFE

Public acceptance of pet cloning will increase, and technology will help lower the cost (now at $10,000 per cat and $20,000 per dog).

PETS AT WORK

Pets are showing up at work at an increasing rate, and companies are offering them—and their owners—pet benefits. Many companies allow employees to take days off to care for sick pets and for pet bereavement. Others provide pet health insurance and pay for petsitters when employees are out of town on business. Those workers who don't have pet-friendly employers can check up on Fido from their desks via Webcams.

TOP TRENDS IN PET GIFTS

■ **Luxurious fabrics** (faux lambskin bedding with an internal warmer)

■ **Designer pet perfumes**

■ **A device (Bowlingual)** that helps you interpret what your dog is saying

■ **Electric toothbrushes and mouthwash** for dogs

SKY NEWS & VIEWS

"The greatest development of the 21st century will be the transcendence of a global or planetary patriotism above nationalism." –futurist Tad Daley

A FACT OF LIFE

Sales of computerized Moon maps and atlases, lunar-phase photos, and Japanese telescopes and accessories for Moon observation have reached numbers not seen since the 1950s and '60s.

COMING TO A LAUNCHPAD NEAR YOU

The door to space tourism is expected to open in this decade. The first private team to invent a rocket that can safely carry three tourists out of Earth's atmosphere (62.5 miles) and back, twice in two weeks, on or before January 1, 2005, will win the $10 million XPrize, offered by the XPrize Foundation in St. Louis, Missouri. Some two dozen teams are in the running (including two from Canada and 15 from the United States). "Really it's just a 15-minute roller-coaster ride," says XPrize Director of Operations Ken Davidian, "that allows you to see black space and the curve of Earth, and experience weightlessness for two to four minutes."

CONTINUED

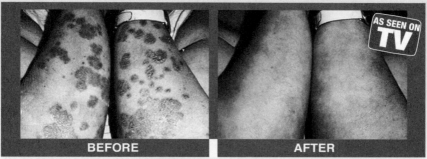

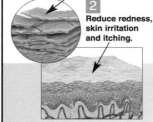

OUR MOOD

"I wouldn't be surprised to see a visceral generational revolt in the next few years."

–Geoffrey Gilmore, director, Sundance
Film Festival, on the tendency of independent films
to forecast trends in mainstream culture

SIGNS OF THE TIMES

■ **Artificial intelligence priests** (robots) in the confessional

■ **Cosmetic surgery gift certificates**

■ **Competitive solitaire**

■ **Corporate consultants** who are paid $1,000 to evaluate how good a dad a man's family thinks he is

THE UNITED STATES: A NATION AT THE CROSSROADS

In response to a growing mistrust of many institutions that form the foundation of our society, America has been undergoing an identity crisis. We have become a re-nation, reinventing ourselves in every manner possible (remodeling, regifting, recycling, reusing, refashioning, renewing). We have sought safe haven in our nostalgic past, our homes, our gardens, our machines, and ourselves.

"Maybe we're living in the past because we feel all freaked out about the future," commented columnist Joel Stein. Where we used to draw sharp lines and make clear categories, we are now a blender nation mixing it all up. Animals have human traits and vice versa, our cars are our clubhouses, the outdoors has come into our homes, we're dressing our furniture with the fabrics we also wear, we're mixing our scientific facts with our spiritual notions, and we're combining academic disciplines with new hybrid branches of study.

"We have one foot in the past, one in the future," says Ellen Sideri of ESP Trendlab. "We're going to see a lot of innovation over the next few years, and I believe that something good is going to come out of it."

With the end of major combat operations in Iraq and Afghanistan, perhaps the process has already begun and we are on the path to global peace and prosperity.

THE CANADIAN PERSPECTIVE

Polls show that Canadians' optimism for the future has reached its lowest point in two decades. Though their overall personal finances have remained steady or gotten better, and though they report increased sexual activity, citizens are still feeling unsettled about the healthcare system, questionable corporate practices, the economy, and the state of education. □□

SO WHAT ELSE IS NEW?

For more statistics, data, and other colorful details of our life and times, go to
www.almanac.com and click on **Article Links 2004.**

Best Fishing Days

The best fishing times are when the ocean tides are restless before their turn and in the first hour of ebbing. All fish in all waters, salt and fresh, feed most heavily at those times.

The best temperatures for different fish species vary widely, of course, and are important mainly if you are going to have your own fishpond. The best temperatures for brook trout are 45° to 65°F. Brown trout and rainbow trout are more tolerant of higher temperatures. Smallmouth black bass do best in cool water. Horned pout take any temperature.

Most of us go fishing when we can get time off, not because it is the best time. But there *are* best times, according to fishing lore:

■ One hour before and one hour after high tides, and one hour before and one hour after low tides. (The times of high tides for Boston are given on pages 44–70 and corrected for your locality on pages 168–169. Inland, the times for high tides correspond with the times the Moon is due south. Low tides are halfway between high tides.)

■ During the "morning rise" (after sunup for a spell) and the "evening rise" (just before sundown and the hour or so after).

■ When the barometer is steady or on the rise. (But, of course, even in a three-day driving northeaster, the fish aren't going to give up feeding. Their hunger clock keeps right on working, and the smart fisherman will find just the right bait.)

■ When there is a hatch of flies—caddis flies or mayflies, commonly. (The fisherman will have to match *his* fly with the hatching flies or go fishless.)

■ When the breeze is from a westerly quarter rather than from the north or east.

■ When the water is still or rippled, rather than during a wind.

■ Starting on the day the Moon is new and continuing through the day it is full.

Moon Between New and Full

- January 1–7
- January 21–February 6
- February 20–March 6
- March 20–April 5
- April 19–May 4
- May 19–June 3
- June 17–July 2
- July 17–31
- August 15–29
- September 14–28
- October 13–27
- November 12–26
- December 11–26

What People Fish For (freshwater)

Bass	35%
Trout	18%
Catfish	11%
All species	9%
Bream	6%
Crapple	6%
Carp/muskie/panfish/ pike/shad/steelhead/ striper	5%
Walleye	5%
Perch	3%
Salmon	2%

–courtesy American Sportfishing Association

THE 2004 EDITION OF

The Old Farmer's Almanac

Established in 1792 and published every year thereafter

ROBERT B. THOMAS (1766–1846), *Founder*

YANKEE PUBLISHING INC.

EDITORIAL, ADVERTISING, AND PUBLISHING OFFICES
P.O. Box 520, 1121 Main Street, Dublin, NH 03444
Phone: 603-563-8111 • Fax: 603-563-8252

EDITOR IN CHIEF: Judson D. Hale Sr.
EDITOR *(13th since 1792)*: Janice Stillman
ART DIRECTOR: Margo Letourneau
SENIOR EDITOR: Mare-Anne Jarvela
COPY EDITOR: Jack Burnett
SENIOR ASSOCIATE EDITOR: Heidi Stonehill
RESEARCH EDITOR: Martie Majoros
ASSISTANT EDITOR: Sarah Perreault
ASTROLOGER: Celeste Longacre
ASTRONOMER: George Greenstein
WEATHER PROGNOSTICATOR: Michael A. Steinberg
WEATHER GRAPHICS AND CONSULTATION:
Accu-Weather, Inc.
CONTRIBUTING EDITORS: Bob Berman, *Astronomy;*
Castle Freeman Jr., *Farmer's Calendar*

PRODUCTION DIRECTOR: Susan Gross
PRODUCTION MANAGER: David Ziarnowski
SENIOR PRODUCTION ARTISTS: Lucille Rines,
Rachel Kipka, Nathaniel Stout
ADVERTISING PRODUCTION ARTIST: Janet Calhoun

WEB SITE: WWW.ALMANAC.COM

CREATIVE DIRECTOR, ON-LINE: Stephen O. Muskie
INTERNET DESIGN COORDINATOR: Lisa Traffie

CONTACT US

We welcome your questions and comments about articles in and topics for this periodical. Mail all editorial correspondence to Editor, The Old Farmer's Almanac, P.O. Box 520, Dublin, NH 03444-0520; fax us at 603-563-8252; or send e-mail to us at almanac@yankeepub.com. The Old Farmer's Almanac can not accept responsibility for unsolicited manuscripts and will not respond to any manuscripts that do not include a stamped and addressed return envelope.

OUR CONTRIBUTORS

Bob Berman, our astronomy editor, is the director of Overlook Observatory in Woodstock and Storm King Observatory in Cornwall, both in New York. In 1976, he founded the Catskill Astronomical Society. Bob will go a long way for a good look at the sky: He has led many aurora and eclipse expeditions, venturing as far as the Arctic and Antarctic.

Castle Freeman Jr., who lives in southern Vermont, has been writing the Almanac's "Farmer's Calendar" essays for more than 20 years. The essays come out of his longtime interest in wildlife and the outdoors, gardening, history, and the life of rural New England. His latest book is *My Life and Adventures* (St. Martin's Press, 2002).

George Greenstein, Ph.D., who has been the Almanac's astronomer for more than 25 years, is the Sidney Dillon Professor of Astronomy at Amherst College in Amherst, Massachusetts. His research has centered on cosmology, pulsars, and other areas of theoretical astrophysics, and on the mysteries of quantum mechanics. He has written three books and many magazine articles on science for the general public.

Celeste Longacre, our astrologer, often refers to astrology as "the world's second-oldest profession." A New Hampshire native, she has been a practicing astrologer for 25 years: "It is a study of timing, and timing is everything." Her book, *Love Signs* (Sweet Fern Publications, 1999), is available on her Web site, www.yourlovesigns.com.

Michael Steinberg, our meteorologist, has been forecasting weather for the Almanac since 1996. In addition to having college degrees in atmospheric science and meteorology, he brings a lifetime of experience to the task: He began making weather predictions when he attended the only high school in the world with weather Teletypes and radar.

Hydrogen Peroxide Can Heal What?

(SPECIAL) – Medical science has discovered that hydrogen peroxide is more than just a disinfectant, it's an amazing healer. Many doctors are using hydrogen peroxide to treat a wide variety of serious ailments such as: **heart problems, clogged arteries, chest pain, allergies, asthma, migraine headaches, vascular headaches, cluster headaches, yeast infections, type II diabetes, emphysema, chronic pain syndromes, and more**.

Average consumers are also discovering that hydrogen peroxide has tons of health, beauty and household uses. A new handbook called *"The Amazing Health and Household Uses of Hydrogen Peroxide"* is now available to the general public. It shows you home remedies using diluted hydrogen peroxide and how to mix it with ordinary household items like baking soda, lemon, vinegar and salt to help:

• Soothe ARTHRITIS PAIN
• Make SORE THROATS feel better
• Ease the pain of BEE STINGS and INSECT BITES
• Treat ATHLETE'S FOOT
• Ease the PAIN OF RHEUMATISM
• Clear up FUNGUS and MINOR INFECTIONS
• Help treat minor BURNS
• Treat BRUISES and RASHES
• Soothe ACHING MUSCLES, JOINTS & SORE FEET

Hydrogen peroxide is truly amazing. Scientists have found it is involved in virtually all of life's vital processes. It stimulates the immune system, helps your body fight off viruses, parasites and bacteria. It also regulates hormones and is involved in the production of energy in the body's cells. That's just a few of the amazing things it does.

It's also a great alternative to harsh toxic chemicals and cleaners around the house. *"The Amazing Health and Household Uses of Hydrogen Peroxide"* also shows you how to make easy peroxide recipes for:
• A powerful bleaching formula for formica

• A fantastic homemade scouring powder
• The perfect drain cleaner for clogged drains
• A dishwasher detergent that makes dishes gleam
• An oven cleaner that eliminates elbow grease
• A great rust remover formula
• A tile cleaner that works like magic
• A little known formula that really cleans old porous tubs
• A solution to help house and garden plants flourish
• Use this formula to clean your pets
• This spray keeps a leftover salad fresher
• Ever wonder what happens to meats and fish before you bring them home? Here's a safety-wash for meat and fish
• A spray that's great for sprouting seeds
• Here's a sanitizing vegetable soak
• A denture soak that works great
• A tooth whitener that makes teeth sparkle
• A super polish for copper and brass
• A spot lifter for coffee, tea and wine stains

You'll learn all this and more in this remarkable book. In addition, you also get an extensive list of qualified doctors across the United States and even some in Canada who regularly use hydrogen peroxide in their practices to treat serious ailments.

Right now you can receive a special press run of *"The Amazing Health and Household Uses of Hydrogen Peroxide"* for only $8.95 plus $1.00 postage and handling. You must be completely satisfied, or simply return it in 90 days for a <u>full refund</u>.

HERE'S HOW TO ORDER: Simply PRINT your name and address and the words "Hydrogen Peroxide" on a piece of paper and mail it along with a check or money order for only $9.95 to: THE LEADER CO., INC., Publishing Division, Dept. HP729, P.O. Box 8347, Canton, OH 44711. VISA or MasterCard send card number and expiration date. Act now. Orders are fulfilled on a first come, first served basis. © 2003 The Leader Co., Inc.

THE 2004 EDITION OF

The Old Farmer's Almanac
Established in 1792 and published every year thereafter

ROBERT B. THOMAS (1766–1846), *Founder*

YANKEE PUBLISHING INC.
P.O. Box 520, 1121 Main Street, Dublin, NH 03444
Phone: 603-563-8111 • Fax: 603-563-8252

GROUP PUBLISHER: John Pierce
PUBLISHER *(23rd since 1792):* Sherin Wight
DIRECT RETAIL SALES MANAGER: Cindy Schlosser
DIRECT RETAIL SALES ASSISTANT: Stacey Korpi
MAIL-ORDER MARKETING MANAGER: Susan Way
MAIL-ORDER/SUBSCRIPTION COORDINATOR: Priscilla Gagnon

ADVERTISING MARKETING REPRESENTATIVES
General and Mail-Order Advertising

Classified Advertising: Gallagher Group
Phone: 203-263-7171 • Fax: 203-263-7174

Midwest & South: Gallagher Group
Phone: 203-263-7171 • Fax: 203-263-7174

Northeast & West: Robert Bernbach
Phone: 914-769-0051 • Fax: 914-769-0691

FOR RETAIL SALES
Contact Cindy Schlosser, 800-729-9265, ext. 126,
or Stacey Korpi, ext. 160.

The Old Farmer's Almanac publications are available at special discounts for bulk purchases for sales promotions or premiums. Contact MeadWestvaco, 800-333-1125.

SUBSCRIBE TO THIS ALMANAC
Subscription rate: 3 years, $15
Choose your region: • National • Western
• Southern • Canadian
Clearly indicate your region with your order.

Payment: Send check or money order (in U.S. funds drawn on a U.S. bank); we also accept Visa, Master-Card, American Express, and Discover/NOVUS
By mail: See address above
Phone: Toll-free at 800-895-9265, ext. 220
E-mail: customerservice@yankeepub.com

See our ad on page 196 for more details.

Jamie Trowbridge, *President;* Judson D. Hale Sr., John Pierce, *Senior Vice Presidents;* Jody Bugbee, Judson D. Hale Jr., Sherin Wight, *Vice Presidents;* Joyce Levesque, *Treasurer.*

Thank you for buying this Almanac!
We hope you find it new, useful, and entertaining.
Thanks, too, to everyone who had a hand in its creation, including advertisers, distributors, printers, and sales and delivery people.

How to Use This Almanac
Anywhere in the United States

■ The calendar pages **(44–71)** are the heart of *The Old Farmer's Almanac*. They present astronomical data and sky sightings for the entire year and are what make this book a true almanac, a "calendar of the heavens." In essence, these pages are unchanged since 1792, when Robert B. Thomas published his first edition. The long columns of numbers and symbols reveal all of Nature's precision, rhythm, and glory—an astronomical look at the year 2004.

–Beth Krommes

Please note: All times given in this edition of the Almanac are for Boston, Massachusetts, and are in Eastern Standard Time (EST), except from 2:00 A.M., April 4, until 2:00 A.M., October 31, when Eastern Daylight Time (EDT) is given. Key Letters (A–E) are provided so that readers can calculate times for their own localities. The following four pages provide detailed explanations.

Seasons of the Year

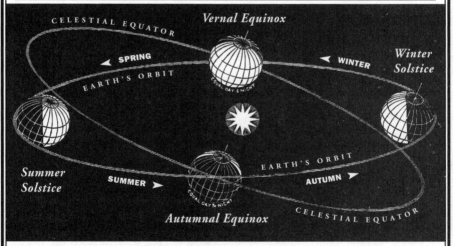

The seasons occur because Earth's axis is tilted with respect to its orbit of the Sun. Thus, the hemispheres take turns reaching their maximum tilt toward the Sun, which occurs at the solstices. The equinoxes mark the intersection of Earth's orbit with the plane of the celestial equator, when the hemispheres equally face the Sun.

■ The Old Farmer's Almanac Web site, **www.almanac.com**, provides a vast array of daily data: astronomical information, including Sun, Moon, and planet rise and set times, for many locations in the United States and Canada, as well as tide predictions for U.S. and Canadian coastlines. Also available are weather forecasts for anywhere in the United States and select locations around the world, plus U.S. and Canadian weather history since 1994. **(continued)**

The Left-Hand Calendar Pages

(Pages 44–70)

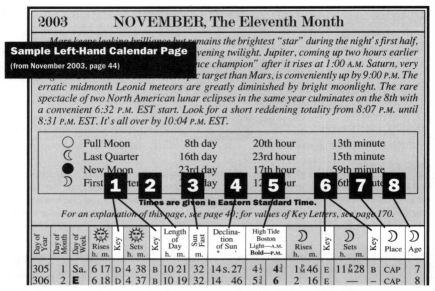

2003 NOVEMBER, The Eleventh Month

Sample Left-Hand Calendar Page
(from November 2003, page 44)

Mars keeps looking brilliance but remains the brightest "star" during the night's first half, ... evening twilight. Jupiter, coming up two hours earlier ... nce champion" after it rises at 1:00 A.M. Saturn, very ... target than Mars, is conveniently up by 9:00 P.M. The erratic midmonth Leonid meteors are greatly diminished by bright moonlight. The rare spectacle of two North American lunar eclipses in the same year culminates on the 8th with a convenient 6:32 P.M. EST start. Look for a short reddening totality from 8:07 P.M. until 8:31 P.M. EST. It's all over by 10:04 P.M. EST.

○ Full Moon	8th day	20th hour	13th minute
☾ Last Quarter	16th day	23rd hour	15th minute
● New Moon	23rd day	17th hour	59th minute
☽ First Quarter	day	ur	6th ute

Times are given in Eastern Standard Time.

For an explanation of this page, see page 40; for values of Key Letters, see page 170.

Day of Year	Day of Month	Day of Week	☀ Rises h. m.	Key	☀ Sets h. m.	Key	Length of Day h. m.	Sun Fast m.	Declination of Sun ° '	High Tide Boston Light—A.M. Bold—P.M.	☽ Rises h. m.	Key	☽ Sets h. m.	Key	☽ Place	☽ Age
305	1	Sa.	6 17	D	4 38	B	10 21	32	14 s.27	4½ / 4¾	1⅛46	E	11⅜28	B	CAP	7
306	2	**E**	6 18	D	4 37	B	10 19	32	14 46	5¾ / 6	2 16	E	—	–	CAP	8

1 Use these two Key Letter columns to calculate the sunrise/sunset times for your locale. Each sunrise/sunset time is assigned a Key Letter whose value is given in minutes in the **Time Corrections** table on **page 170**. Find your city in the table, or the city nearest you, and add or subtract those minutes to Boston's sunrise or sunset time.

E X A M P L E :

■ To find the time of sunrise in Denver, Colorado, on November 1, 2003:

Sunrise, Boston, with Key Letter D (above)	6:17 A.M. EST
Value of Key Letter D for Denver (p. 171)	+ 11 minutes
Sunrise, Denver	6:28 A.M. MST

2 This column shows how long the Sun is above the horizon in Boston. To determine your city's length of day, find the sunrise/sunset Key Letter values for your city on **page 170**. Add or subtract the sunset value to Boston's length of day. Then sim-

ply *reverse* the sunrise sign (from minus to plus, or plus to minus) and add (or subtract) this value to the result of the first step.

E X A M P L E :

■ To find the length of day in Richmond, Virginia, on November 1, 2003:

Length of day, Boston (above)	10:21
Sunset Key Letter B (p. 173)	+ 32 minutes
	10:53
Reverse sunrise Key Letter D (p. 173, +17 to –17)	– 17 minutes
Length of day, Richmond (10 hr., 36 min.)	10:36

3 The Sun Fast column is for changing sundial time to clock time in Boston. A sundial reads natural time, or Sun time, which is neither Standard nor Daylight time except by coincidence. From a sundial reading, subtract the minutes given in the Sun Fast column to get Boston clock time, and use Key Letter C in the table on **page 170** to convert the time to your city.

E X A M P L E :

■ To change sundial time to clock time in Boston, or Salem, Oregon, on November 1, 2003:

Sundial reading, Nov. 1 (Boston or Salem)	12:00 noon
Subtract Sun Fast (p. 40)	– 32 minutes
Clock time, Boston	11:28 A.M. EST
Use Key Letter C for Salem (p. 173)	+ 27 minutes
Clock time, Salem	11:55 A.M. PST

4 This column gives the degrees and minutes of the Sun from the celestial equator at noon EST or EDT.

5 The High Tide column gives the times of daily high tides in Boston. For example, on November 1, the first high tide occurs at 4:30 A.M. and the second occurs at 4:45 P.M. (A dash under High Tide indicates that high water occurs on or after midnight and so is recorded on the next day.) Figures for calculating high tide times and heights for localities other than Boston are given in the **Tide Corrections** table on **page 168.**

6 Use these two Key Letter columns to calculate the moonrise/moonset times for localities other than Boston. (A dash indicates that moonrise/moonset occurs on or after midnight and so is recorded on the next day.) Use the same procedure as explained in #1 for calculating your moonrise/moonset time, then factor in an additional correction based on longitude (see table below). For the longitude of your city, see **page 170.**

Longitude of city	Correction minutes
58° – 76°	0
77° – 89°	+1
90° – 102°	+2
103° – 115°	+3
116° – 127°	+4
128° – 141°	+5
142° – 155°	+6

E X A M P L E :

■ To determine the time of moonrise in Lansing, Michigan, on November 1, 2003:

Moonrise, Boston, with Key Letter E (p. 40)	1:46 P.M. EST
Value of Key Letter E for Lansing (p. 172)	+ 54 minutes
Correction for Lansing longitude 84° 33'	+ 1 minute
Moonrise, Lansing	2:41 P.M. EST

Use the same procedure to determine the time of moonset.

–Beth Krommes

7 The Moon's place is its *astronomical,* or *actual,* placement in the heavens. (This should not be confused with the Moon's *astrological* place in the zodiac, as explained on **page 189.**) All calculations in this Almanac are based on astronomy, not astrology, except for the information on **pages 188, 189,** and **190.**

In addition to the 12 constellations of the astronomical zodiac, five other abbreviations may appear in this column: Auriga **(AUR),** a northern constellation between Perseus and Gemini; Cetus **(CET),** which lies south of the zodiac, just south of Pisces and Aries; Ophiuchus **(OPH),** a constellation primarily north of the zodiac but with a small corner between Scorpius and Sagittarius; Orion **(ORI),** a constellation whose northern limit first reaches the zodiac between Taurus and Gemini; and Sextans **(SEX),** which lies south of the zodiac except for a corner that just touches it near Leo.

8 The last column gives the Moon's age, which is the number of days since the previous new Moon. (The average length of the lunar month is 29.53 days.)

(c o n t i n u e d)

The Right-Hand Calendar Pages

(Pages 45–71)

■ Throughout the **Right-Hand Calendar Pages** are groups of symbols that represent notable celestial events. The symbols and names of the principal planets and aspects are:

☉	**Sun**	♆	**Neptune**
○ ● ☾	**Moon**	♇	**Pluto**
☿	**Mercury**	♂	**Conjunction (on**
♀	**Venus**		**the same celestial**
⊕	**Earth**		**longitude)**
♂	**Mars**	☊	**Ascending node**
♃	**Jupiter**	☋	**Descending node**
♄	**Saturn**	☍	**Opposition (180**
♅	**Uranus**		**degrees apart)**

For example, ♂♅☾ next to November 2, 2003 (see opposite page), means that a conjunction (♂) of Uranus (♅) and the Moon (☾) occurs on that date, when they are aligned along the same celestial longitude and appear to be closest together in the sky.

−Beth Krommes

The Seasons of 2003–2004

Fall 2003 . . . . **Sept. 23, 6:47 A.M. EDT**
Winter 2003 . . . . **Dec. 22, 2:04 A.M. EST**
Spring 2004 . . . . **Mar. 20, 1:49 A.M. EST**
Summer 2004 . . . . . . **June 20, 8:57 P.M. EDT**
Fall 2004 . . . . **Sept. 22, 12:30 P.M. EDT**
Winter 2004 . . . . **Dec. 21, 7:42 A.M. EST**

Earth at Perihelion and Aphelion 2004

■ Earth will be at perihelion on January 4, 2004, when it will be 91,400,193 miles from the Sun. Earth will be at aphelion on July 5, 2004, when it will be 94,507,612 miles from the Sun.

Movable Feasts and Fasts for 2004

Septuagesima Sunday . . . . . **Feb. 8**
Shrove Tuesday . . . . **Feb. 24**
Ash Wednesday . . . . **Feb. 25**
Palm Sunday . . . . **Apr. 4**
Good Friday . . . . **Apr. 9**
Easter . . . . **Apr. 11**
Rogation Sunday . . . . **May 16**
Ascension Day . . . . **May 20**
Whitsunday–Pentecost . . . . **May 30**
Trinity Sunday . . . . **June 6**
Corpus Christi . . . . **June 10**
First Sunday in Advent . . . **Nov. 28**

Chronological Cycles for 2004

Dominical Letter . . . . **D/C**
Epact **8**
Golden Number (Lunar Cycle) . . **10**
Roman Indiction **12**
Solar Cycle **25**
Year of Julian Period **6717**

Era	Year	Begins
Byzantine	7513	. . Sept. 14
Jewish (A.M.)* . . .	5765	. . Sept. 15
Chinese (Lunar) .	4702	. . . Jan. 22
[Year of the Monkey]		
Roman (A.U.C.) . .	2757	. . . Jan. 14
Nabonassar	2753	. . . Apr. 22
Japanese	2664	. . . . Jan. 1
Grecian		
(Seleucidae) . . .	2316	. . Sept. 14
		(or Oct. 14)
Indian (Saka)	1926	. . . Mar. 21
Diocletian	1721	. . Sept. 11
Islamic (Hegira)*	1425	. . . Feb. 21

---

*Year begins at sunset.

■ Day of the month.

■ Day of the week.

■ The bold letter in this column is the Dominical Letter, a traditional ecclesiastical designation for Sunday. The letter for 2003 is E, because the first Sunday of the year falls on the fifth day of January. The letter for 2004, a leap year, is D through February, then reverts to C.

■ Notable celestial events appear as these symbols. (Conjunction of Uranus and the Moon.)

■ Sundays and special holy days generally appear in this typeface.

■ Religious feasts appear in this typeface.

■ Civil holidays appear in this typeface.

■ Noteworthy historical events, folklore, and legend appear in this typeface.

■ Proverbs, poems, and adages appear in this typeface.

■ First high tide at Boston is 10.8 feet; second high tide is 10.3 feet.

■ Weather prediction rhyme. **(For detailed regional forecasts, see pages 124–139.)**

What moistens the lip
and what brightens the eye?
What calls back the past,
like the rich pumpkin pie? –J. G. Whittier

D.M.	D.W.	Dates, Feasts, Fasts, Aspects, Tide Heights	Weather ↓
1	Sa.	All Saints' • Sadie Hawkins Day • ♂ ♅ ℂ • Tides { 9.2 / 10.1	A
2	E	21st 𝕾. af. 𝕻. • ♂ ⊕ ℂ • Tides { 9.1 / 9.8	scoop
3	M.	All Souls' • ♂ ♂ ℂ • First national auto show, held in New York City, 1900	of
4	Tu.	Election Day • James Ritty received a patent for a cash register, 1879	vanilla
5	W.	ℂ on Eq. • Bryan Adams born, 1959 • Tides { 9.6 / 9.6	on
6	Th.	*The barber shows you the mirror, but it's too late to raise a squawk.* • { 9.9 / 9.6	northern
7	Fr.	Last spike of the transcontinental Canadian Pacific Railway driven at Craigellachie, B.C., 1885	hills.
8	Sa.	Full Beaver ○ • Eclipse ℂ • ⊕ stat. • Tides { 10.1 / 9.4	gives
9	E	22nd 𝕾. af. 𝕻. • ℂ at ☍ • Sally Tompkins born, 1833	the
10	M.	ℂ at apo. • S.S. Edmund Fitzgerald sank in storm, entire crew of 29 lost, 1975 •	snow-
11	Tu.	St. Martin • Veterans Day • Indian Summer • Tides { 9.1 / 10.0	blower
12	W.	Largest iceberg on record (208x60 miles) discovered by U.S.S. Glacier, 1956 •	salesman
13	Th.	ℂ rides high • ♂ ♄ ℂ • Tides { 8.6 / 9.6	thrills.
14	Fr.	First performance of a Western theatrical production in North America, 1606 •	The
15	Sa.	Explorer Zebulon Pike spotted a mountain he called Grand Peak, later renamed Pikes Peak, 1806	sight
16	E	23rd 𝕾. af. 𝕻. • Skunks hibernate now. • Tides { 8.3 / 9.2	of
17	M.	St. Hugh of Lincoln • Computer mouse patented, 1970 • { 8.4 / 9.2	white,
18	Tu.	♂ ♃ ℂ • Captain Nathaniel B. Palmer discovered Antarctica, 1820 •	however
19	W.	*If there be ice in November that will bear a duck, There will be nothing thereafter but sleet and muck.*	meager,
20	Th.	ℂ on Eq. • First nighttime photograph taken from airplane, 1925 • { 10.0 / 10.0	makes
21	Fr.	North Carolina became the 12th state, 1789 • Tides { 10.8 / 10.3 •	the

For an explanation of terms used in the Almanac, see the glossaries on pages 84 and 92.

Predicting Earthquakes

■ Note the dates, in the **Right-Hand Calendar Pages,** when the Moon rides high or runs low. The date of the high begins the most likely five-day period of earthquakes in the Northern Hemisphere; the date of the low indicates a similar five-day period in the Southern Hemisphere. Also noted each month are the days when the Moon is on the celestial equator, indicating the most likely two-day earthquake periods in both hemispheres.

Forecasting the Almanac Weather

■ We derive our weather forecasts from a secret formula devised by the founder of this Almanac in 1792, enhanced by the most-modern scientific calculations based on so-

–Beth Krommes

lar activity and current meteorological data. We believe that nothing in the universe occurs haphazardly but that there is a cause-and-effect pattern to all phenomena, thus making long-range weather forecasts possible. However, neither we nor anyone else has as yet gained sufficient insight into the mysteries of the universe to predict the weather with anything resembling total accuracy.

2003 NOVEMBER, The Eleventh Month

Mars keeps leaking brilliance but remains the brightest "star" during the night's first half, after slowly improving Venus sets in evening twilight. Jupiter, coming up two hours earlier each month, now rules as the "brilliance champion" after it rises at 1:00 A.M. Saturn, very bright in Gemini and a better telescopic target than Mars, is conveniently up by 9:00 P.M. The erratic midmonth Leonid meteors are greatly diminished by bright moonlight. The rare spectacle of two North American lunar eclipses in the same year culminates on the 8th with a convenient 6:32 P.M. EST start. Look for a short reddening totality from 8:07 P.M. until 8:31 P.M. EST. It's all over by 10:04 P.M. EST.

○	Full Moon	8th day	20th hour	13th minute
☾	Last Quarter	16th day	23rd hour	15th minute
●	New Moon	23rd day	17th hour	59th minute
☽	First Quarter	30th day	12th hour	16th minute

Times are given in Eastern Standard Time.

For an explanation of this page, see page 40; for values of Key Letters, see page 170.

Day of Year	Day of Month	Day of Week	☼ Rises h. m.	Key	☼ Sets h. m.	Key	Length of Day h. m.	Sun Fast m.	Declination of Sun ° '	High Tide Boston Light—A.M.	Bold—P.M.	☽ Rises h. m.	Key	☽ Sets h. m.	Key	☽ Place	☽ Age
305	1	Sa.	6 17	D	4 38	B	10 21	32	14 s. 27	4½	**4¾**	1 P.M. 46	E	11 P.M. 28	B	CAP	7
306	2	**E**	6 18	D	4 37	B	10 19	32	14 46	5¾	**6**	2 16	E	—	–	CAP	8
307	3	M.	6 20	D	4 35	B	10 15	32	15 05	6¾	**7**	2 40	D	12 A.M. 37	C	AQU	9
308	4	Tu.	6 21	D	4 34	B	10 13	32	15 23	7¾	**8**	3 01	D	1 43	C	AQU	10
309	5	W.	6 22	D	4 33	B	10 11	32	15 42	8½	**9**	3 21	C	2 47	D	PSC	11
310	6	Th.	6 23	D	4 32	B	10 09	32	16 00	9¼	**9¾**	3 41	C	3 50	D	PSC	12
311	7	Fr.	6 25	D	4 31	B	10 06	32	16 18	10	**10½**	4 01	B	4 52	E	PSC	13
312	8	Sa.	6 26	D	4 30	A	10 04	32	16 35	10½	**11**	4 23	B	5 54	E	ARI	14
313	9	**E**	6 27	D	4 28	A	10 01	32	16 53	11¼	**11¾**	4 49	A	6 57	E	ARI	15
314	10	M.	6 28	D	4 27	A	9 59	32	17 10	11¾	—	5 19	A	8 00	E	TAU	16
315	11	Tu.	6 30	D	4 26	A	9 56	32	17 26	12¼	**12¼**	5 56	A	9 02	E	TAU	17
316	12	W.	6 31	D	4 25	A	9 54	32	17 42	1	**1**	6 40	A	10 00	E	TAU	18
317	13	Th.	6 32	D	4 24	A	9 52	31	17 58	1¾	**1¾**	7 32	A	10 54	E	GEM	19
318	14	Fr.	6 33	D	4 23	A	9 50	31	18 14	2¼	**2½**	8 31	B	11 A.M. 40	E	GEM	20
319	15	Sa.	6 35	D	4 23	A	9 48	31	18 30	3¼	**3¼**	9 36	B	12 P.M. 19	E	CAN	21
320	16	**E**	6 36	D	4 22	A	9 46	31	18 45	4	**4**	10 44	B	12 52	E	CAN	22
321	17	M.	6 37	D	4 21	A	9 44	31	19 00	4¾	**5**	11 P.M. 54	C	1 21	D	LEO	23
322	18	Tu.	6 38	D	4 20	A	9 42	31	19 15	5¾	**6**	—	–	1 46	D	LEO	24
323	19	W.	6 40	D	4 19	A	9 39	30	19 29	6¾	**7**	1 A.M. 05	C	2 09	D	VIR	25
324	20	Th.	6 41	D	4 18	A	9 37	30	19 42	7½	**8**	2 18	D	2 33	C	VIR	26
325	21	Fr.	6 42	D	4 18	A	9 36	30	19 55	8¼	**8¾**	3 34	E	2 58	C	VIR	27
326	22	Sa.	6 43	D	4 17	A	9 34	30	20 08	9¼	**9¾**	4 53	E	3 27	B	VIR	28
327	23	**E**	6 44	D	4 16	A	9 32	29	20 21	10	**10½**	6 16	E	4 02	B	LIB	0
328	24	M.	6 45	D	4 16	A	9 31	29	20 33	10¾	**11½**	7 39	E	4 46	A	LIB	1
329	25	Tu.	6 47	D	4 15	A	9 28	29	20 45	11¾	—	8 59	E	5 41	A	OPH	2
330	26	W.	6 48	D	4 15	A	9 27	29	20 57	12½	**12½**	10 07	E	6 47	A	SAG	3
331	27	Th.	6 49	E	4 14	A	9 25	28	21 08	1¼	**1½**	11 03	E	8 00	B	SAG	4
332	28	Fr.	6 50	E	4 14	A	9 24	28	21 19	2¼	**2½**	11 A.M. 45	E	9 14	B	CAP	5
333	29	Sa.	6 51	E	4 13	A	9 22	28	21 29	3¼	**3½**	12 P.M. 18	E	10 26	C	CAP	6
334	30	**E**	6 52	E	4 13	A	9 21	27	21 s. 39	4¼	**4½**	12 P.M. 45	D	11 P.M. 34	C	AQU	7

NOVEMBER hath 30 days. 2003

What moistens the lip
and what brightens the eye?
What calls back the past,
like the rich pumpkin pie? –J. G. Whittier

D. M.	D. W.	Dates, Feasts, Fasts, Aspects, Tide Heights	*Weather* ↓
1	Sa.	**All Saints'** • Sadie Hawkins Day • ☌♆☾ • Tides { 9.2 10.1	*A*
2	**E**	**21st S. af. P.** • ☌♅☾ • Tides { 9.1 9.8 •	*scoop*
3	M.	**All Souls'** • ☌♂☾ • First national auto show, held in New York City, 1900 •	*of*
4	Tu.	Election Day • James Ritty received a patent for a cash register, 1879 •	*vanilla*
5	W.	☾ on Eq. • Bryan Adams born, 1959 • Tides { 9.6 9.6 •	*on*
6	Th.	*The barber shows you the mirror, but it's too late to raise a squawk.* • { 9.9 9.6	*northern*
7	Fr.	Last spike of the transcontinental Canadian Pacific Railway driven at Craigellachie, B.C., 1885	*hills*
8	Sa.	**Full Beaver** ○ • **Eclipse** ☾ • ♅ stat. • Tides { 10.1 9.4	*gives*
9	**E**	**22nd S. af. P.** • ☾ at ☊ • Sally Tompkins born, 1833	*the*
10	M.	☾ at apo. • S.S. *Edmund Fitzgerald* sank in storm, entire crew of 29 lost, 1975 •	*snow-*
11	Tu.	**St. Martin** • **Veterans Day** • Indian Summer • Tides { 9.1 10.0	*blower*
12	W.	Largest iceberg on record (208x60 miles) discovered by U.S.S. *Glacier,* 1956 •	*salesman*
13	Th.	☾ rides high • ☌♄☾ • Tides { 8.6 9.6 •	*thrills.*
14	Fr.	First performance of a Western theatrical production in North America, 1606 • { 8.4 9.4 •	*The*
15	Sa.	Explorer Zebulon Pike spotted a mountain he called Grand Peak, later renamed Pikes Peak, 1806	*sight*
16	**E**	**23rd S. af. P.** • Skunks hibernate now. • Tides { 8.3 9.2 •	*of*
17	M.	**St. Hugh of Lincoln** • Computer mouse patented, 1970 • { 8.4 9.2	*white,*
18	Tu.	☌♃☾ • Captain Nathaniel B. Palmer discovered Antarctica, 1820 •	*however*
19	W.	*If there be ice in November that will bear a duck, There will be nothing thereafter but sleet and muck.*	*meager,*
20	Th.	☾ on Eq. • First nighttime photograph taken from airplane, 1925 • { 10.0 10.0	*makes*
21	Fr.	North Carolina became the 12th state, 1789 • Tides { 10.8 10.3 •	*the*
22	Sa.	Statue of Liberty began role as first U.S. lighthouse to use electricity, 1886 • { 11.5 10.6	*skiers*
23	**E**	**24th S. af. P.** • **New** ● • Eclipse ☉ •	*eager*
24	M.	**St. Clement** • ☌☿☾ • Tides { 12.3 10.7 •	*beavers.*
25	Tu.	☌♀☾ • Ireland voted to legalize divorce, 1995 •	*Snowmobilers*
26	W.	☾ runs low • Archaeologist Howard Carter opened second doorway to tomb of Tutankhamen, 1922	*sing*
27	Th.	**Thanksgiving** • CARE organization founded, 1945 • { 10.2 11.7	*Hosanna*
28	Fr.	☌♆☾ • Ferdinand Magellan reached Pacific through newly discovered strait, 1520 •	*for*
29	Sa.	☌♅☾ • Former Beatle George Harrison died, 2001 • Tides { 9.5 10.5	*frozen*
30	**E**	**1st S. in Advent** • Lucy Maud Montgomery born in P.E.I., 1874	*manna.*

Happy is said to be the family which can eat onions together.
–Charles Dudley Warner, American author

Farmer's Calendar

■ The news has no mercy. The more of it there is, the worse it gets. The morning paper, the local six-o'clock broadcast, which only a few years ago you could safely sleep through, now scare you out of your wits. What does the news tell you? It tells you that you're never out of danger. The world in all its aspects is either actively malign or lethally indifferent; either way, its course with you will be measured in degrees of calamity. Not only in its content does the news appall. Even more alarming is its method: a kind of cinema gone mad, a St. Vitus's Dance of obsessive, repetitive images and words, all run at top speed, that would be terrifying if they were used to document the manufacture of oatmeal.

It wasn't always so. I have before me *The Vermont Phoenix* for Thursday, November 18, 1911. Published in Brattleboro, Vermont, the *Phoenix* took seriously its mission to give readers news of local importance. "Mr. and Mrs. A. F. Cheney have returned from their visit in Springfield, Mass.," I read. "J. A. Veinot is building a henhouse for F. W. Smith." "Charles Alexander has returned from his vacation." So it goes, for 17 column inches.

Certainly it's restful. Certainly the contrast it offers with the murder, mayhem, and misfortune of journalism today is striking. Do you like it? Don't be too sure. Perhaps we get what we want. The placid annals of our grandparents' time may be for us like so much of the real life of another age: great stuff if you can stay awake.

Mercury is readily seen below Venus during the first half of the month, and Venus finally gets conspicuously high at dusk beginning midmonth. The Geminid meteors on the 13th, like all other major showers this year, are washed out by a bright Moon. Mars enters Pisces and dims to below zero magnitude. Starring roles now go to brilliant Jupiter, which rises by midnight, and especially to Saturn, which rises soon after nightfall and reaches opposition on the final night of the year. Sitting atop the zodiac with rings wide open, Saturn won't offer such optimal viewing conditions for another 28 years. Winter begins with the solstice on the 22nd at 2:04 A.M. EST.

○	Full Moon	8th day	15th hour	37th minute
☾	Last Quarter	16th day	12th hour	42nd minute
●	New Moon	23rd day	4th hour	43rd minute
☽	First Quarter	30th day	5th hour	3rd minute

Times are given in Eastern Standard Time.

For an explanation of this page, see page 40; for values of Key Letters, see page 170.

Day of Year	Day of Month	Day of Week	☼ Rises h. m.	Key	☼ Sets h. m.	Key	Length of Day h. m.	Sun Fast m.	Declination of Sun ° '	High Tide Boston Light—A.M. Bold—P.M.		☽ Rises h. m.	Key	☽ Sets h. m.	Key	☽ Place	☽ Age
335	1	M.	6 53	E	4 13	A	9 20	27	21 s. 48	5¼	5½	1 M 07	D	—	–	AQU	8
336	2	Tu.	6 54	E	4 12	A	9 18	27	21 57	6¼	6½	1 28	C	12 M 40	C	PSC	9
337	3	W.	6 55	E	4 12	A	9 17	26	22 06	7¼	7½	1 47	C	1 43	D	CET	10
338	4	Th.	6 56	E	4 12	A	9 16	26	22 15	8	8½	2 07	B	2 44	E	PSC	11
339	5	Fr.	6 57	E	4 12	A	9 15	25	22 23	8¾	9¼	2 28	B	3 46	E	ARI	12
340	6	Sa.	6 58	E	4 12	A	9 14	25	22 30	9½	10	2 52	B	4 48	E	ARI	13
341	7	**E**	6 59	E	4 12	A	9 13	25	22 37	10	10¾	3 21	A	5 51	E	TAU	14
342	8	M.	7 00	E	4 11	A	9 11	24	22 43	10¾	11¼	3 55	A	6 54	E	TAU	15
343	9	Tu.	7 01	E	4 11	A	9 10	24	22 49	11¼	12	4 37	A	7 54	E	TAU	16
344	10	W.	7 02	E	4 12	A	9 10	23	22 55	12	—	5 27	A	8 50	E	GEM	17
345	11	Th.	7 03	E	4 12	A	9 09	23	23 01	12½	12½	6 24	A	9 38	E	GEM	18
346	12	Fr.	7 04	E	4 12	A	9 08	22	23 05	1¼	1¼	7 28	A	10 20	E	CAN	19
347	13	Sa.	7 05	E	4 12	A	9 07	22	23 09	2	2	8 34	B	10 54	E	CAN	20
348	14	**E**	7 05	E	4 12	A	9 07	21	23 13	2¾	2¾	9 42	B	11 24	E	LEO	21
349	15	M.	7 06	E	4 12	A	9 06	21	23 16	3½	3½	10 M 50	C	11 A 49	D	LEO	22
350	16	Tu.	7 07	E	4 13	A	9 06	20	23 19	4¼	4½	—	–	12 M 12	D	LEO	23
351	17	W.	7 08	E	4 13	A	9 05	20	23 21	5¼	5½	12 M 00	D	12 34	D	VIR	24
352	18	Th.	7 08	E	4 13	A	9 05	19	23 23	6	6½	1 11	D	12 58	C	VIR	25
353	19	Fr.	7 09	E	4 14	A	9 05	19	23 25	7	7½	2 26	E	1 23	B	VIR	26
354	20	Sa.	7 09	E	4 14	A	9 05	18	23 26	7¾	8½	3 44	E	1 54	B	LIB	27
355	21	**E**	7 10	E	4 14	A	9 04	18	23 26	8¾	9½	5 06	E	2 32	A	OPH	28
356	22	M.	7 10	E	4 15	A	9 05	17	23 26	9¾	10¼	6 27	E	3 21	A	OPH	29
357	23	Tu.	7 11	E	4 16	A	9 05	17	23 26	10½	11¼	7 43	E	4 22	A	SAG	0
358	24	W.	7 11	E	4 16	A	9 05	16	23 25	11½	—	8 47	E	5 34	A	SAG	1
359	25	Th.	7 12	E	4 17	A	9 05	16	23 24	12¼	12¼	9 37	E	6 50	B	CAP	2
360	26	Fr.	7 12	E	4 17	A	9 05	15	23 22	1	1¼	10 15	E	8 06	B	CAP	3
361	27	Sa.	7 12	E	4 18	A	9 06	15	23 20	2	2	10 45	E	9 19	C	AQU	4
362	28	**E**	7 13	E	4 19	A	9 06	14	23 17	2¾	3	11 10	D	10 27	D	AQU	5
363	29	M.	7 13	E	4 19	A	9 06	14	23 13	3¾	4	11 32	C	11 M 32	D	AQU	6
364	30	Tu.	7 13	E	4 20	A	9 07	13	23 10	4½	5	11 A 52	C	—	–	CET	7
365	31	W.	7 13	E	4 21	A	9 08	13	23 s. 05	5½	6	12 M 12	C	12 A 35	D	PSC	8

DECEMBER hath 31 days. 2003

Granny's come to our house,
And ho! my lawzy-daisy!
All the childern round the place
Is ist a-runnin' crazy! –James Whitcomb Riley

D. M.	D. W.	Dates, Feasts, Fasts, Aspects, Tide Heights	*Weather* ↓
1	M.	☌ ♂ ☾ • The Christmas Club savings account began, 1909 • { 9.2 / 9.4	*There's*
2	Tu.	St. Viviana • ☾ on Eq. • First controlled, self-sustained nuclear chain reaction, 1946 •	*a*
3	W.	Oberlin Collegiate Institute became first coeducational college in U.S., 1833 • { 9.3 / 9.0	*run on*
4	Th.	Cardinal de Richelieu died, 1642 • Marcel Marceau appeared on television, 1955	*winter*
5	Fr.	Phi Beta Kappa founded at the College of William and Mary, 1776 •	*underwear.*
6	Sa.	St. Nicholas • ☾ at ☊ • Agnes Moorehead born, 1906 • { 9.8 / 8.9	*We*
7	E	2nd S. in Advent • ☾ at apo. • Tides { 10.0 / 8.9	*need*
8	M.	St. Ambrose • **Full Cold** ○ • *A full Moon eats clouds.* • { 10.0 / 8.8	*some*
9	Tu.	☿ Gr. Elong. (21° E.) • Christmas seals sold for first time, 1907 • { 10.1 / 8.8 •	*like*
10	W.	St. Eulalia • ☾ rides high • ☌ ♄ ☾ • { 10.0 / —	*reindeer*
11	Th.	Joe DiMaggio announced his retirement from baseball, 1951 • Tides { 8.7 / 10.0 •	*on*
12	Fr.	☌ ♇ ☉ • Father Edward Flanagan founded a home for boys in Omaha, Nebr., 1917 •	*the*
13	Sa.	St. Lucy • Anthony B. Heinsbergen born, 1894 •	*tundra wear!*
14	E	3rd S. in Advent • Halcyon Days • Tides { 8.6 / 9.6 •	*A*
15	M.	☌ ♃ ☾ • *Superman* movie premiered, 1978 • Tides { 8.7 / 9.5 •	*teaser,*
16	Tu.	Beware the Pogonip. • *The wise man sits on the hole in his carpet.* • Tides { 8.9 / 9.4	*then*
17	W.	Ember Day • ☾ on Eq. • ☿ stat. • Termination of Project Blue Book, 1969	*back*
18	Th.	Ty Cobb born, 1886 • John William Draper took first photo of the Moon, 1839 • Tides { 9.8 / 9.4	*in*
19	Fr.	The National Hockey League played its first games, 1917 • Ember Day • Tides { 10.4 / 9.6	*the*
20	Sa.	Ember Day • First day of Chanukah • ☾ at ☋ •	*freezer.*
21	E	4th S. in Advent • Tides { 11.5 / 10.0 •	*Bearable*
22	M.	**Winter Solstice** • ☾ at perig. • *An early winter, a surly winter.* • { 11.9 / 10.2	*for*
23	Tu.	**New** ● • "Account of a Visit from St. Nicholas" published, 1823 •	*caroling.*
24	W.	☾ runs low • First great fire of San Francisco, 1849 • Tides { 12.1 / —	*Flurries,*
25	Th.	Christmas Day • ☌ ♆ ☾ • ☌ ♀ ☾ •	*floods,*
26	Fr.	**Boxing Day (Canada)** • **First day of Kwanzaa** • ☿ in inf. ☌ • { 10.1 / 11.5	*and*
27	Sa.	St. John • ☌ ♅ ☾ • Radio City Music Hall opened in New York City, 1932	*muddy*
28	E	1st S. af. Ch. • Woodrow Wilson born, 1856 •	*floors—*
29	M.	Holy Innocents • *He only truly lives who lives in peace.* • { 9.4 / 9.6	*hurry up,*
30	Tu.	☾ on Eq. • ☌ ♂ ☾ • ☌ ♀ ♆ • { 9.2 / 9.1 •	*2004!*
31	W.	St. Sylvester • ♄ at ☍ • Ottawa selected by Queen Victoria as capital of Province of Canada, 1857	

Farmer's Calendar

■ *December 2.* A gray, still day at winter's doorstep. Took the dogs to the little wooded pond at the top of the hill. Nobody around. We followed the dirt road that runs alongside the water to its end—about a half-mile. Both dogs do the whole trip with their noses intently in the dirt. They quarter avidly back and forth across the road. It's not recreation for them but serious business. It's what they do.

Recent temperatures in the 20s have begun to freeze the pond over. A windowpane of ice now seems to go clear across. You couldn't walk on it, but it will support a small stone. I pick one up and shy it sidearm out over the pond as though I were aiming to make it skip on the water. The stone lands and slides freely over the ice toward the middle of the pond. As it slides, it makes—or the ice beneath it makes—a peculiar quavering, whistling sound, resonant and surprisingly loud, almost like the noise of an enormous musical saw.

What makes that noise? I imagine it's from waves induced in the thin ice by the stone's passing across it, the sound amplified by the little air space between the ice and the water below, or by the water itself. The new-frozen pond becomes a sound chamber, a giant cello. It's an effect that is evident only briefly. Another few cold days and the ice will get thicker. The pond will fall silent. I try another stone. *Whoo-oo-oo-uh,* goes the pond. The dogs hear it. They look up, but it doesn't hold their interest. They're impatient. They feel it's time to get moving.

2004 JANUARY, The First Month

A busy sky-year begins with Earth reaching its near point to the Sun (perihelion) on January 4. Venus blazes conspicuously in the southwest after sunset and can be seen passing in front of green Uranus on the 15th, a treat through binoculars. Jupiter, in Leo, rises at or soon after 10:00 P.M. on the 1st and a little after 8:00 P.M. by month's end. Orange medium-bright Mars, in Pisces, floats in the south at nightfall. Saturn enjoys its best month of the year, rising at sunset and remaining out all night in Gemini. It's now at peak glory for this entire half-century period, with wide-open rings for telescope users. The crescent Moon performs a lovely conjunction with Venus on the 24th and with Mars on the 27th.

○ Full Moon	7th day	10th hour	40th minute
☾ Last Quarter	14th day	23rd hour	46th minute
● New Moon	21st day	16th hour	5th minute
☽ First Quarter	29th day	1st hour	3rd minute

Times are given in Eastern Standard Time.

For an explanation of this page, see page 40; for values of Key Letters, see page 170.

Day of Year	Day of Month	Day of Week	☼ Rises h. m.	Key	☼ Sets h. m.	Key	Length of Day h. m.	Sun Fast m.	Declination of Sun ° '	High Tide Boston Light—A.M. Bold—P.M.		☾ Rises h. m.	Key	☾ Sets h. m.	Key	☾ Place	☾ Age
1	1	Th.	7 13	E	4 22	A	9 09	13	23 s.01	6½	7	12ᴾ̫32	B	1ᴹ̫37	E	PSC	9
2	2	Fr.	7 14	E	4 23	A	9 09	12	22 56	7¼	7¾	12 56	B	2 40	E	ARI	10
3	3	Sa.	7 14	E	4 24	A	9 10	12	22 50	8	8¾	1 22	A	3 42	E	TAU	11
4	4	**D**	7 14	E	4 25	A	9 11	11	22 44	8¾	9½	1 55	A	4 45	E	TAU	12
5	5	M.	7 14	E	4 26	A	9 12	11	22 38	9½	10¼	2 34	A	5 46	E	TAU	13
6	6	Tu.	7 13	E	4 26	A	9 13	10	22 31	10¼	11	3 22	A	6 44	E	GEM	14
7	7	W.	7 13	E	4 27	A	9 14	10	22 23	11	11½	4 18	A	7 35	E	GEM	15
8	8	Th.	7 13	E	4 29	A	9 16	9	22 15	11½	—	5 20	A	8 19	E	GEM	16
9	9	Fr.	7 13	E	4 30	A	9 17	9	22 07	12¼	12¼	6 26	B	8 56	E	CAN	17
10	10	Sa.	7 13	E	4 31	A	9 18	9	21 59	12¾	1	7 34	B	9 27	E	LEO	18
11	11	**D**	7 13	E	4 32	A	9 19	8	21 50	1½	1½	8 42	C	9 53	E	LEO	19
12	12	M.	7 12	E	4 33	A	9 21	8	21 40	2¼	2¼	9 51	D	10 17	D	LEO	20
13	13	Tu.	7 12	E	4 34	A	9 22	7	21 30	3	3	11ᴾ̫00	D	10 39	D	VIR	21
14	14	W.	7 11	E	4 35	A	9 24	7	21 20	3¾	4	—	–	11 01	C	VIR	22
15	15	Th.	7 11	E	4 36	A	9 25	7	21 09	4½	5	12ᴬ̫11	E	11 25	B	VIR	23
16	16	Fr.	7 11	E	4 37	A	9 26	6	20 58	5½	6	1 25	E	11ᴬ̫52	B	LIB	24
17	17	Sa.	7 10	E	4 39	A	9 29	6	20 46	6½	7	2 43	E	12ᴾ̫25	A	LIB	25
18	18	**D**	7 10	E	4 40	A	9 30	6	20 35	7½	8	4 02	E	1 07	A	OPH	26
19	19	M.	7 09	E	4 41	A	9 32	5	20 23	8½	9¼	5 18	E	2 01	A	OPH	27
20	20	Tu.	7 08	E	4 42	A	9 34	5	20 10	9¼	10	6 27	E	3 06	A	SAG	28
21	21	W.	7 08	E	4 43	A	9 35	5	19 56	10¼	11	7 23	E	4 21	B	SAG	0
22	22	Th.	7 07	E	4 45	A	9 38	4	19 43	11¼	12	8 07	E	5 39	B	CAP	1
23	23	Fr.	7 06	D	4 46	A	9 40	4	19 29	12		8 42	E	6 55	C	CAP	2
24	24	Sa.	7 06	D	4 47	A	9 41	4	19 15	12¾	1	9 09	D	8 07	C	AQU	3
25	25	**D**	7 05	D	4 49	A	9 44	4	19 00	1½	1¾	9 33	D	9 16	D	AQU	4
26	26	M.	7 04	D	4 50	A	9 46	3	18 45	2¼	2½	9 54	C	10 21	D	PSC	5
27	27	Tu.	7 03	D	4 51	A	9 48	3	18 30	3	3½	10 14	C	11ᴾ̫25	D	PSC	6
28	28	W.	7 02	D	4 52	A	9 50	3	18 14	4	4¼	10 35	B	—	–	PSC	7
29	29	Th.	7 01	D	4 54	A	9 53	3	17 59	4¾	5¼	10 57	B	12ᴹ̫28	E	ARI	8
30	30	Fr.	7 00	D	4 55	A	9 55	2	17 42	5½	6¼	11 23	A	1 31	E	ARI	9
31	31	Sa.	6 59	D	4 56	A	9 57	2	17 s.26	6½	7¼	11ᴬ̫53	A	2ᴹ̫34	E	TAU	10

JANUARY hath 31 days. 2004

Chill airs and wintry winds! my ear
Has grown familiar with your song;
I hear it in the opening year,
I listen, and it cheers me long. –Henry Wadsworth Longfellow

D. M.	D. W.	Dates, Feasts, Fasts, Aspects, Tide Heights	*Weather* ↓
1	Th.	New Year's Day • **Circumcision** • {9.2 8.3 •	*Sunshine,*
2	Fr.	**St. Basil** • ☾ at ☊ • Author Isaac Asimov born, 1920	*flurries,*
3	Sa.	☾ at apo. • *Deny self for self's sake.* • Social reformer Lucretia Mott born, 1793 •	*and*
4	D	**2nd S. af. Ch.** • ♃ stat. • ⊕ at perihelion	*frozen-*
5	M.	**St. Elizabeth Ann Seton** • Twelfth Night • Tides {9.7 8.4 •	*pipe*
6	Tu.	**Epiphany** • ☿ stat. • ☌ ♄ ☾ • {9.9 8.6	*worries.*
7	W.	Distaff Day • **Full Wolf** ○ • ☾ runs high • Tides {10.1 8.7	*Teasing*
8	Th.	U.S. victory, Battle of New Orleans, 1815 • *Button up to the chin 'til May comes in.*	*easing—*
9	Fr.	Connecticut became 5th state in Union, 1788 • Richard Nixon born, 1913 •	*coastal*
10	Sa.	First aerial photography, 1911 • RCA introduced the 45 rpm record, 1949 • {8.9 10.2	*blow,*
11	D	**1st S. af. Ep.** • U.S. report on smoking and health released, 1964 •	*inland*
12	M.	Plough Monday • ☌ ♃ ☾ • Mystery writer Agatha Christie died, 1976 •	*snow!*
13	Tu.	**St. Hilary** • ☾ on Eq. • National Geographic Society founded, 1888 •	*Melt-*
14	W.	☌ ♀ ♅ • *Dr. Dolittle* author, Hugh Lofting, born, 1886 • Tides {9.6 9.4	*song*
15	Th.	Gray whales migrate, Calif. • *The cat in gloves catches no mice.* • Tides {9.8 9.2	*won't*
16	Fr.	☾ at ☋ • Last day of "The Great Snowstorm" that struck the East Coast, 1831 •	*last*
17	Sa.	☿ Gr. Elong. (24° W.) • Benjamin Franklin born, 1706 • {10.3 8.9 •	*long.*
18	D	**2nd S. af. Ep.** • Eugene Ely first to land a plane on a ship, 1911	*Chilled*
19	M.	**Martin Luther King Jr.'s Birthday (observed)** • ☾ at perig. • ☌ ☿ ☾ •	*to*
20	Tu.	☾ runs low • *Fame is a magnifying glass.* • Tides {11.3 9.6 •	*the*
21	W.	**New** ● • Singer Peggy Lee died, 2002 • Tides {11.6 9.8 •	*core—*
22	Th.	**St. Vincent** • Chinese New Year • Macintosh computer introduced, 1984 •	*worth*
23	Fr.	☌ ♅ ☾ • Fact-finding guru Joseph Nathan Kane born, 1899 • {11.5 — •	*waiting*
24	Sa.	☌ ♀ ☾ • Patent 1,404,539 granted for the Eskimo pie, 1922 • Tides {10.1 11.2	*for!*
25	D	**3rd S. af. Ep.** • *You can not unscramble eggs.* • {10.0 10.7 •	*Sled*
26	M.	**Conversion of Paul** • **Sts. Timothy & Titus** • ☾ on Eq. •	*dogs*
27	Tu.	☌ ♂ ☾ • Mozart born, 1756 • Michael Jackson's hair caught fire, 1984	*mush*
28	W.	**St. Thomas Aquinas** • Manitoba first province to grant women suffrage, 1916	*through*
29	Th.	☾ at ☊ • Outward Bound USA founder Joshua Miner died, 2002 • {9.1 8.2	*rain*
30	Fr.	"Hi-Yo, Silver!" heard for first time on radio when *The Lone Ranger* debuted, 1933 • {8.9 7.9	*and*
31	Sa.	☾ at apo. • Raccoons mate now. • Retailer Timothy Eaton died, 1907 • {8.9 7.8	*slush!*

Farmer's Calendar

■ Five years later, the recovery of the forest is more evident than its destruction. Its damage wasn't mortal, after all. At the time, that wasn't clear. It was on January 7, 1998, that a winter storm arrived out of the northwest, bringing not snow but a cold rain that froze when it landed. Nothing unusual in that; we were having an ice storm. We have plenty of ice storms. But this one went on for four days.

By the time the storm ended, it was obvious that this region had taken a hit of historic proportions. Because of a temperature inversion in which the evergreen forests on higher elevations stayed a little warmer than forests lower down, freezing was concentrated on hardwood stands, loading each tree with, literally, tons of ice. Branches, tops, trunks of mature trees failed and broke under the weight; smaller trees simply went over. That happened over a belt that stretched from Buffalo to New Brunswick.

In the Green Mountains near my home, the wreckage was frightening. Big trees were snapped off at their crowns, smaller trees were bent to the ground or uprooted. Smashed branches and trunks lay everywhere. The damage to the forest had the ominous, wanton quality of vandalism, as though a gang of giants had rampaged through the woods spreading destruction aimlessly, for fun.

It was hard to see how the woods in those mountains could survive that kind of injury. They did survive, and that's good. But if another storm like the Ice of '98 shouldn't happen again for a long, long time—that would be all right, too.

2004 — FEBRUARY, The Second Month

Venus grows higher and brighter, now remaining up for three hours after sunset. Mars steadily fades while crossing into Aries. Saturn remains glorious, standing high up at nightfall and reaching its nightly apex nearly overhead around 9:00 P.M. Jupiter rises at 7:00 P.M. at midmonth and remains prominent all night, joined loosely by the Moon on the 7th and 8th. The Moon also serves as guide and companion to Venus on the 23rd, Mars on the 25th, and Saturn on the 29th. By month's end, daylight increases by three to four minutes a day in most of the United States and four to five minutes a day in Canada. The year's most outstanding array of stars, centered in Orion, now float optimally high soon after nightfall.

○ Full Moon	6th day	3rd hour	47th minute
☾ Last Quarter	13th day	8th hour	40th minute
● New Moon	20th day	4th hour	18th minute
☽ First Quarter	27th day	22nd hour	24th minute

Times are given in Eastern Standard Time.

For an explanation of this page, see page 40; for values of Key Letters, see page 170.

Day of Year	Day of Month	Day of Week	Rises h. m.	Key	Sets h. m.	Key	Length of Day h. m.	Sun Fast m.	Declination of Sun ° '	High Tide Boston Light—A.M. Bold—P.M.		Rises h. m.	Key	Sets h. m.	Key	Place	Age
32	1	D	6 58	D	4 58	A	10 00	2	17 s.09	7½	8	12 ᴾ𝗆30	A	3 ᴬ𝗆36	E	TAU	11
33	2	M.	6 57	D	4 59	A	10 02	2	16 52	8¼	9	1 14	A	4 35	E	TAU	12
34	3	Tu.	6 56	D	5 00	A	10 04	2	16 34	9	9¾	2 07	A	5 29	E	AUR	13
35	4	W.	6 55	D	5 01	A	10 06	2	16 16	9¾	10½	3 08	A	6 16	E	GEM	14
36	5	Th.	6 54	D	5 03	A	10 09	2	15 58	10½	11¼	4 14	B	6 55	E	CAN	15
37	6	Fr.	6 53	D	5 04	A	10 11	2	15 40	11¼	11¾	5 23	B	7 28	E	CAN	16
38	7	Sa.	6 52	D	5 05	A	10 13	2	15 22	11¾	—	6 33	C	7 56	E	LEO	17
39	8	D	6 51	D	5 07	B	10 16	1	15 03	12½	12½	7 42	D	8 21	D	LEO	18
40	9	M.	6 49	D	5 08	B	10 19	1	14 44	1	1¼	8 52	D	8 43	D	VIR	19
41	10	Tu.	6 48	D	5 09	B	10 21	1	14 25	1¾	2	10 03	E	9 06	C	VIR	20
42	11	W.	6 47	D	5 11	B	10 24	1	14 05	2½	2¾	11 ᴾ𝗆16	E	9 29	B	VIR	21
43	12	Th.	6 46	D	5 12	B	10 26	1	13 45	3¼	3¾	—	–	9 54	B	VIR	22
44	13	Fr.	6 44	D	5 13	B	10 29	1	13 25	4	4½	12 ᴬ𝗆31	E	10 24	B	LIB	23
45	14	Sa.	6 43	D	5 14	B	10 31	1	13 05	5	5¾	1 48	E	11 02	A	SCO	24
46	15	D	6 42	D	5 16	B	10 34	1	12 44	6	6¾	3 03	E	11 ᴬ𝗆50	A	OPH	25
47	16	M.	6 40	D	5 17	B	10 37	1	12 23	7	8	4 13	E	12 ᴾ𝗆49	A	SAG	26
48	17	Tu.	6 39	D	5 18	B	10 39	2	12 02	8¼	9	5 12	E	1 58	B	SAG	27
49	18	W.	6 37	D	5 20	B	10 43	2	11 41	9¼	10	6 00	E	3 14	B	CAP	28
50	19	Th.	6 36	D	5 21	B	10 45	2	11 20	10¼	10¾	6 38	E	4 30	B	CAP	29
51	20	Fr.	6 34	D	5 22	B	10 48	2	10 58	11	11½	7 08	E	5 44	C	AQU	0
52	21	Sa.	6 33	D	5 23	B	10 50	2	10 37	11¾	—	7 33	D	6 55	D	AQU	1
53	22	D	6 31	D	5 25	B	10 54	2	10 15	12¼	12½	7 55	D	8 03	D	PSC	2
54	23	M.	6 30	D	5 26	B	10 56	2	9 53	1	1¼	8 16	C	9 09	D	CET	3
55	24	Tu.	6 28	D	5 27	B	10 59	2	9 31	1¾	2	8 36	B	10 14	E	PSC	4
56	25	W.	6 27	D	5 28	B	11 01	2	9 09	2½	2¾	8 58	B	11 ᴾ𝗆18	E	ARI	5
57	26	Th.	6 25	D	5 30	B	11 05	3	8 47	3	3½	9 22	B	—	–	ARI	6
58	27	Fr.	6 24	D	5 31	B	11 07	3	8 24	4	4½	9 51	A	12 ᴬ𝗆22	E	TAU	7
59	28	Sa.	6 22	D	5 32	B	11 10	3	8 02	4¾	5½	10 25	A	1 25	E	TAU	8
60	29	D	6 21	D	5 33	B	11 12	3	7 s.39	5¾	6½	11 ᴬ𝗆06	A	2 ᴬ𝗆25	E	TAU	9

FEBRUARY hath 29 days. 2004

Serene will be our days and bright,
And happy will our nature be,
When love is an unerring light,
And joy its own security. –William Wordsworth

D. M.	D. W.	Dates, Feasts, Fasts, Aspects, Tide Heights	Weather ↓
1	D	4th S. af. Ep. • Voice message exchange system patented, 1983 •	*Hit*
2	M.	Candlemas • Groundhog Day • ☌♆☉ • Tides { 9.1 8.0	*the*
3	Tu.	☾ rides high • Calcutta Railway opened, 1855 • Tides { 9.4 8.2 •	*deck!*
4	W.	Winter Olympics opened in U.S. (Lake Placid, N.Y.) for first time, 1932 • { 9.8 8.5	*Snow*
5	Th.	St. Agatha • *Welcome is the best cheer.* • Tides { 10.1 8.9 •	*up to*
6	Fr.	Full Snow ○ • "You've Lost That Lovin' Feeling" topped charts, 1965	*your neck!*
7	Sa.	Author Charles Dickens born, 1812 • First untethered space walk, 1984 • Tides { 10.5 —	*It's*
8	D	Septuagesima • ☌♃☾ • { 9.5 10.5	*variable;*
9	M.	☾ on Eq. • Office of Commissioner of Fish and Fisheries formed in U.S., 1871 • { 9.7 10.4	*some*
10	Tu.	Garry Kasparov began chess match against computer *Deep Blue*, 1996 • { 10.0 10.2	*might*
11	W.	First use of anthracite coal as household fuel, 1808 • Tides { 10.1 9.9 •	*say*
12	Th.	☾ at ☋ • Abraham Lincoln born, 1809 • { 10.2 9.4 •	*terrible!*
13	Fr.	*It is bad luck to fall out of a 13th story window on Friday.* • Tides { 10.2 9.0	*Mercury*
14	Sa.	St. Valentine • Sts. Cyril & Methodius •	*plummets,*
15	D	Sexagesima • ☌☿♆ • Susan B. Anthony born, 1820	*snow*
16	M.	George Washington's Birthday (observed) • ☾ runs low • ☾ at perig. • { 10.3 8.7	*on*
17	Tu.	Eighth prime minister of Canada, Wilfrid Laurier, died, 1919 • Winter's back breaks. •	*the*
18	W.	☌♆☾ • Hiroyuki Goto recited pi to 42,195 digits, 1995 • { 10.9 9.5	*summits.*
19	Th.	*Luck is loaned, not owned.* • Knights of Pythias founded, 1864 • Tides { 11.1 9.8	*This*
20	Fr.	New ● • An auto-airplane combination, Arrowbile, completed for testing, 1937	*week's*
21	Sa.	☌♅☉ • First telephone book issued, 1878 • { 11.1 — •	*bright*
22	D	Quinquagesima • Islamic New Year • ☾ on Eq. •	*and*
23	M.	Pure Monday • ☌♀☾ • Cato Street plot foiled, 1820 •	*beamish.*
24	Tu.	Shrove Tuesday • "When You Wish Upon a Star" recorded, 1940 • { 10.1 9.8 •	*This*
25	W.	Ash Wednesday • ☾ at ☊ • ☌♂☾ •	*one's*
26	Th.	*A year of snow, a year of plenty.* • *Les Misérables* author, Victor Hugo, born, 1802 • { 9.5 8.6	*not*
27	Fr.	Italian government asked public for ideas on how to save the Leaning Tower of Pisa, 1964 •	*for*
28	Sa.	☾ at apo. • Baltimore and Ohio Railroad incorporated, 1827 • { 8.9 7.7 •	*the*
29	D	1st S. in Lent • Sunday of Orthodoxy •	*squeamish!*

If I have seen further, it is by standing upon the shoulders of giants.
–Isaac Newton, English physicist

Farmer's Calendar

■ The highest point in the state of Vermont is Mount Mansfield, a massive peak whose various buttresses and approaches take up parts of four different townships. The upper reaches of Mansfield are thought by the fanciful to look like the face of a man lying on his back with his head resting on the height and his feet in, roughly, Montreal. Thus, Mount Mansfield has its Forehead, its Nose, its Adam's Apple. The summit is the Chin, which rises 4,393 feet above sea level. Or, rather, the summit's elevation *was* 4,393 feet. A couple of years ago, a revised elevation was published, based on new maps made with satellites and computers. Now Mount Mansfield stands at a little over 4,395 feet. All these years, we were wrong about the height of the biggest mountain in the state.

Here, surely, we have a rueful metaphor of man's quest for the truth. "What do you know, for sure?" the old-timer asks his neighbor in the famous joke, to which his neighbor, evidently a species of rural philosopher, replies, "Not a damn thing!" Yes, indeed. If we are honest, most of us admit that as we put on age and experience, certainty becomes an ever scarcer commodity. More than that, certainty becomes a prize that, like some mysterious, hypothetical particle in the most abstruse physics, eludes us the more, the more we seek it. One had thought that the mountains—grand and enduring as they are—constituted a solid piece of data. Not at all. We learn that if we keep looking for the truth, we will find more of it than we want or need.

MARCH, The Third Month

Jupiter, at its year's maximum brilliance, comes to opposition on the night of March 3–4. Venus, growing brighter, reaches its greatest angular separation from the Sun on the 29th, setting more than four hours after sunset. Mercury is easily visible as the only "star" far below Venus in late evening twilight after the 14th, and optimal from the 20th to the 31st. Saturn is highest at nightfall and sets around 2:00 A.M., and Mars moves into Taurus. The Moon has wonderful close meetings with Venus on the 24th and Mars on the 25th. Late this month, all five bright planets are arrayed along the zodiac like a string of pearls in evening twilight. Spring begins with the vernal equinox on the 20th at 1:49 A.M. EST.

○	Full Moon	6th day	18th hour	14th minute
☾	Last Quarter	13th day	16th hour	1st minute
●	New Moon	20th day	17th hour	41st minute
☽	First Quarter	28th day	18th hour	48th minute

Times are given in Eastern Standard Time.

For an explanation of this page, see page 40; for values of Key Letters, see page 170.

Day of Year	Day of Month	Day of Week	☼ Rises h. m.	Key	☼ Sets h. m.	Key	Length of Day h. m.	Sun Fast m.	Declination of Sun ° '	High Tide Boston Light—A.M.	Bold—P.M.	☽ Rises h. m.	Key	☽ Sets h. m.	Key	☽ Place	☽ Age
61	1	M.	6 19	D	5 35	B	11 16	3	7 s.16	6¾	**7½**	11 A.M. 55	A	3 A.M. 21	E	AUR	10
62	2	Tu.	6 17	D	5 36	B	11 19	3	6 53	7½	**8¼**	12 P.M. 53	A	4 10	E	GEM	11
63	3	W.	6 16	D	5 37	B	11 21	4	6 30	8½	**9¼**	1 57	B	4 52	E	CAN	12
64	4	Th.	6 14	D	5 38	B	11 24	4	6 07	9¼	**10**	3 05	B	5 28	E	CAN	13
65	5	Fr.	6 12	D	5 39	B	11 27	4	5 44	10	**10½**	4 16	C	5 57	E	LEO	14
66	6	Sa.	6 11	D	5 41	B	11 30	4	5 21	10¾	**11¼**	5 27	C	6 23	D	LEO	15
67	7	**C**	6 09	D	5 42	B	11 33	5	4 57	11½	**11¾**	6 38	D	6 47	D	LEO	16
68	8	M.	6 07	D	5 43	B	11 36	5	4 34	**12¼**	—	7 51	D	7 09	C	VIR	17
69	9	Tu.	6 06	D	5 44	B	11 38	5	4 10	12½	**12¾**	9 05	E	7 32	B	VIR	18
70	10	W.	6 04	D	5 45	B	11 41	5	3 47	1¼	**1¾**	10 21	E	7 57	B	VIR	19
71	11	Th.	6 02	C	5 46	B	11 44	6	3 23	2	**2½**	11 P.M. 38	E	8 26	B	LIB	20
72	12	Fr.	6 01	C	5 48	B	11 47	6	3 00	2¾	**3¼**	—	–	9 01	A	SCO	21
73	13	Sa.	5 59	C	5 49	B	11 50	6	2 36	3¾	**4½**	12 A.M. 55	E	9 45	A	OPH	22
74	14	**C**	5 57	C	5 50	B	11 53	6	2 12	4¾	**5½**	2 06	E	10 40	A	SAG	23
75	15	M.	5 55	C	5 51	B	11 56	7	1 49	5¾	**6¾**	3 08	E	11 A.M. 46	A	SAG	24
76	16	Tu.	5 54	C	5 52	B	11 58	7	1 25	7	**7¾**	3 58	E	12 P.M. 58	B	SAG	25
77	17	W.	5 52	C	5 53	B	12 01	7	1 01	8	**8¾**	4 38	E	2 13	B	CAP	26
78	18	Th.	5 50	C	5 55	B	12 05	7	0 37	9	**9¾**	5 09	E	3 26	C	AQU	27
79	19	Fr.	5 49	C	5 56	C	12 07	8	0 s.14	10	**10½**	5 35	D	4 38	C	AQU	28
80	20	Sa.	5 47	C	5 57	C	12 10	8	0 n.10	10¾	**11¼**	5 58	D	5 46	D	AQU	0
81	21	**C**	5 45	C	5 58	C	12 13	8	0 34	11½	**11¾**	6 19	C	6 52	D	PSC	1
82	22	M.	5 43	C	5 59	C	12 16	9	0 57	**12¼**	—	6 39	B	7 58	E	PSC	2
83	23	Tu.	5 42	C	6 00	C	12 18	9	1 21	12½	**1**	7 00	B	9 03	E	PSC	3
84	24	W.	5 40	C	6 01	C	12 21	9	1 45	1¼	**1½**	7 23	B	10 08	E	ARI	4
85	25	Th.	5 38	C	6 03	C	12 25	10	2 08	1¾	**2¼**	7 49	A	11 P.M. 12	E	TAU	5
86	26	Fr.	5 36	C	6 04	C	12 28	10	2 32	2½	**3**	8 21	A	—	–	TAU	6
87	27	Sa.	5 35	C	6 05	C	12 30	10	2 55	3¼	**3¾**	8 59	A	12 A.M. 14	E	TAU	7
88	28	**C**	5 33	C	6 06	C	12 33	10	3 19	4	**4¾**	9 45	A	1 12	E	AUR	8
89	29	M.	5 31	C	6 07	C	12 36	11	3 42	5	**5¾**	10 39	A	2 03	E	GEM	9
90	30	Tu.	5 29	C	6 08	C	12 39	11	4 05	6	**6¾**	11 A.M. 39	B	2 48	E	GEM	10
91	31	W.	5 28	B	6 09	C	12 41	11	4 n.28	7	**7¾**	12 P.M. 45	B	3 A.M. 26	E	CAN	11

MARCH hath 31 days. 2004

There's a path that leads to Nowhere
In a meadow that I know,
Where an inland river rises
And the stream is still and slow. –Corinne Roosevelt Robinson

D. M.	D. W.	Dates, Feasts, Fasts, Aspects, Tide Heights	Weather ↓
1	M.	**St. David** • ☾ rides high • ☌♄☾ • Tides {8.7 7.7 •	*Brace*
2	Tu.	**St. Chad** • Oversized gorilla carried girl to top of Empire State Bldg. in *King Kong,* 1933	*yourself:*
3	W.	Ember Day • ☿ in sup. ☌ • Tides {9.3 8.3 •	*Nor'easter*
4	Th.	♃ at ☍ • Nuclear-power plant began operation in Antarctica, 1962 •	*knocks*
5	Fr.	**St. Piran** • Ember Day • *A good teacher is worth two books.* • {10.1 9.3 •	*you*
6	Sa.	Ember Day • **Full Worm** ○ • ☌♃☾ • Tides {10.5 9.8 •	*on*
7	**C**	**2nd S. in Lent** • ♄ stat. • Tides {10.7 10.2 •	*your*
8	M.	**St. Perpetua** • ☾ on Eq. • Actress Lynn Redgrave born, 1943 •	*keister!*
9	Tu.	First Japanese ambassador to U.S. arrived in San Francisco, 1860 • Tides {10.6 10.7 •	*Use*
10	W.	☾ at ☋ • William Knox bowled a perfect 300 game, 1913 • Tides {10.8 10.4 •	*this*
11	Th.	☾ at perig. • Naval Unit Commendation awarded to light cruiser U.S.S. *Helena,* 1945	*hiatus—*
12	Fr.	Singer Paul McCartney married photographer Linda Eastman, 1969 • Tides {10.8 9.5 •	*a*
13	Sa.	*A pet lamb makes a cross ram.* • "Uncle Sam" appeared in cartoon for first time, 1852 •	*new*
14	**C**	**3rd S. in Lent** • Tides {10.3 8.6 •	*storm's*
15	M.	Beware the Ides of March • ☾ runs low • Maine became the 23rd state, 1820 • {10.1 8.6	*here*
16	Tu.	Prisoner-of-war Col. Floyd J. Thompson released from N. Vietnam after almost nine years, 1973 •	*to*
17	W.	**St. Patrick** • ☌♆☾ • Eruption of Mt. Agung in Bali, 1963 •	*inundate*
18	Th.	☌♅☾ • Maud Farris-Luse died at 115 years, 56 days, in 2002 • Tides {10.5 9.6 •	*us!*
19	Fr.	**St. Joseph** • Academy Awards first televised, 1953 • Tides {10.6 10.0 •	*That*
20	Sa.	**Vernal Equinox** • **New** ● • Libby Riddles won the Iditarod, 1985 •	*UFO,*
21	**C**	**4th S. in Lent** • ☾ on Eq. • Tides {10.6 10.4 •	*the*
22	M.	☌☿☾ • Gambling made illegal in Boston, 1630 • {10.3 —	*experts*
23	Tu.	*Halifax Gazette* became Canada's first newspaper, 1752 • Tides {10.4 10.0	*say,*
24	W.	☾ at ☊ • ☌♀☾ • ♇ stat. • Tides {10.2 9.5 •	*is*
25	Th.	**Annunciation** • ☌♂☾ • Tides {9.9 9.1 •	*called*
26	Fr.	Dr. Jonas Salk announced development of polio vaccine, 1953 • Tides {9.6 8.6	*the*
27	Sa.	☾ at apo. • *Don't say that spring has come until you can put your foot on nine daisies.* •	*"Sun,"*
28	**C**	**5th S. in Lent** • ☌♄☾ • Tides {8.9 7.8 •	*but*
29	M.	☾ rides high • ☿ Gr. Elong. (19° E.) • ♀ Gr. Elong. (46° E.) • {8.8 7.7 •	*it's*
30	Tu.	Queensboro Bridge, the first double-decker, opened in N.Y.C., 1909 • {8.7 7.8 •	*gone*
31	W.	*The seeds of great things are often small.* • Philosopher René Descartes born, 1596 •	*away.*

Farmer's Calendar

■ Some days in March, the weather seems to want to show you everything it's got, like a show-off kid. The sky changes with a kind of headlong speed that is almost cinematic: You're watching a weather movie and the film is running on fast-forward. Blue sky and bright sun give way to gray clouds and quick, driving snow, which give way to more blue sky, which is followed by more snow. The little winter birds, chickadees and sparrows, are tossed about on the fresh wind, along with last year's leaves. They blow by in streams, tumbling. You'll have a whole day's weather in half an hour, and because the month is March, that weather will be flamboyant: You'll go through winter and well into spring, and back, and forth again, in the course of a single day.

Maybe the crazy flux of days like these is owing to the season—the equinox, when Earth's attitude toward the Sun puts the cold side of the year in uneasy balance with the warm. Again like a young person, talented but confused, the year can't figure out what it wants to be from one day to the next, so it decides to be everything at once, all the time. The resulting drama is exciting for the onlooker. These are good days in which to be outdoors, as the rush and change overhead lift your spirits. But after a while, the spectacle wears you down. You begin to wish the day would pick a line and stick to it rather than go through the entire repertoire over and over. No chance. The year is young, and so is the kid, and both will go where they will go. You can ride along, but you can't drive.

APRIL, The Fourth Month

The first week of April offers several notable sights: All five naked-eye planets remain simultaneously visible for the final time for many years to come. Mercury concludes its best evening apparition of the year. Venus, now unbelievably brilliant, floats near the famous Seven Sisters star cluster in Taurus. Mars, nearly 200 times dimmer than Venus, hovers to Venus's upper left the entire month, both joined by the crescent Moon on the 23rd. Jupiter has a superb month, brilliant to the naked eye and striking through a telescope. It is high up at nightfall in the east and reaches its apex more than halfway up in the southern sky at 10:00 P.M. The Moon joins it on the 29th.

○	Full Moon	5th day	7th hour	3rd minute
☾	Last Quarter	11th day	23rd hour	46th minute
●	New Moon	19th day	9th hour	21st minute
☽	First Quarter	27th day	13th hour	32nd minute

After 2:00 A.M. on April 4, Eastern Daylight Time (EDT) is given.

For an explanation of this page, see page 40; for values of Key Letters, see page 170.

Day of Year	Day of Month	Day of Week	☼ Rises h. m.	Key	☼ Sets h. m.	Key	Length of Day h. m.	Sun Fast m.	Declination of Sun ° '	High Tide Boston Light—A.M.	Bold—P.M.	☽ Rises h. m.	Key	☽ Sets h. m.	Key	☽ Place	☽ Age
92	1	Th.	5 26	B	6 11	C	12 45	12	4 N.51	7¾	**8½**	1 P.M. 54	B	3 A.M. 57	E	LEO	12
93	2	Fr.	5 24	B	6 12	C	12 48	12	5 14	8¾	**9¼**	3 05	C	4 24	E	LEO	13
94	3	Sa.	5 23	B	6 13	C	12 50	12	5 37	9½	**10**	4 17	D	4 48	D	LEO	14
95	4	**C**	6 21	B	7 14	D	12 53	13	6 00	11¼	**11½**	6 30	D	6 11	D	VIR	15
96	5	M.	6 19	B	7 15	D	12 56	13	6 23	**12**	—	7 45	E	6 34	C	VIR	16
97	6	Tu.	6 18	B	7 16	D	12 58	13	6 46	12¼	**12¾**	9 02	E	6 58	B	VIR	17
98	7	W.	6 16	B	7 17	D	13 01	13	7 08	1	**1½**	10 22	E	7 26	B	LIB	18
99	8	Th.	6 14	B	7 18	D	13 04	14	7 31	1¾	**2¼**	11 P.M. 42	E	7 59	A	LIB	19
100	9	Fr.	6 12	B	7 20	D	13 08	14	7 53	2½	**3¼**	—	–	8 41	A	OPH	20
101	10	Sa.	6 11	B	7 21	D	13 10	14	8 16	3½	**4¼**	12 A.M. 58	E	9 34	A	SAG	21
102	11	**C**	6 09	B	7 22	D	13 13	15	8 38	4½	**5¼**	2 04	E	10 37	A	SAG	22
103	12	M.	6 08	B	7 23	D	13 15	15	8 59	5½	**6¼**	2 58	E	11 A.M. 48	A	SAG	23
104	13	Tu.	6 06	B	7 24	D	13 18	15	9 21	6½	**7½**	3 40	E	1 P.M. 02	B	CAP	24
105	14	W.	6 04	B	7 25	D	13 21	15	9 43	7¾	**8½**	4 13	E	2 15	C	CAP	25
106	15	Th.	6 03	B	7 26	D	13 23	16	10 04	8¾	**9½**	4 40	D	3 26	C	AQU	26
107	16	Fr.	6 01	B	7 27	D	13 26	16	10 25	9¾	**10¼**	5 03	D	4 34	D	AQU	27
108	17	Sa.	5 59	B	7 29	D	13 30	16	10 46	10¾	**11**	5 24	D	5 40	D	PSC	28
109	18	**C**	5 58	B	7 30	D	13 32	16	11 07	11½	**11¾**	5 43	C	6 45	E	PSC	29
110	19	M.	5 56	B	7 31	D	13 35	16	11 28	**12¼**	—	6 04	B	7 50	E	PSC	0
111	20	Tu.	5 55	B	7 32	D	13 37	17	11 48	12¼	**12¾**	6 26	B	8 55	E	ARI	1
112	21	W.	5 53	B	7 33	D	13 40	17	12 08	1	**1½**	6 51	B	9 59	E	ARI	2
113	22	Th.	5 52	B	7 34	D	13 42	17	12 28	1½	**2¼**	7 20	A	11 P.M. 03	E	TAU	3
114	23	Fr.	5 50	B	7 35	D	13 45	17	12 48	2¼	**2¾**	7 55	A	—	–	TAU	4
115	24	Sa.	5 49	B	7 36	D	13 47	17	13 08	3	**3½**	8 38	A	12 A.M. 03	E	TAU	5
116	25	**C**	5 47	B	7 38	D	13 51	18	13 27	3¾	**4¼**	9 28	A	12 57	E	AUR	6
117	26	M.	5 46	B	7 39	D	13 53	18	13 47	4½	**5¼**	10 26	A	1 44	E	GEM	7
118	27	Tu.	5 44	B	7 40	D	13 56	18	14 06	5¼	**6**	11 A.M. 29	B	2 23	E	CAN	8
119	28	W.	5 43	B	7 41	D	13 58	18	14 24	6¼	**7**	12 P.M. 36	B	2 57	E	CAN	9
120	29	Th.	5 42	B	7 42	D	14 00	18	14 43	7¼	**8**	1 44	C	3 25	E	LEO	10
121	30	Fr.	5 40	B	7 43	D	14 03	18	15 N.02	8¼	**8¾**	2 P.M. 54	C	3 A.M. 49	D	LEO	11

APRIL hath 30 days. 2004

Again the blackbirds sing; the streams
Wake, laughing, from their winter dreams,
And tremble in the April showers
The tassels of the maple flowers. –John Greenleaf Whittier

D. M.	D. W.	Dates, Feasts, Fasts, Aspects, Tide Heights	*Weather* ↓
1	Th.	All Fools' • *It is an equal failing to trust everybody and to trust nobody.* • {9.3 8.7 •	*The*
2	Fr.	☌♃☾ • Bread riot in Richmond, Va., 1863 • Tides {9.7 9.3 •	*poet*
3	Sa.	St. Richard of Chichester • Pony Express began, 1860 • {10.1 9.9	*claims*
4	C	**Palm Sunday** • ☾ on Eq. • **Daylight Saving Time begins, 2:00 A.M.**	*that*
5	M.	Full Pink ○ • Sec. of State Colin Powell born, 1937 • Tides {10.7 — •	*April's*
6	Tu.	First day of Passover • ☿ stat. • {11.1 10.8 •	*cruel,*
7	W.	☾ at ☋ • ☾ at perig. • Sahara Desert sand began falling in Switzerland, 2002 •	*but*
8	Th.	Maundy Thursday • Clint Eastwood elected mayor of Carmel, Calif., 1986 •	*now*
9	Fr.	**Good Friday** • NASA introduced first seven astronauts to press, 1959 •	*she's*
10	Sa.	*Gidget* premiered, 1959 • Trans-Canada Air Lines created by Parliament, 1937 •	*nice*
11	C	**Easter** • Orthodox Easter • ☾ runs low • Tides {10.7 9.1	*and*
12	M.	Easter Monday • Charles A. Gayler received patent for fireproof safe, 1833 •	*flirty;*
13	Tu.	☌♆☾ • Thomas Jefferson born, 1743 • Alewives run, Cape Cod, Mass. •	*she*
14	W.	N.J. passed first law providing state aid for public roads, 1891 • Tides {9.9 9.2 •	*has*
15	Th.	☌⛢☾ • *It does not always rain when a pig squeals.* • Tides {9.9 9.5 •	*her*
16	Fr.	☿ in inf. ☌ • Composer Henry Mancini born, 1924 • Tides {10.0 9.9	*rains,*
17	Sa.	☾ on Eq. • Minot's Light in Mass. swept away during storm, 1851 • Tides {10.1 10.2	*her*
18	C	**1st S. af. Easter** • First "washateria" opened, 1934 •	*breezes*
19	M.	New ● • Eclipse ☉ • Great fire in Toronto started, 1904 •	*cool,*
20	Tu	☾ at ☊ • Retailer Stanley Marcus born, 1905 • Tides {10.4 9.8 •	*and*
21	W.	Ashes of *Star Trek* creator, Gene Roddenberry, journeyed into space, 1997 •	*sometimes*
22	Th.	*Sirius* became first ship to complete trek across Atlantic solely by steam, 1838 •	*downright*
23	Fr.	St. George • ☾ at apo. • ☌♀☾ • Tides {10.0 8.9 •	*dirty!*
24	Sa.	Robert B. Thomas born, 1766 • "La Marseillaise" composed, 1792 • Tides {9.7 8.6 •	*Is*
25	C	**2nd S. af. Easter** • ☾ rides high • ☌♄☾ •	*she*
26	M.	St. Mark • *A new broom sweeps clean, but the old brush knows all the corners.* •	*nasty*
27	Tu	Babe Ruth Day, 1947 • Civil rights activist Coretta Scott King born, 1927 • {9.0 8.1 •	*or*
28	W.	101-day voyage of balsawood raft *Kon-Tiki* began, 1947 • Tides {8.9 8.3	*nifty?*
29	Th.	☌♃☾ • ☿ stat. • Prisoners liberated at Dachau, 1945 • Tides {9.1 8.7	*Or*
30	Fr.	Louisiana joined Union as 18th state, 1812 • Tides {9.3 9.2 •	*fifty-fifty?*

Jewelry takes people's minds off your wrinkles.
–Sonja Henie, Norwegian figure skater

Farmer's Calendar

■ In the waste places beside the road, a moraine of sand and gravel, scraped off the road by the snowplows, accumulates over the winter. It's a bitter, barren ground, a tiny desert. Nothing should be able to grow there. But on those unpromising roadsides, where they lie in the pale spring sun, little yellow flowers appear while in the woods the snow still lingers. The coltsfoot *(Tussilago farfara)* comes up with the skunk cabbage. They are the first of the first flowers in the year. But though the skunk cabbage, by its look, is hardly a flower at all, the coltsfoot is the real thing.

It's easy to miss the coltsfoot. You don't look for a flower to grow in the sterile till that is its habitat. And it's a small flower, a few inches high, with, at first, no leaves but only a spindly stalk. Odd brown scales like those of asparagus clasp the stalk, at the top of which the yellow pom-pom of a flower nods. The flower endures for a week or so. When it has gone by, the plant's leaves appear. The size of your hand, and vaguely heart-shaped, the leaves give the plant its name; somebody thought they looked like a colt's hoof or perhaps its track. That is no very compelling resemblance, to be sure, but the flower is a good mimic in another way. The coltsfoot's bloom looks much like a dandelion: same yellow, same single flower made up of small radiating petals. But the coltsfoot comes a good six weeks before the dandelion. For a moment, when you pass it clinging to its poverty-stricken heap of dirt, you think you've skipped ahead from April to June and missed the spring altogether.

2004 MAY, The Fifth Month

Venus attains its greatest brilliancy on the 2nd at magnitude –4.5. During this month, the evening star drops dramatically lower each evening at nightfall, as it speeds in retrograde motion toward its momentous passage in front of the Sun early next month. Telescopes now show Venus as a dramatic, ever-larger crescent, lit from behind by the Sun. Mars and Saturn, both in Gemini and sinking lower each evening, float together the final half of the month. Look for the crescent Moon between them and Venus on the 21st in fading twilight. A total lunar eclipse on the 4th will not be visible from most of the United States and Canada.

○	Full Moon	4th day	16th hour	33rd minute
☾	Last Quarter	11th day	7th hour	4th minute
●	New Moon	19th day	0 hour	52nd minute
☽	First Quarter	27th day	3rd hour	57th minute

Times are given in Eastern Daylight Time.

For an explanation of this page, see page 40; for values of Key Letters, see page 170.

Day of Year	Day of Month	Day of Week	☼ Rises h. m.	Key	☼ Sets h. m.	Key	Length of Day h. m.	Sun Fast m.	Declination of Sun ° '	High Tide Boston Light—A.M.	Bold—P.M.	☽ Rises h. m.	Key	☽ Sets h. m.	Key	☽ Place	☽ Age
122	1	Sa.	5 39	B	7 44	D	14 05	18	15N.20	9	**9½**	4 P.M. 05	D	4 A.M. 12	D	VIR	12
123	2	**C**	5 38	B	7 45	D	14 07	19	15 38	10	**10¼**	5 18	E	4 34	C	VIR	13
124	3	M.	5 36	A	7 46	D	14 10	19	15 55	10¾	**11**	6 35	E	4 57	B	VIR	14
125	4	Tu.	5 35	A	7 48	D	14 13	19	16 12	11½	**11¾**	7 55	E	5 23	B	VIR	15
126	5	W.	5 34	A	7 49	D	14 15	19	16 29	**12½**	—	9 18	E	5 54	B	LIB	16
127	6	Th.	5 32	A	7 50	D	14 18	19	16 46	12½	**1¼**	10 39	E	6 33	A	SCO	17
128	7	Fr.	5 31	A	7 51	D	14 20	19	17 02	1½	**2**	11 P.M. 52	E	7 23	A	OPH	18
129	8	Sa.	5 30	A	7 52	D	14 22	19	17 18	2¼	**3**	—	–	8 24	A	SAG	19
130	9	**C**	5 29	A	7 53	D	14 24	19	17 34	3¼	**4**	12 A.M. 53	E	9 36	A	SAG	20
131	10	M.	5 28	A	7 54	D	14 26	19	17 50	4¼	**5**	1 40	E	10 A.M. 51	B	CAP	21
132	11	Tu.	5 27	A	7 55	D	14 28	19	18 06	5¼	**6**	2 16	E	12 P.M. 06	B	CAP	22
133	12	W.	5 25	A	7 56	D	14 31	19	18 21	6¼	**7¼**	2 45	E	1 18	C	AQU	23
134	13	Th.	5 24	A	7 57	D	14 33	19	18 35	7½	**8¼**	3 09	D	2 26	D	AQU	24
135	14	Fr.	5 23	A	7 58	E	14 35	19	18 50	8½	**9**	3 30	D	3 32	D	PSC	25
136	15	Sa.	5 22	A	7 59	E	14 37	19	19 04	9½	**10**	3 50	C	4 37	D	CET	26
137	16	**C**	5 21	A	8 00	E	14 39	19	19 17	10¼	**10½**	4 10	B	5 41	E	PSC	27
138	17	M.	5 20	A	8 01	E	14 41	19	19 31	11	**11¼**	4 31	B	6 45	E	ARI	28
139	18	Tu.	5 19	A	8 02	E	14 43	19	19 44	11¾	12	4 54	B	7 49	E	ARI	29
140	19	W.	5 19	A	8 03	E	14 44	19	19 56	**12½**	—	5 22	A	8 53	E	TAU	0
141	20	Th.	5 18	A	8 04	E	14 46	19	20 09	12½	**1¼**	5 54	A	9 54	E	TAU	1
142	21	Fr.	5 17	A	8 05	E	14 48	19	20 22	1¼	**1¾**	6 34	A	10 51	E	TAU	2
143	22	Sa.	5 16	A	8 06	E	14 50	19	20 33	1¾	**2½**	7 22	A	11 P.M. 40	E	AUR	3
144	23	**C**	5 15	A	8 07	E	14 52	19	20 44	2½	**3¼**	8 17	A	—	–	GEM	4
145	24	M.	5 15	A	8 08	E	14 53	19	20 55	3¼	**4**	9 18	A	12 A.M. 22	E	CAN	5
146	25	Tu.	5 14	A	8 09	E	14 55	19	21 06	4	**4¾**	10 23	B	12 57	E	CAN	6
147	26	W.	5 13	A	8 10	E	14 57	19	21 16	4¾	**5½**	11 A.M. 29	B	1 26	E	LEO	7
148	27	Th.	5 13	A	8 11	E	14 58	18	21 26	5¾	**6¼**	12 P.M. 36	C	1 51	D	LEO	8
149	28	Fr.	5 12	A	8 12	E	15 00	18	21 35	6½	**7¼**	1 44	D	2 14	D	LEO	9
150	29	Sa.	5 11	A	8 12	E	15 01	18	21 44	7½	**8**	2 54	D	2 35	D	VIR	10
151	30	**C**	5 11	A	8 13	E	15 02	18	21 53	8½	**8¾**	4 08	E	2 57	C	VIR	11
152	31	M.	5 10	A	8 14	E	15 04	18	22N.02	9¼	**9¾**	5 P.M. 25	E	3 A.M. 21	B	VIR	12

MAY hath 31 days. 2004

My lilac trees are old and tall;
I cannot reach their bloom at all.
They send their perfume over trees
And roofs and streets, to find the bees. –Louise Driscoll

D. M.	D. W.	Dates, Feasts, Fasts, Aspects, Tide Heights	Weather ↓
1	Sa.	May Day • Great Britain was formed, 1707 • Tides {9.7 / 9.9 •	*Glory!*
2	C	**3rd S. af. Easter** • ☾ on Eq. • ♀ Gr. Bril. •	*Sun's*
3	M.	Sts. Philip & James • **Invention of the Holy Cross** • Tides {10.4 / 11.2 •	*the*
4	Tu.	**Full Flower** ○ • Eclipse ☾ • ☾ at ☋ • {10.6 / 11.7 •	*story.*
5	W.	**Cinco de Mayo** • ♃ stat. • *The first dish pleaseth all.* • {10.7 / —	*Rumors*
6	Th.	☾ at perig. • Eurotunnel, a.k.a. "Chunnel," opened, 1994 • {12.0 / 10.6 •	*of*
7	Fr.	First exhibit by "Group of Seven" artists, 1920 • Bigfoot reported seen in Hollis, N.H., 1977	*thunder-*
8	Sa.	St. Julian of Norwich • ☾ runs low • V-E Day, 1945 •	*boomers.*
9	C	**4th S. af. Easter** • Thomas Blood stole Crown Jewels, 1671	*Showery*
10	M.	☌♆☾ • *It is not common for hens to have pillows.* • Tides {10.9 / 9.4 •	*and*
11	Tu.	Glacier National Park, Mont., established, 1910 • {10.4 / 9.3 • **Three**	*flowery,*
12	W.	☌♅☾ • S. Maroney swam from Cuba to Florida in 24.5 hours, 1997 • **Chilly**	*with*
13	Th.	Sandstorm in N.J., 1866 • Pope John Paul II shot, 1981 • **Saints**	*lightning*
14	Fr.	St. Matthias • ☾ on Eq. • ☿ Gr. Elong. (26° W.) • {9.6 / 9.8 •	*almost*
15	Sa.	*The prudent man does not make the goat his gardener.* • Tides {9.5 / 10.0 •	*hourly.*
16	C	**Rogation S.** • ☌☿☾ • Tides {9.5 / 10.2 •	*Summer*
17	M.	☾ at ☊ • ♆ stat. • ♀ stat. • Tides {9.4 / 10.3 •	*heat*
18	Tu.	Masses feared end of world during passage of Halley's Comet, 1910 • {9.4 / 10.3 •	*makes*
19	W.	**New** ● • First Jumping Frog Jubilee in Calaveras County, Calif., 1928 •	*school-*
20	Th.	Ascension • Orthodox Ascension • Fountain pen patented, 1830 •	*kids*
21	Fr.	☾ at apo. • ☌♀☾ • Wrestler/actor Mr. T born, 1952 •	*gripers—*
22	Sa.	☾ rides high • ☌♂☾ • ☌♄☾ • Tides {10.0 / 8.8 •	*now*
23	C	**1st S. af. Asc.** • Botanist Carolus Linnaeus born, 1707 • {9.8 / 8.6	*you'll*
24	M.	**Victoria Day (Canada)** • ☌♂♄ • Tides {9.6 / 8.5 •	*need*
25	Tu.	St. Bede • Daniel Goodwin climbed Chicago's Sears Tower using suction cups, 1981 •	*your*
26	W.	Shavuot • Actor John Wayne born, 1907 • Tides {9.3 / 8.6	*windshield*
27	Th.	☌♃☾ • *Some are weatherwise, some are otherwise.* • Tides {9.2 / 8.9	*wipers!*
28	Fr.	"When a Man Loves a Woman," by Percy Sledge, topped charts, 1966 • {9.2 / 9.3 •	*Clear:*
29	Sa.	☾ on Eq. • Bartholomeu Dias, Portuguese discoverer of Cape of Good Hope, drowned, 1500	*Early*
30	C	**Whit S.** • **Pentecost** • Orthodox Pentecost •	*peas*
31	M.	Visit. of Mary • **Memorial Day (observed)** • ☾ at ☋ • {9.8 / 11.1	*appear.*

Farmer's Calendar

■ The premises from which these monthly items issue include a house of the kind called a Cape Cod cottage. If you have spent much time in New England, you've seen these houses; perhaps you live in one. The Cape is the commonplace, vernacular housing of its era, the suburban ranch of bygone days. It's an oblong box, one-and-a-half or two stories, with a simple, symmetrical floor plan based on a central hall with matching front rooms on both sides and a big kitchen in the rear.

The outside of the house, in front, recapitulates the interior. There are two bays, each lighted by two windows, with the front entrance centered between them. Visually, the front entrance is the focal point of the house. Visually, it is the focal point, but in every other way, the front entrance is irrelevant. Nobody enters or leaves the house by it; you come in by a door in the gable end. The front door is nearly a trompe l'oeil. It might be painted on the front of the house for all the real use it gets.

Once a year, around this time, I open the front door of this house just to prove to myself that I can do it. The door creaks open cautiously, stiffly, like an old man getting out of a car at the end of a long ride. I sweep the past winter's accumulation of debris off the doorstep and close the door again. Closed it will stay. These famous old houses with their front entrances that are no entrances at all amount to a kind of sly architectural jest on the part of a people who appreciated the sly and took it wherever they found it.

Venus crosses the face of the Sun on the 8th for the first time since 1882 (see "Venus Touches the Sun," page 78). Doing so, it transitions from the evening to the morning sky, where it will remain for the rest of the year. This month of maximum sunshine could be titled "month of vanishing planets." Jupiter alone remains conspicuous in the west at nightfall; all the remaining bright planets now sink into the Sun's glare, joining the newly vanished winter constellations. Impossibly dim planet Pluto comes to opposition on the 11th in Ophiuchus; a large telescope is needed to see it. Look for the Moon to join lonely Jupiter on the 23rd. Summer begins with the solstice on the 20th at 8:57 P.M. EDT.

○ Full Moon	3rd day	0 hour	20th minute
☾ Last Quarter	9th day	16th hour	2nd minute
● New Moon	17th day	16th hour	27th minute
☽ First Quarter	25th day	15th hour	8th minute

Times are given in Eastern Daylight Time.

For an explanation of this page, see page 40; for values of Key Letters, see page 170.

Day of Year	Day of Month	Day of Week	☀ Rises h. m.	Key	☀ Sets h. m.	Key	Length of Day h. m.	Sun Fast m.	Declination of Sun ° '	High Tide Boston Light—A.M. **Bold—P.M.**		☽ Rises h. m.	Key	☽ Sets h. m.	Key	☽ Place	☽ Age
153	1	Tu.	5 10	A	8 15	E	15 05	18	22 N.10	10¼	**10½**	6 ᴘ 46	E	3 ᴀ 49	B	LIB	13
154	2	W.	5 10	A	8 16	E	15 06	18	22 18	11¼	**11¼**	8 10	E	4 24	A	SCO	14
155	3	Th.	5 09	A	8 16	E	15 07	18	22 25	12	—	9 29	E	5 08	A	OPH	15
156	4	Fr.	5 09	A	8 17	E	15 08	17	22 32	12¼	**1**	10 38	E	6 05	A	SAG	16
157	5	Sa.	5 09	A	8 18	E	15 09	17	22 38	1	**1¾**	11 ᴘ 33	E	7 15	A	SAG	17
158	6	**C**	5 08	A	8 18	E	15 10	17	22 44	2	**2¾**	—	–	8 32	B	CAP	18
159	7	M.	5 08	A	8 19	E	15 11	17	22 50	3	**3¾**	12 ᴀ 15	E	9 50	B	CAP	19
160	8	Tu.	5 08	A	8 20	E	15 12	17	22 55	4	**4¾**	12 47	D	11 ᴀ 06	B	AQU	20
161	9	W.	5 07	A	8 20	E	15 13	16	23 00	5	**5¾**	1 13	D	12 ᴘ 17	C	AQU	21
162	10	Th.	5 07	A	8 21	E	15 14	16	23 05	6	**6¾**	1 36	D	1 24	D	PSC	22
163	11	Fr.	5 07	A	8 21	E	15 14	16	23 09	7	**7¾**	1 56	C	2 30	D	CET	23
164	12	Sa.	5 07	A	8 22	E	15 15	16	23 12	8	**8½**	2 16	B	3 34	E	PSC	24
165	13	**C**	5 07	A	8 22	E	15 15	16	23 15	9	**9¼**	2 36	B	4 37	E	ARI	25
166	14	M.	5 07	A	8 23	E	15 16	15	23 18	10	**10**	2 59	B	5 41	E	ARI	26
167	15	Tu.	5 07	A	8 23	E	15 16	15	23 20	10¾	**10¾**	3 25	A	6 45	E	TAU	27
168	16	W.	5 07	A	8 23	E	15 16	15	23 22	11½	**11½**	3 56	A	7 47	E	TAU	28
169	17	Th.	5 07	A	8 24	E	15 17	15	23 24	12	—	4 33	A	8 45	E	TAU	0
170	18	Fr.	5 07	A	8 24	E	15 17	15	23 26	12	**12¾**	5 19	A	9 37	E	AUR	1
171	19	Sa.	5 07	A	8 24	E	15 17	14	23 26	12¾	**1½**	6 12	A	10 21	E	GEM	2
172	20	**C**	5 07	A	8 24	E	15 17	14	23 26	1½	**2**	7 11	A	10 58	E	CAN	3
173	21	M.	5 08	A	8 25	E	15 17	14	23 26	2	**2¾**	8 14	B	11 29	E	CAN	4
174	22	Tu.	5 08	A	8 25	E	15 17	14	23 26	2¾	**3½**	9 20	B	11 ᴘ 55	E	LEO	5
175	23	W.	5 08	A	8 25	E	15 17	13	23 25	3½	**4¼**	10 26	C	—	–	LEO	6
176	24	Th.	5 08	A	8 25	E	15 17	13	23 24	4¼	**5**	11 ᴀ 32	C	12 ᴀ 18	D	LEO	7
177	25	Fr.	5 09	A	8 25	E	15 16	13	23 22	5	**5¾**	12 ᴘ 39	D	12 39	C	VIR	8
178	26	Sa.	5 09	A	8 25	E	15 16	13	23 20	6	**6½**	1 49	D	1 00	C	VIR	9
179	27	**C**	5 09	A	8 25	E	15 16	13	23 17	7	**7¼**	3 01	E	1 22	B	VIR	10
180	28	M.	5 10	A	8 25	E	15 15	12	23 14	8	**8¼**	4 18	E	1 47	B	LIB	11
181	29	Tu.	5 10	A	8 25	E	15 15	12	23 11	8¾	**9¼**	5 39	E	2 17	B	LIB	12
182	30	W.	5 11	A	8 25	E	15 14	12	23 N.07	9¾	**10**	7 ᴘ 00	E	2 ᴀ 55	A	SCO	13

JUNE hath 30 days. 2004

These are the fields of light, and laughing air,
And yellow butterflies, and foraging bees,
And whitish, wayward blossoms winged as these,
And pale green tangles like a seamaid's hair. –Charles G. D. Roberts

D. M.	D. W.	Dates, Feasts, Fasts, Aspects, Tide Heights	*Weather* ↓
1	Tu.	Tennessee statehood, 1796 • Helen Keller, deaf/blind lecturer, died, 1968 •	*North*
2	W.	Ember Day • Queen Elizabeth II coronated, 1953 • Tides { 10.2 / 12.0 •	*is*
3	Th.	**Full Strawberry** ○ • ☾ at perig. • { 10.4 / — •	*drizzling,*
4	Fr.	Ember Day • Tiananmen Square massacre, 1989 • Tides { 12.2 / 10.4 •	*South*
5	Sa.	**St. Boniface** • Ember Day • ☾ runs low • *The talker sows, the silent reaps.*	*sizzling.*
6	**C**	**Trinity • Orthodox All Saints'** • D Day, 1944 • { 11.9 / 10.1 •	*Wed-*
7	M.	☌♆☾ • Reigning British monarchs visit U.S. for first time, 1939 •	*dings*
8	Tu.	☌⛢☾ • ♀ in inf. ☌ • ♀ transit over ☉ • { 11.0 / 9.8	*and*
9	W.	Church of England fully adopted *Book of Common Prayer,* 1549 •	*commencements*
10	Th.	**Corpus Christi** • ☾ on Eq. • ⛢ stat. • { 9.9 / 9.7 •	*require*
11	Fr.	**St. Barnabas** • ♇ at ☍ • Sir Barton won triple crown, 1919 •	*jackets:*
12	Sa.	Bryan Allen was first to cross the English Channel in a pedal-powered aircraft, 1979 • { 9.2 / 9.8	*maybe*
13	**C**	**2nd S. af. P.** • ☾ at ☊ • Tides { 9.0 / 9.9 •	*tents!*
14	M.	Engineer Thomas J. Kelly, dubbed "father of the lunar module," born, 1929 • { 8.9 / 10.0	*First*
15	Tu.	Writer Bill Arp born, 1826 • Fire on riverboat *General Slocum* killed 1,021 in 1904 •	*day*
16	W.	*If your head is wax, don't walk in the Sun.* • Soviet dancer Rudolf Nureyev defected, 1961 •	*of*
17	Th.	**New** ● • ☾ at apo. • The Nile was said to rise on this day each year.	*summer*
18	Fr.	☾ rides high • ☿ in sup. ☌ • National postal strike in Canada, 1924	*could*
19	Sa.	☌♄☾ • Wham-O filed to register Hula Hoop trademark, 1958 • Tides { 10.1 / 8.8	*be*
20	**C**	**3rd S. af. P.** • **Summer Solstice** • ☌♂☾ • { 10.0 / 8.7 •	*a*
21	M.	*The Parent Trap* movie debuted, 1961 • *He who rides the tiger can never dismount.*	*bummer.*
22	Tu.	**St. Alban** • Pilot/writer Anne Morrow Lindbergh born, 1906 • Tides { 9.9 / 8.8	*Take*
23	W.	☌♃☾ • First U.S. national lipreading tournament, Philadelphia, Pa., 1926 • { 9.7 / 8.9	*a*
24	Th.	**Nativ. John the Baptist** • **Midsummer Day** • { 9.6 / 9.1 •	*hike—*
25	Fr.	☾ on Eq. • John Tyler became first president to marry while in office, 1844 • { 9.4 / 9.5	*this*
26	Sa.	Humanitarian Pearl S. Buck born, 1892 • *If you would be loved, love and be lovable.* • { 9.4 / 9.8	*is*
27	**C**	**4th S. af. P.** • "O Canada" approved as national anthem, 1980 •	*weather*
28	M.	**St. Irenaeus** • ☾ at ☋ • Cholera epidemic began in N.Y.C., 1832	*anyone*
29	Tu.	**Sts. Peter & Paul** • ♀ stat. • Tides { 9.5 / 11.2	*would*
30	W.	Thousands watched Charles Blondin walk across Niagara Falls on a tightrope, 1859 • { 9.7 / 11.6	*like.*

A journey is like marriage. The certain way to be wrong is to think you control it. –John Steinbeck, American writer

Farmer's Calendar

■ Success in life comes only with effort, self-denial, and grim perseverance. So we are asked to believe, at any rate; and, with due allowance for sheer, dumb luck, the proposition is mainly true. But the lazy man has also his reward—smaller, less negotiable, but satisfactory in its own way, and especially welcome as a kind of end run around the rigorous principle above.

One June some years ago, I found myself dangerously behindhand in the grass-cutting department. Normally the lawn on this place begins to need mowing in the last part of April. But this year, owing (in small part) to the press of other business and (in large part) to slovenliness, moral inertia, and a really remarkable talent for putting things off, it was late May before I so much as got around to discovering that the lawn mower wouldn't start. It spent the next two weeks in the shop, where they also know a thing or two about inertia. By mid-June, the unshorn grass waved luxuriantly in the breezes. The lawn was no lawn—it was a savanna. It was a standing affront to good order. But, I found, it was also a place of color and varied design far exceeding what it would have been had I given it timely care. For my neglect had allowed ten thousand humble flowers that ought to have been cut down to grow and bloom. Blue ajuga, purple and white violets, dandelions, and bluets sported across the green field and gave it new life and motion. Through its manager's fecklessness, the lawn ceased to be a featureless green plot and had become the flag of the republic of indolence.

JULY, The Seventh Month

Earth reaches its annual far point (aphelion) from the Sun on the 5th. The reddish planets Mars and Mercury are extremely close on the 10th but are low in evening twilight; try with binoculars. During the first hour of nightfall, look for the year's best showing of man-made satellites. Some 300 are visible, one every minute or two. Meanwhile, as Jupiter sinks low in the west at nightfall, Venus comes storming back just before dawn after its historic June transit. Dramatically higher each morning, it reaches greatest brilliancy on the 14th, bright enough to cast shadows on white surfaces in rural settings away from artificial lights.

○	Full Moon	2nd day	7th hour	9th minute
☾	Last Quarter	9th day	3rd hour	34th minute
●	New Moon	17th day	7th hour	24th minute
☽	First Quarter	24th day	23rd hour	37th minute
○	Full Moon	31st day	14th hour	5th minute

Times are given in Eastern Daylight Time.

For an explanation of this page, see page 40; for values of Key Letters, see page 170.

Day of Year	Day of Month	Day of Week	☼ Rises h. m.	Key	☼ Sets h. m.	Key	Length of Day h. m.	Sun Fast m.	Declination of Sun ° '	High Tide Boston Light—A.M.	Bold—P.M.	☽ Rises h. m.	Key	☽ Sets h. m.	Key	☽ Place	☽ Age
183	1	Th.	5 11	A	8 25	E	15 14	12	23N.03	10¾	**11**	8 P.M. 15	E	3 A.M. 45	A	OPH	14
184	2	Fr.	5 12	A	8 25	E	15 13	12	22 58	11¾	12	9 18	E	4 49	A	SAG	15
185	3	Sa.	5 12	A	8 24	E	15 12	11	22 53	**12¾**	—	10 07	E	6 04	A	SAG	16
186	4	**C**	5 13	A	8 24	E	15 11	11	22 48	12¾	**1½**	10 45	E	7 25	B	CAP	17
187	5	M.	5 14	A	8 24	E	15 10	11	22 42	1¾	**2½**	11 14	E	8 45	B	CAP	18
188	6	Tu.	5 14	A	8 23	E	15 09	11	22 36	2¾	**3½**	11 P.M. 38	D	10 00	C	AQU	19
189	7	W.	5 15	A	8 23	E	15 08	11	22 30	3¾	**4¼**	—	–	11 A.M. 11	D	AQU	20
190	8	Th.	5 16	A	8 23	E	15 07	11	22 23	4½	**5¼**	12 A.M. 00	D	12 P.M. 19	D	PSC	21
191	9	Fr.	5 16	A	8 22	E	15 06	10	22 15	5½	**6**	12 20	C	1 25	D	PSC	22
192	10	Sa.	5 17	A	8 22	E	15 05	10	22 07	6½	**7**	12 41	C	2 29	E	ARI	23
193	11	**C**	5 18	A	8 21	E	15 03	10	21 59	7½	**7¾**	1 03	B	3 34	E	ARI	24
194	12	M.	5 19	A	8 21	E	15 02	10	21 51	8½	**8¾**	1 27	B	4 38	E	TAU	25
195	13	Tu.	5 19	A	8 20	E	15 01	10	21 43	9½	**9½**	1 57	A	5 40	E	TAU	26
196	14	W.	5 20	A	8 20	E	15 00	10	21 33	10¼	**10¼**	2 32	A	6 40	E	TAU	27
197	15	Th.	5 21	A	8 19	E	14 58	10	21 24	11	**11**	3 15	A	7 34	E	AUR	28
198	16	Fr.	5 22	A	8 18	E	14 56	10	21 14	11¾	**11¾**	4 06	A	8 20	E	GEM	29
199	17	Sa.	5 23	A	8 18	E	14 55	9	21 03	**12¼**	—	5 04	A	8 59	E	GEM	0
200	18	**C**	5 24	A	8 17	E	14 53	9	20 52	12½	**1**	6 07	B	9 32	E	CAN	1
201	19	M.	5 25	A	8 16	E	14 51	9	20 41	1	**1¾**	7 12	B	9 59	E	LEO	2
202	20	Tu.	5 25	A	8 15	E	14 50	9	20 30	1¾	**2¼**	8 18	C	10 23	D	LEO	3
203	21	W.	5 26	A	8 14	E	14 48	9	20 19	2¼	**3**	9 25	C	10 44	D	LEO	4
204	22	Th.	5 27	A	8 13	E	14 46	9	20 07	3	**3½**	10 31	D	11 04	C	VIR	5
205	23	Fr.	5 28	A	8 13	E	14 45	9	19 54	3¾	**4¼**	11 A.M. 38	D	11 25	C	VIR	6
206	24	Sa.	5 29	A	8 12	E	14 43	9	19 42	4½	**5**	12 P.M. 48	E	11 P.M. 48	B	VIR	7
207	25	**C**	5 30	A	8 11	D	14 41	9	19 28	5½	**6**	2 01	E	—	–	VIR	8
208	26	M.	5 31	A	8 10	D	14 39	9	19 15	6½	**6¾**	3 18	E	12 A.M. 15	B	LIB	9
209	27	Tu.	5 32	A	8 09	D	14 37	9	19 01	7½	**7¾**	4 36	E	12 48	A	SCO	10
210	28	W.	5 33	A	8 08	D	14 35	9	18 47	8½	**8¾**	5 53	E	1 32	A	OPH	11
211	29	Th.	5 34	A	8 07	D	14 33	9	18 33	9½	**9¾**	7 00	E	2 28	A	SAG	12
212	30	Fr.	5 35	A	8 05	D	14 30	9	18 18	10½	**10¾**	7 55	E	3 37	A	SAG	13
213	31	Sa.	5 36	A	8 04	D	14 28	9	18N.03	11½	**11¾**	8 P.M. 38	E	4 A.M. 55	B	CAP	14

JULY hath 31 days. 2004

How they shouted! What rejoicing!
How the old bell shook the air,
Till the clang of freedom ruffled,
The calmly gliding Delaware! –Unknown

D. M.	D. W.	Dates, Feasts, Fasts, Aspects, Tide Heights	*Weather* ↓
1	Th.	**Canada Day** • ☾ at perig. • Tides {9.9 / 11.9} •	*Rocket's*
2	Fr.	**Full Buck** ○ • ☾ runs low • First solo balloon flight around world completed, 2002	*red*
3	Sa.	**St. Thomas** • Dog Days begin. • Idaho became 43rd state, 1890 • {10.2 / —}	*glare!*
4	C	**5th S. af. P.** • **Independence Day** • ☌♆☾ •	*Warm*
5	M.	☌♅☾ • ⊕ at aphelion • A. Ashe won at Wimbledon, 1975 • {11.8 / 10.3}	*and*
6	Tu.	Pirate Capt. Kidd captured, 1699 • Fires in Québec brought smoke to NE U.S., 2002 • {11.4 / 10.2}	*fair.*
7	W.	Hammerfest, Norway (known as northernmost town in world), granted town status, 1789 •	*Can't*
8	Th.	☾ on Eq. • ☌♄☉ • Cornscateous air is everywhere. • Tides {10.2 / 9.9}	*be*
9	Fr.	Actor Rod Steiger died, 2002 • Argentina declared its independence from Spain, 1816	*beat*
10	Sa.	☾ at ☊ • ☌☿♂ • Mildred Benson, author of 23 Nancy Drew books, born, 1905 •	*if*
11	C	**6th S. af. P.** • *All strangers are relations to each other.* • {8.7 / 9.6}	*you*
12	M.	114°F in Basin, Wyo., 1900 • Comedian Bill Cosby born, 1937 • Tides {8.5 / 9.6} •	*like*
13	Tu.	☌♀☾ • Basketball player Frank Ramsey born, 1931 • Tides {8.4 / 9.7} •	*the*
14	W.	**Bastille Day** • ☾ at apo. • ♀ Gr. Bril. • Tides {8.4 / 9.8} •	*heat.*
15	Th.	**St. Swithin** • *St. Swithin's day if thou be fair, for 40 days 'twill rain nae mair.* •	*Boiling,*
16	Fr.	☾ rides high • First parking meters installed, Oklahoma City, Okla., 1935 •	*broiling,*
17	Sa.	**New** ● • Nils Bohlin, inventor of safer seat belt, born, 1920 • Tides {8.7 / —}	*sun-*
18	C	**7th S. af. P.** • ☌♂☾ • Fireworks banned in Cleveland, 1908	*tan-*
19	M.	☌☿☾ • Plant breeder Elwyn Meader died, 1996 • Tides {10.2 / 9.0} •	*oiling!*
20	Tu.	Mel Fisher's crew found sunken *Atocha* off Fla., loaded with silver, gold, and emeralds, 1985	*Thunder-*
21	W.	☌♃☾ • Violinist Isaac Stern born, 1920 • Tides {10.1 / 9.3} •	*storms*
22	Th.	**St. Mary Magdalene** • ☾ on Eq. • Tides {10.0 / 9.5} •	*are*
23	Fr.	Ulysses S. Grant died, 1885 • Disney's *Tarzan* became first all-digital film, 1999 • {9.8 / 9.7}	*fierce*
24	Sa.	*Luck is like having a rice dumpling fly into your mouth.* • Tides {9.6 / 10.0} •	*and*
25	C	**8th S. af. P.** • ☾ at ☋ • Tides {9.3 / 10.2}	*frequent;*
26	M.	**St. Anne** • ☿ Gr. Elong. (27° E.) • Tides {9.2 / 10.5} •	*vacationers*
27	Tu	Korean War Armistice, 1953 • "Bugs Bunny" cartoon debuted, 1940 • {9.1 / 10.8}	*wonder*
28	W.	7.8 earthquake in NE China killed 242,000 in 1976 • Tides {9.1 / 11.1} •	*where*
29	Th.	**St. Martha** • ☾ runs low • *Extremes meet.* • Tides {9.3 / 11.4} •	*the*
30	Fr.	☾ at perig. • New York Yacht Club founded, 1844 • Tides {9.6 / 11.7} •	*week*
31	Sa.	**St. Ignatius of Loyola** • **Full Thunder** ○ • ☌♆☾ •	*went.*

Farmer's Calendar

■ Across the road, one of the neighbors is mowing his field with a tractor. He works from the edge toward the middle, driving around and around the steadily shrinking island of standing grass at the approximate center of the mowing. It's fun to watch. It may even be fun to do, within reason. Not today, however, it seems. The tractor stops abruptly. Milton jumps off and begins running, away from his machine and toward the road. He's no kid, and yet he's moving fast. The abandoned tractor idles in place. Milton didn't even wait to shut off the engine. Has he suddenly remembered to call his broker? Did his morning coffee land wrong? No, nothing like that. He has driven over a nest of yellow jackets.

Yellow jackets are any of several species of small yellow-and-black-bodied wasps of the family Vespidae. They live like honeybees in colonies of as many as several thousand workers and a single queen. Often, yellow jackets build their communal nests underground in old mouse holes. The nest is the nursery of the next generation of yellow jackets, and the wasps protect it with a fury and a concentration no other insect in these parts can muster. Each of these little devils owns a sting that makes a bee sting feel like a gentle caress. When an intruder passes near or over their nest, the yellow jackets attack, not singly but by squadrons. They go for unprotected skin: your hands, your ears, your neck, your ankles. You can't drive them away. All you can do is run. Milton didn't stop until he was halfway to Boston.

2004 AUGUST, The Eighth Month

Neptune in Capricornus reaches opposition and its nearest approach to Earth on the 5th; Uranus in Aquarius, faintly visible to the naked eye in dark skies, arrives at its own opposition on the 27th. The Perseid meteor shower on the night of August 11–12 will be unhampered by a late-rising waning crescent Moon. Best viewing is after midnight. Meanwhile, Jupiter vanishes in the evening sky after a final low meeting with the Moon on the 17th, while Venus soars spectacularly in the east before dawn, where it reaches greatest elongation on the 17th. Also in the predawn sky, Saturn returns just to the right of the thin crescent Moon on the 13th and forms a nice conjunction with Venus on the 30th and 31st.

☾	Last Quarter	7th day	18th hour	1st minute
●	New Moon	15th day	21st hour	24th minute
☽	First Quarter	23rd day	6th hour	12th minute
○	Full Moon	29th day	22nd hour	22nd minute

Times are given in Eastern Daylight Time.

For an explanation of this page, see page 40; for values of Key Letters, see page 170.

Day of Year	Day of Month	Day of Week	☼ Rises h. m.	Key	☼ Sets h. m.	Key	Length of Day h. m.	Sun Fast m.	Declination of Sun ° '	High Tide Boston Light—A.M.	Bold—P.M.	☽ Rises h. m.	Key	☽ Sets h. m.	Key	☽ Place	☽ Age
214	1	**C**	5 37	A	8 03	D	14 26	9	17N.48	**12½**	—	9 PM 11	E	6 AM 17	B	CAP	15
215	2	M.	5 38	A	8 02	D	14 24	9	17 33	12¾	**1¼**	9 38	D	7 36	C	AQU	16
216	3	Tu.	5 39	A	8 01	D	14 22	9	17 17	1½	**2**	10 01	D	8 51	C	AQU	17
217	4	W.	5 40	A	8 00	D	14 20	10	17 01	2½	**3**	10 22	C	10 02	D	PSC	18
218	5	Th.	5 41	A	7 58	D	14 17	10	16 45	3¼	**3¾**	10 43	B	11 AM 10	D	PSC	19
219	6	Fr.	5 42	A	7 57	D	14 15	10	16 28	4	**4½**	11 05	B	12 PM 17	E	PSC	20
220	7	Sa.	5 43	A	7 56	D	14 13	10	16 11	5	**5½**	11 29	B	1 23	E	ARI	21
221	8	**C**	5 44	A	7 54	D	14 10	10	15 54	6	**6¼**	11 PM 57	A	2 28	E	ARI	22
222	9	M.	5 45	A	7 53	D	14 08	10	15 37	7	**7¼**	—	–	3 32	E	TAU	23
223	10	Tu.	5 46	A	7 52	D	14 06	10	15 19	7¾	**8**	12 AM 30	A	4 33	E	TAU	24
224	11	W.	5 48	A	7 50	D	14 02	10	15 01	8¾	**9**	1 11	A	5 29	E	TAU	25
225	12	Th.	5 49	A	7 49	D	14 00	11	14 43	9¾	**9¾**	1 59	A	6 18	E	AUR	26
226	13	Fr.	5 50	A	7 48	D	13 58	11	14 25	10½	**10½**	2 55	A	6 59	E	GEM	27
227	14	Sa.	5 51	B	7 46	D	13 55	11	14 06	11¼	**11¼**	3 57	B	7 34	E	CAN	28
228	15	**C**	5 52	B	7 45	D	13 53	11	13 48	**12**	12	5 03	B	8 03	E	CAN	0
229	16	M.	5 53	B	7 43	D	13 50	11	13 29	12½	—	6 09	B	8 27	D	LEO	1
230	17	Tu.	5 54	B	7 42	D	13 48	12	13 10	12½	**1**	7 16	C	8 49	D	LEO	2
231	18	W.	5 55	B	7 40	D	13 45	12	12 50	1¼	**1¾**	8 23	D	9 10	D	VIR	3
232	19	Th.	5 56	B	7 39	D	13 43	12	12 30	2	**2¼**	9 31	D	9 30	C	VIR	4
233	20	Fr.	5 57	B	7 37	D	13 40	12	12 10	2¾	**3**	10 40	E	9 52	B	VIR	5
234	21	Sa.	5 58	B	7 36	D	13 38	12	11 50	3½	**3¾**	11 AM 51	E	10 17	B	VIR	6
235	22	**C**	5 59	B	7 34	D	13 35	13	11 30	4¼	**4½**	1 PM 06	E	10 48	A	LIB	7
236	23	M.	6 00	B	7 32	D	13 32	13	11 10	5¼	**5½**	2 22	E	11 PM 26	A	LIB	8
237	24	Tu.	6 01	B	7 31	D	13 30	13	10 49	6¼	**6½**	3 38	E	—	–	SCO	9
238	25	W.	6 02	B	7 29	D	13 27	13	10 28	7¼	**7½**	4 47	E	12 AM 15	A	SAG	10
239	26	Th.	6 03	B	7 27	D	13 24	14	10 07	8¼	**8½**	5 45	E	1 17	A	SAG	11
240	27	Fr.	6 04	B	7 26	D	13 22	14	9 46	9¼	**9½**	6 32	E	2 31	B	SAG	12
241	28	Sa.	6 06	B	7 24	D	13 18	14	9 25	10¼	**10½**	7 08	E	3 50	B	CAP	13
242	29	**C**	6 07	B	7 23	D	13 16	15	9 03	11¼	**11½**	7 37	E	5 10	B	AQU	14
243	30	M.	6 08	B	7 21	D	13 13	15	8 42	**12**	—	8 02	D	6 27	C	AQU	15
244	31	Tu.	6 09	B	7 19	D	13 10	15	8N.20	12½	**1**	8 PM 24	C	7 AM 40	D	AQU	16

AUGUST hath 31 days. 2004

Where' er you walk, cool gales shall fan the glade;
Trees, where you sit, shall crowd into a shade;
Where' er you tread, the blushing flowers shall rise,
And all things flourish where you turn your eyes. –Alexander Pope

D. M.	D. W.	Dates, Feasts, Fasts, Aspects, Tide Heights	Weather ↓
1	C	9th S. af. P. • Lammas Day • {10.2 / —}	• *Thunder*
2	M.	☌♅☾ • Olivia Newton-John's "Magic" topped charts, 1980 • {11.8 / 10.4}	*wakes*
3	Tu.	At 2:47 A.M., Calvin Coolidge was sworn in as president by his father at Vermont homestead, 1923 •	*us,*
4	W.	☾ on Eq. • Major geomagnetic storm, 1972 • Tides {11.1 / 10.4} •	*Old*
5	Th.	♆ at ☍ • Civil War gun turret and artifacts of U.S.S. *Monitor* recovered, 2002 • {10.6 / 10.2}	*Sol*
6	Fr.	Transfiguration • ☾ at ☊ • First electric-chair execution, 1890 •	*bakes*
7	Sa.	Name of Jesus • Silver discovered in northern Ontario, 1903 • {9.3 / 9.7} •	*us.*
8	C	10th S. af. P. • *The best fish swims near the bottom.* • {8.7 / 9.4}	*Days*
9	M.	St. Dominic • ☿ stat. • 113°F, Perryville, Tenn., 1930 • {8.3 / 9.3}	*are*
10	Tu.	St. Laurence • Artist James Wilson Morrice born, 1865 • {8.1 / 9.2}	*equatorial,*
11	W.	St. Clare • Dog Days end. • ☾ at apo. • ☌♀☾ •	*spawning*
12	Th.	☾ rides high • Movie producer/director Cecile B. DeMille born, 1881 •	*brownouts*
13	Fr.	☌♄☾ • "L'il Abner" comic strip debuted, 1934 • Tides {8.4 / 9.8} •	*and*
14	Sa.	*Dry bread is better with love than fried chicken with fear and trembling.* •	*editorials.*
15	C	Assumption • New ● • Tides {8.9 / 10.2} •	*Find*
16	M.	☌☿♂ • Siamese twins arrived in Boston, Mass., to start U.S. tour, 1829 • {9.2 / —}	*some*
17	Tu.	Cat Nights begin. • ♀ Gr. Elong. (46° W.) • Tides {10.3 / 9.5} •	*shade*
18	W.	☌♃☾ • Explorer Meriwether Lewis born, 1774 • {10.3 / 9.7} •	*or*
19	Th.	☾ on Eq. • U.S.S. *Constitution* captured H.M.S. *Guerrière* during War of 1812 • {10.3 / 10.0}	*be*
20	Fr.	Sompom Saekow, founder of first Thailand monkey-training school, died, 2002 •	*sautéed.*
21	Sa.	☾ at ☋ • *A good mind possesses a kingdom.* • Tides {9.9 / 10.3} •	*In*
22	C	12th S. af. P. • Stephen C. Rockefeller married Anne Marie Rasmussen, 1959	*this*
23	M.	☿ in inf. ☌ • *Ranger I* lunar probe launched, 1961 • {9.2 / 10.4} •	*furnace*
24	Tu.	St. Bartholomew • Archbishop Geoffrey Plantagenet born, 1113 • {9.0 / 10.5}	*up to*
25	W.	*Star Trek*'s Patrick Stewart married producer Wendy Neuss, 2000 • {8.9 / 10.6} •	*bed we*
26	Th.	☾ runs low • F. Gasparro, Lincoln Memorial penny engraver, born, 1909 • {9.0 / 10.8}	*go,*
27	Fr.	☾ at perig. • ♅ at ☍ • C. G. Conn received patent for an all-metal clarinet, 1889	*like*
28	Sa.	St. Augustine of Hippo • ☌♆☾ • {9.6 / 11.3} •	*Shadrach,*
29	C	Full Sturgeon ○ • ☌♅☾ • Tides {10.1 / 11.4} •	*Meshach,*
30	M.	St. John the Baptist • Civil rights leader Roy Wilkins born, 1901 • {10.4 / —}	*and*
31	Tu.	☾ on Eq. • ☌♀♄ • ♇ stat. • Tides {11.4 / 10.6}	*Abednego!*

Farmer's Calendar

■ There is a killer in the woods of New England—a monster of aggression and ferocity—and uniquely armed. Fortunately, it's a very small monster. A short-tailed shrew *(Blarina brevicauda)* could curl up comfortably in a half-cup measure. A big one weighs three-quarters of an ounce. In form, the shrew is a cross between a mole and a weasel, having the mole's thick, soft gray fur and the weasel's speedy, sinuous motion. But the shrew has traits all its own, as well, including a long pointed nose and a mouthful of tiny, needle-like teeth.

It has also a supercharged, hyperactive way of life fueled by one of the most extravagant metabolisms in nature. The shrew is in permanent overdrive. One researcher measured the heart rates of anesthetized short-tailed shrews: The mean was 760 beats per minute. Shrews don't hibernate; they seem scarcely to sleep. What they do is eat, fight, and reproduce—all with the pedal right down on the floor at all times. They devour any kind of meat they can kill, from insects and earthworms to other shrews.

As if its basic endowment of powers weren't enough, the short-tailed shrew (but not other species) has a secret weapon. Glands in its lower jaw secrete venom that flows into its victims as it bites them. This shrew is, as far as is known, the only mammal with a poisonous bite. The poison is no joke, either; even for people, the bite is painful and possibly dangerous. This extraordinary little beast is the cobra of the mammal world. If the shrew were the size of, say, a Ford Escort... well, it won't bear thinking about.

2004 SEPTEMBER, The Ninth Month

The morning sky is definitely the center of the action. On the 1st, Venus and Saturn hang out close together one-third of the way up the eastern sky at 5:30 A.M., with Mercury far below them but getting higher each dawn as this innermost world begins its best morning showing of the year. On the 10th, an eye-catching triangle formed by the Moon, Venus, and Saturn hovers high above an extremely close conjunction of Mercury and Leo's blue star, Regulus. Three mornings later, on the 13th, Mercury meets the crescent Moon. Binoculars show Venus very near Cancer's Beehive star cluster from the 12th to the 14th. Autumn begins with the equinox on the 22nd at 12:30 P.M. EDT.

◖	Last Quarter	6th day	11th hour	11th minute
●	New Moon	14th day	10th hour	29th minute
◗	First Quarter	21st day	11th hour	54th minute
○	Full Moon	28th day	9th hour	9th minute

Times are given in Eastern Daylight Time.

For an explanation of this page, see page 40; for values of Key Letters, see page 170.

Day of Year	Day of Month	Day of Week	☼ Rises h. m.	Key	☼ Sets h. m.	Key	Length of Day h. m.	Sun Fast m.	Declination of Sun ° '	High Tide Boston Light—A.M. Bold—P.M.		☽ Rises h. m.	Key	☽ Sets h. m.	Key	Place	Age
245	1	W.	6 10	B	7 17	D	13 07	16	7 N.58	1¼	1¾	8ᴮ45	C	8ᴹ51	D	CET	17
246	2	Th.	6 11	B	7 16	D	13 05	16	7 36	2	2½	9 06	B	10 00	E	PSC	18
247	3	Fr.	6 12	B	7 14	D	13 02	16	7 14	2¾	3	9 29	B	11ᴹ07	E	ARI	19
248	4	Sa.	6 13	B	7 12	D	12 59	17	6 52	3½	3¾	9 56	B	12ᴹ14	E	ARI	20
249	5	C	6 14	B	7 11	D	12 57	17	6 30	4½	4¾	10 27	A	1 20	E	TAU	21
250	6	M.	6 15	B	7 09	D	12 54	17	6 08	5¼	5½	11 05	A	2 23	E	TAU	22
251	7	Tu.	6 16	B	7 07	D	12 51	18	5 45	6¼	6½	11ᴮ51	A	3 21	E	TAU	23
252	8	W.	6 17	B	7 05	C	12 48	18	5 23	7¼	7½	—	–	4 13	E	AUR	24
253	9	Th.	6 18	B	7 04	C	12 46	18	5 00	8¼	8¼	12ᴬ44	A	4 57	E	GEM	25
254	10	Fr.	6 19	B	7 02	C	12 43	19	4 37	9	9¼	1 44	A	5 34	E	CAN	26
255	11	Sa.	6 20	B	7 00	C	12 40	19	4 15	10	10	2 49	B	6 05	E	CAN	27
256	12	C	6 21	B	6 58	C	12 37	19	3 52	10¾	10¾	3 56	B	6 31	E	LEO	28
257	13	M.	6 22	B	6 57	C	12 35	20	3 29	11¼	11½	5 03	C	6 53	D	LEO	29
258	14	Tu.	6 23	B	6 55	C	12 32	20	3 06	12	—	6 11	D	7 15	D	LEO	0
259	15	W.	6 25	B	6 53	C	12 28	20	2 43	12¼	12½	7 20	D	7 35	C	VIR	1
260	16	Th.	6 26	B	6 51	C	12 25	21	2 19	12¾	1¼	8 29	E	7 57	B	VIR	2
261	17	Fr.	6 27	B	6 50	C	12 23	21	1 56	1½	1¾	9 42	E	8 21	B	VIR	3
262	18	Sa.	6 28	B	6 48	C	12 20	21	1 33	2¼	2½	10ᴬ56	E	8 50	A	LIB	4
263	19	C	6 29	C	6 46	C	12 17	22	1 10	3	3¼	12ᴹ13	E	9 25	A	LIB	5
264	20	M.	6 30	C	6 44	C	12 14	22	0 46	4	4¼	1 29	E	10 10	A	SCO	6
265	21	Tu.	6 31	C	6 43	C	12 12	22	0 N.23	5	5¼	2 40	E	11ᴮ08	A	OPH	7
266	22	W.	6 32	C	6 41	C	12 09	23	0 S.00	6	6¼	3 40	E	—	–	SAG	8
267	23	Th.	6 33	C	6 39	C	12 06	23	0 24	7	7¼	4 29	E	12ᴬ16	B	SAG	9
268	24	Fr.	6 34	C	6 37	C	12 03	24	0 47	8¼	8½	5 08	E	1 32	B	CAP	10
269	25	Sa.	6 35	C	6 35	C	12 00	24	1 10	9¼	9½	5 38	E	2 49	B	CAP	11
270	26	C	6 36	C	6 34	C	11 58	24	1 34	10¼	10½	6 04	D	4 06	C	AQU	12
271	27	M.	6 37	C	6 32	B	11 55	25	1 57	11	11¼	6 26	D	5 20	C	AQU	13
272	28	Tu.	6 38	C	6 30	B	11 52	25	2 20	11¾	—	6 47	C	6 31	D	PSC	14
273	29	W.	6 40	C	6 28	B	11 48	25	2 44	12	12½	7 08	B	7 40	E	PSC	15
274	30	Th.	6 41	C	6 27	B	11 46	26	3 S.07	12¾	1¼	7ᴮ30	B	8ᴹ49	E	PSC	16

SEPTEMBER hath 30 days. 2004

Little drops of water,
Little grains of sand,
Make the mighty ocean
And the pleasant land. –Julia A. Fletcher Carney

D. M.	D. W.	Dates, Feasts, Fasts, Aspects, Tide Heights	Weather ↓
1	W.	☿ stat. • Saskatchewan became a province of Canada, 1905 • Tides {11.1 / 10.7 •	*No,*
2	Th.	Charles Burton and co. started 3-year, pole-to-pole expedition, 1979 • {10.7 / 10.5 •	*the*
3	Fr.	**St. Gregory the Great** • ☾ at ☊ • *Never cut what can be untied.*	*planet*
4	Sa.	Ten-year-old Barney Flaherty became first newsboy in U.S., for New York *Sun,* 1833 •	*hasn't*
5	C	**14th S. af. P.** • Comedian Bob Newhart born, 1929	*tipped:*
6	M.	**Labor Day** • President McKinley shot, 1901 • Tides {8.5 / 9.2 •	*Gardens*
7	Tu.	☾ at apo. • 109°F, Weldon, N.C., 1954 • Tides {8.1 / 9.0 •	*get*
8	W.	☾ rides high • *He who shuns labor labors doubly.* • Tides {7.9 / 9.0 •	*nipped.*
9	Th.	**St. Omer** • ☌ ♄ ☾ • ☿ Gr. Elong. (18° W.) • Tides {8.0 / 9.1 •	*But*
10	Fr.	☌ ♀ ☾ • Evolutionary theorist Stephen Jay Gould born, 1941 •	*summer's*
11	Sa.	**Sts. Protus & Hyacinth** • Terrorist attacks on U.S., 2001 • {8.5 / 9.7	*lease*
12	C	**15th S. af. P.** • ☌ ☿ ☾ • Tides {8.9 / 10.0 •	*has*
13	M.	Chiang Kai-shek became president of China, 1943 • *The Chocolate Soldier* opened in N.Y.C., 1909 •	*not*
14	Tu.	**Holy Cross** • **New** ● • *Fevers come on horseback but go away on foot.* •	*run*
15	W.	Ember Day • ☾ on Eq. • ☌ ♂ ☉ • Tides {10.4 / 10.2 •	*out;*
16	Th.	**Rosh Hashanah** • Edward Elliott caught 97-pound blue catfish in S.D., 1959 •	*enjoy*
17	Fr.	Ember Day • ☾ at ☋ • City of Boston founded, 1630 • Tides {10.4 / 10.7 •	*its*
18	Sa.	Ember Day • Actress Greta Garbo born, 1905 • {10.2 / 10.8 •	*satisfactions.*
19	C	**16th S. af. P.** • Bissell carpet sweeper patented, 1876 •	*The*
20	M.	**St. Eustace** • *In deep waters, men find great pearls.* • {9.5 / 10.7 •	*morning*
21	Tu.	Harvest Home • ☌ ♃ ☉ • Explorer Louis Joliet born, 1645 • {9.1 / 10.5 •	*chill*
22	W.	**Autumnal Equinox** • ☾ runs low • ☾ at perig. • Boxer Tunney beat Dempsey, 1927 •	*is*
23	Th.	Time capsule buried at New York World's Fair, 1938 • Tides {8.8 / 10.3 •	*just*
24	Fr.	☌ ♆ ☾ • *As September, so the coming March.* • Tides {9.0 / 10.5 •	*a*
25	Sa.	**Yom Kippur** • ☌ ♅ ☾ • Sequoia National Park established, 1890 •	*tout—*
26	C	**17th S. af. P.** • World's oldest alligator on record died at age 66 in 1978 •	*a*
27	M.	**St. Vincent de Paul** • *Tonight Show* debuted, 1954 • {10.3 / 10.9	*preview*
28	Tu.	**Full Harvest** ○ • ☾ on Eq. • First photograph of a comet, 1858 • {10.6 / —	*of*
29	W.	**St. Michael** • *Brevity is the soul of wit.* • Tides {10.8 / 10.8 •	*coming*
30	Th.	**St. Sophia** • **Succoth** • ☾ at ☊ • {10.5 / 10.7 •	*attractions.*

When you come to a fork in the road, take it. –Yogi Berra, American baseball player

Farmer's Calendar

■ Vegetable gardening is fun because you succeed at it, not by overcoming or outwitting nature, but by understanding, anticipating, and cooperating with it. You are not in a wrestling match with the garden; you're dancing with it. As in dancing, too, the gardener shares his activity with others similarly engaged. And unless he is a kind of Fred Astaire of the garden, he will be humbled.

At this time of the year, for example, the fields and farm stands are crowded with fat orange pumpkins, basketball-size, keg-size. Local pumpkin patches have once more brought forth a bountiful harvest of this most prized and charismatic squash.

Not this patch, though. My pumpkin hills show no more than a couple of specimens the size of a regulation baseball. It was the old story: The time was out of joint. Pumpkin culture is gardening's minuet—a figure stately, complex, and prolonged. No step can be mistimed or the whole evolution fails. In June, when pumpkin vines must make their growth, mine tarried. In July, when the vines must begin to grow their fruit, mine slumbered. In mid-August, they suddenly awoke and began to set fruit—far too late. No basketballs for me this year.

But I will not be discouraged by my neighbors' flourishing pumpkin crop. Rather, I will concentrate. I will resolve not to do differently next year, but to do the same better: more water, more compost, more topdressing. For the gardener, there is always another year, as for the dancer there is always another ball. The former, however, can buy his pumpkins off a truck.

2004   OCTOBER, The Tenth Month

Jupiter emerges at dawn in its new home of Virgo, and by month's end so does fainter Mars. Saturn at midmonth starts to rise at midnight, and by Halloween, aided by the ending of Daylight Saving Time, it starts appearing at 10:00 P.M. The midmonth new Moon provides darkness for the year's best views of the Milky Way, assisted by October's low humidity levels and clear air. Meanwhile, early risers can enjoy brilliant Venus, fading but conspicuously high in the hours before dawn. The entire United States and Canada experience a total lunar eclipse on the 27th, with the umbral phase starting at 9:14 P.M. EDT and totality beginning at 10:23 P.M. EDT, at which point the Moon should turn coppery red.

☾	Last Quarter	6th day	6th hour	12th minute
●	New Moon	13th day	22nd hour	48th minute
☽	First Quarter	20th day	17th hour	59th minute
○	Full Moon	27th day	23rd hour	7th minute

After 2:00 A.M. on October 31, Eastern Standard Time (EST) is given.

For an explanation of this page, see page 40; for values of Key Letters, see page 170.

Day of Year	Day of Month	Day of Week	☼ Rises h. m.	Key	☼ Sets h. m.	Key	Length of Day h. m.	Sun Fast m.	Declination of Sun ° '	High Tide Boston Light—A.M. Bold—P.M.		☽ Rises h. m.	Key	☽ Sets h. m.	Key	Place	Age
275	1	Fr.	6 42	C	6 25	B	11 43	26	3 s.30	1½	1¾	7ᴹ55	B	9ᴹ57	E	ARI	17
276	2	Sa.	6 43	C	6 23	B	11 40	26	3 53	2¼	2½	8 25	A	11ᴹ04	E	TAU	18
277	3	**C**	6 44	C	6 22	B	11 38	27	4 17	3	3¼	9 00	A	12ᴹ09	E	TAU	19
278	4	M.	6 45	C	6 20	B	11 35	27	4 40	3¾	4	9 42	A	1 11	E	TAU	20
279	5	Tu.	6 46	C	6 18	B	11 32	27	5 03	4¾	4¾	10 33	A	2 06	E	AUR	21
280	6	W.	6 47	C	6 16	B	11 29	27	5 26	5½	5¾	11ᴹ30	A	2 53	E	GEM	22
281	7	Th.	6 48	C	6 15	B	11 27	28	5 49	6½	6¾	—	–	3 32	E	GEM	23
282	8	Fr.	6 49	C	6 13	B	11 24	28	6 12	7½	7¾	12ᴹ33	B	4 05	E	CAN	24
283	9	Sa.	6 51	C	6 11	B	11 20	28	6 35	8½	8½	1 38	B	4 32	E	LEO	25
284	10	**C**	6 52	C	6 10	B	11 18	29	6 57	9¼	9½	2 45	B	4 56	D	LEO	26
285	11	M.	6 53	C	6 08	B	11 15	29	7 20	10	10¼	3 53	C	5 18	D	LEO	27
286	12	Tu.	6 54	C	6 06	B	11 12	29	7 43	10½	11	5 02	D	5 38	D	VIR	28
287	13	W.	6 55	D	6 05	B	11 10	29	8 05	11¼	11¾	6 12	D	6 00	C	VIR	0
288	14	Th.	6 56	D	6 03	B	11 07	30	8 27	12	—	7 24	E	6 23	B	VIR	1
289	15	Fr.	6 58	D	6 02	B	11 04	30	8 50	12½	12½	8 40	E	6 50	B	VIR	2
290	16	Sa.	6 59	D	6 00	B	11 01	30	9 12	1¼	1¼	9 59	E	7 24	A	LIB	3
291	17	**C**	7 00	D	5 58	B	10 58	30	9 34	2	2	11ᴹ17	E	8 07	A	SCO	4
292	18	M.	7 01	D	5 57	B	10 56	30	9 55	2¾	3	12ᴹ32	E	9 01	A	OPH	5
293	19	Tu.	7 02	D	5 55	B	10 53	31	10 17	3¾	3¾	1 36	E	10 07	A	SAG	6
294	20	W.	7 03	D	5 54	B	10 51	31	10 38	4¾	5	2 29	E	11ᴹ20	B	SAG	7
295	21	Th.	7 05	D	5 52	B	10 47	31	11 00	5¾	6	3 10	E	—	–	CAP	8
296	22	Fr.	7 06	D	5 51	B	10 45	31	11 21	7	7¼	3 42	E	12ᴹ37	B	CAP	9
297	23	Sa.	7 07	D	5 49	B	10 42	31	11 42	8	8¼	4 08	D	1 53	C	AQU	10
298	24	**C**	7 08	D	5 48	B	10 40	31	12 02	9	9¼	4 30	D	3 06	C	AQU	11
299	25	M.	7 09	D	5 46	B	10 37	31	12 23	9¾	10¼	4 51	C	4 16	D	PSC	12
300	26	Tu.	7 11	D	5 45	B	10 34	32	12 43	10½	11	5 11	C	5 25	D	PSC	13
301	27	W.	7 12	D	5 44	B	10 32	32	13 04	11¼	11¾	5 33	B	6 33	E	PSC	14
302	28	Th.	7 13	D	5 42	B	10 29	32	13 23	12	—	5 56	B	7 40	E	ARI	15
303	29	Fr.	7 14	D	5 41	B	10 27	32	13 43	12½	12¾	6 24	A	8 48	E	ARI	16
304	30	Sa.	7 16	D	5 40	B	10 24	32	14 03	1¼	1¼	6 56	A	9 55	E	TAU	17
305	31	**C**	6 17	D	4 38	B	10 21	32	14 s.22	2	1	6ᴹ36	A	9ᴹ58	E	TAU	18

OCTOBER hath 31 days. 2004

The hollow winds begin to blow,
The clouds look black, the glass is low;
The soot falls down, the spaniels sleep,
And spiders from their cobwebs peep. –Dr. Edward Jenner

D. M.	D. W.	Dates, Feasts, Fasts, Aspects, Tide Heights	Weather ↓
1	Fr.	St. Gregory • National Aeronautics and Space Administration (NASA) founded, 1958 •	*A*
2	Sa.	Woodchucks hibernate now. • *The Twilight Zone* premiered, 1959 • { 9.7 / 10.2 •	*soaking,*
3	C	18th S. af. P. • Writer Thomas Wolfe born, 1900 • { 9.2 / 9.9 •	*and*
4	M.	St. Francis of Assisi • *If the birds be silent, expect thunder.* • { 8.7 / 9.5	*we're*
5	Tu.	☾ at apo. • ☿ in sup. ☌ • Tides { 8.3 / 9.1 •	*not*
6	W.	☾ rides high • J. Charles began 30 years of waving to motorists in Berkeley, Calif., 1962	*joking.*
7	Th.	☌♄☾ • Cellist Yo-Yo Ma born, 1955 • Tides { 7.9 / 8.8 •	*Autumn*
8	Fr.	*Many a man's tongue has broken his nose.* • President Franklin Pierce died, 1869 •	*colors*
9	Sa.	American Humane Association organized, 1877 • Tides { 8.3 / 9.2 •	*really*
10	C	19th S. af. P. • ☌♀☾ • *Lassie Come Home* premiered, 1943	*glow*
11	M.	**Columbus Day** • **Thanksgiving Day (Canada)** • Historic Bartram's Garden began, 1728	*when*
12	Tu.	☾ on Eq. • ☌♃☾ • *A smart fly never lights on a boiling pot.* •	*coated*
13	W.	**New ●** • Eclipse ☉ • Boston Pilgrims won first World Series, 1903 •	*with*
14	Th.	☾ at ☋ • Prime Minister Lester Pearson won Nobel Peace Prize, 1957 • Tides { 10.9 / —	*a*
15	Fr.	**First day of Ramadan** • *We all fade as the leaf.* • Mata Hari executed for spying, 1917 •	*dust*
16	Sa.	*Sun-Times* published first Ann Landers column by Eppie Lederer, 1955 • Tides { 10.4 / 11.4 •	*of*
17	C	20th S. af. P. • ☾ at perig. • A. Einstein came to U.S., 1933	*snow!*
18	M.	St. Luke • St. Ignatius of Antioch • St. Luke's little summer. •	*Sneak*
19	Tu.	☾ runs low • Poet Edna St. Vincent Millay died, 1950 • Tides { 9.5 / 10.9 •	*a*
20	W.	Humorist Art Buchwald born, 1925 • Louisiana Purchase ratified by U.S. Senate, 1803	*peek*
21	Th.	☌♆☾ • First planetarium opened, Deutsches Museum, Munich, Germany, 1923 •	*at*
22	Fr.	*No camel route is long, with good company.* • First national horse show opened in N.Y.C., 1883 •	*peak*
23	Sa.	☌⛢☾ • Cumberland mine disaster, 1958 • Tides { 9.3 / 10.1 •	*this*
24	C	21st S. af. P. • ♆ stat. • Tides { 9.7 / 10.2 •	*week:*
25	M.	☾ on Eq. • Entertainer Minnie Pearl born, 1912 • Tides { 10.1 / 10.2 •	*Frankly,*
26	Tu.	Gospel singer Mahalia Jackson born, 1911 • Erie Canal fully opened, 1825 • { 10.5 / 10.2 •	*my*
27	W.	**Full Hunter's ○** • Eclipse ☾ • ☾ at ☊ • { 10.7 / 10.1	*dearie,*
28	Th.	Sts. Simon & Jude • Harvard College founded, 1636 • Tides { 10.7 / — •	*it's*
29	Fr.	Journalist Joseph Pulitzer died, 1911 • Star of India sapphire stolen, 1964 • { 9.9 / 10.6	*dank*
30	Sa.	*Lost time is never found again.* • The "Perfect Storm" reached maximum intensity, 1991 •	*and*
31	C	All Hallows Eve • **Daylight Saving Time ends, 2:00 A.M.** • { 9.2 / 10.1	*dreary.*

Farmer's Calendar

■ The autumn leaves that each year turn the hills and valleys into a great silent peal of color are one of nature's most famous shows. They have their stage, their cast, their audience—and they have their critics. Not every year's production is found to measure up. Last fall, for example, the colors in my neighborhood were generally thought to be disappointing. There wasn't the variety of color; many trees simply turned yellow or brown. And what colors *did* appear weren't as bright as in other years, especially the reds. Finally, last year's leaves fell quickly, and so the foliage season was short. Many experts blamed the unusually dry summer. A dry year leads to poor autumn color, the authorities said. That makes sense, I thought.

But here observe a curious point. A few years before this recent autumn shortfall of color, we had another poor year for foliage. Once again, the leaves were said to be "faded," "rusty." (I saved the news reports, you see; in this job, you learn to think ahead.) Back then, however, the experts agreed that the cause of the unsatisfactory color was a *wet* summer, with unusually heavy rainfall. Too much rain means poor color, the foresters said. That makes sense, I thought.

Hang on, though. Shouldn't it be one way or the other? Yes, it should, and if interpreting a season's leaf-show were entirely a matter of science, it would. But this enterprise isn't entirely about science: It's criticism. The critic is also part of the audience. He's a consumer, and if he likes the show, and especially if he doesn't, he wants to know why.

NOVEMBER, The Eleventh Month

A party in Virgo: Venus and Jupiter, the night's two brightest "stars," celebrate Jupiter's predawn return with a tight conjunction on the 4th and 5th, above Virgo's brightest star, Spica. The crescent Moon joins them on the 9th, occulting Jupiter as seen from parts of North America. The next morning presents a vertical lineup (top to bottom) of Jupiter, Venus, the Moon, and Mars. Meanwhile, Saturn begins sliding backward in retrograde motion. Mercury is barely visible above the extremely low, slender crescent Moon and Scorpius's red star, Antares, on the 13th around 5:00 P.M. Southern observers will enjoy a higher, more visible target. The erratic Leonid meteor shower is not expected to be visible this year.

☾	Last Quarter	5th day	0 hour	53rd minute
●	New Moon	12th day	9th hour	27th minute
☽	First Quarter	19th day	0 hour	50th minute
○	Full Moon	26th day	15th hour	7th minute

Times are given in Eastern Standard Time.

For an explanation of this page, see page 40; for values of Key Letters, see page 170.

Day of Year	Day of Month	Day of Week	☼ Rises h. m.	Key	☼ Sets h. m.	Key	Length of Day h. m.	Sun Fast m.	Declination of Sun ° '	High Tide Boston Light—A.M.	**Bold—P.M.**	☽ Rises h. m.	Key	☽ Sets h. m.	Key	☽ Place	☽ Age
306	1	M.	6 18	D	4 37	B	10 19	32	14 s.41	1½	**1¾**	7 P.M. 23	A	10 A.M. 57	E	TAU	19
307	2	Tu.	6 19	D	4 36	B	10 17	32	15 00	2¼	**2½**	8 18	A	11 A.M. 47	E	AUR	20
308	3	W.	6 21	D	4 34	B	10 13	32	15 19	3¼	**3¼**	9 18	B	12 P.M. 29	E	GEM	21
309	4	Th.	6 22	D	4 33	B	10 11	32	15 38	4	**4**	10 22	B	1 04	E	CAN	22
310	5	Fr.	6 23	D	4 32	B	10 09	32	15 56	5	**5**	11 P.M. 28	B	1 33	E	CAN	23
311	6	Sa.	6 24	D	4 31	B	10 07	32	16 14	5¾	**6**	—	–	1 58	E	LEO	24
312	7	**C**	6 26	D	4 30	A	10 04	32	16 31	6¾	**7**	12 A.M. 34	C	2 20	D	LEO	25
313	8	M.	6 27	D	4 29	A	10 02	32	16 49	7½	**7¾**	1 41	C	2 40	D	LEO	26
314	9	Tu.	6 28	D	4 28	A	10 00	32	17 06	8¼	**8½**	2 49	D	3 01	C	VIR	27
315	10	W.	6 29	D	4 27	A	9 58	32	17 22	9	**9½**	4 00	E	3 23	B	VIR	28
316	11	Th.	6 31	D	4 26	A	9 55	32	17 39	9¾	**10¼**	5 15	E	3 49	B	VIR	29
317	12	Fr.	6 32	D	4 25	A	9 53	31	17 55	10½	**11**	6 34	E	4 20	A	LIB	0
318	13	Sa.	6 33	D	4 24	A	9 51	31	18 11	11¼	**11¾**	7 55	E	4 59	A	SCO	1
319	14	**C**	6 34	D	4 23	A	9 49	31	18 26	**12**	—	9 15	E	5 50	A	OPH	2
320	15	M.	6 36	D	4 22	A	9 46	31	18 42	12¾	**12¾**	10 26	E	6 54	A	SAG	3
321	16	Tu.	6 37	D	4 21	A	9 44	31	18 57	1½	**1¾**	11 A.M. 25	E	8 08	B	SAG	4
322	17	W.	6 38	D	4 20	A	9 42	31	19 11	2½	**2¾**	12 P.M. 10	E	9 26	B	CAP	5
323	18	Th.	6 39	D	4 19	A	9 40	30	19 25	3½	**3¾**	12 45	E	10 43	B	CAP	6
324	19	Fr.	6 40	D	4 19	A	9 39	30	19 39	4½	**4¾**	1 13	D	11 P.M. 57	C	AQU	7
325	20	Sa.	6 42	D	4 18	A	9 36	30	19 52	5½	**6**	1 36	D	—	–	AQU	8
326	21	**C**	6 43	D	4 17	A	9 34	30	20 05	6¾	**7**	1 57	D	1 A.M. 07	D	AQU	9
327	22	M.	6 44	D	4 17	A	9 33	29	20 18	7½	**8**	2 17	C	2 15	D	CET	10
328	23	Tu.	6 45	D	4 16	A	9 31	29	20 30	8½	**9**	2 37	B	3 22	E	PSC	11
329	24	W.	6 46	D	4 15	A	9 29	29	20 43	9¼	**9¾**	3 00	B	4 29	E	ARI	12
330	25	Th.	6 48	D	4 15	A	9 27	29	20 54	10	**10½**	3 25	A	5 36	E	ARI	13
331	26	Fr.	6 49	E	4 14	A	9 25	28	21 06	10½	**11¼**	3 56	A	6 42	E	TAU	14
332	27	Sa.	6 50	E	4 14	A	9 24	28	21 17	11¼	**11¾**	4 33	A	7 47	E	TAU	15
333	28	**C**	6 51	E	4 14	A	9 23	28	21 27	11¾	—	5 17	A	8 47	E	TAU	16
334	29	M.	6 52	E	4 13	A	9 21	27	21 37	12½	**12½**	6 09	A	9 41	E	AUR	17
335	30	Tu.	6 53	E	4 13	A	9 20	27	21 s.46	1¼	**1¼**	7 P.M. 08	A	10 A.M. 26	E	GEM	18

NOVEMBER hath 30 days. 2004

Orchards have shared their treasures,
The fields, their yellow grain,
So open wide the doorway—
Thanksgiving comes again! –Unknown

D. M.	D. W.	Dates, Feasts, Fasts, Aspects, Tide Heights	Weather ↓
1	M.	All Saints' • Earthquake, Lisbon, Portugal, 1755 • *Fortune is fickle.* •	*Bright*
2	Tu.	All Souls' • Election Day • ☾ rides high • ☾ at apo. • { 8.5 / 9.5 •	*days*
3	W.	☌♄☾ • Detroit–Windsor tunnel opened, 1930 • Tides { 8.3 / 9.2 •	*of*
4	Th.	☌♃♀ • Abraham Lincoln married Mary Todd in Springfield, Ill., 1842 • { 8.1 / 8.9	*sun*
5	Fr.	Songwriter George M. Cohan died, 1942 • *An elephant never forgets.* • Tides { 8.1 / 8.8	*and*
6	Sa.	Sadie Hawkins Day • 98-mph winds, Block Island, R.I., 1953 • { 8.2 / 8.9	*haze.*
7	**C**	**23rd S. af. P.** • "Galloping Gertie" bridge collapsed, 1940 •	*Silver*
8	M.	♄ stat. • X-rays discovered by physicist Wilhelm Roentgen, 1895 • { 9.1 / 9.3	*drops*
9	Tu.	☾ on Eq. • ☌♃☾ • ☌♀☾ • Tides { 9.7 / 9.6 •	*turn*
10	W.	☌♂☾ • 70 tornadoes churned across eastern U.S., 2002 • { 10.3 / 9.9 •	*white*
11	Th.	St. Martin of Tours • **Veterans Day** • ☾ at ☋ • ♅ stat.	*and*
12	Fr.	Indian Summer • **New** ● • Canadarm, a robotic arm, launched into space, 1981	*float;*
13	Sa.	☌☿☾ • Walt Disney's *Fantasia* premiered, 1940 • { 11.7 / 10.3 •	*time*
14	**C**	**24th S. af. P.** • ☾ at perig. • Tides { 11.9 / — •	*to*
15	M.	☾ runs low • First U.S. poultry show began, Boston, 1849 • Tides { 10.1 / 11.8	*put*
16	Tu.	Oklahoma admitted to the Union, 1907 • "The Sound of Music" opened on Broadway, 1959 •	*away*
17	W.	St. Hugh of Lincoln • ☌♆☾ • Tides { 9.6 / 11.0 •	*the*
18	Th.	Four standard time zones adopted for the U.S., 1883 • Pres. Chester A. Arthur died, 1886	*boat.*
19	Fr.	☌♅☾ • *Don't argue with your bread and butter.* • { 9.3 / 10.1 •	*Pilgrims*
20	Sa.	☿ Gr. Elong. (22° E.) • William Bundy received patent for employees' time recorder, 1888	*suffered*
21	**C**	**25th S. af. P.** • ☾ on Eq. • "Tweety Bird" debuted, 1942 •	*their*
22	M.	*Good things require time.* • Skunks hibernate now. • Tides { 9.9 / 9.5 •	*first*
23	Tu.	St. Clement • ☾ at ☊ • Food rationing ended, 1945 • { 10.1 / 9.5	*year—*
24	W.	Painter Toulouse-Lautrec born, 1864 • First national Thanksgiving celebration, 1863	*be*
25	Th.	**Thanksgiving** • *Gratitude is the memory of the heart.* • { 10.4 / 9.3	*thankful*
26	Fr.	**Full Beaver** ○ • *Casablanca* premiered, 1942 • Tides { 10.4 / 9.2 •	*that*
27	Sa.	Guitarist Jimi Hendrix born, 1942 • Penn Station opened in N.Y.C., 1910 • { 10.4 / 9.1 •	*it's*
28	**C**	**1st S. in Advent** • Grand Ole Opry made radio debut, 1925	*warm*
29	M.	☾ rides high • Actor Cary Grant died, 1986 • Tides { 8.9 / 10.0 •	*and*
30	Tu.	☾ at apo. • ☌♄☾ • ☿ stat. • Tides { 8.7 / 9.8 •	*clear.*

Radical historians now tell the story of Thanksgiving from the point of view of the turkey. –Mason Cooley, U.S. aphorist

Farmer's Calendar

■ According to Article II, Section 2 of the Constitution, the president "shall have the Power to grant Reprieves and Pardons for Offenses against the United States. . . ." Now, it is true that the history of presidential pardons is not one of the more creditable chapters in the annals of the republic. Too often, pardons have gone to dubious characters who have been helpful in getting the president into the office that empowers him to draw a veil over their misdeeds (and his own). There is one honorable exception, however—a presidential pardon that the most cynical can hardly impugn. I refer to the traditional annual pardon of the White House Thanksgiving turkey.

Evidently, it was President Harry Truman who in 1947 began the practice of selecting a turkey at Thanksgiving time that would be spared to live out its full life. More recently, a pair of birds have been pardoned. So far, so good. But a question comes up. What have these turkeys done that they are being pardoned for? What Offenses against the United States have they committed? Turkeys are not part of the dreary entourage of fixers, grafters, and all-purpose scoundrels who commonly follow in the oily wake of the Chief Executive. Turkeys are . . . poultry.

Clearly, the president's traditional Thanksgiving-turkey pardon isn't about the turkeys. It's about the president. He needs play, like everybody else. Hence the turkey pardon. It's good for the Boss. And, when you consider the alternative, it's not a bad deal for the birds, either.

2004 DECEMBER, The Twelfth Month

Saturn rises by 7:00 P.M. in midmonth, becoming brighter and telescopically larger as it heads for its mid-January opposition. Ideal moonless conditions prevail for the reliable one-a-minute, all-night Geminid meteors on the night of the 13th–14th. On the predawn morning stage, Venus ventures close to Mars from the 5th to the 7th and close to Mercury starting on the 26th in a leisurely three-week conjunction that becomes extraordinarily compact in January. The event caps Mercury's period of fairly good visibility that began in midmonth. Winter, and the longest night of 2004, arrives with the solstice on the 21st at 7:42 A.M. EST, even though the year's earliest sunset occurs two weeks earlier.

☾	Last Quarter	4th day	19th hour	53rd minute
●	New Moon	11th day	20th hour	29th minute
☽	First Quarter	18th day	11th hour	40th minute
○	Full Moon	26th day	10th hour	6th minute

Times are given in Eastern Standard Time.

For an explanation of this page, see page 40; for values of Key Letters, see page 170.

Day of Year	Day of Month	Day of Week	☼ Rises h. m.	Key	☼ Sets h. m.	Key	Length of Day h. m.	Sun Fast m.	Declination of Sun ° '	High Tide Boston Light—A.M.	Bold—P.M.	☽ Rises h. m.	Key	☽ Sets h. m.	Key	☽ Place	☽ Age
336	1	W.	6 54	E	4 12	A	9 18	27	21 s.55	2	**2**	8 P.M. 10	B	11 A.M. 04	E	CAN	19
337	2	Th.	6 55	E	4 12	A	9 17	26	22 04	2¾	**2¾**	9 14	B	11 A.M. 34	E	CAN	20
338	3	Fr.	6 56	E	4 12	A	9 16	26	22 13	3½	**3½**	10 19	B	12 P.M. 00	E	LEO	21
339	4	Sa.	6 57	E	4 12	A	9 15	25	22 21	4¼	**4¼**	11 P.M. 24	C	12 22	D	LEO	22
340	5	**C**	6 58	E	4 12	A	9 14	25	22 28	5	**5¼**	—	–	12 43	D	LEO	23
341	6	M.	6 59	E	4 12	A	9 13	25	22 35	5¾	**6¼**	12 A.M. 30	D	1 03	C	VIR	24
342	7	Tu.	7 00	E	4 12	A	9 12	24	22 42	6¾	**7**	1 37	D	1 23	C	VIR	25
343	8	W.	7 00	E	4 11	A	9 11	24	22 48	7½	**8**	2 48	E	1 46	B	VIR	26
344	9	Th.	7 02	E	4 12	A	9 10	23	22 54	8¼	**8¾**	4 04	E	2 14	B	LIB	27
345	10	Fr.	7 03	E	4 12	A	9 09	23	22 59	9	**9¾**	5 23	E	2 49	A	LIB	28
346	11	Sa.	7 04	E	4 12	A	9 08	22	23 04	10	**10½**	6 45	E	3 34	A	SCO	0
347	12	**C**	7 04	E	4 12	A	9 08	22	23 08	10¾	**11½**	8 03	E	4 34	A	OPH	1
348	13	M.	7 05	E	4 12	A	9 07	21	23 12	11¾	—	9 10	E	5 46	A	SAG	2
349	14	Tu.	7 06	E	4 12	A	9 06	21	23 15	12¼	**12½**	10 03	E	7 06	B	SAG	3
350	15	W.	7 06	E	4 12	A	9 06	21	23 18	1¼	**1½**	10 44	E	8 27	B	CAP	4
351	16	Th.	7 07	E	4 13	A	9 06	20	23 21	2¼	**2½**	11 15	E	9 44	C	CAP	5
352	17	Fr.	7 08	E	4 13	A	9 05	20	23 23	3¼	**3½**	11 A.M. 40	D	10 P.M. 58	D	AQU	6
353	18	Sa.	7 09	E	4 14	A	9 05	19	23 25	4¼	**4½**	12 P.M. 02	D	—	–	AQU	7
354	19	**C**	7 09	E	4 14	A	9 05	19	23 26	5¼	**5½**	12 23	C	12 A.M. 07	D	PSC	8
355	20	M.	7 10	E	4 14	A	9 04	18	23 26	6¼	**6½**	12 43	B	1 15	D	PSC	9
356	21	Tu.	7 11	E	4 15	A	9 04	18	23 26	7	**7¾**	1 05	B	2 21	E	ARI	10
357	22	W.	7 11	E	4 15	A	9 04	17	23 26	8	**8½**	1 29	B	3 27	E	ARI	11
358	23	Th.	7 11	E	4 16	A	9 05	17	23 25	8¾	**9½**	1 57	A	4 33	E	TAU	12
359	24	Fr.	7 12	E	4 17	A	9 05	16	23 24	9½	**10¼**	2 32	A	5 38	E	TAU	13
360	25	Sa.	7 12	E	4 17	A	9 05	16	23 23	10¼	**11**	3 14	A	6 40	E	TAU	14
361	26	**C**	7 12	E	4 18	A	9 06	15	23 20	11	**11½**	4 04	A	7 36	E	AUR	15
362	27	M.	7 13	E	4 19	A	9 06	15	23 18	11½	—	5 00	A	8 24	E	GEM	16
363	28	Tu.	7 13	E	4 19	A	9 06	14	23 14	12¼	**12¼**	6 02	B	9 03	E	GEM	17
364	29	W.	7 13	E	4 20	A	9 07	14	23 11	12¾	**12¾**	7 05	B	9 36	E	CAN	18
365	30	Th.	7 13	E	4 21	A	9 08	13	23 06	1½	**1½**	8 10	B	10 03	E	LEO	19
366	31	Fr.	7 13	E	4 22	A	9 09	13	23 s.00	2¼	**2¼**	9 P.M. 14	B	10 A.M. 26	E	LEO	20

DECEMBER hath 31 days. 2004

But Winter has yet brighter scenes—he boasts
Splendors beyond what gorgeous Summer knows;
Or Autumn with his many fruits, and woods
All flushed with many hues. –William Cullen Bryant

D. M.	D. W.	Dates, Feasts, Fasts, Aspects, Tide Heights	*Weather* ↓
1	W.	Capt. Edward L. Beach, author of *Run Silent, Run Deep,* died, 2002 • Tides {8.5 / 9.6 •	*Gully*
2	Th.	St. Viviana • Napoleon crowned Emperor of France, 1804 • {8.4 / 9.3	*washers:*
3	Fr.	*The worst bug in our heads is humbug.* • Meteorologist Cleveland "Old Probabilities" Abbe born, 1838	*Wear*
4	Sa.	"Boss" Tweed escaped from jail, 1875 • Tides {8.4 / 8.9 •	*galoshers!*
5	C	**2nd S. in Advent** • ☌♂♀ • {8.6 / 8.9 •	*Mild,*
6	M.	St. Nicholas • ☾ on Eq. • First international football game, 1873 • {8.9 / 8.9	*then*
7	Tu.	St. Ambrose • **National Pearl Harbor Remembrance Day** • Occn. ♃☾	*wild.*
8	W.	First day of Chanukah • ☾ at ☋ • Tides {10.0 / 9.3 •	*Polar*
9	Th.	☌♂☾ • First Heisman Trophy awarded to Jay Berwanger, 1935 • {10.6 / 9.6	*shower*
10	Fr.	☌♀☾ • ☿ in inf. ☌ • *Keep conscience clear, then never fear.*	*yields*
11	Sa.	New ● • Annie Jump Cannon, who cataloged over 225,000 stars, born, 1863 • {11.6 / 10.0	*to*
12	C	**3rd S. in Advent** • ☾ at perig. • Tides {11.9 / 10.1	*solar*
13	M.	St. Lucia • ☾ runs low • ☌♇☉ • Tides {12.1 / — •	*power.*
14	Tu.	Halcyon Days • George Washington died, 1799 • *Art imitates Nature.* •	*Crisp*
15	W.	Ember Day • ☌♆☾ • Baseball player Dick Stuart, a.k.a. Dr. Strangeglove, died, 2002	*with*
16	Th.	☌♅☾ • Earthquake in Miss. River Valley near New Madrid, Mo., 1811	*flurrying—*
17	Fr.	Ember Day • First heart, lung, and liver transplant, 1986 • {9.8 / 10.5 •	*everyone's*
18	Sa.	Ember Day • Actress Betty Grable born, 1916 • {9.7 / 9.9 •	*hurrying*
19	C	**4th S. in Advent** • ☾ on Eq. • Tides {9.6 / 9.4 •	*to*
20	M.	☿ stat. • Missouri imposed $1 per year tax on bachelors, 1820 • {9.7 / 9.1	*finish*
21	Tu.	**Winter Solstice** • ☾ at ☊ • Bowell became Canada's prime minister, 1894	*shopping,*
22	W.	First colonial naval officers appointed, 1775 • Beware the Pogonip. • {9.8 / 8.7 •	*but*
23	Th.	Airplane *Voyager* finished first nonstop around-the-world flight without refueling, 1986 •	*it's*
24	Fr.	*If you would have guests merry with cheer, be so yourself, or so at least appear.*	*sopping.*
25	Sa.	**Christmas Day** • Wind today brings a fruitful year. •	*May*
26	C	**Boxing Day (Canada)** • **Full Cold** ○ • ☾ rides high • Tides {10.1 / 8.7 •	*your*
27	M.	St. John • ☾ at apo. • Tides {10.1 / — •	*Christmas*
28	Tu.	Holy Innocents • ☌♄☾ • Westminster Abbey consecrated, 1065 •	*cacti*
29	W.	☌☿♀ • ☿ Gr. Elong. (22° W.) • Texas became 28th state, 1845 • {8.7 / 9.9	*thrive*
30	Th.	–13°F, N.Y.C., 1917 • Guitarist Bo Diddley born, 1928 • Tides {8.7 / 9.7 •	*in*
31	Fr.	St. Sylvester • *With the old Almanack and the old Year, leave thy old Vices, tho' ever so dear.*	*2005!*

Farmer's Calendar

■ Some weather signs are—or purport to be—mere formulas: Enter the data, get the value. For example, the larva of the little brown isabella tiger moth, the famous woolly bear caterpillar. It's supposed to predict the severity of each year's winter. See what fraction of the caterpillar's length in the present year is brown, what black, and you know whether the winter to come will be hard or mild. Does anybody believe this? No. The woolly bears themselves don't believe it. But it's comforting because it's quantitative and so offers a kind of travesty of science.

The better weather signs are otherwise. They're not fake science, they're fake art. That is to say, they're subtle. The day before a big winter storm, the afternoon light will sometimes take on a strange, yellow look. It's a brassy, metallic cast that comes over the sky, an off-look, like a jaundice. The sky isn't cloudy exactly, but neither is it clear. Rather, it has a kind of sheen, almost a greasy feeling. As the brief winter afternoon wears on, the sky, which had been still, becomes windy and darkens. Real clouds arrive. At dusk or a little later, the snow begins.

When I see that odd, greasy sky, I know snow will be falling within six or seven hours. But I am conscious of having done a lousy job of describing the particular condition I have in mind. I know it when I see it, but I don't know how to explain it. Clearly, we are far beyond the woolly bear and its spurious precision. The woolly bear is a poor weather sign, but it's easy. The greasy sky is a good weather sign, but you have to be a poet to read it.

Holidays and Observances

A selected list of commemorative days, with federal holidays denoted by *.

Jan. 1	New Year's Day*
Jan. 17	Benjamin Franklin's Birthday
Jan. 19	Martin Luther King Jr.'s Birthday *(observed)**
Feb. 2	Groundhog Day; Guadalupe-Hidalgo Treaty Day *(N.Mex.)*
Feb. 12	Abraham Lincoln's Birthday
Feb. 14	St. Valentine's Day
Feb. 15	Susan B. Anthony's Birthday *(Fla.; Wis.)*
Feb. 16	George Washington's Birthday *(observed)**
Feb. 24	Mardi Gras *(Baldwin & Mobile Counties, Ala.; La.)*
Mar. 2	Texas Independence Day; Town Meeting Day *(Vt.)*
Mar. 15	Andrew Jackson Day *(Tenn.)*
Mar. 17	St. Patrick's Day; Evacuation Day *(Suffolk Co., Mass.)*
Mar. 29	Seward's Day *(Alaska)*
Apr. 2	Pascua Florida Day
Apr. 13	Thomas Jefferson's Birthday
Apr. 19	Patriots Day *(Maine; Mass.)*
Apr. 21	San Jacinto Day *(Tex.)*
Apr. 30	National Arbor Day
May 1	May Day
May 8	Truman Day *(Mo.)*
May 9	Mother's Day
May 15	Armed Forces Day
May 22	National Maritime Day
May 24	Victoria Day *(Canada)*
May 31	Memorial Day *(observed)**
June 5	World Environment Day
June 11	King Kamehameha I Day *(Hawaii)*
June 14	Flag Day
June 17	Bunker Hill Day *(Suffolk Co., Mass.)*
June 19	Emancipation Day *(Tex.)*
June 20	Father's Day; West Virginia Day
July 1	Canada Day
July 4	Independence Day*
July 24	Pioneer Day *(Utah)*
Aug. 2	Colorado Day
Aug. 9	Victory Day *(R.I.)*
Aug. 16	Bennington Battle Day *(Vt.)*
Aug. 19	National Aviation Day
Aug. 26	Women's Equality Day
Sept. 6	Labor Day*
Sept. 9	Admission Day *(Calif.)*
Sept. 12	Grandparents Day
Sept. 17	Citizenship Day
Oct. 4	Child Health Day
Oct. 9	Leif Eriksson Day
Oct. 11	Columbus Day *(observed)**; Thanksgiving Day *(Canada)*; Native Americans Day *(S.Dak.)*
Oct. 18	Alaska Day
Oct. 24	United Nations Day
Oct. 31	Halloween; Nevada Day
Nov. 2	Election Day
Nov. 4	Will Rogers Day *(Okla.)*
Nov. 11	Veterans Day*
Nov. 19	Discovery Day *(Puerto Rico)*
Nov. 25	Thanksgiving Day*
Nov. 26	Acadian Day *(La.)*
Nov. 28	John F. Kennedy Day *(Mass.)*
Dec. 7	National Pearl Harbor Remembrance Day
Dec. 15	Bill of Rights Day
Dec. 17	Wright Brothers Day
Dec. 25	Christmas Day*
Dec. 26	Boxing Day *(Canada)*; First day of Kwanzaa

Religious Observances

Epiphany	Jan. 6
Islamic New Year	Feb. 22
Ash Wednesday	Feb. 25
Palm Sunday	Apr. 4
First day of Passover	Apr. 6
Good Friday	Apr. 9
Easter	Apr. 11
Orthodox Easter	Apr. 11
Whitsunday–Pentecost	May 30
Rosh Hashanah	Sept. 16
Yom Kippur	Sept. 25
First day of Ramadan	Oct. 15
First day of Chanukah	Dec. 8
Christmas Day	Dec. 25

What's So Special About May 5?

On this day, the United States and Mexico celebrate unity and patriotism.

Some people believe that a short battle in a small town in Mexico on May 5, 1862, helped determine the outcome of the U.S. Civil War. *That* truth about the outcome will never be known, but what *is* true is that the events of that day fostered a friendship between the two countries that still endures.

The circumstances leading up to the fight on that day, now known as Cinco de Mayo (or the "Fifth of May"), are rooted in Mexico's struggle for stability after gaining independence from Spain in 1821. Because that hard-won freedom was not easy to maintain, Mexico sought and received loans from England, France, and even Spain.

At the same time, political unrest within Mexico itself took a toll on the young country. In the mid-1830s, the region that became Texas seceded from Mexico. That revolt and years of turmoil eventually led to the Mexican-American War, which began in 1846 and ended two years later with a U.S. victory—and a nearly bankrupt Mexican treasury. A severe economic crisis in the 1850s dealt another crippling blow to the weakened finances. By 1861, President Benito Juárez saw no alternative but to suspend payment of all foreign debt for two years.

Juárez's plan was not accepted by the ruling monarchies in England, France, and Spain, however. In 1862, each country sent military forces to Mexico to demand repayment. When the armies arrived in the port city of Veracruz, representatives from England and Spain reconsidered their demands, accepted warrants offered by Juárez, and departed. But some 4,500 French troops sent by Napoleon III (nephew of Napoleon Bonaparte) refused to compromise. The emperor had a grand plan.

Napoleon III saw his opportunity in the U.S. Civil War, which was also raging at this time. Because he detested the Union and favored the Confederacy, he decided to establish a French empire in Mexico and support the South by helping to keep its ports open, among other goals.

On the morning of May 5, General Lorenz led the French Army, some 6,000 trained infantrymen, inland, headed for Mexico City. Lorenz planned to rest his men at the town of Puebla, about 100 miles east of the capital.

President Juárez had anticipated the French invasion. He ordered General Ignacio Zaragoza to defend Puebla. Zaragoza's army, composed of about 3,500 mestizos and Zapotec Indians armed with tools and farm implements, would have appeared no match for the highly trained invaders, but they were not alone. The Mexican cavalry, under Brigadier General Porfirio Díaz (who later became the country's president and dictator), was also there to defend the homeland.

The Mexicans had significant advantages—they were on high ground, and the surrounding area was thick with mud, the result of a recent thunderstorm. As the Mexicans waited, the French footsoldiers surged forward but became mired in the muck. At this decisive moment, Zaragosa ordered Díaz and the cavalry to charge. To compound the chaos, the Mexicans stirred hundreds of cattle to stampede.

Known as La Batalla de Puebla, or the Battle of Puebla, the fighting continued for almost half a day. When it was over, many French lay dead and many more had retreated. The small, untrained Mexican defenders rejoiced in their victory: They had defeated the most powerful army in the world!

Cinco de Mayo rallied and unified the Mexican people. Unfortunately, it signaled the beginning—not the end—of a long struggle. One year later, a reinforced French army came back and took over Mexico City, establishing a monarchy in the capital. Juárez fled to the north, where he and his militia so effectively harassed the French regime that it was unable to support the Confederacy at any time during its reign. In 1867, a grateful President Lincoln sent 50,000 Union troops to the Mexican border to expel the French. Napoleon III, realizing he had no choice, withdrew his soldiers, and the sovereignty of Mexico was restored. ☐☐

¡Viva México!

These days, on Cinco de Mayo, Mexicans and Mexican Americans celebrate courage, perseverance, and loyalty. In some communities, the battle scene is re-created. In many towns in both countries, there are parades, street festivals, and colorful folk dances with mariachi music. Children enjoy piñatas. And what would a party be without food? Always, traditional Mexican dishes are served, such as enchiladas, frijoles, and tamales.

CELEBRATE CINCO DE MAYO

Join in the fun of fiesta. For traditional Mexican recipe suggestions, go to **www.almanac.com** and click on **Article Links 2004.**

We're looking for people to—

Write Children's Books

By Kristi Holl

If you've ever dreamed of writing for children, here's your chance to test that dream. . . and find out if you have the aptitude to make it a reality. If you do, we'll teach you how to crack one of today's most rewarding markets for new writers.

The $2 billion children's market

The tremendous recent success of children's books has made the general public aware of what we've known for years: There's a huge market out there. And there's a growing need for new writers trained to create the nearly $2 billion of children's books purchased every year. . . plus the stories and articles needed by more than 600 publishers of magazines for and about children and teenagers.

Who are these needed writers? They're ordinary people like you and me.

"But am I good enough?"

Fifteen years ago, I was where you may be now. My occasional thoughts of writing had been pushed down by self-doubt, and I didn't know where to turn for help. Then, on an impulse, I sent for the Institute's free writing aptitude test and it turned out to be the spark I needed. I took their course and my wonderful author-instructor helped me to discover, step-by-step, that my everyday life— probably not much different from yours—was an endless creative resource for my writing!

The promise that paid off

The Institute made the same promise to me that they'll make to you, if you demonstrate basic writing aptitude: *You will complete at least one manuscript suitable to submit to editors by the time you finish the course.*

I really didn't expect to be published before I finished the course, but

Kristi Holl, a graduate of our course, has published 24 books and more than 180 stories and articles. She is now an instructor at the Institute.

I was. I sold three stories. And I soon discovered that that was not unusual at the Institute. Now, as a graduate and a nationally published author of 24 children's books, and more than 180 stories and articles, I'm teaching: I'm passing along what I've learned to would-be writers like you.

One-on-one training with your own instructor

My fellow instructors—all of them professional writers or editors—work with their students the same way I work with mine: When you've completed an assignment on your own schedule, at your own pace, you send it to me. I read it and reread it to make sure I get everything out of it that you've put into it. Then I edit it line-by-line and send you a detailed letter explaining my edits. I point out your strengths and show you how to shore up your weaknesses. Between your pushing and my pulling, you learn how to write—and how to market what you write.

I am the living proof

What I got from my instructor at the Institute changed me from a "wannabe" into a nationally published writer. While there's no guarantee that every student will have the same success, we're showered with letters like these from current and former students.

"Since graduating from your course," says Heather Klassen, Edmonds, WA, "I've sold 125 stories to magazines for children and teenagers."

"Before this, I didn't know if my work was typical or bland, or if there was even a spark of life in it," writes Kate Spanks, Maple Ridge, BC. "I now have over 30 articles published. . . .."

". . .a little bird. . .has just been given freedom"

"This course has helped me more than I can say," says Jody Drueding, Boston, MA. "It's as if a little bird that was locked up inside of me has just been given the freedom of the garden."

". . .I was attracted by the fact that you require an aptitude test," says Nikki Arko, Raton, NM. "Other schools sign you up as long as you have the money to pay, regardless of talent or potential."

"I'd take the course again in a heartbeat!"

"My most recent success has been the publication of the novel I started for my last Institute assignment," writes Jennifer Jones, Homer, NY. "Thank you for giving me the life I longed for."

"I'd take the course again in a heartbeat!", says Tonya Tingey, Woodruff, UT. "It made my dream a reality."

Don't let your dream die— send for your free test today!

If life as a successful writer is your dream, here's your chance to test that dream. We've developed a revealing aptitude test based on our 34 years of experience. Just fill out and mail the coupon below to receive your free test and a 32-page introduction to our course, *Writing for Children and Teenagers,* and 80 of our instructors. *There is no obligation.*

Get both free

Institute of Children's Literature
93 Long Ridge Road
West Redding, CT 06896-0812

Yes, please send me your free Writing Aptitude Test and illustrated brochure. I understand I'm under no obligation, and no salesperson will visit me.

Please circle one and print name clearly:

Mr.   Mrs.   Ms.   Miss   E9542

Name _____

Street _____

City _____

State _____ Zip _____

COPYRIGHT © ICL 2003, A DIVISION OF THE INSTITUTE, INC.

Recommended for college credits by the Connecticut Board for State Academic Awards and approved by the Connecticut Commissioner of Higher Education.

VENUS TOUCHES THE SUN

One of the "Greatest Shows on Earth"

BY BOB BERMAN

−JPL/NASA

When it comes to sky spectacles, there are rare events—a so-called "great comet" that comes along every 15 or 20 years, or a total solar eclipse that might happen twice in your lifetime—and then there are the extraordinary occurrences of the type we'll experience on June 8. On that day, for the first time in 121½ years, the Sun will be partially eclipsed by the planet Venus. Such a phenomenon is called a transit, or crossing, and nobody alive today has ever seen a transit of Venus.

A transit of Venus occurs if Venus arrives at an inferior conjunction (passing between Earth and the Sun) at precisely one of the two spots along its tilted orbit that perfectly intersect the Earth-Sun plane. Venus's orbit is such that its transits have two distinctions: 1) they occur only in June or December, and 2) they occur in a double cycle, or in a pair. There are eight years minus two days between the two transits in each pair, and the pairs alternate between 121½ and 105½ years apart (measured from the date of the second transit of a pair to the date of the first transit in the next pair).

The last pair of Venus transits occurred in December 1874 and December 1882. On June 8, 2004, the first half of the next double cycle occurs again. Eight years from then, on June 6, 2012, a second transit will complete that cycle—and that's it for more than a lifetime. Fully 105½ years will pass before anyone on Earth sees Venus transit the Sun again.

Because we've now waited the maximum interval between transits, it had better be good—and it will be if you have the Sun in your sky during at least part of the event, the sky is clear of cloud cover, and you have eye protection on hand (*never* look at the Sun without a filter).

(c o n t i n u e d)

The appeal and impact of this rare SPECTACLE lie in its display of the grand clockwork machinery of the SOLAR SYSTEM.

In this view of Venus *(left)*, its north pole is at the center. The planet's highest mountain, Maxwell Montes, is in the bright spot just below.

Approximate size of Venus compared with the Sun

A Heavenly Hat Trick

Only three objects periodically cross the Sun's face. The Moon does it every year or so. The planet Mercury crosses the Sun 13 times each century; for the past 40 years, however, only one Mercury transit has been visible from Earth's Western Hemisphere. And transits by Venus, the rarest, happen 13 times every 1,000 years, on average.

If all three of these conditions are met, you'll see a perfectly round Venus creep across the Sun like an ambulatory sunspot. You don't need binoculars or a telescope, although you can magnify the image nicely with either of these if they're equipped with an effective solar filter.

As Venus creeps along, you'll view its 22-mile-per-second orbital motion. This will speedily propel it into the morning sky, where it will be a riveting predawn spectacle just a few weeks later. In an extended encore performance after the transit, our nearest planetary neighbor will remain dazzling from July through October.

Venus will be at its closest point to Earth during the transit, some 26 million miles away. Its width of nearly one arc-minute will make it look "only" 30 times smaller than the Sun. Try this: See if you can perceive it as a black disk rather than as a speck or point (again, with eye protection). If you can, you will see the only planet whose shape can ever be discerned with just the naked eye!

Unlike total solar eclipses or major displays of the northern lights, this rare spectacle is not visually gorgeous. Venus won't seem large. It will look about the size of a penny on the goal line of a football field, as seen from midfield. The transit will offer no visible hint that this is a substantial world, nearly Earth's twin in size. Its appeal and impact lie in its display of the grand clockwork machinery of the solar system—and in the fact that nobody has seen this in more than 120 years.

The View from . . . Where?

If the Venus transit lasted just a few minutes, only half the world (those in daylight) would be able to see it, assuming the sky were clear. For the unfortunate half, it would be night. But because a Venus transit unfolds over about six hours, an additional quarter of Earth's inhabitants can glimpse at least part of it.

(continued)

Families Have Saved Up To 50% On Heating Costs
And never have to buy fuel—wood, oil, gas, kerosene—ever again!

REPLACE OLD & INEFFICIENT HEAT

Hydro-Sil is a unique room-by-room heating system that can **save you hundreds of dollars** in home heating costs. It can replace or supplement your electric heat, gas or oil furnace and woodstoves.

Hydro-Sil heating works like this: inside the heater case is a sealed copper tube filled with a harmless silicone fluid that will never spill, leak, boil or freeze. **It's permanent. You'll never run out.** Running through the liquid is a variable watt hydroelectric element that is _only_ being supplied a _proportional_ amount of power on an as-needed basis. When Hydro-Sil is turned on, the silicone liquid is quickly heated, and with its heat retention qualities, continues to heat after the Hydro element shuts off. Hydro-Sil's room-by-room technology greatly increases energy savings and comfort.

Many Families are Benefitting — You can too!

• **F. Smalley (Mass):** *"A company that advertises the truth* saved me 50% compared to my gas heat. I found it hard to believe until my power bill came. Thanks a million!"

• **R. Hanson (Ind):** "I cannot begin to tell you how pleased I am with Hydro-Sil...the first time in 25 years our electric bill was reduced... *saved $635, over 40%!"*

• **A. Consalves (Mass):** "We updated our existing standard electric heat, removing 20 electric heaters and replacing them with Hydro-Sil. *Wow – what a difference!* We received a substantial reduction of our electric bill. I have recommended Hydro-Sil to many people!"

ORDER BY: Phone • Website • Mail
☐Check ☐MasterCard ☐VISA

800-627-9276 OR **www.hydrosil.com**

MAIL TO: HYDRO-SIL, P.O. BOX 662, FORT MILL, SC 29715

Seasonal Discount Available Now!

Your benefits with Hydro-Sil:

• **Slash Heating Cost – Up to 50%**
• **Lifetime Warranty – no service calls**
• **Safe – complete peace of mind**
• **Clean – no fumes – no smoke**
• **U.L. Listed**
• **Preassembled – ready to use**
• **No furnaces – ducts – chimney**
• **Portable (110V) or permanent (220V)**
• **Whole House Heating or Single Room**
• **Room by Room Control**

PERMANENT 220 VOLT	Approx. Area To Heat	Discount Price	Quantity
8´ 2000 watts	250-300 sq. ft.	$269	
6´ 1500 watts	180-250 sq. ft.	$239	
5´ 1250 watts	130-180 sq. ft.	$229	
4´ 1000 watts	100-130 sq. ft.	$209	
3´ 750 watts	75-100 sq. ft.	$189	
2´ 500 watts	50-75 sq. ft.	$169	
Thermostats – CALL for options and exact heater needed			
PORTABLE 110 VOLT – Thermostat Included			
5´ Hydro–Max 750 -1500 watts		$219	
4´ Convector – Dual watt		$179	
3´ 750 watts – Silicone		$179	
$15.00 shipping per heater		$ _____	
Total Amount		$ _____	

Acct. No. _____ Ex. _____

Name _____

Address _____

Phone _____

So where will it be visible from on June 8?

IN THE EAST. The best vantage points in North America will be on the East Coast and especially in the Northeast. The farther east you go, the higher the Sun will be in the sky when the transit ends. One of the best viewing sites will be Canada's Maritime Provinces, where the Sun will rise at around 5:30 A.M. with Venus still well within its disk and with more than 90 minutes of the transit remaining. From the Maritimes to Florida, the transit will continue until Venus encounters the Sun's edge at around 7:05 A.M. and totally passes beyond it 20 minutes later.

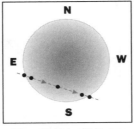

Approximate path Venus will take across the Sun on June 8, 2004.

IN THE MIDDLE. Observations in the Midwest will be spotty; the eastern regions have the potential for better visibility than western areas, contingent on such factors as an unobstructed horizon, steady air, and the quality of the viewing equipment. Still there are no guarantees, because unlike with total solar eclipses, the areas of visibility are not precisely defined, and the transit ends and Venus departs the edge of the Sun at nearly sunrise.

IN THE WEST. People who live west of the Rockies in the United States and Canada will see none of it.

AROUND THE WORLD. Assuming that clear skies prevail, nearly all of Europe and Asia will see the whole thing, and as a bonus, the Sun will be high overhead when it happens.

There's Always Next Time

If you miss this transit cycle, don't despair. The second half, in June 2012, will be visible from all of North America.

Sneak Preview

Venus will be visible this spring in the evening sky. It's exceptionally high and brilliant from March through May after sunset and will reveal dreamlike moon phases through even the smallest telescope. You can watch it mutate from a tiny Venusian half-moon shape in March to a stunning little crescent in early May to a skinny yet dramatically big crescent in late May. Of all these phases, a "new" Venus—showing its dark side alone (like a new Moon)—is the rarest of all, and that's exactly what will appear on the morning of June 8.

Bob Berman's latest book is *Strange Universe* (Henry Holt and Company). He is also the author of *Cosmic Adventure* (Quill, 2000).

SAVE YOUR SIGHT

Don't you dare stare at the Sun without eye protection! For tips on where to get inexpensive transit glasses and recommendations on using filters, go to www.almanac.com and click on Article Links 2004.

Astronomical Glossary

Aphelion (Aph.): The point in a planet's orbit that is farthest from the Sun.

Apogee (Apo.): The point in the Moon's orbit that is farthest from Earth.

Celestial Equator (Eq.): The circle around the celestial sphere that is halfway between the celestial poles. It can be thought of as the plane of Earth's equator projected out onto the sphere.

Celestial Sphere: An imaginary sphere projected into space that represents the entire sky, with an observer on Earth at its center. All celestial bodies other than Earth are imagined as being on its inside surface.

Conjunction: The time at which two or more celestial bodies appear closest in the sky. (Dates for conjunctions are given in the Right-Hand Calendar Pages 45–71; sky sightings of closely aligned bodies are given in the descriptive text at the top of the Left-Hand Calendar Pages 44–70.) **Inferior (Inf.):** Mercury or Venus is between the Sun and Earth. **Superior (Sup.):** The Sun is between a planet and Earth.

Declination: The celestial latitude of an object in the sky, measured in degrees north or south of the celestial equator; analogous to latitude on Earth. The Almanac gives the Sun's declination at noon.

Dominical Letter: A letter from A to G, denoting Sundays in the ecclesiastical calendar for a given year, determined by the date on which the first Sunday falls. If it falls on January 1, the letter (for the year) is A; if it falls on January 2, the letter is B; and so on.

Eclipse, Lunar: The full Moon enters the shadow of Earth, which cuts off all or part of the Moon's light. **Total:** The Moon passes completely through the **umbra** (central dark part) of Earth's shadow. **Partial:** Only part of the Moon passes through the umbra. **Penumbral:** The Moon passes through only the penumbra (area of partial darkness surrounding the umbra).

Eclipse, Solar: Earth enters the shadow of the new Moon, which cuts off all or part of the Sun's light. **Total:** Earth passes through the umbra (central dark part) of the Moon's shadow, resulting in totality for observers within a narrow band on Earth. **Annular:** The Moon appears silhouetted against the Sun, with a ring of sunlight showing around it. **Partial:** The Moon blocks only part of the Sun.

Ecliptic: The apparent annual path of the Sun around the celestial sphere. The plane of the ecliptic is tipped 23½° from the celestial equator.

Elongation: The difference in degrees between the celestial longitudes of a planet and the Sun. **Greatest Elongation (Gr. Elong.):** The greatest apparent distance of a planet from the Sun, as seen from Earth.

Epact: A number from 1 to 30 that indicates the Moon's age on January 1 at Greenwich, England; used for determining the date of Easter.

Equinox: When the Sun crosses the celestial equator. This occurs two times each year: **Vernal** around March 21 and **Autumnal** around September 23.

Evening Star: A planet that is above the western horizon at sunset and less than 180° east of the Sun in right ascension.

Golden Number: A number in the 19-year cycle of the Moon, used for determining the date of Easter. (The Moon repeats its phases approximately every 19 years.) Add 1 to any given year and divide the result by 19; the remainder is the Golden Number. If there is no remainder, the Golden Number is 19.

Julian Period: A period of 7,980 years beginning January 1, 4713 B.C. Devised in 1583 by Joseph Scaliger, it provides a chronological basis for the study of ancient history. To find the Julian year, add 4,713 to any year. **(continued on page 86)**

How A Breakthrough New Combination of 3 Powerful Healing Herbs Can...

Flush Prostate Disorders Out Of Your Body!

...And Trigger Rapid Healing Of Even The Most Enlarged Prostate!

Thanks to a stunning new product developed by a San Diego company, if you suffer from prostate disorders, you can now get <u>rapid and dramatic relief!</u>

Yes it's true! There's a new, just released prostate supplement that is so incredibly <u>powerful</u>, it can actually <u>flush out</u> the dangerous toxins that scientists say cause prostate disorders for men over 45. This new supplement, is <u>so potent</u> experts believe it can...

Trigger Rapid Healing Of Prostate Disorders... Even If Other Treatments Have Failed You!

According to leading researcher Dr. Michael Ernest, this new supplement is so effective because "it helps rid the body of the <u>mutant hormone DHT</u> that attacks the prostate tissue and causes it to become diseased!"

The new product is called *Nature's Prostate Remedy*™ and it is a scientifically formulated combination of <u>three</u> of the world's most powerful and <u>clinically documented</u> prostate healing herbs, plus seven other miracle nutrients, all shown to rejuvenate the prostate!

Here is a breakdown of the truly remarkable "prostate defenders" contained in *Nature's Prostate Remedy*.

Prostate Defender #1

The first healing herb is called *Pygeum africanum*. Dozens of clinical studies document that *Pygeum* is a safe, effective herb that <u>shrinks enlarged prostate tissue</u>, and relieves pain and swelling. This healing herb is so effective, that over 80% of all doctors' prescriptions for prostate enlargement in France contain *Pygeum* extract!

Prostate Defender #2

This second healing herb contained in *Nature's Prostate Remedy* is called *Urtica dioica* extract and studies show that when combined with *Pygeum*, this dynamic "healing-duo" is so profoundly effective that it creates a fortress around the <u>prostate that shields it from toxins and other cellular invaders!</u>

But wait, it gets better! The herb Saw Palmetto is one of the most highly effective natural prostate treatments available. In fact, over 20 clinical studies credit Saw Palmetto with as high as a...

90% Success Rate In Treating Men With An Enlarged Prostate!

Therefore, the formulators of *Nature's Prostate*

- ✓ **No More Frequent Middle-Of-The-Night Trips To The Bathroom!**
- ✓ **No More Sudden -- *Even Uncontrollable* -- Urges To Urinate!**
- ✓ **No More Dignity-Robbing Incontinence!**
- ✓ **No More Pain and Discomfort!**
- ✓ **No More Sexual Dysfunction!**

Remedy added...

Prostate Defender #3

Saw Palmetto extract, the third powerful healing herb contained in *Nature's Prostate Remedy*. Clinical studies show that Saw Palmetto plays a vital role in flushing out the dangerous hormone DHT.

Now, with *Nature's Prostate Remedy*, you can have the combined force of <u>all three of these scientifically documented healing herbs</u>...working simultaneously in your body to heal your prostate condition.

100% Satisfaction Guaranteed!

Take an entire <u>120 days</u> and <u>experience for yourself</u> the dramatic relief *Nature's Prostate Remedy* will bring to you... <u>without risking a single penny!</u> If you're not 100% satisfied, we'll promptly send you a full, no-questions asked refund!

Get A <u>FREE</u> 64 Page Health Book Just For Trying It!

It's called *Prostate Healing Miracles* (a $14.95 value) – and it's YOURS FREE with your order.

Copyright © 2000 by Active Health Labs. These statements have not been evaluated by the FDA. This product is not intended to diagnose, treat, cure or prevent any disease.

Moon on Equator: The Moon is on the celestial equator.

Moon Rides High/Runs Low: The Moon is highest above or farthest below the celestial equator.

Moonrise/Moonset: The Moon's rising above or descending below the horizon.

Moon's Phases: The continually changing appearance of the Moon, caused by the different angles at which it is illuminated by the Sun. **First Quarter:** The right half of the Moon is illuminated, as seen from the Northern Hemisphere. **Full:** The Sun and the Moon are in opposition; the entire disk of the Moon is illuminated as viewed from Earth. **Last Quarter:** The left half of the Moon is illuminated, as seen from the Northern Hemisphere. **New:** The Sun and the Moon are in conjunction; the entire disk of the Moon is darkened as viewed from Earth.

Moon's Place, Astronomical: The actual position of the Moon within the constellations on the celestial sphere. **Astrological:** The astrological position of the Moon within the zodiac according to calculations made more than 2,000 years ago. Because of precession of the equinoxes and other factors, this is not the Moon's actual position in the sky.

Morning Star: A planet that is above the eastern horizon at sunrise and less than 180° west of the Sun in right ascension.

Node: Either of the two points where a body's orbit intersects the ecliptic. **Ascending:** The body is moving from south to north of the ecliptic. **Descending:** The body is moving from north to south of the ecliptic.

Occultation (Occn.): The eclipse of a star or planet by the Moon or another planet.

Opposition: The Moon or a planet appears on the opposite side of the sky from the Sun (elongation 180°).

Perigee (Perig.): The point in the Moon's orbit that is closest to Earth.

Perihelion (Perih.): The point in a planet's orbit that is closest to the Sun.

Precession: The slowly changing position of the stars and equinoxes in the sky resulting from variations in the orientation of Earth's axis.

Right Ascension (R.A.): The celestial longitude of an object in the sky, measured eastward along the celestial equator in hours of time from the vernal equinox; analogous to longitude on Earth.

Roman Indiction: A number in a 15-year cycle, established January 1, A.D. 313, as a fiscal term. Add 3 to any given year in the Christian era and divide by 15; the remainder is the Roman Indiction. If there is no remainder, it is 15.

Solar Cycle: A period of 28 years in the Julian calendar, at the end of which the days of the month return to the same days of the week.

Solstice, Summer: The Sun reaches its greatest declination (23½°) north of the celestial equator. **Winter:** The Sun reaches its greatest declination (23½°) south of the celestial equator.

Stationary (Stat.): The apparent halted movement of a planet against the background of the stars as it reaches opposition, shortly before it appears to move backward (retrograde motion).

Sun Fast/Slow: When a sundial reading is behind (slow) or ahead of (fast) clock time.

Sunrise/Sunset: The visible rising and setting of the Sun's upper limb across the unobstructed horizon of an observer whose eyes are 15 feet above ground level.

Twilight: The interval of time following sunset and preceding sunrise, during which the sky is partially illuminated. The three ranges of twilight are **civil** (from sunset/sunrise to when the Sun is 6° below the horizon), **nautical** (greater than 6° and ending at 12°), and **astronomical** (greater than 12° and ending at 18°—full darkness). (See page 92 to calculate twilight times in your area.) □ □

Plant a New Career...
and Watch It Grow!

Learn Professional Landscaping at Home.

Turn your gardening hobby into a new career with nationally accredited Education Direct's at-home training. Learn the skills you need to start your own home-based business or get a great job tending plants. You can earn up to $30,000 a year doing work you love! *

Enter a growing field.

Opportunities in landscaping services are projected to increase 29% by 2010! Begin your new career by training with the Education Direct Professional Landscaper program.

- Learn at the pace that fits your lifestyle best.
- Learn with expert instruction and specialized materials, including DesignWare® Software and preparation materials for the (PGMS) Certified Groundskeeper Exam.
- Learn at home. The entire career-training program comes to you in easy-to-manage sections. You never need to enter a classroom!

* Growth figures represent a ten-year period ending 2010. Source: *National Industry-Occupation Employment Matrix*, a publication of the U.S. Bureau of Labor Statistics. All salary information is based on the *Occupational Outlook Handbook*, a publication of the U.S. Department of Labor. Individual student earnings vary.

Get FREE information, with no obligation. For fastest service, call

1·800·572·1685 ext. 3770

or visit our website at **www.EduDirect-usa.com.** Online, enter ID#AA2S93S, or complete and return the coupon today.

Yes I would like to receive free information on the Education Direct program below. Please check ONE only! No obligation.

☐ 102 Professional Landscaper

Or choose one of these other training programs:

ASSOCIATE IN SPECIALIZED BUSINESS OR TECHNOLOGY DEGREE
- ☐ 61 Accounting
- ☐ 60 Business Management
- ☐ 396 Veterinary Technician (AST)

CAREER DIPLOMA PROGRAMS
- ☐ 390 Bookkeeping
- ☐ 59 Catering/Gourmet Cooking

- ☐ 03 Child Day Care Management
- ☐ 395 Dog Obedience Trainer/Instructor
- ☐ 06 Electrician
- ☐ 30 Floral Design
- ☐ 07 High School
- ☐ 15 Home Inspector
- ☐ 27 PC Repair

- ☐ 84 Pharmacy Technician
- ☐ 40 Photographer
- ☐ 58 Private Investigator
- ☐ 160 Professional Bridal Consultant
- ☐ 31 Professional Locksmithing
- ☐ 70 Small Business Management
- ☐ 389 Spanish *
- ☐ 88 Veterinary Assistant
- ☐ 22 Wildlife/Forestry Conservation

*Certificate Program

THOMSON
EDUCATION DIRECT

Dept. AA2S93S
925 Oak Street
Scranton, PA 18515-0700

Name _____ Age _____
Street _____ Apt. # _____
City _____ State ____ Zip _____
Phone ( ) _____
E-Mail _____

514A

Bright Stars

Transit Times

■ This table shows the time (EST or EDT) and altitude of a star as it transits the meridian (i.e., reaches its highest elevation while passing over the horizon's south point) at Boston on the dates shown. The transit time on any other date differs from that of the nearest date listed by approximately four minutes per day. To find the time of a star's transit for your location, convert its time at Boston using Key Letter C.*

Star	Constellation	Magnitude	Time of Transit (EST/EDT) Boldface–P.M. Lightface–A.M.						Altitude (degrees)
			Jan. 1	Mar. 1	May 1	July 1	Sept. 1	Nov. 1	
Altair	Aquila	0.8	**12:51**	8:55	5:56	1:56	**9:48**	**4:48**	56.3
Deneb	Cygnus	1.3	**1:42**	9:46	6:46	2:47	**10:39**	**5:39**	92.8
Fomalhaut	Psc. Aus.	1.2	**3:57**	**12:01**	9:01	5:01	12:53	**7:54**	17.8
Algol	Perseus	2.2	**8:07**	**4:12**	**1:12**	9:12	5:08	12:08	88.5
Aldebaran	Taurus	0.9	**9:35**	**5:39**	**2:39**	10:39	6:35	1:36	64.1
Rigel	Orion	0.1	**10:13**	**6:17**	**3:17**	11:18	7:14	2:14	39.4
Capella	Auriga	0.1	**10:15**	**6:19**	**3:19**	11:19	7:16	2:16	93.6
Bellatrix	Orion	1.6	**10:24**	**6:28**	**3:28**	11:28	7:25	2:25	54.0
Betelgeuse	Orion	var. 0.4	**10:54**	**6:58**	**3:58**	11:58	7:54	2:55	55.0
Sirius	Can. Maj.	−1.4	**11:44**	**7:48**	**4:48**	**12:48**	8:44	3:44	31.0
Procyon	Can. Min.	0.4	12:41	**8:41**	**5:42**	**1:42**	9:38	4:38	52.9
Pollux	Gemini	1.2	12:47	**8:47**	**5:48**	**1:48**	9:44	4:44	75.7
Regulus	Leo	1.4	3:10	**11:10**	**8:11**	**4:11**	**12:07**	7:07	59.7
Spica	Virgo	var. 1.0	6:27	2:31	**11:27**	**7:27**	**3:23**	10:23	36.6
Arcturus	Bootes	−0.1	7:17	3:22	12:18	**8:18**	**4:14**	11:14	66.9
Antares	Scorpius	var. 0.9	9:30	5:34	2:34	**10:31**	**6:27**	**1:27**	21.3
Vega	Lyra	0	11:38	7:42	4:42	12:38	**8:34**	3:35	86.4

Risings and Settings

■ To find the time of a star's rising at Boston on any date, subtract the interval shown at right from the star's transit time on that date; add the interval to find the star's setting time. To find the rising and setting times for your city, convert the Boston transit times above using the Key Letter* shown at right before applying the interval. The directions in which the stars rise and set, shown for Boston, are generally useful throughout the United States. Deneb, Algol, Capella, and Vega are circumpolar stars—they never set but appear to circle the celestial north pole.

Star	Interval (h. m.)	Rising Key	Rising Dir.	Setting Key	Setting Dir.
Altair	6:36	B	EbN	E	WbN
Fomalhaut	3:59	E	SE	D	SW
Aldebaran	7:06	B	ENE	D	WNW
Rigel	5:33	D	EbS	B	WbS
Bellatrix	6:27	B	EbN	D	WbN
Betelgeuse	6:31	B	EbN	D	WbN
Sirius	5:00	D	ESE	B	WSW
Procyon	6:23	B	EbN	D	WbN
Pollux	8:01	A	NE	E	NW
Regulus	6:49	B	EbN	D	WbN
Spica	5:23	D	EbS	B	WbS
Arcturus	7:19	A	ENE	E	WNW
Antares	4:17	E	SEbE	A	SWbW

*The values of Key Letters are given in the Time Corrections table (page 170).

-Beth Krommes

Are you over 55?

"Look What Seniors Can Get Free!"

Washington DC (Special) An amazing new book reveals thousands of little-known Government giveaways for people over 55.

Each year, lots of these benefits are NOT given away simply because people don't know they're available... and the government doesn't advertise them.

Many of these fabulous freebies can be yours regardless of your income or assets. Entitled "Free for Seniors", the book tells you all about such goodies as how you can:

▶ Get free prescription drugs. (This one alone could save you thousands of dollars!)

▶ Get free dental care... for yourself AND for your grandkids.

▶ Get up to $800 for food.

▶ How you can get free legal help.

▶ How to get some help in paying your rent, wherever you live.

▶ How to get up to $15,000 free money to spruce up your home!

▶ Here's where to get $1,800 to keep you warm this winter.

▶ Access the very best research on our planet on how you can live longer.

▶ Are you becoming more forgetful? Here's valuable free information you should get now.

▶ Stop high blood pressure and cholesterol worries from ruling your life.

▶ Free help if you have arthritis of any type.

▶ Incontinence is not inevitable. These free facts could help you.

▶ Free eye treatment.

▶ Depression: Being down in the dumps is common, but it doesn't have to be a normal part of growing old.

▶ Free medical care from some of the very best doctors in the world for Alzheimer's, cataracts, or heart disease.

▶ New Cancer Cure? Maybe! Here's how to find out what's known about it to this point.

▶ Promising new developments for prostate cancer.

▶ Get paid $100 a day plus expenses to travel overseas!

▶ Up to $5,000 free to help you pay your bills.

▶ Free and confidential help with your sex life.

▶ Impotence? Get confidential help... Free therapies, treatments, implants, and much more.

▶ Hot Flashes? This new research could help you now!

▶ Find out if a medicine you're taking could be affecting your sex life.

There's more! Much, much more, and "Free for Seniors" comes with a solid no-nonsense guarantee. Send for your copy today and examine it at your leisure. Unless it makes or saves you AT LEAST ten times it's cost, simply return it for a full refund within 90 days.

To get your copy of "Free for Seniors", send your name and address along with a check or money-order for only $12.95 plus $3.98 postage and handling (total of $16.93) to: FREE FOR SENIORS, Dept. FS3473, 718 - 12th Street N.W., Box 24500, Canton, Ohio 44701.

To charge to your VISA or MasterCard, include your card number, expiration date, and signature. For even faster service, have your credit card handy and call toll-free 1-800-772-7285, Ext. FS3473.

Want to save even more? Do a favor for a friend or relative and order 2 books for only $20 postpaid.   ©2003 TCO FS0267S13

http://www.trescocorp.com

Eclipses

■ There will be four eclipses in 2004, two of the Sun and two of the Moon. Solar eclipses are visible only in certain areas and require eye protection to be viewed safely. Lunar eclipses are technically visible from the entire night side of Earth, but during a penumbral eclipse, the dimming of the Moon's illumination is slight.

1 **Partial eclipse of the Sun, April 19.** This eclipse will not be visible in the United States or Canada.

2 **Total eclipse of the Moon, May 4.** This eclipse will not be visible from most of the United States or Canada.

3 **Partial eclipse of the Sun, October 13.** Visible from Alaska and Hawaii. In both Alaska and Hawaii, the eclipse will begin about 6:00 P.M. local time and end about sunset.

4 **Total eclipse of the Moon, October 27–28.** The beginning of the umbral phase will be visible in North America except in the extreme Northwest. The end of the eclipse will be visible throughout North America. The Moon enters penumbra at 8:06 P.M. EDT (5:06 P.M. PDT) and enters umbra at 9:14 P.M. EDT (6:14 P.M. PDT).

The Moon enters totality at 10:23 P.M. EDT (7:23 P.M. PDT) and leaves totality at 11:45 P.M. EDT (8:45 P.M. PDT). Finally, the Moon leaves umbra at 12:54 A.M. EDT (9:54 P.M. PDT) and leaves penumbra at 2:03 A.M. EDT (11:03 P.M. PDT).

Full-Moon Dates

	2004	2005	2006	2007	2008
Jan.	7	25	14	3	22
Feb.	6	23	12	2	20
Mar.	6	25	14	3	21
Apr.	5	24	13	2	20
May	4	23	13	2 & 31	19
June	3	22	11	30	18
July	2 & 31	21	10	29	18
Aug.	29	19	9	28	16
Sept.	28	17	7	26	15
Oct.	27	17	6	26	14
Nov.	26	15	5	24	13
Dec.	26	15	4	23	12

Principal Meteor Showers

Shower	Best Viewing	Point of Origin	Date of Maximum*	Peak Rate (/hr.)**	Associated Comet
Quadrantid	Predawn	N	Jan. 4	80	—
Lyrid	Predawn	S	Apr. 22	12	Thatcher
Eta Aquarid	Predawn	SE	May 4	20	Halley
Delta Aquarid	Predawn	S	July 30	10	—
Perseid	Predawn	NE	Aug. 11–13	75	Swift-Tuttle
Draconid	Late evening	NW	Oct. 9	6	Giacobini-Zinner
Orionid	Predawn	S	Oct. 21–22	25	Halley
Taurid	Midnight	S	Nov. 9	6	Encke
Leonid	Predawn	S	Nov. 18	20	Tempel-Tuttle
Andromedid	Late evening	S	Nov. 25–27	5	Biela
Geminid	All night	NE	Dec. 13–14	65	—
Ursid	Predawn	N	Dec. 22	12	Tuttle

*May vary by one or two days in either direction.
**Approximate.

"If I told you that I can end a lifetime of foot pain instantly, you probably wouldn't believe me..."

"Half a million other men and women didn't either... until they tried this revolutionary European discovery that positively killed their foot pain dead!

"Don't live with foot pain a moment longer! If you're ready to recapture the vitality and energy that healthy feet provide, I'll give you 60 days to try the remarkable foot support system I discovered in Europe. You will immediately experience relief and freedom from foot ailments. I GUARANTEE IT!

"How can I make such an unprecedented guarantee? Because I personally lived in constant, agonizing foot pain for years

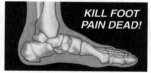 **KILL FOOT PAIN DEAD!** before my exciting discovery. What started out as simple aching from corns and calluses grew into full-blown, incapacitating misery only a few other foot pain sufferers could understand.

"Believe me, I tried all the so-called remedies I could get my hands on (and feet into), but none of them really worked. It wasn't until my wife and I took a trip to Europe that I discovered a remarkable invention called Flexible Featherspring® Foot Supports. Invented in Germany, these custom-formed foot supports absorb shock as they cradle your feet as if on a cushion of air.

Harvey Rothschild,
Founder of Featherspring Int'l.

"Imagine my complete surprise as I slipped a pair of custom-formed Feathersprings into my shoes for the first time and began the road to no more pain. The tremendous pain and pressure I used to feel every time I took a step was gone! I could scarcely believe how great a relief I felt even after walking several hours. And after just a few days of use, my pain disappeared totally - *and has never returned.*

"Whatever your problem– corns, calluses, bunions, pain in the balls of your feet, toe cramps, fallen arches, burning nerve endings, painful ankles, back aches, or just generally sore, aching feet and legs – *my Feathersprings are guaranteed to end your foot pain or you don't pay a penny.*

"But don't just take my word for it: Experience for yourself the immediate relief and renewed energy that Feathersprings provide. Send for your FREE kit today on our no risk, 60-day trial offer!"

Visit our web site at: www.featherspring.com or call us toll free at: 1-800-628-4693

Please send FREE INFORMATION KIT!

FEATHERSPRING INTERNATIONAL, INC.
712 N. 34th Street, Dept. OF014
Seattle, WA 98103-8881

Name _____

Address _____

City _____ State ____ Zip _____

Look for a **LARGE PINK ENVELOPE** containing all the details. No obligation. No salesperson will call.

© FEATHERSPRING, 712 N. 34th Street, Seattle, WA 98103-8881

The Twilight Zone

How to determine the length of twilight and the times of dawn and dark.

■ Twilight is the period of time between dawn and sunrise, and again between sunset and dark. Both dawn and dark are defined as moments when the Sun is 18 degrees below the horizon. The latitude of a place and the time of year determine the length of twilight. To find the latitude of your city or the city nearest you, consult the **Time Corrections** table, **page 170.** Use that figure in the chart below with the appropriate date, and you will have the length of twilight in your area.

	Length of Twilight (hours and minutes)								
Latitude	Jan. 1 to Apr. 10	Apr. 11 to May 2	May 3 to May 14	May 15 to May 25	May 26 to July 22	July 23 to Aug. 3	Aug. 4 to Aug. 14	Aug. 15 to Sept. 5	Sept. 6 to Dec. 31
25° N to 30° N	1 20	1 23	1 26	1 29	1 32	1 29	1 26	1 23	1 20
31° N to 36° N	1 26	1 28	1 34	1 38	1 43	1 38	1 34	1 28	1 26
37° N to 42° N	1 33	1 39	1 47	1 52	1 59	1 52	1 47	1 39	1 33
43° N to 47° N	1 42	1 51	2 02	2 13	2 27	2 13	2 02	1 51	1 42
48° N to 49° N	1 50	2 04	2 22	2 42	—	2 42	2 22	2 04	1 50

■ To determine when dawn will break and when dark will descend, apply the length of twilight to the times of sunrise and sunset. Follow the instructions given in **How to Use This Almanac, page 39,** to determine sunrise/sunset times for your locality. Subtract the length of twilight from the time of sunrise for dawn. Add the length of twilight to the time of sunset for dark. (See examples at right.)

	Boston, Mass. (latitude 42° 22')	Oshkosh, Wis. (latitude 44° 1')
Sunrise, August 1	5:37 A.M.	5:40 A.M.
Length of twilight	−1:52	−2:13
Dawn breaks	3:45 A.M. EDT	3:27 A.M. CDT
Sunset, August 1	8:03 P.M.	8:15 P.M.
Length of twilight	+1:52	+2:13
Dark descends	9:55 P.M. EDT	10:28 P.M. CDT

Tidal Glossary

Apogean Tide: A monthly tide of decreased range that occurs when the Moon is at apogee (farthest from Earth).

Diurnal Tide: A tide with one high water and one low water in a tidal day of approximately 24 hours.

Mean Lower Low Water: The arithmetic mean of the lesser of a daily pair of low waters, observed over a specific 19-year cycle called the National Tidal Datum Epoch.

Neap Tide: A tide of decreased range that occurs twice a month, when the Moon is in quadrature (during its first and last quarters, when the Sun and the Moon are at right angles to each other relative to Earth).

Perigean Tide: A monthly tide of increased range that occurs when the Moon is at perigee (closest to Earth).

Semidiurnal Tide: A tide with one high water and one low water every half day. East

Coast tides, for example, are semidiurnal, with two highs and two lows during a tidal day of approximately 24 hours.

Spring Tide: A tide of increased range that occurs at times of syzygy each month. Named not for the season of spring but from the German *springen* ("to leap up"), a spring tide also brings a lower low water.

Syzygy: The nearly straight-line configuration that occurs twice a month, when the Sun and the Moon are in conjunction (on the same side of Earth at the new Moon) and when they are in opposition (on opposite sides of Earth at the full Moon). In both cases, the gravitational effects of the Sun and the Moon reinforce each other, and tidal range is increased.

Vanishing Tide: A mixed tide of considerable inequality in the two highs and two lows, so that the lower high (or higher low) may become indistinct or appear to vanish.

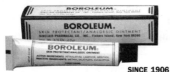

The Visible Planets

■ Listed here for Boston are the times (EST/EDT) of the visible rising and setting of the planets Venus, Mars, Jupiter, and Saturn on the 1st, 11th, and 21st of each month. The approximate times of their visible rising and setting on other days can be found by interpolation. The capital letters that appear beside the times are Key Letters and are used to convert the times for other localities (see pages 40 and 170). For definitions of morning and evening stars, see the Glossary on page 84.

Venus has its best year since 1882. Dominated by the historical June 8 transit, 2004 is a rare year when our sister planet optimally blazes twice. First, as a dazzling, high-up evening star (from January through May), it reaches greatest elongation 46 degrees from the Sun on March 29 and greatest brilliancy at magnitude −4.5 on May 2. Then, as a lofty morning star (from late June through December), it reaches greatest brilliancy on July 14 and greatest elongation on August 17.

Mars has an off year. After its historic close-approach last August, Mars spends the year fading, until it vanishes in mid-July and slinks behind the Sun on September 15. After that, the orange world slowly exits the solar glare into the morning sky and is visible again in mid-November. During the year, Mars speeds from Pisces in January to Scorpius in December. Two conjunctions, best seen with binoculars, pair the dim orange world with Mercury on July 10 and with Venus on December 5.

Venus

Boldface—p.m. / Lightface—a.m.		
Jan.........1 set **7:03** A	July ....1 rise 3:29 A
Jan.......11 set **7:28** B	July .....11 rise 3:00 A
Jan.......21 set **7:53** B	July .....21 rise 2:39 A
Feb........1 set **8:19** C	Aug.......1 rise 2:24 A
Feb......11 set **8:41** C	Aug.....11 rise 2:18 A
Feb......21 set **9:02** D	Aug.....21 rise 2:18 A
Mar ......1 set **9:21** D	Sept.......1 rise 2:25 A
Mar .....11 set **9:42** D	Sept.....11 rise 2:37 A
Mar .....21 set **10:01** E	Sept.....21 rise 2:52 B
Apr.........1 set **10:18** E	Oct ....1 rise 3:10 B
Apr......11 set **11:29** E	Oct ......11 rise 3:30 B
Apr......21 set **11:32** E	Oct ......21 rise 3:51 B
May.......1 set **11:24** E	Nov ....1 rise 3:15 C
May.....11 set **11:01** E	Nov .....11 rise 3:37 C
May.....21 set **10:18** E	Nov .....21 rise 4:01 D
June......1 set **9:06** E	Dec........1 rise 4:25 D
June.....11 rise 4:54 A	Dec......11 rise 4:50 D
June.....21 rise 4:07 A	Dec......21 rise 5:14 E
	Dec......31 rise 5:37 E

Mars

Boldface—p.m. / Lightface—a.m.		
Jan.........1 set **11:53** A	July ....1 set **9:55** E
Jan.......11 set **11:46** A	July .....11 set **9:34** E
Jan.......21 set **11:39** A	July .....21 set **9:12** D
Feb........1 set **11:32** A	Aug.......1 set **8:47** D
Feb......11 set **11:26** A	Aug.....11 set **8:23** D
Feb......21 set **11:20** A	Aug.....21 set **7:59** D
Mar ......1 set **11:15** A	Sept.......1 set **7:31** D
Mar .....11 set **11:09** A	Sept.....11 set **7:06** C
Mar .....21 set **11:03** A	Sept.....21 rise 6:20 C
Apr.........1 set **10:56** B	Oct ....1 rise 6:14 C
Apr......11 set **11:49** B	Oct ......11 rise 6:08 C
Apr......21 set **11:40** C	Oct ......21 rise 6:02 C
May.......1 set **11:30** C	Nov ....1 rise 4:56 D
May.....11 set **11:19** D	Nov .....11 rise 4:51 D
May.....21 set **11:06** E	Nov .....21 rise 4:46 D
June......1 set **10:50** E	Dec........1 rise 4:41 D
June.....11 set **10:33** E	Dec......11 rise 4:37 D
June.....21 set **10:15** E	Dec......21 rise 4:33 E
	Dec......31 rise 4:29 E

Mercury continues its custom of darting in and out of the Sun's glare. In 2004, the broiling ruddy world is easy to see in the evening sky after sunset from March 14 to April 10, with the best period from March 20 to 31. Far less favorable is its evening apparition from July 3 to 25, although a meeting with Mars on the 10th should be interesting through binoculars. Its final evening performance in November is extremely poor. As a morning star, Mercury's best appearances of 2004 occur the first three weeks of September, followed by the last half of December. Mercury will be very low and difficult to see throughout January, and its May apparition is essentially nonexistent.

DO NOT CONFUSE 1) Saturn with Castor or Pollux. Saturn is brighter and doesn't twinkle. 2) Mars with Saturn during their meeting in Gemini in the last half of May. Mars is dimmer and noticeably orange. 3) Venus and a sunspot, during Venus's crossing of the Sun's face on June 8. Venus will appear perfectly round. 4) Mercury with Mars on July 10. Mercury is brighter. 5) Venus with Jupiter on November 4 and 5 in the predawn east. Venus is brighter.

Jupiter, in Leo, has a splendid year, rising by 11:00 P.M. in January and by 9:00 P.M. in February, and remaining conspicuous through July. It is especially brilliant within two months of its opposition on March 4, when it is out all night in the southern midnight sky. After sinking into the obscurity of evening twilight in August and vanishing behind the Sun on September 21, the planet emerges before dawn in October in its new home of Virgo. By year's end, it is rising by 1:00 A.M.

Saturn, like Mars, has no opposition this year, but in Saturn's case it doesn't matter. The ringed world is gorgeous, its rings wide open and its nightly elevation ultrahigh in its northerly home of Gemini. Having reached opposition on New Year's Eve, Saturn remains conspicuous all winter. It becomes strictly an evening object during spring, vanishes in June, and reappears in the east before dawn in August. By November, it rises again before midnight and is prominent throughout winter.

			Boldface—P.M.			Lightface—A.M.			
Jan.........1	rise	9:57	B	July 1	set 11:34	D	Jan.........1	set 7:16	E	July 1	set 8:43	E

Jan.........1	rise	9:57	B	July 1	set	11:34	D	Jan.........1	set	7:16	E	July 1	set	8:43	E
Jan.......11	rise	9:17	B	July 11	set	10:58	D	Jan.......11	set	6:33	E	July 11	rise	5:09	A
Jan.......21	rise	8:36	B	July 21	set	10:22	D	Jan.......21	set	5:51	E	July 21	rise	4:36	A
Feb.........1	rise	7:48	B	Aug 1	set	9:44	C	Feb.........1	set	5:05	E	Aug 1	rise	4:00	A
Feb......11	rise	7:04	B	Aug 11	set	9:08	C	Feb......11	set	4:24	E	Aug 11	rise	3:27	A
Feb......21	rise	6:19	B	Aug 21	set	8:34	C	Feb......21	set	3:43	E	Aug 21	rise	2:53	A
Mar 1	rise	5:37	B	Sept.......1	set	7:55	C	Mar 1	set	3:07	E	Sept.......1	rise	2:16	A
Mar 11	set	5:58	D	Sept.....11	set	7:21	C	Mar 11	set	2:28	E	Sept.....11	rise	1:41	A
Mar 21	set	5:16	D	Sept.....21	set	6:46	C	Mar 21	set	1:49	E	Sept.....21	rise	1:06	A
Apr.......1	set	4:30	D	Oct 1	rise	6:04	C	Apr.......1	set	1:08	E	Oct 1	rise	12:27	A
Apr......11	set	4:49	D	Oct 11	rise	5:36	C	Apr......11	set	1:31	E	Oct 11	rise	11:50	A
Apr......21	set	4:08	D	Oct 21	rise	5:07	C	Apr......21	set	12:51	E	Oct 21	rise	11:13	A
May.......1	set	3:28	D	Nov 1	rise	3:35	C	May.......1	set	12:15	E	Nov 1	rise	9:31	A
May.....11	set	2:49	D	Nov 11	rise	3:06	C	May.....11	set	11:39	E	Nov 11	rise	8:52	A
May.....21	set	2:10	D	Nov 21	rise	2:36	C	May.....21	set	11:04	E	Nov 21	rise	8:11	A
June.......1	set	1:28	D	Dec........1	rise	2:05	C	June.......1	set	10:26	E	Dec........1	rise	7:30	A
June.....11	set	12:47	D	Dec......11	rise	1:33	C	June.....11	set	9:51	E	Dec......11	rise	6:48	A
June.....21	set	12:10	D	Dec......21	rise	1:01	C	June.....21	set	9:17	E	Dec......21	rise	6:06	A
				Dec......31	rise	12:27	C					Dec......31	rise	5:23	A

THE
EASIEST-EVER
EDIBLE
GARDEN

PLANT ONCE.
PICK FOREVER.

Although people know that most vegetables are grown as annuals and planted and harvested during the same growing season, we often forget about the perennials. Once established, these plants will provide a bountiful harvest every year for many years—without needing to be replanted. Three that are easy to grow are asparagus, horseradish, and rhubarb.

by George and Becky Lohmiller

THE GROUND RULES

Asparagus, horseradish, and rhubarb are seldom bothered by insects and diseases, and all require about the same growing conditions: a sunny location and a deep soil that is rich in organic matter. Because these hardy edibles will be occupying the same spot for years, put them either at the end of your garden, where they won't interfere with the soil preparation and growing of annual vegetables, or in a place of their own. Each one is an attractive ornamental, suitable as a border planting in front of a wall or fence or as a background for flowers.

ASPARAGUS

■ Asparagus is relatively expensive at the grocery store and loses quality quickly after picking, so if you love it, grow your own! An asparagus bed is a long-term investment. Many plantings last 30 years or more and can produce up to one-half pound of spears per foot of row over the eight-week harvest period in spring and early summer.

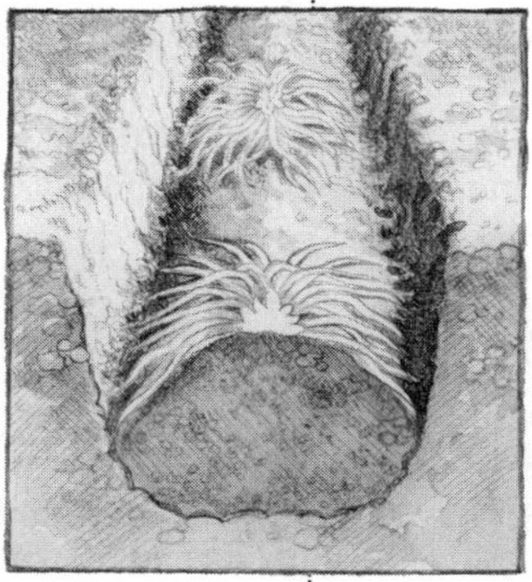

In early spring, plant asparagus deep to protect the crown from the deep cultivation needed for weed control. For each row of asparagus desired, dig a trench 12 inches deep and 12 to 18 inches wide. Allow three feet between rows. Fill the trench half full of rich organic soil with the top slightly mounded **(see il-lustration at right)**. Place each asparagus crown on top of the mound, and spread the roots away from the crown. Space one-year-old roots 12 to 14 inches apart. Cover with two inches of soil. As the shoots grow, fill in around them, until the soil is level with the ground.

–Renée Quintal Daily

An asparagus bed is a long-term investment. Many plantings last 30 years or more.

–Johnny's Selected Seeds

(continued)

To establish a strong root system, don't harvest spears in the same year you plant them. In the second season, harvest them for three to four weeks and then stop. During the third year, the bed should be in full production.

Harvest the spears by snapping them off near the ground when they are six to eight inches tall and more than one-half inch thick. Stop picking when the only spears that remain are thin and spindly (leave them to grow into the feathery fern that nourishes the roots). Cut the fern back to the ground after it yellows in late fall.

HORSERADISH

■ Store-bought versions of this condiment can not compare with the penetrating aroma and spicy hot taste of freshly dug and prepared horseradish root. Prepared horseradish will last in the refrigerator for four to six months, and longer in the freezer.

For long, well-shaped roots, plant horseradish in deeply cultivated soil enriched with compost or manure. In early spring, plant pieces of root at a 45-degree angle four to five inches deep and 24 inches apart, with the fatter top end of the root pointing up **(see illustration at right)**. Planted in early spring, horseradish can be dug in late fall or left in the ground for harvesting anytime— providing the ground isn't frozen.

—Renée Quintal Daily

The easiest way to prepare horseradish for the table is in the blender. Use the thick, fleshy white roots. Peel and cube enough root to fill the blender half full, and add a small amount of water and one or two ice cubes. As the root is ground, strong fumes are released by enzyme activity, so do the preparation in a well-ventilated area. When you

Planted in early spring, horseradish can be dug in late fall or left in the ground for harvesting anytime.

—The Herb Gardener, Storey Publishing

(continued)

Why wait ten months?

Now you can have rich, dark compost _in just 14 days!_

With the amazing ComposTumbler, you'll have bushels of crumbly, ready-to-use compost — _in just 14 days!_ (And, in the ten months it takes to make compost the old way, your ComposTumbler can produce _hundreds of pounds_ of rich food for your garden!)

Say good-bye to that messy, open compost pile (and to the flies, pests, and odors that come along with it!) Bid a happy farewell to the strain of trying to turn over heavy, wet piles with a pitchfork.

Compost the Better Way

Compost-making with the ComposTumbler is neat, quick and easy!

Gather up leaves, old weeds, kitchen scraps, lawn clippings, etc. and toss them into the roomy 18-bushel drum. Then, once each day, give the ComposTumbler's _gear-driven_ handle a few easy spins.

The ComposTumbler's Magic

Inside the ComposTumbler, carefully positioned mixing fins blend materials, pushing fresh mixture to the core where the temperatures are the hottest (up to 160°) and the composting bacteria most active.

After just 14 days, open the door, and you'll find an abundance of dark, sweet-smelling "garden gold" — ready to enrich and feed your garden!

NEW SMALLER SIZE!

Now there are 2 sizes. The 18-bushel original ComposTumbler and the NEW 9.5-bushel Compact ComposTumbler. Try either size risk-free for 30 days!

See for yourself! Try the ComposTumbler risk-free with our 30-Day Home Trial!

Call Toll-Free 1-800-880-2345

NOW ON SALE— SAVE UP TO $115!

like the consistency, add two to three tablespoons of white vinegar and one-quarter teaspoon of salt for each cup of grated root. The vinegar stops the enzyme action, so if you like mild horseradish, add it right away; if you prefer it hot and spicy, wait three minutes after grinding. Serve it fresh to add zest to meats, fish, salads, and dips. There won't be a dry eye in the house.

Beware: Many folks find that horseradish is all too easy to grow and a big problem when they want to get rid of it. Horseradish has a large taproot that grows straight down under the plant, with secondary roots that may grow out horizontally for three feet or more. When the taproot is harvested, even the tiniest pieces of secondary roots left in the ground can sprout new plants that will quickly overrun a garden. The best way to avoid this disaster is to plant horseradish in its own bed, or corral it in a bottomless barrel at the end of the garden.

Even the tiniest pieces of secondary horseradish roots left in the ground can sprout new plants that will quickly overrun a garden.

RHUBARB

■ For rhubarb lovers, nothing beats the flavor of pie, sauce, jam, and jelly made from homegrown, freshly picked rhubarb. Northern areas of the country are best suited for growing rhubarb because the plant requires a cold dormant period to trigger spring growth and give the tender new stalks, or petioles, their characteristic pink or red color. However, southern gardeners can grow it as an annual.

The best time to start a new rhubarb planting is in early spring as soon as the ground can be worked. Space the crowns three feet apart, with the buds an inch or two below the soil surface **(see illustration at right)**. For the roots to grow and store energy, don't harvest any stalks the first season, and harvest only sparingly the second year. You can harvest a full crop the third season. Picking rhubarb is easy: Simply grab a stalk near the base and pull it sharply to the side, as you would pull a stalk of celery from the bunch.

–Renée Quintal Daily

(continued)

Black Listed Cancer Treatment Could Save Your Life

Baltimore, MD— As unbelievable as it seems the key to stopping many cancers has been around for over 30 years. Yet it has been banned. Blocked. And kept out of your medicine cabinet by the very agency designed to protect your health—the FDA.

In 1966, the senior oncologist at a prominent New York hospital rocked the medical world when he developed a serum that **"shrank cancer tumors in 45 minutes!"** 90 minutes later they were gone...Headlines hit every major paper around the world. Time and again this life saving treatment worked miracles, but the FDA ignored the research and hope he brought and shut him down.

You read that right. He was not only shut down—but also forced out of the country where others benefited from his discovery. How many other treatments have they been allowed to hide?

Decades ago, European research scientist Dr. Johanna Budwig, a six-time Nobel Award nominee, discovered a totally natural formula that not only protects against the development of cancer, but has helped people all over the world diagnosed with incurable cancer—now lead normal lives.

After 30 years of study, Dr. Budwig discovered that the blood of seriously ill cancer patients was deficient in certain substances and nutrients. Yet, healthy blood always contained these ingredients. It was the lack of these nutrients that allowed cancer cells to grow wild and out of control.

By simply eating a combination of two natural and delicious foods (found on page 134) not only can cancer be prevented—but in case after case it was actually healed! "Symptoms of cancer, liver dysfunction, and diabetes were completely alleviated." Remarkably, what Dr. Budwig discovered was a totally natural way for eradicating cancer.

However, when she went to publish these results so that everyone could benefit—**she was blocked by manufacturers with heavy financial stakes!** For over 10 years now her methods have proved effective—yet she is denied publication—blocked by the giants who don't want you to read her words.

What's more, the world is full of expert minds like Dr. Budwig who have pursued cancer remedies and come up with remarkable natural formulas and diets that work for hundreds and thousands of patients. *How to Fight Cancer & Win* author William Fischer has studied these methods and revealed their secrets for you—so that you or someone you love may be spared the horrors of conventional cancer treatments.

As early as 1947, Virginia Livingston, M.D., isolated a cancer-causing microbe. She noted that every cancer sample analyzed (whether human or other animal) contained it.

This microbe—a bacteria that is actually in each of us from birth to death—multiplies and promotes cancer when the immune system is weakened by disease, stress, or poor nutrition. Worst of all, the microbes secrete a special hormone protector that short-circuits our body's immune system—allowing the microbes to grow undetected for years. No wonder so many patients are riddled with cancer by the time it is detected. But there is hope even for them...

Turn to page 82 of *How to Fight Cancer & Win* for the delicious diet that can help stop the formation of cancer cells and shrink tumors.

They walked away from traditional cancer treatments...and were healed! Throughout the pages of *How to Fight Cancer & Win* you'll meet real people who were diagnosed with cancer—suffered through harsh conventional treatments—turned their backs on so called modern medicine—only to be miraculously healed by natural means! Here is just a sampling of what others have to say about the book.

"We purchased *How to Fight Cancer & Win*, and immediately my husband started following the recommended diet for his just diagnosed colon cancer. He refused the surgery that our doctors advised. Since following the regime recommended in the book he has had no problems at all, cancer-wise. If not cured, we believe the cancer has to be in remission."—*Thelma B.*

"I bought *How to Fight Cancer & Win* and this has to be the greatest book I've ever read. I have had astounding results from the easy to understand knowledge found in this book. My whole life has improved drastically and I have done so much for many others. The information goes far beyond the health thinking of today."—*Hugh M.*

"I can't find adequate words to describe my appreciation of your work in providing *How to Fight Cancer & Win*. You had to do an enormous amount of research to bring this vast and most important knowledge to your readers.

My doctor found two tumors on my prostate with a high P.S.A. He scheduled a time to surgically remove the prostate, but I canceled the appointment. Instead I went on the diet discussed in the book combined with another supplement. Over the months my P.S.A. has lowered until the last reading was one point two."—*Duncan M.*

"In my 55 years as a Country Family Physician, I have never read a more 'down to earth,' practical resume of cancer prevention and treatments, than in this book. It needs to be studied worldwide for the prevention of cancer by all researchers who are looking for a cure."—*Edward S.,MD*

"As a cancer patient who has been battling lymphatic cancer on and off for almost three years now, I was very pleased to stumble across *How to Fight Cancer & Win*. The book was inspiring, well-written and packed with useful information for any cancer patient looking to maximize his or her chances for recovery."—*Romany S.*

"I've been incorporating Dr. Budwig's natural remedy into my diet and have told others about it. Your book is very informative and has information I've never heard about before (and I've read many books on the cancer and nutrition link). Thanks for the wonderful information."—*Molly G.*

Don't waste another minute. Claim your book today and you will be one of the lucky few who no longer have to wait for cures that get pushed "underground" by big business and money hungry giants.

To get your copy of *How to Fight Cancer & Win* call **1-888-821-3609 and ask for code PD91** to order by credit card. Or write "Fight Cancer—Dept. PD91" on a plain piece of paper with your name, address, phone number (in case we have a question about your order) and mail it with a check for $19.95 plus $5.00 shipping to: **Agora Health Books, Dept. PD91, P.O. Box 925, Frederick, MD 21705-9838.**

If you are not completely satisfied, return the book within one year for a complete and total refund—no questions asked. This will probably be the most important information you and your loved ones receive—so order today.

©2003 Agora Health Books, LLC

A SPORTS BARB

In baseball, a rhubarb is a heated on-field argument or controversy.

You can trick rhubarb into producing an extra off-season crop by potting up a plant (those with larger-diameter roots work best) in a large container in November and leaving it outside to experience several 32°F nights. Then put it into a basement or other dark area that stays between 50° and 65°F. Cover the top of the pot with more soil, or sawdust or other mulch, and keep it moist. In four to six weeks, the forced stalks will be bright pink, tender, and exceptionally tasty. In the spring, return the plant to the garden.

It's true that rhubarb leaves can be poisonous to eat, but they are not harmful to touch. They can be safely composted with no harm to the pile, or laid out between garden rows to restrict weeds. ☐☐

George and Becky Lohmiller, who write the essays in *The Old Farmer's Almanac Gardening Calendar,* run a garden center and landscaping business in Hancock, New Hampshire.

IN THE KITCHEN. For recipes using these vegetables, visit **www.almanac.com** and click on **Article Links 2004.**

Frosts and Growing Seasons

Courtesy of National Climatic Center

■ Dates given are normal averages for a light freeze (32°F); local weather and topography may cause considerable variations. The possibility of frost occurring after the spring dates and before the fall dates is 50 percent. The classification of freeze temperatures is usually based on their effect on plants, with the following commonly accepted categories: **Light freeze:** 29° to 32°F—tender plants killed. **Moderate freeze:** 25° to 28°F—widely destructive effect on most vegetation. **Severe freeze:** 24°F and colder—heavy damage to most plants.

City	State	Growing Season (days)	Last Spring Frost	First Fall Frost	City	State	Growing Season (days)	Last Spring Frost	First Fall Frost
Mobile	AL	273	Feb. 27	Nov. 26	North Platte	NE	136	May 11	Sept. 24
Juneau	AK	133	May 16	Sept. 26	Las Vegas	NV	259	Mar. 7	Nov. 21
Phoenix	AZ	309	Feb. 5	Dec. 15	Concord	NH	121	May 23	Sept. 22
Tucson	AZ	274	Feb. 28	Nov. 29	Newark	NJ	219	Apr. 4	Nov. 10
Pine Bluff	AR	234	Mar. 19	Nov. 8	Carlsbad	NM	223	Mar. 29	Nov. 7
Eureka	CA	325	Jan. 30	Dec. 15	Los Alamos	NM	157	May 8	Oct. 13
Sacramento	CA	290	Feb. 14	Dec. 1	Albany	NY	144	May 7	Sept. 29
San Francisco	CA	*	*	*	Syracuse	NY	170	Apr. 28	Oct. 16
Denver	CO	157	May 3	Oct. 8	Fayetteville	NC	212	Apr. 2	Oct. 31
Hartford	CT	167	Apr. 25	Oct. 10	Bismarck	ND	129	May 14	Sept. 20
Wilmington	DE	198	Apr. 13	Oct. 29	Akron	OH	168	May 3	Oct. 18
Miami	FL	*	*	*	Cincinnati	OH	195	Apr. 14	Oct. 27
Tampa	FL	339	Jan. 28	Jan. 3	Lawton	OK	217	Apr. 1	Nov. 5
Athens	GA	224	Mar. 28	Nov. 8	Tulsa	OK	218	Mar. 30	Nov. 4
Savannah	GA	250	Mar. 10	Nov. 15	Pendleton	OR	188	Apr. 15	Oct. 21
Boise	ID	153	May 8	Oct. 9	Portland	OR	217	Apr. 3	Nov. 7
Chicago	IL	187	Apr. 22	Oct. 26	Carlisle	PA	182	Apr. 20	Oct. 20
Springfield	IL	185	Apr. 17	Oct. 19	Williamsport	PA	168	Apr. 29	Oct. 15
Indianapolis	IN	180	Apr. 22	Oct. 20	Kingston	RI	144	May 8	Sept. 30
South Bend	IN	169	May 1	Oct. 18	Charleston	SC	253	Mar. 11	Nov. 20
Atlantic	IA	141	May 9	Sept. 28	Columbia	SC	211	Apr. 4	Nov. 2
Cedar Rapids	IA	161	Apr. 29	Oct. 7	Rapid City	SD	145	May 7	Sept. 29
Topeka	KS	175	Apr. 21	Oct. 14	Memphis	TN	228	Mar. 23	Nov. 7
Lexington	KY	190	Apr. 17	Oct. 25	Nashville	TN	207	Apr. 5	Oct. 29
Monroe	LA	242	Mar. 9	Nov. 7	Amarillo	TX	197	Apr. 14	Oct. 29
New Orleans	LA	289	Feb. 20	Dec. 5	Denton	TX	231	Mar. 25	Nov. 12
Portland	ME	143	May 10	Sept. 30	San Antonio	TX	265	Mar. 3	Nov. 24
Baltimore	MD	231	Mar. 26	Nov. 13	Cedar City	UT	134	May 20	Oct. 2
Worcester	MA	172	Apr. 27	Oct. 17	Spanish Fork	UT	156	May 8	Oct. 12
Lansing	MI	140	May 13	Sept. 30	Burlington	VT	142	May 11	Oct. 1
Marquette	MI	159	May 12	Oct. 19	Norfolk	VA	239	Mar. 23	Nov. 17
Duluth	MN	122	May 21	Sept. 21	Richmond	VA	198	Apr. 10	Oct. 26
Willmar	MN	152	May 4	Oct. 4	Seattle	WA	232	Mar. 24	Nov. 11
Columbus	MS	215	Mar. 27	Oct. 29	Spokane	WA	153	May 4	Oct. 5
Vicksburg	MS	250	Mar. 13	Nov. 18	Parkersburg	WV	175	Apr. 25	Oct. 18
Jefferson City	MO	173	Apr. 26	Oct. 16	Green Bay	WI	143	May 12	Oct. 2
Fort Peck	MT	146	May 5	Sept. 28	Janesville	WI	164	Apr. 28	Oct. 10
Helena	MT	122	May 18	Sept. 18	Casper	WY	123	May 22	Sept. 22
Blair	NE	165	Apr. 27	Oct. 10	*Frosts do not occur every year.				

Outdoor Planting Table
2 0 0 4

The best time to plant flowers and vegetables that bear crops *above ground* is during the *light* of the Moon; that is, from the day the Moon is new to the day it is full. Flowering bulbs and vegetables that bear crops *below ground* should be planted during the *dark* of the Moon; that is, from the day after it is full to the day before it is new again. The Moon Favorable columns at right give these days, which are based on the Moon's phases for 2004 and the safe periods for planting in areas that receive frost. Consult **page 103** for dates of frosts and lengths of growing seasons. See the **Left-Hand Calendar Pages 44–70** for the exact days of the new and full Moons.

Aboveground Crops Marked (*)

(E) means early   (L) means late

Map shading corresponds to shading of date columns.

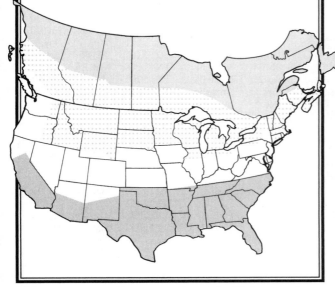

* Barley	
* Beans	(E)
	(L)
Beets	(E)
	(L)
* Broccoli plants	(E)
	(L)
* Brussels sprouts	
* Cabbage plants	
Carrots	(E)
	(L)
* Cauliflower plants	(E)
	(L)
* Celery plants	(E)
	(L)
* Collards	(E)
	(L)
* Corn, sweet	(E)
	(L)
* Cucumbers	
* Eggplant plants	
* Endive	(E)
	(L)
* Flowers	
* Kale	(E)
	(L)
Leek plants	
* Lettuce	
* Muskmelons	
Onion sets	
* Parsley	
Parsnips	
* Peas	(E)
	(L)
* Pepper plants	
Potatoes	
* Pumpkins	
Radishes	(E)
	(L)
* Spinach	(E)
	(L)
* Squashes	
Sweet potatoes	
* Swiss chard	
* Tomato plants	
Turnips	(E)
	(L)
* Watermelons	
* Wheat, spring	
* Wheat, winter	

Planting Dates	Moon Favorable	Planting Dates	Moon Favorable	Planting Dates	Moon Favorable	Planting Dates	Moon Favorable
2/15-3/7	2/20-3/6	3/15-4/7	3/20-4/5	5/15-6/21	5/19-6/3, 6/17-21	6/1-30	6/1-3, 6/17-30
3/15-4/7	3/20-4/5	4/15-30	4/19-30	5/7-6/21	5/19-6/3, 6/17-21	5/30-6/15	5/30-6/3
8/7-31	8/15-29	7/1-21	7/1-2, 7/17-21	6/15-7/15	6/17-7/2	—	
2/7-29	2/7-19	3/15-4/3	3/15-19	5/1-15	5/5-15	5/25-6/10	6/4-10
9/1-30	9/1-13, 9/29-30	8/15-31	8/30-31	7/15-8/15	7/15-16, 8/1-14	6/15-7/8	6/15-16, 7/3-8
2/15-3/15	2/20-3/6	3/7-31	3/20-31	5/15-31	5/19-31	6/1-25	6/1-3, 6/17-25
9/7-30	9/14-28	8/1-20	8/15-20	6/15-7/7	6/17-7/2		
2/11-3/20	2/20-3/6, 3/20	3/7-4/15	3/20-4/5	5/15-31	5/19-31	6/1-25	6/1-3, 6/17-25
2/11-3/20	2/20-3/6, 3/20	3/7-4/15	3/20-4/5	5/15-31	5/19-31	6/1-25	6/1-3, 6/17-25
2/15-3/7	2/15-19, 3/7	3/7-31	3/7-19	5/15-31	5/15-18	5/25-6/10	6/4-10
8/1-9/7	8/1-14, 8/30-9/7	7/7-31	7/7-16	6/15-7/21	6/15-16, 7/3-16	6/15-7/8	6/15-16, 7/3-8
2/15-3/7	2/20-3/6	3/15-4/7	3/20-4/5	5/15-31	5/19-31	6/1-25	6/1-3, 6/17-25
8/7-31	8/15-29	7/1-8/7	7/1-2, 7/17-31	6/15-7/21	6/17-7/2, 7/17-21	—	
2/15-29	2/20-29	3/7-31	3/20-31	5/15-6/30	5/19-6/3, 6/17-30	6/1-30	6/1-3, 6/17-30
9/15-30	9/15-28	8/15-9/7	8/15-29	7/15-8/15	7/17-31, 8/15		
2/11-3/20	2/20-3/6, 3/20	3/7-4/7	3/20-4/5	5/15-31	5/19-31	6/1-25	6/1-3, 6/17-25
9/7-30	9/14-28	8/15-31	8/15-29	7/1-8/7	7/1-2, 7/17-31	—	
3/15-31	3/20-31	4/1-17	4/1-5	5/10-6/15	5/19-6/3	5/30-6/20	5/30-6/3, 6/17-20
8/7-31	8/15-29	7/7-21	7/17-21	6/15-30	6/17-30	—	
3/7-4/15	3/20-4/5	4/7-5/15	4/19-5/4	5/7-6/20	5/19-6/3, 6/17-20	5/30-6/15	5/30-6/3
3/7-4/15	3/20-4/5	4/7-5/15	4/19-5/4	6/1-30	6/1-3, 6/17-30	6/15-30	6/17-30
2/15-3/20	2/20-3/6, 3/20	4/7-5/15	4/19-5/4	5/15-31	5/19-31	6/1-25	6/1-3, 6/17-25
8/15-9/7	8/15-29	7/15-8/15	7/17-31, 8/15	6/7-30	6/17-30	—	
3/15-4/7	3/20-4/5	4/15-30	4/19-30	5/7-6/21	5/19-6/3, 6/17-21	6/1-30	6/1-3, 6/17-30
2/11-3/20	2/20-3/6, 3/20	3/7-4/7	3/20-4/5	5/15-31	5/19-31	6/1-15	6/1-3
9/7-30	9/14-28	8/15-31	8/15-29	7/1-8/7	7/1-2, 7/17-31	6/25-7/15	6/25-7/2
2/15-4/15	2/19, 3/7-19, 4/6-15	3/7-4/7	3/7-19, 4/6-7	5/15-31	5/15-18	6/1-25	6/4-16
2/15-3/7	2/20-3/6	3/1-31	3/1-6, 3/20-31	5/15-6/30	5/19-6/3, 6/17-30	6/1-30	6/1-3, 6/17-30
3/15-4/7	3/20-4/5	4/15-5/7	4/19-5/4	5/15-6/30	5/19-6/3, 6/17-30	6/1-30	6/1-3, 6/17-30
2/1-29	2/7-19	3/1-31	3/7-19	5/15-6/7	5/15-18, 6/4-7	6/1-25	6/4-16
2/20-3/15	2/20-3/6	3/1-31	3/1-6, 3/20-31	5/15-31	5/19-31	6/1-15	6/1-3
1/15-2/4	1/15-20	3/7-31	3/7-19	4/1-30	4/6-18	5/10-31	5/10-18
1/15-2/7	1/21-2/6	3/7-31	3/20-31	4/15-5/7	4/19-5/4	5/15-31	5/19-31
9/15-30	9/15-28	8/7-31	8/15-29	7/15-31	7/17-31	7/10-25	7/17-25
3/1-20	3/1-6, 3/20	4/1-30	4/1-5, 4/19-30	5/15-6/30	5/19-6/3, 6/17-30	6/1-30	6/1-3, 6/17-30
2/10-29	2/10-19	4/1-30	4/6-18	5/1-31	5/5-18	6/1-25	6/4-16
3/7-20	3/20	4/23-5/15	4/23-5/4	5/15-31	5/19-31	6/1-30	6/1-3, 6/17-30
1/21-3/1	2/7-19	3/7-31	3/7-19	4/15-30	4/15-18	5/15-6/5	5/15-18, 6/4-5
10/1-21	10/1-12	9/7-30	9/7-13, 9/29-30	8/15-31	8/30-31	7/10-31	7/10-16
2/7-3/15	2/20-3/6	3/15-4/20	3/20-4/5, 4/19-20	5/15-31	5/19-31	6/1-25	6/1-3, 6/17-25
10/1-21	10/13-21	8/1-9/15	8/15-29, 9/14-15	7/17-9/7	7/17-31, 8/15-29	7/20-8/15	7/20-31
3/15-4/15	3/20-4/5	4/15-30	4/19-30	5/15-6/15	5/19-6/3	6/1-30	6/1-3, 6/17-30
3/23-4/6	4/6	4/21-5/9	5/5-9	5/15-6/15	5/15-18, 6/4-15	6/1-30	6/4-16
2/7-3/15	2/20-3/6	3/15-4/15	3/20-4/15	5/1-31	5/1-4, 5/19-31	5/15-31	5/19-31
3/7-20	3/20	4/7-30	4/19-30	5/15-31	5/19-31	6/1-15	6/1-3
1/20-2/15	2/7-15	3/15-31	3/15-19	4/7-30	4/7-18	5/10-31	5/10-18
9/1-10/15	9/1-13, 9/29-10/12	8/1-20	8/1-14	7/1-8/15	7/3-16, 8/1-14	—	
3/15-4/7	3/20-4/5	4/15-5/7	4/19-5/4	5/15-6/30	5/19-6/3, 6/17-30	6/1-30	6/1-3, 6/17-30
2/15-29	2/20-29	3/1-20	3/1-6, 3/20	4/7-30	4/19-30	5/15-6/10	5/19-6/3
10/15-12/7	10/15-27, 11/12-26	9/15-10/20	9/15-28, 10/13-20	8/11-9/15	8/15-29, 9/14-15	8/5-30	8/15-29

CREATURES THAT LIVE ON BLOOD

Facts and fallacies about three bloodsuckers that love to get under our skin.

There is nothing more horrid than a creature so rude that it would suck the very blood from our veins. Vampire bats, mosquitoes, and ticks—these are the bloodthirsty monsters of our nightmares, our horror movies, our picnics gone awry. If we are to overcome our fears of these miniature menaces, we must know the facts about them.

—illustrated by Kristin Kest

by Christine Schultz

For centuries, we have loved to hate

the vampire bat.

HE HAS SO OCCUPIED OUR IMAGINATIONS THAT THE myths about him have transformed him into the embodiment of evil. As far back as A.D. 300, members of the Mayan culture sculpted fang-toothed, bat-headed men. In 17th-century Latin American culture, vampire bats were linked with witchcraft. Then, in 1897, Bram Stoker dramatized the myth so chillingly in the tale of Dracula that none of our necks

has seemed safe since.

Calm your fears. Vampire bats live only in Central and South America. They prefer to lap blood from the feet, nose, or ear tips of cattle, horses, and pigs, not people—unless they are rabid.

Of the approximately 1,000 bat species, only three are vampire bats that survive solely on blood. Each night, they emerge after dark and follow their heat-sensitive noses to within a short distance of their prey. They land, hunch their backs high, and tiptoe across the ground. With supersharp teeth, they slice a piece

of skin from their sleeping victim, and then use their well-grooved tongues to lap up half their body weight in blood—about two tablespoons for these tiny one-ounce bats.

If they didn't carry rabies, equine diseases, and a bad reputation, vampire bats might be considered regular charmers. After all, these creatures greet each other with hugs, share meals with less-well-fed cavemates, suckle orphan bats, and rest 80 percent of the time. Even their blood-sipping habit has a benefit. Scientists have learned to synthesize vampires' anticlotting serum (the anticoagu-lant is called draculin) into a drug that aids heart-attack sufferers. Thus, the vampire bat is truly a romantic rogue after our own hearts.

The maddening mosquito, by contrast, is anything but romantic.

WITH AN ESTIMATED 1 TRILLION mosquitoes of more than 2,500 species (100 or so known to transfer germs to people) having evolved since before the dinosaurs, it should not be surprising that they carry all sorts of diseases (encephalitis, malaria, West Nile virus, yellow fever), making them one of our worst enemies. Never mind that male mosquitoes feed only on nectar, not on us. Never mind that the hard-working female mosquitoes are not trying to bother *us* but simply nourishing their developing eggs with rich protein. No, the best publicity campaign could not lessen the malice we feel toward mosquitoes.

During the short summers of the Canadian arctic, the swarms of these critters are so intense that an unsuspecting man could be attacked some 9,000 times per minute, thereby losing half his blood in two hours. Elsewhere, the female mosquito seeks blood every three or four days, attacking around nightfall by zeroing in her keen chemosensors on the combination of carbon dioxide, body heat, and lactic acid that we emit.

She prefers to dine on wrists and ankles, where blood vessels are nearer to the skin's surface. She doesn't bite but pierces our capillaries with her needle-like proboscis, which is equipped with six serrated stylets. The pumps in her head and thorax draw out about one millionth of a gallon of blood. To make matters worse, she spits an anticoagulant under our skin, leaving us with whatever disease she is

SATURDAY AFTERNOON SERIALS

THE CLIFFHANGERS

BILL ELLIOTT

NON-STOP ACTION

12-15 CHAPTER SERIALS

$27.95
ANY 2-**$50.00** PPD.

COMPLETE -
UNCUT ON 1 VIDEO TAPE
4-5 HOURS RUNNING TIME

BUY 10 PICK ONE FREE

THE GREEN HORNET
13-chapter serial   1940
Gordon Jones

THE GREEN HORNET STRIKES AGAIN
15-chapter serial   1940
Warren Hull

THE OREGON TRAIL
15-chapter serial   1939
Johnny Mack Brown

THE MIRACLE RIDER
15-chapter serial   1935
Tom Mix

THE PHANTOM RIDER
15-chapter serial   1936
Buck Jones

WHITE EAGLE
15-chapter serial   1941
Buck Jones

THE PHANTOM
15-chapter serial   1943
Tom Tyler

THE SPIDER'S WEB
15-chapter serial   1940
Warren Hull

THE SHADOW
15-chapter serial   1940
Victor Jory

ZORRO RIDES AGAIN
12-chapter serial   1937
John Carroll

MYSTERY MOUNTAIN
12-chapter serial   1934
Ken Maynard

HURRICANE EXPRESS
12-chapter serial   1932
John Wayne

VALLEY OF VANISHING MEN
15-chapter serial   1942
Bill Elliott

OVERLAND WITH KIT CARSON
15-chapter serial   1939
Bill Elliott

THE GR. ADV. OF WILD BILL HICKOK
15-chapter serial   1938
Bill Elliott

FLASH GORDON
13-chapter serial   1936
Buster Crabbe

FLASH GR'S TRIP TO MARS
15-chapter serial   1938
Buster Crabbe

FLASH CONQUERS UNIVERSE
12-chapter serial   1940
Buster Crabbe

SPY SMASHER
12-chapter serial   1942
Kane Richmond

GHOST OF ZORRO
12-chapter serial   1949
Clayton Moore

TO ORDER:
PHONE 724-349-4455 OR FAX 724-357-8406
OR SEND CHECK OR MONEY ORDER TO:
JIM SPOTTS, RARE SERIALS - FA

Free Shipping
USA Only

60 JACOBS LANE, P.O. BOX 477, PENN RUN, PA 15765
website: www.rareserials.com   E-MAIL: jspotts@rareserials.com

MasterCard VISA

carrying or, at the very least, with an irritating itch.

Italian folklore holds that sleeping with a pig will protect you from malaria by diverting the mosquitoes. Recent scientific studies have shown that catnip may throw mosquitoes off our scent, but the only certain reprieve from this worrisome whiner is to squash it flat, and that, thank goodness, is easy enough to do.

That's more than can be said for a dreadful, head-burrowing bloodsucker,

the terrible tick.

NUZZLING CLOSE AND DRINKING DEEPLY of your essence for up to a week, she expects you, as a good host, to stand quietly by while she first hacks away at you with her cutting tools (called cheliceral digits), and then inserts a syringelike hypostome to

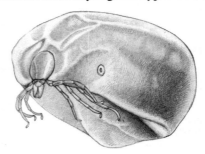

dribble her anticlotting saliva under your skin. Her backward-pointing teeth will lock her head in place, making it particularly difficult for you to disengage your visitor's swelling enthusiasm. If you indulge her fully, she will grow to a plump jellybean size and 200 times her original weight. Then, unable to maintain her passionate embrace, she will abandon you to the laying of up to 2,000 eggs.

Though in coming days she will indulge twice more by waving her feet alluringly from the end of a stalk in a "questing" pose, she will not choose you again as a host. You will remember her only by a lingering, itching sore and perhaps (if she were a deer tick or a western black-legged tick) by that unpleasant case of Lyme disease she gave you, or (if she were a Rocky Mountain wood tick, an American dog tick, or a Lone-Star tick) by that bothersome case of Rocky Mountain spotted fever you now have. "There's no doubt that ticks can be dangerous," says Robert Lane, an entomologist at the University of California at Berkeley, "but for those of us who study them, they're also enthralling." Enthralling or not, just remember that of the 200 or so tick species in the United States, not one is your friend. The best way to convey this is to pull out your buddy with a fine-point tweezer firmly positioned on both sides of her little blood-guzzling head. □□

Christine Schultz, who writes for numerous magazines, is fascinated by the habits of the bloodsucking critters near her home in Mississippi but would prefer that they keep to themselves.

ANOTHER SUCKER

What has 32 brains, 4 sets of eyes, and 3 jaws? The leech. To learn more, go to **www.almanac.com** and click on **Article Links 2004.**

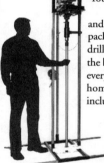

WHERE'S THE RAIN?

BY TOM KONVICKA

O ver the past few years throughout North America, that question—where's the rain?—has been on just about everyone's lips. Dry or drought conditions have reached record or near-record levels in many parts of the United States and Canada. At least ten U.S. cities have set new calendar-year minimum precipitation records. The year 2002 was the driest in Colorado since 1895 (when records began), and the third or fourth driest in 108 years in Arizona, Nebraska, Nevada, and Wyoming. In January 2003, farmers in Canada's prairies, now in their third year of drought, were advised to brace for grasshoppers and sawflies. And in cities and towns in both countries, water moratoriums were instituted.

So where's the rain? Some would say that it's right over our heads. They would be proponents of precipitation enhancement through weather modification, or, to put it simply, making rain.

A modification, or change, in the weather is either planned or accidental. In the latter case, the mixture of pollution from industry and transportation causes unanticipated changes such as acid rain. Planned weather modification occurs when a team of scientists designs an experiment and then attempts to change the weather.

To make rain, scientists need appropriate conditions, specific chemicals or agents, and a delivery system. First, the "right" cloud needs to be identified. The best candidate is a cloud layer in which supercooled water is present, or where the ambient temperature is between 32° and –40°F.

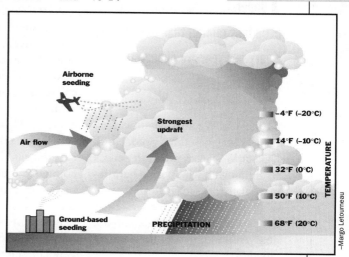

Seeding agents form ice particles that melt as they fall and so become rain *(above)*. The Mojave Desert, California, in 2000 *(opposite)*.

—Wallace Garrison/Index Stock

continued

The agents of change are either silver iodide (AgI) or dry ice. Silver iodide is a chemical with a crystalline structure close to that of ice. It is possible to create a "smoke" of silver iodide particles that will contain many potential freezing nuclei. Dry ice, with a temperature near −108°F, will instantly convert supercooled water to ice, which will fall to the ground as rain.

The seeding agents must be dispersed within the cloud layer. The most common delivery method is by aircraft, which places the seeding material directly where it needs to be. A major player in the "rainmaking"

smoke that becomes airborne in the wind, but their ability to place seeding agents in the appropriate part of the cloud is questionable.

Weather-modification companies in the United States claim increases in rainfall of 9 to 20 percent in the summer, and increases in snowfall of 10 to 15 percent in the winter.

I t is not easy for man to understand that it takes but a little less rainfall than normal over a very few years to change the face of the land.

–from the archives of The Old Farmer's Almanac

business is Weather Modification, Inc. (WMI), based in Fargo, North Dakota. WMI uses two Piper Seneca II aircraft with wingtip and burn-in-place flare racks to create the smoke of silver iodide particles, as well as a radar facility at Elmdale Airpark near Abilene, Texas, to identify clouds to be seeded.

Ground-based generators are also used to seed clouds. They emit a

WMI operated the West Central Texas Rainfall Enhancement Program from May through September in 2001, 2002, and 2003. The company estimates that this operation, which covers a nine-county area near Abilene and San Angelo, Texas, resulted in a 25 percent increase in rain in 2002. North American Weather Consultants of Sandy, Utah, boasts as high as a 25 percent increase in their tropical experiments. Cloudquest, a research company founded by Canadian-born Graeme Mather, claims increases of 40 to 60 percent in experiments conducted in South Africa in 1995–96. Although independent scientific verification of these claims is lacking, even skeptics must admit that cloud seeding

continued on page 117

WHERE DOES WATER COME FROM?

Ask people where their water comes from and some will say "the faucet" or "a bottle." True enough, but this is where some of our water originates:

- **If you live in Boston or New York City, you are drinking treated water from voluminous reservoirs many miles from the city centers.**

- **If you live in Cape Coral, Florida, you are drinking desalinated water produced by reverse osmosis, a process whereby seawater is forced through a membrane to remove minerals and salt.**

- **If you live in Chicago, you are drinking water pumped from Lake Michigan and then treated.**

- **If you live in New Orleans, the water piped to your faucet comes from the Mississippi River, which flows past cities and industrial areas for hundreds of miles before being treated.**

- **If you live in South Dakota, Wyoming, Nebraska, Colorado, Oklahoma, Kansas, New Mexico, or Texas, you may be drinking water from the ancient Ogallala aquifer, the level of which has dropped hundreds of feet in the last 50 years.**

- **Areas of Orange County and Los Angeles, California, use reclaimed treated sewage effluent for irrigation and to recharge groundwater supplies.**

- **If you drink bottled water, you may be surprised to learn that it may not be from pure mountain springs but from municipal supplies. Aquafina, by PepsiCo., is municipal water from Wichita, Kansas, and other places; Dasani, produced by The Coca-Cola Company, flows from taps in Queens, New York, and Jacksonville, Florida. Both brands use high-tech reverse osmosis to filter out contaminants.**

–compiled by Galen H. McGovern

–Coca-Cola Company

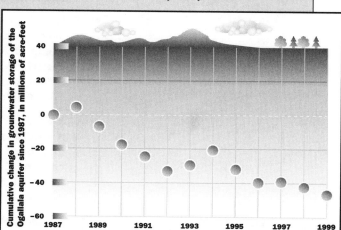

–Margo Letourneau

Groundwater depletion in the Ogallala aquifer from 1987–99 was severe: One acre-foot equals 325,851 gallons of water.

WHERE DOES WATER GO?

"Down the drain," some would say. Maybe so, eventually, but this is about volume. Here's some news about how much we use:

TYPICAL WATER USE (based on national averages):

TOILET	TYPICAL	WATER-CONSERVING
Daily per person use	18.8 gallons	9.1 gallons

SHOWER		
Daily per person use	11.6 gallons	

BATHTUB		
Daily per person use	1.2 gallons*	

FAUCET (KITCHEN, BATHROOMS, LAUNDRY ROOM)		
Daily per person use	10.9 gallons	

WASHING MACHINE	TYPICAL	WATER-CONSERVING
Daily per person use	15 gallons	9.2 gallons

DISHWASHER		
Daily per person use	1 gallon	

*The average volume used per bath is 24 gallons.

—Mauritius/Index Stock

outdoors than homes without swimming pools.

- Filling a swimming pool (depending on size) requires thousands of gallons of water. A typical 20x20-foot pool that is 5 feet deep contains almost 15,000 gallons of water.

CAR WASH
- A standard garden hose uses 10 gallons or more per minute. You could easily use 100 gallons of water or more during a 10-minute car wash.

- A typical commercial car wash uses between 15 and 45 gallons of water per car.

SWIMMING POOL
- Homes with swimming pools use 58 percent more water

GARDEN AND LAWN

■ Vegetable crop require-
ments range from 6 inches
of water per growing sea-
son for radishes to 24
inches for tomatoes and wa-
termelons. Lawns typically
require 1 inch of water per
week. The volume in gallons
depends on the area. For example, for 1 square foot of
ground, radishes would use
3.74 gallons, and a tomato
or watermelon plant would
use 15 gallons for the growing season. A 10,000-
square-foot lawn would use
6,233 gallons per week, if
there were no rain.

—compiled by Galen H. McGovern

continued from page 114

works in some cases. Indeed, few scientists doubt our ability to "change" the weather, albeit inconsistently and on a limited scale.

Scientists are also working to predict drought, but this is difficult because drought results from an intricate interplay of ingredients. **Part of the solution is in the study of global weather patterns. Certain global circulation patterns tend to recur, and a systematic relationship between them is called a teleconnection.** These teleconnection patterns are frequent and reliable enough to make long-range drought prediction possible.

American editor and essayist Charles Dudley Warner observed

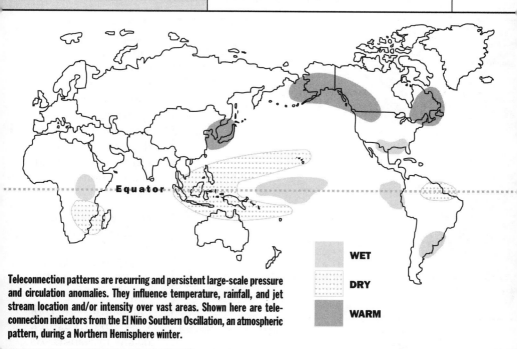

Equator

WET

DRY

WARM

Teleconnection patterns are recurring and persistent large-scale pressure and circulation anomalies. They influence temperature, rainfall, and jet stream location and/or intensity over vast areas. Shown here are tele-connection indicators from the El Niño Southern Oscillation, an atmospheric pattern, during a Northern Hemisphere winter.

—Margo Letourneau

that "everybody talks about the weather, but nobody does anything about it." Thanks to weather modification, that's changing. The irony is that the effects of our unintentional alteration of weather, including air pollution, acid rain, and ozone depletion, far exceed the effects achieved through planned modification. If Warner were alive today, he might say, "Everybody talks about the weather, but nobody does much about it unless they don't intend to."

ONE PROBLEM WE'D ALL LIKE TO HAVE

I know what's wrong, my dear, but I really do not know how to turn it off.

–Albert Einstein, American physicist (1879–1955), to his cat, which disliked rain

DEFINING DROUGHT

A drought is defined by the severity of its effects:

■ **Meteorological drought** occurs when less than 75 percent of the "normal" 30-year-average precipitation amount is observed over a specified time frame. The levels of precipitation that define drought vary, because of different climate types involved. For example, meteorological drought in Florida is not the same as it is in Nebraska.

■ **Agricultural drought** means that the amount of soil moisture is not adequate to meet the needs of crops. The result is a reduction in yield or quality.

■ **Hydrological drought** occurs when surface and subsurface water supplies are low. Using water for other purposes such as irrigation, recreation, and navigation can make the situation worse. Deforestation and dam construction also contribute.

■ **Socioeconomic drought** occurs when water shortages begin to affect the day-to-day life of society. Examples include water rationing in New York City or livestock deaths in Kansas. As

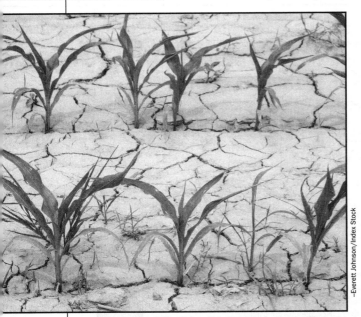

Evidence of agricultural drought in Montgomery County, Maryland, in July 2000.

—Everett Johnson/Index Stock

the demand for water increases, so will the risk of socioeconomic drought.

WHY DOESN'T IT RAIN?

■ **Topography** is partially to blame. A mountain range promotes drought on its leeward side as moisture in the form of water vapor is lifted over the windward side, where the rising motion causes the water vapor to be precipitated out. **As the air descends on the leeward side, it not only contains much less water vapor, but because of the sinking motion, it releases less precipitation. Meteorologists call this a "rain shadow."**

Evidence of hydrological drought in 1991 at Lake Shasta, the largest man-made reservoir in California.

■ **The spotty nature of summer thunderstorms** has an effect. Over weeks or months, popcorn thunderstorms create a patchwork pattern in which ample rainfall occurs at some points, but scant amounts fall "down

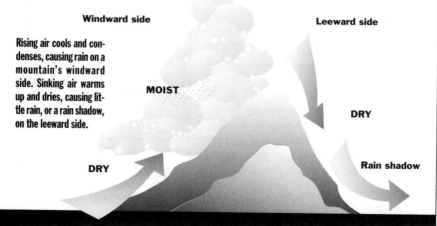

Windward side   **Leeward side**

Rising air cools and condenses, causing rain on a mountain's windward side. Sinking air warms up and dries, causing little rain, or a rain shadow, on the leeward side.

MOIST

DRY

DRY   Rain shadow

—Margo Letourneau

A cumulonimbus cloud is a source of heavy, localized rain, thunder, lightning, and hail.

the road." A bumper crop can be harvested on one side of town, with crops withering on the opposite side.

■ **Seasonal climatic change,** such as a well-defined wet/dry seasonal alteration, is also part of the picture. In Southeast Asia, a seasonal reversal of wind, known as a monsoon, marks the transition from winter to summer and can bring relentless and torrential rains. During the cool season, much less rain falls.

> **Clouds that thunder do not always rain.**
> –*Armenian proverb*

WEATHER MODIFICATION AS DAMAGE CONTROL

■**Cloud seeding** is not just about making rain. In 1996, Weather Modification, Inc., contracted with the Alberta (Canada) Severe Weather Management Society, a consortium of insurance companies, to conduct the Alberta Hail Suppression Project. The contract called for WMI to provide cloud seeding and related services for the purpose

A large hailstone.

of reducing hail damage in south-central Alberta. The target area stretched from LaCombe in the north to High River in the south, with priority given to the cities of Calgary and Red Deer. The Society's interest was in reducing property damage and resulting insurance claims. (In 1991, claims for hail damage in Calgary reached $486 million.)

Hailstone damage.

The scientific hypothesis used in the project is based on the concept of "beneficial competition." This assumes that there is a lack of natural ice nuclei in the cloud and that the injection of silver iodide will result in the production of a significant number of artificial ice nuclei. **The natural and artificial ice crystals compete for the available supercooled water in the cloud. As a result, the hailstones in the seeded storm are smaller and cause less damage.**

Hailstones before seeding.

Overall, the results of hail-suppression projects are inconclusive. Computer models, however, tend to give credibility to the beneficial-competition hypothesis, and WMI was awarded another contract to continue efforts through 2007. (Notably, a similar project conducted in North Dakota by WMI resulted in a 45 percent decrease in insurance payments for crop loss due to hail damage.)

Hailstones after seeding.

–Margo Letourneau

JUST IN CASE YOU'RE WONDERING . . .

Scientists have had mixed results in attempting to modify some weather conditions.

> When the well's dry, we know the worth of water.
>
> *–Benjamin Franklin, American statesman (1706–1790)*

- ■ **HURRICANES.** Experiments have proven inconclusive, and only limited research is being done.

- ■ **LIGHTNING.** Experiments have not yielded any practical applications.

- ■ **FOG.** Attempts to dissipate or disperse fog are routine at some airports.

- ■ **TORNADOES.** No viable hypothesis for tornado mitigation exists, and scientific experiments have not progressed outside of the laboratory.

Tom Konvicka is a meteorologist and writer in Pineville, Louisiana.

□□

SOAK UP KNOWLEDGE
To learn more about weather modification and the cause of drought, go to **www.almanac.com** and click on **Articles Links 2004.**

General Weather Forecast

2 0 0 3 – 2 0 0 4

(For detailed regional forecasts, see pages 124–139.)

This year will bring extreme temperatures. The southwest will have one of its hottest years ever, with a very warm year in the Rockies, on average. Much of the east and midwest will have a cold winter but hot summer. The northeast and mid-Atlantic will get less snow than last winter. Although most of the country will receive near- or above-normal rainfall, expect below-normal precipitation in the Rockies and Desert Southwest.

November through March, overall, will be much colder than normal in the northeast, Great Lakes, and midwest, and somewhat colder than normal elsewhere east of the Rockies except for Florida, which will be milder than normal. The entire western part of the country will be milder than normal. The period will start cold, with below-normal temperatures, on average, just about everywhere east of the Rockies through January. Meanwhile, the west will be exceptionally mild, with one of the warmest Januarys on record. February and March will have near-normal temperatures in most of the country.

Precipitation will be much above normal in Florida and eastern Georgia, and above normal in the rest of Georgia, much of New England, and Upstate New York; across the Great Lakes; and in the central Great Plains and Pacific Northwest. Precipitation will be below normal from the southwest eastward to Alabama; from South Carolina northward to New York City; and in the Ohio Valley, the Northern Great Plains, and the Rockies.

Snowfall will be above normal in northern New England and Upstate New York; from Norfolk, Virginia, southwestward into the Smokies; in northern portions of Arizona and New Mexico; from the foothills of the Rockies eastward across the central Great Plains; and in the Pacific Northwest. Snowfall will be below normal in other areas that receive snow.

April and May will be much warmer than normal in the northeastern part of the nation and in southern California, and above normal in most places east of the Mississippi and in the Desert Southwest. The Pacific Northwest and the Rockies and their foothills will be cooler than normal. Elsewhere, temperatures will be close to normal. Florida will be much wetter than normal, with above-normal rainfall from the Gulf Coast northeastward to Atlantic City and in western Washington state. Rainfall will be well below normal in northern Arkansas and near or slightly below normal elsewhere.

June through August will be hotter than normal in the northeast and mid-Atlantic states, across the Great Lakes and Northern Great Plains, in the Desert Southwest, and in southern California. Temperatures will be cooler than normal in Florida, Arkansas, and Oklahoma, and in interior parts of California, Oregon, and Washington state. Elsewhere, temperatures will be slightly above normal.

Rainfall will be much above normal in parts of Florida and Oklahoma, and above normal in Washington state, the Desert Southwest, Tennessee, the northern Great Lakes, the mid-Atlantic, and much of New England. Elsewhere, rainfall will be below normal.

September through October will be cooler than normal in the Great Plains, Rockies, and Pacific Northwest, and warmer than normal elsewhere. Rainfall will be below normal in southern California, Oregon, the southern Rockies, New Mexico, and west Texas, and from New York City to Baltimore, and near normal in Florida. Rainfall will be much greater than normal from the Carolinas westward to Oklahoma. Elsewhere, rainfall will be slightly greater than normal.

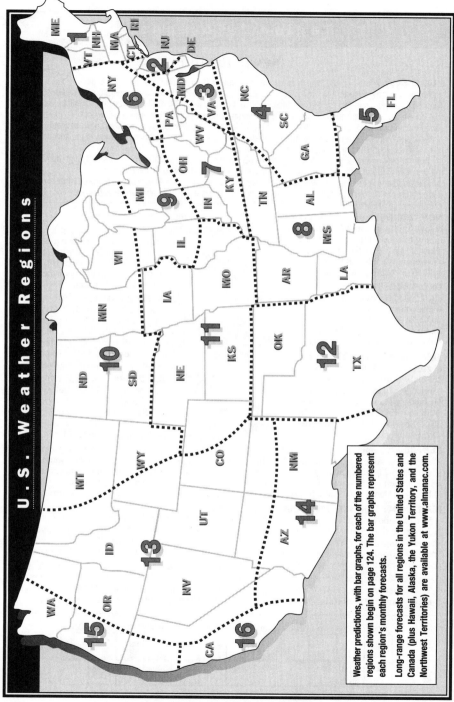

U.S. Weather Regions

Weather predictions, with bar graphs, for each of the numbered regions shown begin on page 124. The bar graphs represent each region's monthly forecasts.

Long-range forecasts for all regions in the United States and Canada (plus Hawaii, Alaska, the Yukon Territory, and the Northwest Territories) are available at www.almanac.com.

New England

SUMMARY: Winter will be two to three degrees colder than normal, on average. Expect especially cold temperatures from November through early January, with the coldest temperatures in mid-December. Temperatures from mid-January through March will be relatively mild. Snowfall and precipitation will be near normal, on average. After widespread snowfall in late November and early December, expect below-normal snow through January. February will be a snowy month, and early March will be marked by heavy wet snow, at least inland.

April and May will be much warmer than normal, on average, despite the chance for snow in the second week of April. The second half of May will be unusually hot.

After a fairly normal June and July, August will be much hotter than usual, with oppressively high humidity in the first half of the month. Other hot periods will occur in early and late June and mid-July.

Hot weather will continue in early September, with warm days in much of the month, followed by near-normal temperatures in October. September will be fairly dry, but October will have above-normal rainfall.

NOV. 2003: Temp. 40° (4° below avg. north; 2° below south); precip. 4" (avg.). 1-4 Sunny, then rain with snow north. 5-17 Mostly cloudy, mild; showers. 18-21 Colder, sunny, then showers, snow showers north. 22-26 Rain to snow, turning very cold. 27-30 Chilly; heavy rain south, snow north.

DEC. 2003: Temp. 26° (7° below avg.); precip. 2" (1.5" below avg.). 1-3 Cold; snow south, flurries north. 4-8 Cold, flurries. 9-11 Snow. 12-20 Cold; sunny south, flurries north. 21-24 Sunny, milder. 25-28 Cold, then mild, snow to rain. 29-31 Cold.

JAN. 2004: Temp. 23° (3° below avg.); precip. 3.5" (0.5" above avg.). 1-6 Partly sunny, cold, flurries. 7-8 Milder. 9-12 Heavy rain and snow. 13-16 January thaw, rain. 17-21 Very cold; snow showers. 22-24 Mild, showers. 25-27 Snow north, then sunny, cold. 28-31 Mild, rain.

FEB. 2004: Temp. 26° (1° below avg.); precip. 4" (1" above avg.). 1-5 Cold; snow north, rain southeast. 6-11 Mild; rain south, snow north. 12-18 Rain, then cold, snow. 19-23 Sunny, seasonable. 24-29 Heavy rain south, heavy snow north.

MAR. 2004: Temp. 40° (2° above avg.); precip. 3.5" (0.5" above avg.). 1-2 Sunny, chilly. 3-7 Northeaster. 8-13 Partly sunny, seasonable; snow showers north. 14-17 Warm, then cold, rain to snow. 18-20 Sunny, seasonable. 21-25 Sunny and cold north, rain and snow south. 26-31 Rain, mild.

APR. 2004: Temp. 51° (2° above avg.); precip. 2.5" (1" below avg.). 1-7 Rain, snow. 8-12 Sunny, warmer. 13-19 Rain, then sunny. 20-25 Chilly, rain. 26-30 Sunny, warm.

MAY 2004: Temp. 61° (4° above avg.); precip. 3" (2" below avg. west; 1" above east). 1-4 Sunny, warm. 5-8 Warm, t-storms. 9-13 Showers. 14-17 Hot, then t-storms. 18-23 Sunny, cool, then hot. 24-31 Rain, then sunny.

JUNE 2004: Temp. 64° (1° below avg.); precip. 4.5" (avg.; 2" above east). 1-6 Showers north, sunny, hot south. 7-13 Cool; rainy periods. 14-19 Partly sunny, showers. 20-22 Rain, cool. 23-26 Hot, then t-storms. 27-30 Warm, showers.

JULY 2004: Temp. 73° (2° above avg.); precip. 3.5" (2" below avg. north; 2" above south). 1-4 Sunny, warm. 5-9 Seasonable, rain south. 10-12 Sunny, hot. 13-18 Humid, t-storms. 19-24 Sunny, hot. 25-31 T-storms, then cooler.

AUG. 2004: Temp. 75° (5° above avg.); precip. 4" (2" above avg. north; 0.5" below south). 1-5 T-storms. 6-15 Heat wave south, showers north. 16-18 Showers, cool. 19-22 Hot south, t-storms north. 23-31 T-storms, then sunny, warm.

SEPT. 2004: Temp. 66° (3° above avg.); precip. 3" (1.5" below avg.). 1-3 Sunny, hot. 4-8 T-storms, then sunny; frost north. 9-12 Showers, chilly. 13-18 Sunny, very warm. 19-25 Very warm, showers. 26-30 Showers; warm south, cool north.

OCT. 2004: Temp. 54° (avg.); precip. 5.5" (2" above avg.). 1-3 Heavy rain. 4-9 Chilly, showers. 10-14 Sprinkles and flurries. 15-19 Rain, warmer. 20-24 Sunny, cool. 25-31 Rain; snow north.

Caribou
Burlington
Boston
Hartford

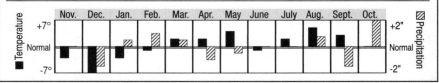

Greater New York–New Jersey

SUMMARY: The first half of the winter will be exceptionally cold, and the second half will have above-normal temperatures. Expect persistent cold from mid-November through early January, with other cold spells in late January and mid-February. Precipitation will be below normal, with near-normal snowfall. Snowy periods will occur in early December and mid- to late January. A northeaster in early March will bring heavy snow inland and mostly rain near the coast.

After wet snow in early April, spring will come quickly, with temperatures in April and May averaging about three degrees above normal.

Overall, the summer will be hot and wet, despite a dry June with near-normal temperatures. Temperatures will continue near normal in July, but heavy thunderstorms will bring double the normal rainfall. After thunderstorms in early August, expect the worst heat wave in several years, with oppressive heat and humidity into midmonth.

September will be delightful, with warm days, comfortably cool nights, and plenty of sunshine. October will be warmer and wetter than normal.

NOV. 2003: Temp. 43° (2° below avg.); precip. 3.5" (avg.). 1-8 Showers, then sunny. 9-13 Warm, showers. 14-17 Sunny, seasonable. 18-23 Rain; snow north. 24-26 Sunny, cold. 27-30 Rain; snow north.

DEC. 2003: Temp. 29° (6° below avg.); precip. 2.5" (1" below avg.). 1-7 Cold, snow, then sunny. 8-13 Flurries, then milder. 14-20 Partly sunny, very cold. 21-27 Milder, rain; snow north. 28-31 Sunny, cold.

JAN. 2004: Temp. 25° (4° below avg.); precip. 2" (1" below avg.). 1-6 Sunny, cold. 7-10 Rain and snow. 11-16 Very cold, then mild with rain. 17-21 Cold, snow showers. 22-28 Mild, then very cold. 29-31 Rain, milder.

FEB. 2004: Temp. 32° (1° above avg.); precip. 3" (0.5" below avg.). 1-4 Snow turning to rain. 5-9 Rain; snow north. 10-12 Sunny, mild. 13-19 Cold; sunny south, snow showers north. 20-25 Sunny, mild. 26-29 Heavy rain; wet snow north.

MAR. 2004: Temp. 41° (1° above avg.); precip. 3.5" (avg.). 1-2 Sunny. 3-7 Northeaster, heavy snow north and west. 8-12 Rain and snow showers. 13-15 Mild, showers. 16-20 Sunny, cold, then mild. 21-24 Cold, rain and snow. 25-31 Mild, rain, then sunny.

APR. 2004: Temp. 53° (3° above avg.); precip. 2.5" (1" below avg.). 1-3 Sunny, warm. 4-7 Chilly, rain and wet snow. 8-12 Sunny, warm. 13-17 Showers, then cooler. 18-20 Sunny, warm. 21-26 Showers. 27-30 Sunny, warm.

MAY 2004: Temp. 63° (3° above avg.); precip. 4" (1" below avg. north; 1" above south). 1-4 Showers, then cool. 5-9 Hot, then t-storms. 10-13 Cooler. 14-17 Hot, then t-storms. 18-20 Sunny. 21-25 Hot; scattered t-storms. 26-31 Rain, then sunny.

JUNE 2004: Temp. 70° (avg.); precip. 1.5" (1" below avg.). 1-5 Sunny, hot. 6-13 Showers, cool. 14-20 Seasonable, showers. 21-24 Hot; scattered t-storms. 25-30 Sunny, warm.

JULY 2004: Temp. 75° (avg.); precip. 7.5" (4" above avg.). 1-3 Sunny, warm. 4-10 Cloudy, cool, heavy rain. 11-18 Warm; heavy t-storms. 19-26 Sunny, hot. 27-31 Cooler, showers.

AUG. 2004: Temp. 79° (6° above avg.); precip. 4" (avg.). 1-3 Partly sunny, t-storms. 4-10 Sunny, hot, humid. 11-16 Hot, humid; scattered t-storms. 17-18 Cool, showers. 19-22 Sunny, hot. 23-28 T-storms, very warm. 29-31 Sunny, very warm.

SEPT. 2004: Temp. 70° (4° above avg.); precip. 1" (2.5" below avg.). 1-4 Sunny, hot. 5-9 T-storms, then sunny, comfortable. 10-14 Showers, then sunny, cool. 15-21 Sunny, warm. 22-30 Very warm, showers, then sunny.

OCT. 2004: Temp. 57° (2° above avg.); precip. 5" (2" above avg.). 1-5 Warm, t-storms. 6-15 Rain, then sunny, cool. 16-21 Rain, warm. 22-24 Sunny, cool. 25-31 Showers.

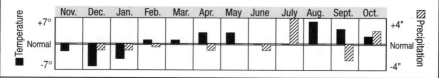

Middle Atlantic Coast

SUMMARY: The coming winter will be another cold one, but with less snow than last winter. Temperatures will average one to two degrees below normal, with well-below-normal temperatures from mid-November through mid-January, and near-normal temperatures from late January through March. The coldest temperatures will be around the New Year, with other especially cold periods in early December and mid-January. Precipitation will be below normal, and most places will also have below-normal snowfall. Southern parts of the region will get more snow than the north, with the best chances for accumulating snow in early December and mid-January.

April and May will be wetter and much warmer than normal, despite the chance for a bit of snow after the first hot spell in early April.

The summer will be hotter than normal, with near-normal rain in the west and above-normal rainfall in the east. Expect record heat in mid- to late June and almost anytime in August, which will be the hottest on record.

September and October will be warmer than normal, with a rather dry September followed by a wet October.

NOV. 2003: Temp. 48° (1° below avg.); precip. 2.5" (0.5" below avg.). 1-4 Chilly, showers. 5-15 Warm, sunny, then showers. 16-19 Sunny, cooler. 20-26 Rain, then sunny, cold. 27-30 Rain, cool.

DEC. 2003: Temp. 33° (6° below avg.); precip. 3.5" (0.5" below north; 1" below south). 1-4 Sunny, cold. 5-10 Very cold; snow. 11-16 Sunny. 17-20 Mild, showers, then sunny, cold. 21-31 Heavy rain, then sunny, very cold.

JAN. 2004: Temp. 31° (3° below avg.); precip. 1.5" (1.5" below avg.). 1-6 Sunny, cold. 7-10 Mild, then cold, rain turning to snow. 11-13 Sunny, cold. 14-16 Warm, t-storms. 17-21 Sunny, then rain and snow. 22-31 Sunny, then rain.

FEB. 2004: Temp. 40° (3° above avg.); precip. 2.5" (0.5" below avg.). 1-12 Mild, partly sunny, a few showers. 13-16 Sunny, cold. 17-23 Rain, then sunny, mild. 24-29 Rain.

MAR. 2004: Temp. 47° (1° above avg.); precip. 3" (0.5" below avg.). 1-6 Chilly, showers. 7-19 Mostly sunny. 20-25 Chilly, rain and flurries. 26-31 Mild, rain.

APR. 2004: Temp. 60° (4° above avg.); precip. 4" (0.5" below avg. north; 1" above south). 1-3 Sunny, hot. 4-7 Rain, cool. 8-11 Sunny, warm. 12-17 Rain, then cool. 18-20 Sunny, warm. 21-22 Rain. 23-30 Warm; sunny north, t-storms south.

MAY 2004: Temp. 68° (3° above avg.); precip. 5" (1" above avg.). 1-5 Sunny, warm. 6-11 T-storms, then sunny, cool. 12-17 Warm, humid, t-storms. 18-20 Sunny. 21-24 Hot, t-storms. 25-27 Rain. 28-31 Sunny.

JUNE 2004: Temp. 76° (2° above avg.); precip. 4" (avg.). 1-5 Sunny, hot. 6-12 Cool, showers. 13-19 Sunny, warm. 20-24 Sunny, record heat. 25-30 T-storms, then sunny.

JULY 2004: Temp. 78.5° (0.5° above avg.); precip. 5.5" (1" above avg.). 1-3 Sunny. 4-9 T-storms. 10-11 Sunny. 12-25 Humid, t-storms. 26-31 More comfortable, then t-storms.

AUG. 2004: Temp. 81.5° (5.5° above avg.); precip. 4.5" (1" below avg. west; 1" above east). 1-3 T-storms. 4-16 Sunny, turning hot, humid. 17-22 Hot, humid, t-storms. 23-31 Very warm, t-storms.

SEPT. 2004: Temp. 73° (3° above avg.); precip. 2.5" (2" below avg. north; avg. south). 1-4 Sunny, very warm. 5-10 Sunny, comfortable. 11-14 Showers, then sunny, cool. 15-21 Sunny, warm. 22-25 Warm, t-storms. 26-30 Sunny, warm.

OCT. 2004: Temp. 61° (2° above avg.); precip. 4" (0.5" above avg. north; 2" above south). 1-5 Warm, t-storms. 6-15 Rain, then sunny, cool. 16-21 Rain. 22-28 Sunny, then showers. 29-31 Very warm, t-storms.

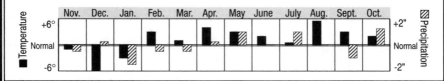

Piedmont and Southeast Coast

SUMMARY: Overall, the winter will be colder than normal. Temperatures from November through mid-January will be four degrees colder than normal, on average, with temperatures from late January through March two degrees milder than normal, on average. Expect drier than normal weather in the north and wetter than normal weather in the south, especially in the southeast. Snowfall will be above normal across the north, due to heavy snow in early December. Elsewhere, expect normal or below-normal snowfall.

April and May will be warmer than normal, with near-normal rainfall in April, then heavy rains in the southeast during May.

June will be dry, with near-normal rainfall in July and August. Temperatures will average a degree or so hotter than normal, thanks to the heat waves in mid- to late June, the middle of August, and late July.

September will be near normal in both temperatures and rainfall. October will be warmer than normal, but with frequent rain, sometimes heavy.

NOV. 2003: Temp. 55° (avg.); precip. 1.5" (1.5" below avg.). 1-5 Showers, then sunny, cool. 6-13 Sunny, warm. 14-17 Sunny, cooler. 18-22 Showers, warm, then cool. 23-25 Cold. 26-30 Showers, mild.

DEC. 2003: Temp. 41° (5° below avg.); precip. 4" (1" above avg. east; 1" below west). 1-3 Sunny; cold north. 4-8 Very cold; snow north, rain south. 9-16 Sunny, very cold then seasonable. 17-20 Showers, mild, then cold. 21-27 Rain. 28-31 Sunny, very cold.

JAN. 2004: Temp. 39° (3° below avg.); precip. 5" (0.5" below avg; 2" above southeast). 1-2 Rain; snow north. 3-6 Sunny, cold. 7-10 Warm, then rain turning to snow. 11-13 Sunny, very cold. 14-16 Rain, mild. 17-21 Sunny, cold, then warm. 22-25 Rain, mild. 26-31 Cold, then rain.

FEB. 2004: Temp. 46° (2° above avg.); precip. 5.5" (avg. north; 4" above south). 1-9 Rain, mild. 10-16 Sunny, cold. 17-27 Showers. 28-29 Heavy rain.

MAR. 2004: Temp. 55° (1° above avg.); precip. 4.5" (1" below avg. north; 1" above south). 1-4 Sunny. 5-9 Rain. 10-13 Chilly; rain south. 14-19 Rain, then sunny. 20-24 Rain, chilly. 25-31 Showers, then sunny.

APR. 2004: Temp. 65° (3° above avg.); precip. 4" (2" above avg. north; 1" below south). 1-4 Sunny, warm. 5-8 T-storms, then sunny, chilly. 9-11 Sunny. 12-16 Rain. 17-30 Sunny, warm.

MAY 2004: Temp. 71° (1° above avg.); precip. 6.5" (1" above avg. north; 5" above south). 1-2 Sunny, warm. 3-7 Warm, t-storms. 8-11 Sunny, cool. 12-15 T-storms. 16-23 Mostly sunny; scattered t-storms. 24-31 T-storms.

JUNE 2004: Temp. 76° (avg.); precip. 1" (3" below avg.). 1-7 Sunny, warm. 8-13 Sunny, cool. 14-19 Warm; scattered t-storms. 20-25 Sunny, very hot, humid. 26-30 T-storms, then comfortable.

JULY 2004: Temp. 80° (avg.); precip. 4.5" (avg.). 1-3 Sunny, warm. 4-17 Seasonable, t-storms. 18-23 Warm; t-storms north. 24-26 Hot; t-storms south. 27-31 Sunny, then t-storms.

AUG. 2004: Temp. 80° (2° above avg.); precip. 4" (2" above avg. east; 1" below west). 1-2 T-storms. 3-7 Sunny, warm. 8-15 Hot; sunny north, t-storms south. 16-21 Sunny, hot. 22-25 Heavy t-storms. 26-31 Sunny, then t-storms.

SEPT. 2004: Temp. 74° (avg.); precip. 3.5" (avg.). 1-4 Warm; sunny north, t-storms south. 5-10 Cool; sunny north, rain south. 11-16 Sunny, cool. 17-21 Sunny, warm. 22-24 Warm, t-storms. 25-30 Sunny, warm.

OCT. 2004: Temp. 66° (2° above avg.); precip. 6.5" (4" above avg.). 1-5 Warm, t-storms. 6-14 Cool, rain, then sunny. 15-24 Cool, rain. 25-31 Sunny, warm.

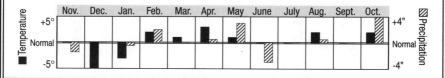

Florida

SUMMARY: Winter will be wet and mild overall, with below-normal temperatures in December and January, and above-normal temperatures in February and March. The best chance for a freeze into central Florida is in mid-January, although we don't expect any major damage. Other cold periods will be in early and late December and early January. Stormy weather will occur in the second week of March, with other especially rainy periods in early and late December, early January, and mid- to late February.

Temperatures in April and May will be near normal in the south and slightly warmer than normal in the north. Expect near-normal rainfall in April, followed by a very wet May.

The summer will continue wet in the south, but the north will be drier than normal. Expect the usual daily thunderstorms scattered about most days in the summer, with widespread heavy downpours in June. The hottest temperatures will occur in mid-June and mid- to late August.

Rainfall in September and October should be near normal, with near-normal temperatures in September and a warm October.

NOV. 2003: Temp. 73° (5° above avg.); precip. 3" (0.5" below avg. north; 2" above south). 1-5 Warm, t-storms. 6-13 Sunny, warm. 14-16 Sunny, cool north. 17-22 Warm; sunny north, t-storms south. 23-25 Cool north, t-storms south. 26-30 Warm, t-storms.

DEC. 2003: Temp. 60.5° (4° below avg. north; 1° below south); precip. 5.5" (3" above avg.). 1-4 Warm, t-storms. 5-11 Cool, rain. 12-17 Sunny, mild. 18-22 Rain. 23-29 Sunny, then rain. 30-31 Sunny, cool.

JAN. 2004: Temp. 59° (2° below avg.); precip. 3" (avg.). 1-7 Rain, then sunny, cold. 8-13 Rain, then sunny; freeze north and central. 14-19 Showers. 20-26 Sunny, mild. 27-31 Warm, showers.

FEB. 2004: Temp. 67° (4° above avg.); precip. 5" (4" above avg. north; avg. south). 1-2 Rain. 3-8 Sunny, warm. 9-16 Showers, then sunny, cool. 17-19 Sunny, warm. 20-24 Sunny south, heavy rain elsewhere. 25-29 Sunny, then t-storms.

MAR. 2004: Temp. 68° (1° above avg.); precip. 6.5" (4" above avg.). 1-8 Showers, cool. 9-14 Heavy rain. 15-21 Sunny. 22-31 Showers, then sunny.

APR. 2004: Temp. 72.5° (1° above avg. north; avg. south); precip. 3" (avg.). 1-4 Sunny, warm.

5-7 T-storms, warm. 8-11 Sunny, cool. 12-16 T-storms, warm. 17-30 Sunny, cool, then warm.

MAY 2004: Temp. 75.5° (1° above avg. north; avg. south); precip. 9" (5" above avg.). 1-4 Sunny, warm. 5-12 Partly sunny; scattered t-storms. 13-18 T-storms. 19-31 Seasonable; scattered t-storms.

JUNE 2004: Temp. 80° (avg.); precip. 7" (5" above avg. south; 3" below north). 1-9 Partly sunny; scattered t-storms. 10-15 Mostly cloudy; heavy t-storms south and central. 16-26 Very warm; scattered t-storms. 27-30 T-storms, cooler.

JULY 2004: Temp. 81° (1° below avg.); precip. 7" (avg.). 1-7 Warm, t-storms. 8-11 Partly sunny. 12-23 Partly sunny; scattered t-storms. 24-31 Warm; scattered t-storms.

AUG. 2004: Temp. 81° (1° below avg.); precip. 7" (2" below avg. north; 2" above south). 1-11 Partly sunny; scattered t-storms. 12-22 Scattered t-storms; hot north. 23-31 T-storms.

SEPT. 2004: Temp. 81° (avg.); precip. 6" (avg.). 1-15 Mostly cloudy, t-storms. 16-22 Partly sunny; scattered t-storms. 23-30 Mostly sunny, warm.

OCT. 2004: Temp. 79° (4° above avg.); precip. 6" (avg.). 1-9 Warm; scattered t-storms. 10-18 Warm, t-storms. 19-21 Sunny, cool. 22-25 Warm, t-storms. 26-31 Sunny, warm.

Jacksonville
Tampa
Orlando
Miami

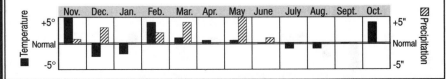

Upstate New York

SUMMARY: Expect a cold, snowy winter, with temperatures two to three degrees below normal, on average, and well-above-normal precipitation and snowfall. Temperatures will be especially cold from the second half of November through mid-December, from late December to early January, and in most of mid-February. Expect frequent snowfalls, with above-normal accumulations every month except February, which will have below-normal snow.

Rain and mild temperatures in early April may bring flooding, but overall April and May will be warm with below-normal rainfall.

The summer will be the opposite extreme of the winter, with temperatures averaging two to three degrees hotter than normal and well-below-normal rainfall. The hottest temperatures will occur in early June, in mid- to late July, and through most of August.

September will start hot and end cool. Overall, the month will be mild and wet. October will also be wet, with near-normal temperatures.

NOV. 2003: Temp. 38° (1° below avg.); precip. 3.5" (1.5" above avg.). 1-7 Partly sunny. 8-14 Warm, showers. 15-20 Rain and snow showers. 21-25 Very cold; heavy lake snows. 26-30 Snow showers.

DEC. 2003: Temp. 20° (7° below avg.); precip. 2" (1" below avg.). 1-10 Very cold; heavy lake snows. 11-17 Partly sunny, flurries. 18-20 Very cold. 21-24 Partly sunny, mild. 25-31 Showers, then windy and cold with snow squalls.

JAN. 2004: Temp. 17° (4° below avg.); precip. 4.5" (2" above avg.). 1-5 Cold; lake snows. 6-9 Mild; rain and snow showers. 10-13 Cold; occasional snow. 14-16 Rain, warm; flooding. 17-21 Cold; snow showers. 22-24 Mild, showers. 25-31 Sunny, cold, then showers, mild.

FEB. 2004: Temp. 23° (avg.); precip. 3.5" (1" above avg.). 1-5 Rain and ice. 6-11 Mild, showers. 12-16 Cold; snow showers. 17-23 Snow, then mild. 24-29 Rain and wet snow.

MAR. 2004: Temp. 31.5° (1.5° below avg.); precip. 3" (avg.). 1-5 Cold; snow showers. 6-11 Snowstorm. 12-17 Showers, mild, then cold. 18-24 Snowstorm, then sunny, cold. 25-31 Mild, then rain, cooler.

APR. 2004: Temp. 47° (2° above avg.); precip. 2" (1" below avg.). 1-4 Rain. 5-12 Sunny, cool, then warm. 13-18 Showers, then cooler. 19-26 Showers. 27-30 Sunny.

MAY 2004: Temp. 59° (3° above avg.); precip. 3.5" (avg.). 1-7 Warm, sunny, then t-storms. 8-12 Showers, cool. 13-25 Showers, then sunny, very warm. 26-31 T-storms, then sunny, warm.

JUNE 2004: Temp. 65° (avg.); precip. 2.5" (1" below avg.). 1-5 Sunny, hot. 6-13 Showers, cool. 14-19 Sunny, nice. 20-24 T-storms, then sunny, warm. 25-30 T-storms, then sunny.

JULY 2004: Temp. 72° (1° above avg.); precip. 2" (1.5" below avg.). 1-6 Warm, t-storms. 7-12 Sunny, warm. 13-19 Very warm; t-storms. 20-26 Sunny, hot, humid. 27-31 Cooler, showers.

AUG. 2004: Temp. 74.5° (6.5° above avg.); precip. 5" (1" above avg.). 1-4 T-storms. 5-9 Sunny, hot. 10-27 Partly sunny; scattered t-storms, very warm. 28-31 Sunny, very warm.

SEPT. 2004: Temp. 65° (4° above avg.); precip. 4.5" (1" above avg.). 1-3 Sunny, hot. 4-7 T-storms, then sunny, cool. 8-13 Chilly, showers. 14-23 Sunny, very warm. 24-30 Rain, turning cooler.

OCT. 2004: Temp. 50° (avg.); precip. 4.5" (1.5" above avg.). 1-9 Showers, then partly sunny. 10-16 Sunny, chilly. 17-21 Showers, mild. 22-25 Sunny, cool. 26-31 T-storms, mild.

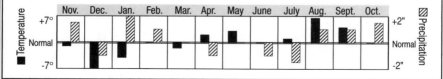

Greater Ohio Valley

SUMMARY: Winter will be two degrees colder than normal, on average. December and early January will be particularly cold, averaging about seven degrees below normal. Temperatures during the rest of the season will be a degree or two milder than normal, on average. Precipitation and snowfall will be near or slightly below normal. The heaviest snowfalls will occur early and late in the season, a few days before Thanksgiving, and in early April.

Other than that early April snow, the month will be nice, with plenty of sunshine, above-normal temperatures, and below-normal rainfall. May will bring more of the same.

The summer will be relatively hot and dry. Expect the hottest temperatures in mid- to late June and late July, and through much of August.

September will continue warm and dry. October will start with heavy rain and be rainier and cooler than normal, on average.

NOV. 2003: Temp. 44.5° (0.5° below avg.); precip. 3.5" (avg.). 1-4 Showers, cool. 5-8 Sunny, warm. 9-12 Very warm, showers. 13-18 Sunny, mild. 19-23 Rain to snow, colder. 24-30 Cold, rain and snow showers.

DEC. 2003: Temp. 27.5° (7.5° below avg.); precip. 1" (2" below avg.). 1-9 Very cold; snow showers. 10-17 Partly sunny, then showers and flurries. 18-24 Sunny, milder. 25-31 Rain turning to snow, then very cold.

JAN. 2004: Temp. 26° (3° below avg.); precip. 3.5" (1" above avg.). 1-7 Sunny, turning milder. 8-12 Showers, then sunny, very cold. 13-15 Heavy rain. 16-22 Rain, snow. 23-31 Rain and snow showers.

FEB. 2004: Temp. 34° (2° above avg.); precip. 3.5" (avg. east; 1" above west). 1-9 Mild, showers. 10-15 Rain turning to snow, then sunny, cold. 16-22 Mild, showers. 23-29 Sunny, then rain.

MAR. 2004: Temp. 42.5° (0.5° below avg.); precip. 3" (1" below avg.). 1-6 Snow north, rain south. 7-12 Cold, rain and snow showers. 13-19 Sunny, mild. 20-24 Chilly, rain. 25-31 T-storms, then sunny.

APR. 2004: Temp. 56.5° (3.5° above avg.); precip. 3" (1" below avg.). 1-6 Turning cold, rain to snow. 7-11 Sunny, nice. 12-19 Showers, then sunny. 20-25 T-storms. 26-30 Sunny, very warm.

MAY 2004: Temp. 65° (2° above avg.); precip. 3.5" (0.5" below avg.). 1-7 Sunny, then showers. 8-11 Chilly; showers south. 12-16 Warm; t-storms north. 17-23 Warm, t-storms. 24-31 Sunny, seasonable.

JUNE 2004: Temp. 72° (1° below avg. east; 1° above west); precip. 3.5" (avg.). 1-6 Sunny, then t-storms. 7-14 Sunny, cool. 15-25 T-storms, then sunny, hot. 26-30 Warm; scattered t-storms.

JULY 2004: Temp. 76.5° (0.5° above avg.); precip. 3.5" (0.5" below avg.). 1-10 Sunny, warm. 11-24 Warm; scattered t-storms. 25-31 Sunny, warm.

AUG. 2004: Temp. 79° (5° above avg.); precip. 2.5" (1" below avg.). 1-8 Showers, then sunny, hot. 9-18 T-storms, then sunny, hot. 19-27 Warm, t-storms. 28-31 Sunny.

SEPT. 2004: Temp. 72° (4° above avg.); precip. 2" (1" below avg.). 1-4 Hot, then t-storms. 5-9 Sunny, nice. 10-13 Chilly, showers. 14-20 Sunny, warm. 21-24 Warm, t-storms. 25-30 Sunny, then t-storms.

OCT. 2004: Temp. 55° (avg. east; 2° below west); precip. 4.5" (2" above avg.). 1-7 Heavy rain, turning cooler. 8-15 Sunny. 16-23 Rain, then sunny. 24-31 Showers.

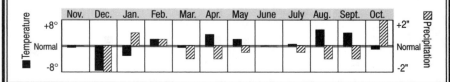

Deep South

SUMMARY: November through March will be a bit colder and drier than normal, with below-normal snowfall in those areas that normally receive snow. November will be relatively mild, followed by a generally cold December and January. Temperatures in February and March will be close to normal, on average. January and February will be the rainiest months, with the best chances for significant snow in the north in early December and in late January.

April and May will be warmer and less rainy than normal, in general, although heavy thunderstorms in May will bring flooding to parts of the south.

The summer will be close to normal, on average, with the usual heat, humidity, and scattered thunderstorms. The hottest periods will be in the latter halves of June and July.

September and October will be warmer than normal with above-normal rainfall, especially in the north.

NOV. 2003: Temp. 58° (4° above avg.); precip. 3.5" (1" above avg. north; 2" below south). 1-7 Sunny, warm. 8-12 T-storms, very warm. 13-19 Sunny, warm. 20-23 Cool, rain; wet snow north. 24-30 Sunny, warm.

DEC. 2003: Temp. 41° (4° below avg.); precip. 3" (2" below avg.). 1-3 Sunny, cold. 4-7 Cold, rain; snow north. 8-16 Sunny, turning milder. 17-21 Rain. 22-31 Showers, then sunny, very cold.

JAN. 2004: Temp. 37° (2° below avg.); precip. 5" (1" below avg. north; 2" above south). 1-6 Rain, turning sunny, cold. 7-13 Rain; snow north, then sunny. 14-21 Rain, then sunny. 22-31 Rain; snow north, chilly.

FEB. 2004: Temp. 44° (1° above avg.); precip. 6.5" (2" above avg.). 1-5 Warm, showers. 6-8 Heavy rain. 9-12 Sunny, mild. 13-15 Showers, then sunny. 16-22 Rain, mild. 23-29 Sunny, then heavy rain.

MAR. 2004: Temp. 51° (1° below avg.; 1° above northwest); precip. 2" (2" below avg.). 1-4 Sunny. 5-10 Showers. 11-17 Sunny, seasonable. 18-31 Rain, then sunny.

APR. 2004: Temp. 63° (1° above avg.); precip. 2" (2.5" below avg.). 1-3 Sunny, warm. 4-9 Showers, then sunny, cool. 10-20 T-storms, then sunny, nice. 21-30 T-storms, then sunny, very warm.

MAY 2004: Temp. 72.5° (1.5° above avg.); precip. 7" (2" below avg. northwest; 7" above southeast). 1-3 Sunny, warm. 4-11 T-storms, then sunny. 12-31 Partly sunny, warm; t-storms.

JUNE 2004: Temp. 77.5° (1.5° below avg. north; 0.5° above south); precip. 3" (0.5" below avg.). 1-6 Partly sunny, warm; t-storms. 7-16 Sunny, very warm. 17-24 T-storms, then sunny, hot. 25-30 Warm, t-storms.

JULY 2004: Temp. 80° (avg.); precip. 3.5" (avg.). 1-16 Partly sunny, warm; scattered t-storms. 17-31 Partly sunny, hot, humid; scattered t-storms.

AUG. 2004: Temp. 81° (1° above avg.); precip. 5" (1" above avg. north; 1" below south). 1-8 Partly sunny; t-storms south. 9-17 Partly sunny; scattered t-storms. 18-25 Partly sunny; t-storms north. 26-31 Very warm; scattered t-storms.

SEPT. 2004: Temp. 75.5° (1.5° above avg.); precip. 4.5" (3" above avg. north; 1" below south). 1-7 Partly sunny, t-storms. 8-16 Sunny, warm. 17-24 Partly sunny; scattered t-storms. 25-30 Sunny, warm.

OCT. 2004: Temp. 64° (1° below avg. north; 1° above south); precip. 6" (3" above avg.). 1-6 Mostly cloudy; scattered t-storms. 7-15 Sunny north, t-storms south. 16-20 Sunny. 21-25 Rain, cool. 26-31 Sunny, then t-storms.

Nashville · Little Rock · Montgomery · Shreveport · Mobile · New Orleans

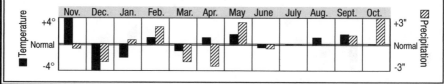

	Nov.	Dec.	Jan.	Feb.	Mar.	Apr.	May	June	July	Aug.	Sept.	Oct.	
Temperature +4° / Normal / -4°													Precipitation +3" / Normal / -3"

Chicago and Southern Great Lakes

SUMMARY: Winter will be cold, with temperatures three degrees below normal, on average. Temperatures will be very cold much of the time from late November through January, with the coldest periods in early December, from about Christmas to New Year, and again in late January. The first half of November, and the months of February and March, will be milder, with temperatures a bit above normal. Precipitation will be slightly above normal, due to a wet February, and snowfall will be near normal. The heaviest snowfalls will occur in late November, early and late December, and mid-January.

April and May will be warmer than usual, with near- to above-normal rainfall.

The summer will be hotter than normal, primarily due to an exceptionally hot August. Rainfall will be very close to normal, with the heaviest rains in July.

September will be wet and mild, with heavy rain to close the month. October will also be wet, but with below-normal temperatures.

NOV. 2003: Temp. 39° (1° below avg.); precip. 3.5" (1" above avg.). 1-6 Showers, then sunny. 7-11 Warm, showers. 12-19 Seasonable, showers. 20-25 Much colder; snow then sunny. 26-30 Flurries.

DEC. 2003: Temp. 20° (8° below avg.); precip. 1.5" (1" below avg.). 1-9 Very cold; snow showers. 10-15 Partly sunny, flurries. 16-23 Turning milder, flurries then sunny. 24-31 Much colder, snow.

JAN. 2004: Temp. 15° (7° below avg.); precip. 2" (0.5" above avg.). 1-5 Sunny, cold. 6-8 Mild, showers. 9-19 Cold, snow. 20-24 Mild, showers. 25-31 Cold, flurries.

FEB. 2004: Temp. 26.5° (1.5° above avg.); precip. 3.5" (2" above avg.). 1-4 Sunny, then rain. 5-10 Mild, showers. 11-15 Cold, flurries, then sunny. 16-18 Rain and snow. 19-26 Seasonable; rain and snow showers. 27-29 Rain and snow.

MAR. 2004: Temp. 37° (avg.); precip. 2.5" (avg.). 1-10 Chilly, periods of snow. 11-18 Sunny, turning warm. 19-23 Rain and snow. 24-31 Mild, showers.

APR. 2004: Temp. 52° (3° above avg.); precip. 3.5" (0.5" above avg.). 1-7 Rain and snow, then sunny, chilly. 8-11 Sunny, warm. 12-16 Showers, then sunny, cool. 17-23 Heavy rain. 24-30 Sunny, very warm.

MAY 2004: Temp. 62° (3° above avg.); precip. 4" (1" above avg. east; 0.5" below west). 1-7 T-storms, warm. 8-11 Cool, showers. 12-24 Warm; scattered t-storms. 25-31 Sunny, warm.

JUNE 2004: Temp. 71° (1° above avg.); precip. 3" (1" below avg.). 1-5 Sunny, hot. 6-14 T-storms, then sunny, cool. 15-19 Warm, t-storms. 20-23 Sunny, hot. 24-30 T-storms, then sunny.

JULY 2004: Temp. 74° (avg.); precip. 5" (1" above avg.). 1-5 Sunny, then t-storms. 6-10 Sunny, nice. 11-17 Warm, t-storms. 18-21 Sunny, nice. 22-24 Sultry, t-storms. 25-31 Partly sunny; scattered t-storms.

AUG. 2004: Temp. 78° (6° above avg.); precip. 3.5" (1" above avg. east; 1" below west). 1-4 Sunny. 5-13 Very warm, t-storms. 14-24 Hot, humid; scattered t-storms. 25-31 Sunny, comfortable, then hot.

SEPT. 2004: Temp. 67° (3° above avg.); precip. 5.5" (2" above avg.). 1-3 Sunny, hot. 4-8 T-storms, then sunny, cool. 9-12 Showers, then chilly. 13-23 Warm, showers. 24-30 Sunny, then heavy rain.

OCT. 2004: Temp. 49° (3° below avg.); precip. 3.5" (0.5" above avg.). 1-6 Showers, turning cool. 7-16 Sunny, cool. 17-22 Rain, cold. 23-31 Sunny, then rain.

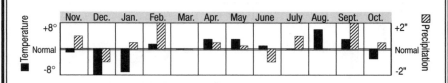

Northern Great Plains–Great Lakes

SUMMARY: Expect substantial variations this winter. Temperatures will be cold in the east, especially in December and January, with below-normal snowfall in Wisconsin and above-normal snowfall in the Upper Peninsula. In Minnesota and the eastern Dakotas, temperatures will be a bit below normal, with near-normal snowfall. In the western part of the region, expect temperatures to be near normal through much of the winter, with a very mild March, but expect more snow than average. The coldest temperatures will occur just after Thanksgiving and between Christmas and New Year.

April will be colder than normal in the west but milder than normal in the east, followed by near-normal temperatures in May. Watch for heavy snow in mid-April.

The summer will be hot. It will be relatively dry in the west, with above-normal rain in the east.

September will be colder than normal in the west, with near-normal temperatures in the east. October will be cold, with heavy snow possible to close the month.

NOV. 2003: Temp. 32° (1° below avg. east; 1° above west); precip. 1.5" (avg.). 1-8 Mild, showers west. 9-12 Snow, colder. 13-16 Cold, snow, then sunny. 17-24 Cold, flurries. 25-27 Sunny, mild. 28-30 Very cold, flurries.

DEC. 2003: Temp. 14° (5° below avg.; 1° below west); precip. 0.75" (0.25" below avg.). 1-8 Snow showers, very cold. 9-12 Mild. 13-15 Showers east. 16-23 Sunny, mild. 24-31 Flurries, then very cold.

JAN. 2004: Temp. 8° (4° below avg.; 2° above west); precip. 0.75" (0.25" below avg.). 1-7 Sunny, turning mild. 8-16 Flurries, very cold. 17-22 Snow showers. 23-26 Sunny, very cold. 27-31 Windy; light snow.

FEB. 2004: Temp. 16° (avg.); precip. 1" (avg.). 1-9 Light snow, cold, then milder. 10-15 Flurries, then sunny, cold. 16-19 Sunny, milder. 20-29 Mild; snow showers.

MAR. 2004: Temp. 33.5° (3° above avg. east; 8° above west); precip. 1" (0.5" below avg.). 1-8 Mild; snow showers. 9-12 Cold, flurries. 13-23 Sunny, mild. 24-31 Showers, then sunny, warm.

APR. 2004: Temp. 44° (3° above avg. east; 3° below west); precip. 2.5" (0.5" above avg.). 1-6 Cold, flurries. 7-9 Sunny, warm. 10-14 Heavy rain and snow. 15-19 Cold, flurries. 20-26 Sunny, very warm. 27-30 Rain.

MAY 2004: Temp. 56° (avg.); precip. 1" (0.5" below avg.). 1-4 Showers. 5-12 Sunny, cool, then warm. 13-25 T-storms, cool. 26-31 Sunny, turning hot.

JUNE 2004: Temp. 66.5° (avg. east; 3° above west); precip. 3.5" (0.5" below avg.). 1-3 Sunny, hot. 4-8 Hot west, t-storms east. 9-16 Comfortable; scattered t-storms. 17-24 T-storms, warm, then cool. 25-30 Sunny, nice.

JULY 2004: Temp. 75.5° (2.5° above avg.); precip. 3.5" (1" above avg. east; 1.5" below west). 1-6 T-storms east, sunny west. 7-14 Sunny, very warm. 15-25 Sunny, hot. 26-31 Hot; scattered t-storms.

AUG. 2004: Temp. 74.5° (3.5° above avg.); precip. 4" (2" above avg. east; 1" below west). 1-10 Warm; scattered t-storms. 11-23 Hot; scattered t-storms. 24-31 T-storms, then sunny, cooler.

SEPT. 2004: Temp. 57.5° (avg. east; 3° below west); precip. 3.5" (avg. east; 1" above west). 1-8 Sunny, warm. 9-12 Chilly, rain. 13-21 Seasonable; scattered t-storms. 22-30 Sunny, cold, then milder.

OCT. 2004: Temp. 40.5° (5.5° below avg.); precip. 2.5" (0.5" above avg.). 1-8 Cold, rain and snow showers. 9-14 Sunny, cool. 15-18 Showers. 19-25 Chilly, rain and snow showers. 26-31 Sunny, then snow.

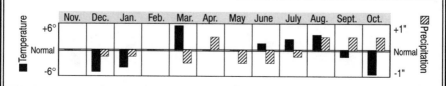

Central Great Plains

SUMMARY: Winter will bring above-normal snowfall. Expect the snowiest periods in mid- to late November, near Thanksgiving, in mid- and late January, and in late February. Watch for heavy snows in the foothills in mid-March and early April. Temperatures will be a degree or two milder than normal, on average, in the foothills and near or a bit colder than normal elsewhere. The coldest temperatures will occur in late December, with record cold possible.

Wet snow will accumulate in mid-April in Iowa and northern Nebraska. Otherwise, expect alternating periods of rain and sunshine. May will have near-normal temperatures, with heavy thunderstorms in midmonth.

The summer will be hot and dry, with much less rainfall than normal in most spots. The hottest temperatures will be in late July and mid-August.

Rainfall will increase in September and October, with heavy snow in the foothills in late September, and perhaps a more widespread snow in late October. Temperatures will be below normal, on average, in September and October, despite a hot start.

NOV. 2003: Temp. 43.5° (2.5° above avg.); precip. 3" (0.5" above avg.). 1-7 Showers, then sunny, warm. 8-11 Warm; heavy rain east, snow west. 12-18 Sunny, mild. 19-22 Snow, much colder. 23-26 Sunny, milder. 27-30 Flurries, then sunny, cool.

DEC. 2003: Temp. 24° (5° below avg.; 1° above west); precip. 0.5" (1" below avg.). 1-5 Snow, cold. 6-9 Cold; flurries. 10-21 Sunny, mild. 22-31 Snow, then record cold.

JAN. 2004: Temp. 21° (3° below avg.; 2° above west); precip. 1" (0.5" below avg.; 1" above west). 1-7 Sunny, mild. 8-12 Cold, flurries. 13-15 Rain turning to snow. 16-19 Sunny, mild. 20-25 Cold, snow. 26-31 Snow west, showers east.

FEB. 2004: Temp. 29° (1° below avg. west; 1° above east); precip. 2" (0.5" above avg.). 1-4 Snow north and west, t-storms southeast. 5-9 Sunny west, showers east. 10-14 Cold, flurries. 15-18 Rain east, snow west. 19-24 Sprinkles east, flurries west. 25-29 Snow north, showers south.

MAR. 2004: Temp. 43° (3° above avg.); precip. 3" (1" above avg.). 1-5 Rain, then flurries. 6-9 Rain east, snow west. 10-12 Sunny. 13-20 Heavy snow west, t-storms east. 21-26 Sunny, then rain. 27-31 Sunny, warm.

APR. 2004: Temp. 52° (3° below avg. west; 3° above east); precip. 3.5" (2" above avg. northeast; 1" below south). 1-5 Cold; snow west, rain east. 6-10 Sunny. 11-15 Rain and snow. 16-20 Sunny. 21-30 Rain, then warm, t-storms.

MAY 2004: Temp. 62° (avg.); precip. 5" (1" above avg.). 1-5 T-storms. 6-10 Sunny, cool. 11-16 Heavy t-storms. 17-25 Sunny, then t-storms. 26-31 Sunny, warm.

JUNE 2004: Temp. 72° (avg.; 4° above west); precip. 2" (2" below avg.). 1-4 Sunny, warm. 5-8 T-storms, then sunny. 9-16 Warm, t-storms. 17-21 Sunny, very warm. 22-24 Hot east, t-storms west. 25-30 Sunny, then showers.

JULY 2004: Temp. 77.5° (0.5° below avg.); precip. 3.5" (1" below avg. north; 1" above south). 1-12 Partly sunny, t-storms. 13-21 Sunny, then t-storms. 22-31 Hot, humid; t-storms.

AUG. 2004: Temp. 78° (3° above avg.); precip. 2" (1.5" below avg.). 1-7 Sunny, comfortable, then hot. 8-23 Hot, humid; scattered t-storms. 24-27 Cool, rain. 28-31 Sunny, hot.

SEPT. 2004: Temp. 64.5° (1° above avg. east; 4° below west); precip. 4.5" (1.5" above avg.). 1-2 Sunny, hot. 3-9 Sunny; cool nights. 10-22 Warm, t-storms. 23-25 Colder; sunny east, heavy snow west. 26-30 Sunny west, heavy rain east.

OCT. 2004: Temp. 52° (3° below avg.); precip. 4" (1" above avg.). 1-7 Cool, showers. 8-15 Sunny. 16-22 Rain, then sunny, cool. 23-31 Turning colder; rain to snow.

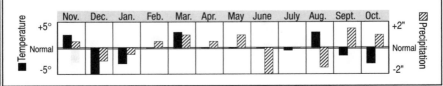

Texas–Oklahoma

SUMMARY: Winter temperatures will be near or slightly colder than normal. The coldest temperatures will occur between Christmas and New Year, with other cold periods in early December and in mid- and late January. Precipitation and snowfall will be slightly below normal. Snow and ice should be limited to the northern half of the region, with the most widespread accumulation around Christmas.

April will be a bit cooler and wetter than normal, with May a bit warmer and drier. Expect very warm weather in late May.

The summer will have near-normal temperatures, with near-normal rainfall in most of the area, but above-normal rainfall from the Metroplex north and eastward. The hottest periods will be in late July and late August, with the greatest threat of a hurricane or tropical storm in mid- to late July.

September and October will be cooler than normal across the north and near normal in the south. Rainfall will be above normal in the northeast and near normal elsewhere.

NOV. 2003: Temp. 58° (2° above avg.); precip. 1" (avg. north; 2" below south). 1-5 Sunny, warm. 6-10 Very warm, t-storms. 11-19 T-storms, snow northwest, then sunny, nice. 20-25 Rain, snow north. 26-30 Sunny, warm, then cool.

DEC. 2003: Temp. 46° (3° below avg.); precip. 0.5" (1" below avg.). 1-7 Turning cold; occasional rain, snow north. 8-13 Sunny, nice. 14-22 Occasional rain south, sunny north. 23-31 Record cold; snow north, rain south.

JAN. 2004: Temp. 42° (2° below avg.); precip. 1.5" (1" below avg. north; 1" above south). 1-4 Rain, then sunny, cold. 5-8 Mild, rain. 9-16 Colder, rain; snow north. 17-24 Sunny north, rain south. 25-31 Cold; snow showers north, rain south.

FEB. 2004: Temp. 51° (1° above avg.); precip. 2" (1" below avg. north; 2" above south). 1-8 Mild, rain. 9-12 Sunny, warm. 13-20 Cold, then seasonable; rain south. 21-26 Sunny, nice. 27-29 Rain; snow north.

MAR. 2004: Temp. 57° (2° above avg. north; 2° below south); precip. 1.5" (1" below avg.). 1-5 Mild, showers. 6-13 Sunny, cool. 14-19 Cold, then mild, rain; snow northwest. 20-25 Light rain. 26-31 Sunny, warm.

APR. 2004: Temp. 64° (2° below avg.); precip. 3.5" (avg. north; 1" above south). 1-9 Chilly, rain, then cloudy. 10-15 Rain, seasonable. 16-24 Sunny, warm. 25-30 Warm, t-storms.

MAY 2004: Temp. 72.5° (avg. north; 1° above south); precip. 4" (0.5" below avg.). 1-8 Warm; scattered t-storms. 9-17 Cool, then warm; showers. 18-25 Sunny, very warm. 26-31 Scattered t-storms.

JUNE 2004: Temp. 80° (avg.); precip. 3.5" (avg.). 1-5 Sunny, very warm. 6-12 Hot north, t-storms south. 13-20 T-storms. 21-30 Sunny, warm.

JULY 2004: Temp. 81.5° (2° below avg. north; avg. south); precip. 4" (4" above avg. northeast; 1" below southwest). 1-16 Partly sunny, warm; scattered t-storms. 17-20 Possible hurricane. 21-31 Sunny, hot.

AUG. 2004: Temp. 83° (avg.); precip. 4" (1" above avg.). 1-6 T-storms, then sunny, warm. 7-21 Humid; scattered t-storms. 22-31 Hot; scattered t-storms.

SEPT. 2004: Temp. 76° (2° below avg. north; 2° above south); precip. 5.5" (5" above avg. northeast; 2" below southwest). 1-7 Turning cooler; sunny north, t-storms south. 8-13 Sunny, warm. 14-23 Warm, humid, t-storms. 24-30 Heavy rain and t-storms.

OCT. 2004: Temp. 65.5° (avg. south; 3° below north); precip. 3" (1" above avg. south; 1" below north). 1-5 Sunny; warm south, cool north. 6-8 Cool, rain. 9-14 Sunny, cool. 15-20 Sunny, warm. 21-27 Rain. 28-31 T-storms, then sunny, cold.

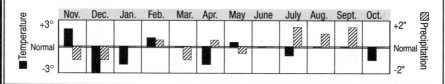

Rocky Mountains

SUMMARY: Winter will be quite a bit milder than normal. Temperatures will average three to five degrees above normal. Despite relatively mild temperatures on average, it will be cold in early to mid-November, late December, and early February. Expect a drier than normal winter with below-normal snowfall. Precipitation will be 30 to 50 percent below normal. The snowiest periods will be in mid-November and early February.

April and May will be a bit cooler and drier than normal. While there will be snow showers in mid-April, there will not be any big spring snowstorms.

The summer will be hotter than normal, with dry weather continuing in the south and near-normal rainfall in the north. The hottest temperatures will occur in early June and in early and mid-July.

September will be noticeably cooler than normal despite a warm start and mild finish. October will be colder than normal in the north, a bit milder than normal in the south. Precipitation should be a bit above normal in the north, a bit below in the south.

NOV. 2003: Temp. 44° (2° above avg.); precip. 0.5" (0.5" below avg.). 1-4 Sunny, warm. 5-7 Rain, cool. 8-12 Cold, snow, then sunny. 13-20 Sunny, mild. 21-30 Snow showers, then sunny, mild.

DEC. 2003: Temp. 32° (4° above avg.); precip. 0.5" (0.5" below avg.). 1-6 Mild; rain north, sunny south. 7-14 Sunny, seasonable. 15-22 Snow showers. 23-31 Cold, flurries.

JAN. 2004: Temp. 33° (7° above avg.); precip. 0.5" (0.5" below avg.). 1-12 Mild; sunny south, showers north. 13-16 Cold, snow showers. 17-21 Mild, sunny, then rain and snow showers. 22-31 Flurries, seasonable.

FEB. 2004: Temp. 34° (5° below avg. east; 1° below west); precip. 1" (0.5" above avg. south; 0.5" below north). 1-8 Cold, snow. 9-15 Mild, showers. 16-20 Snow showers. 21-29 Sunny, mild, then colder.

MAR. 2004: Temp. 42° (3° above avg.); precip. 1.5" (0.5" below avg.). 1-8 Sunny, seasonable. 9-25 Seasonable; rain and snow showers. 26-31 Sunny, warm.

APR. 2004: Temp. 47° (1° below avg.); precip. 1.5" (0.5" below avg.). 1-10 Rain, then sunny, cool. 11-14 Chilly, rain and snow showers.

15-19 Sunny, mild. 20-25 Showers, then sunny, warm. 26-30 Showers, then sunny, cool.

MAY 2004: Temp. 56° (1° below avg.); precip. 2" (avg.). 1-6 Sunny, turning warm. 7-13 Showers, then cooler. 14-25 T-storms, then sunny, cool. 26-31 Sunny, hot.

JUNE 2004: Temp. 68.5° (2.5° above avg.); precip. 1" (0.5" below avg.). 1-7 Sunny, hot. 8-17 T-storms, then sunny, hot. 18-26 Cooler; scattered t-storms. 27-30 Sunny, warm.

JULY 2004: Temp. 76° (2° above avg.); precip. 0.5" (0.5" below avg.). 1-7 Sunny, hot. 8-21 Hot; scattered t-storms. 22-31 T-storms, then sunny, very warm.

AUG. 2004: Temp. 71.5° (2° below avg. north; 1° above south); precip. 1.5" (0.5" below avg. south; 1" above north). 1-6 Very warm; scattered t-storms. 7-20 Cooler, showers. 21-31 Sunny, very warm.

SEPT. 2004: Temp. 59° (4° below avg.); precip. 1.5" (2" above avg. north; 0.5" below south). 1-6 Sunny, very warm. 7-24 Cool, showers. 25-30 Sunny, milder.

OCT. 2004: Temp. 52° (1° above avg. south; 3° below north); precip. 1" (avg.). 1-4 Cool, showers. 5-15 Sunny, seasonable. 16-26 Warm, rain, then cooler. 27-31 Cold, rain and snow showers.

Boise ⊙

Salt Lake City ⊙

⊙ Reno

Grand Junction ⊙

Las Vegas ⊙

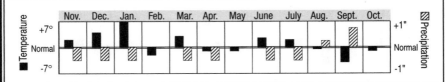

Desert Southwest

SUMMARY: Winter will be quite mild, with temperatures two to three degrees above normal, on average. The coldest periods will be in mid-November, late December, late January, and late February. Precipitation will be below normal, with above-normal snowfall in the north. Expect some snow in high elevations in early to mid-November, with snow in the north and east near Christmas, in mid-January, and in late February.

April and May will be warm and dry, with above-normal temperatures and below-normal rainfall.

The summer will be a hot one, with temperatures two to three degrees above normal, on average. The hottest temperatures will occur in early June, mid-June, and mid-July. June will be relatively dry, but thunderstorm activity will become a bit more widespread from July into mid-August, bringing most spots some much-needed rain.

September will be cooler than normal, with relatively warm temperatures in October. Expect above-normal rainfall in the west, with less rain than normal in the east.

NOV. 2003: Temp. 60.5° (3.5° above avg.); precip. 0.4" (0.2" below avg.). 1-4 Sunny, warm. 5-8 T-storms, then sunny. 9-12 Very cold, rain and snow. 13-19 Sunny. 20-30 Showers, then sunny, warm.

DEC. 2003: Temp. 49.5° (1.5° above avg.); precip. 0.6" (0.4" below avg.). 1-5 Sunny, warm. 6-10 Sunny; cool east, warm west. 11-21 Sunny, mild. 22-27 Showers, heavy snow mountains, then sunny, cold. 28-31 Rain and snow showers.

JAN. 2004: Temp. 50° (3° above avg.); precip. 0.7" (0.3" below avg.). 1-7 Sunny, mild. 8-13 Showers, then warm. 14-25 Rain and snow showers, then sunny, mild. 26-31 Snow showers north; partly sunny, cold.

FEB. 2004: Temp. 53° (1° above avg.); precip. 0.4" (0.2" below avg.). 1-3 Showers. 4-8 Sunny, then showers. 9-13 Mostly cloudy, mild. 14-24 Showers, then sunny. 25-29 Turning colder, mountain snow.

MAR. 2004: Temp. 61° (5° above avg. west; 1° above east); precip. 0.1" (0.5" below avg.). 1-7 Sunny, warm. 8-11 Sunny, cool. 12-17 Sunny, warm. 18-31 Showers, then partly sunny, warm.

APR. 2004: Temp. 67° (1° above avg.); precip. 0.3" (0.1" below avg.). 1-11 Partly sunny; scattered t-storms. 12-20 Warm, clouds and sun, scattered t-storms. 21-24 Sunny, warm. 25-30 Showers, then sunny, cool.

MAY 2004: Temp. 75° (1° above avg.); precip. 0.2" (0.1" below avg.). 1-7 Sunny, very warm. 8-14 T-storms east; sunny, warm. 15-24 Scattered t-storms, then sunny, warm. 25-31 Partly sunny, warm; scattered t-storms.

JUNE 2004: Temp. 88° (4° above avg.); precip. 0.2" (0.1" below avg.). 1-5 Sunny, hot. 6-14 Partly sunny, hot; scattered t-storms west. 15-18 Partly sunny, hot; scattered t-storms east. 19-30 Partly sunny, hot; scattered t-storms.

JULY 2004: Temp. 90° (2° above avg.); precip. 1.1" (0.1" above avg.). 1-10 Partly sunny, hot; scattered t-storms. 11-14 Partly sunny, very warm; scattered t-storms. 15-21 Partly sunny, hot; scattered t-storms. 22-26 Partly sunny, very warm; scattered t-storms. 27-31 T-storms.

AUG. 2004: Temp. 88° (1° above avg.); precip. 1.8" (0.3" above avg.). 1-7 Partly sunny, very warm; scattered t-storms. 8-21 Partly sunny, warm, t-storms. 22-31 Sunny, hot.

SEPT. 2004: Temp. 79° (2° below avg.); precip. 0.5" (0.5" below avg.). 1-3 Sunny, hot. 4-9 Partly sunny, warm; scattered t-storms west. 10-17 Mostly sunny, warm; scattered t-storms east. 18-22 Sunny, seasonable. 23-30 T-storms, cool.

OCT. 2004: Temp. 70° (2° above avg.); precip. 1" (1" above avg. west; 0.5" below east). 1-4 Sunny, cool. 5-8 Warm west, scattered t-storms east. 9-20 Sunny, very warm. 21-27 T-storms, cooler. 28-31 Sunny, cool.

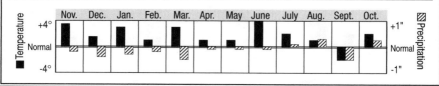

Pacific Northwest

SUMMARY: Winter will be relatively mild. Although most days will be milder than normal, cold air will dominate between Christmas and New Year, in early February, and in early to mid-November. Expect above-normal precipitation, with most spots getting more snow than normal. The most widespread snow will occur during late December and early February, with the heaviest rainfalls in mid-November, early and mid-January, and early February.

April and May will be a bit cooler than normal, with above-normal rainfall in most spots due to a storm in mid-to late April.

The summer will feature near-normal temperatures, with more rain than usual in the north and less in the south. The hottest temperatures will occur in mid- and late July, with other very warm spells in mid-June and early July.

September will be cooler than normal, with above-normal rainfall in most of the region. October will start with cool temperatures and heavy rain, but the rest of the month will be drier than normal with above-normal temperatures.

NOV. 2003: Temp. 45.5° (0.5° below avg.); precip. 6.5" (2" above avg. north; 1" below south). 1-7 Cloudy, light rain. 8-10 Partly sunny, chilly. 11-16 Rain, mild. 17-18 Colder, rain and snow. 19-22 Partly sunny, cold. 23-30 Light rain, warm, then cool.

DEC. 2003: Temp. 46° (4° above avg.); precip. 5.5" (1" above avg. north; 2" below south). 1-5 Rain, mild. 6-10 Occasional sunshine, cool. 11-25 Rain, mild. 26-31 Cold, sunny, then snow.

JAN. 2004: Temp. 47° (6° above avg.); precip. 10" (4" above avg.). 1-6 Stormy; heavy rain. 7-14 Mild; occasional rain. 15-21 Heavy rain, warm. 22-31 Sunny intervals, showers.

FEB. 2004: Temp. 44° (avg.); precip. 4.5" (avg.). 1-4 Cold, rain and snow. 5-9 Some sunshine, then rain and snow. 10-22 Mostly cloudy, light rain. 23-29 Clouds and sun, sprinkles.

MAR. 2004: Temp. 47° (avg.); precip. 3.5" (avg.). 1-7 Seasonable, light rain. 8-20 Rain and occasional sunshine. 21-25 Rain. 26-31 Partly sunny; scattered showers.

APR. 2004: Temp. 49° (1° below avg.); precip. 2.5" (1" above avg. north; 1" below south). 1-7 Partly sunny, seasonable. 8-11 Cool, showers. 12-18 Sunny, warm. 19-24 Rain. 25-30 Cool, showers.

MAY 2004: Temp. 55° (1° below avg.); precip. 2" (0.5" above avg.). 1-4 Cool, showers. 5-12 Sunny, then showers, cool. 13-17 Sunny, nice. 18-22 Showers, cool. 23-26 Sunny, warm. 27-31 Rain.

JUNE 2004: Temp. 62° (1° below avg.); precip. 1.5" (1" above avg. north; 0.5" below south). 1-5 Cool, t-storms. 6-10 Partly sunny, showers. 11-14 Sunny, very warm. 15-22 Showers, cool. 23-25 Sunny, warm. 26-30 Showers.

JULY 2004: Temp. 70° (2° above avg.); precip. 0.5" (0.5" below avg.). 1-5 Sunny, very warm. 6-10 Sunny, nice. 11-16 Sunny, hot. 17-23 Showers, then sunny, cool. 24-31 Hot, then showers.

AUG. 2004: Temp. 68° (1° below avg.); precip. 1.5" (1" above avg. north; avg. south). 1-19 Sunny, seasonable. 20-31 Showers, cool.

SEPT. 2004: Temp. 62° (2° below avg.); precip. 3" (2" above avg. north; 0.5" below south). 1-6 Sunny, nice. 7-22 Mostly cloudy, showers. 23-30 Sunny, then showers.

OCT. 2004: Temp. 57° (avg. north; 2° above south); precip. 3" (0.5" above avg. north; 1" below south). 1-6 Rain, cool. 7-12 Partly sunny, seasonable. 13-18 Warm, rain. 19-31 Partly sunny, showers.

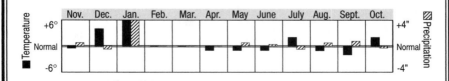

California

SUMMARY: Winter will be one of the mildest ever in southern California, with temperatures three to five degrees above normal, on average. Elsewhere, temperatures won't be quite as mild but will still be two to three degrees above normal. The coldest temperatures will occur in late December. Rainfall and mountain snowfall will be below normal, with the stormiest periods from late December to early January and in the first half of February.

Temperatures in April and May will be well above normal near the coast but a bit cooler than normal in the Valley and the desert. Expect widespread showers in mid- to late April, with scattered showers in early to mid-May.

The summer will be dry, with temperatures near normal inland and well above normal near the coast. Expect hot temperatures just about everywhere in early July, with other hot periods in early and mid-August.

Temperatures will be warmer than normal in September and October, with hot spells in early September and early to mid-October. The best chances for rain are in early and late September and late October.

NOV. 2003: Temp. 56.5° (2° below avg. north; 3° above south); precip. 1.5" (1" below avg.). 1-9 Showers, warm, then cooler. 10-17 Sunny, seasonable. 18-21 Low clouds and fog. 22-30 Sunny, warm.

DEC. 2003: Temp. 52° (2° above avg.); precip. 1.5" (1" below avg.). 1-11 Sunny, warm. 12-18 Showers north, sunny south. 19-22 Showers. 23-31 Chilly, then rain.

JAN. 2004: Temp. 54° (5° above avg.); precip. 2" (1.5" below avg.). 1-8 Mild; rain north, haze south. 9-17 Partly sunny, mild. 18-23 Mild; showers north, sunny south. 24-31 Sunny, seasonable.

FEB. 2004: Temp. 54.5° (4° above avg. west; 1° above east); precip. 4.5" (1.5" above avg.). 1-5 T-storms. 6-8 Partly sunny, seasonable. 9-12 Heavy t-storms. 13-16 Showers. 17-29 Sunny, turning warm.

MAR. 2004: Temp. 59° (5° above avg. west; 3° above east); precip. 1" (1.5" below avg.). 1-14 Sunny, warm. 15-24 Cooler; showers north, partly sunny south. 25-29 Partly sunny, warm. 30-31 Showers.

APR. 2004: Temp. 60.5° (4° above avg. west; 1° above east); precip. 1" (0.5" below avg.). 1-6 Sunny, warm. 7-15 Sunny, seasonable. 16-20 Showers. 21-23 Partly sunny, warm. 24-30 Showers, then cool.

MAY 2004: Temp. 63.5° (3° above avg. west; 2° below east); precip. 0.3" (0.3" below avg.). 1-5 Sunny, warm. 6-14 Showers, then sunny. 15-20 Mostly cloudy; scattered t-storms north. 21-31 Mostly sunny, seasonable.

JUNE 2004: Temp. 68.5° (3° above avg. west; avg. east); precip. 0" (0.1" below avg.). 1-10 Mostly sunny, seasonable. 11-17 Sunny; hot inland. 18-30 Sunny, warm.

JULY 2004: Temp. 72.5° (4° above avg. west; 1° above east); precip. 0" (avg.). 1-6 Partly sunny, hot. 7-31 Mostly sunny, warm.

AUG. 2004: Temp. 71° (4° above avg. west; 2° below east); precip. 0" (avg.). 1-6 Mostly sunny, t-storms inland, warm southwest, hot elsewhere. 7-11 Mostly sunny, seasonable. 12-15 Mostly cloudy, cool inland. 16-20 Warm; scattered t-storms. 21-31 Hazy sunshine, warm.

SEPT. 2004: Temp. 67.5° (3° above avg. west; 2° below east); precip. 1.3" (2" above avg. south). 1-5 Sunny, hot. 6-14 Partly sunny; scattered t-storms. 15-22 Sunny, warm. 23-30 Mostly sunny, seasonable; scattered showers south.

OCT. 2004: Temp. 65° (3° above avg.); precip. 0.1" (1" below avg. north; 0.5" below south). 1-3 Mostly cloudy. 4-11 Sunny, hot. 12-18 Sunny, warm. 19-31 Partly sunny; scattered t-storms south.

San Francisco

Fresno

Los Angeles

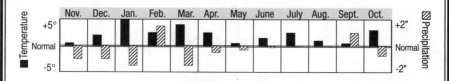

HOW TO FEEL GOOD
ALL OVER

Whether you've got a headache, a stuffed sinus, a burn on the roof of your mouth, a hacking cough, hiccups, a swollen joint, or a blood blister on a toe, one of these simple solutions should help you get back into tip-top shape.

by Steve Calechman

FROM THE TOP OF YOUR HEAD ...

■ **Feel a headache coming on? Pinch yourself. Specifically, put the squeeze on the webbed area between the thumb and first finger of either hand. Hold it for 30 seconds. Pressure applied here will stimulate nerve impulses to the brain and relax blood vessel dilation. Your headache won't have a chance to settle in.**

UP YOUR NOSE

■ When your head feels under pressure and your nose is all stuffed up, and even your teeth hurt, you don't have a common cold. You have a sinus infection. To get relief, mix ½ teaspoon of salt into 1 cup of water. (Use cool water if you're stuffed up but have no discharge. If the mucus is thick, use warm water to help liquefy it.) Bring the mixture into the shower and set it to the side. Turn on the hot water and let it hit your face for three to five minutes. Hot water helps liquefy and drain the mucus. Now pour some salt water into a cupped hand and inhale, so the water goes up your nose. This alleviates irritation, washes out the mucus, and kills bacteria. Spit out what goes down into your throat, and gargle with the rest of the salt water to clear your throat. You can do this snorting/gargling routine up to four times a day.

IN YOUR MOUTH

■ Who hasn't burned the roof of his or her mouth on a hot piece of pizza? To relieve that singed skin, put equal amounts of water and hydrogen peroxide in a glass. Take a sip, and swish the solution around in your mouth. The mixture helps dissolve dead tissue, and its fizziness is soothing. To avoid the chance of upsetting your stomach or getting minor heartburn, spit out the solution instead of swallowing it.

Seltzer also works. It won't kill bacteria, but it's soothing and you can swallow it without worry.

DOWN YOUR THROAT

■ A quick, easy way to quiet a dry, hacking cough is to chew gingerroot. Cut off a quarter-inch piece, trim off the peel, and put it into your mouth. Chew it slowly; the juice will feel hot in the mouth and throat, and the cough will be gone in a minute. The ginger brings blood to the throat and helps soothe it. When you're finished chewing, spit out the pulp.

continued

IN YOUR CHEST

■ We can never have too many remedies for hiccups, so here's another. Swallow a teaspoonful or small packet's worth of dry sugar. The sugar will suck water from the tissue in the back of your throat, stimulating nerves that relax your diaphragm, which is in spasm.

AT YOUR JOINTS

■ Square ice cubes never sit quite right on swollen wrists, ankles, and other body parts—so make your own flexible cold pack. Fill a resealable plastic bag with 3 parts water and 1 part rubbing alcohol, and put it into the freezer. The mixture will form into a slushy compound that will conform to any part of the body. When the swelling goes down, pop the bag back into the freezer till the next time. (There's always a next time.)

TO THE TIPS OF YOUR FINGERS AND TOES

■ When a painful blood blister forms under a fingernail or toenail, get a small metal paper clip (not a plastic-coated one) and straighten out one end of it. Light a match and, while holding the clip with a pair of tweezers or pliers, heat the straightened end. Touch the hot metal tip to the surface of the nail just above the half-moon, so that it goes through. The blood will drain and relief will be yours.

Steve Calechman, who frequently writes on natural health subjects for *Men's Health* and other magazines, rendered a case of hiccups mute almost instantly with a packet of sugar.

□□

SCIATICA RELIEF!

If you want to get relief from Sciatica and have suffered symptoms such as: pain in the buttocks, pain in lower back, pain shooting down one or both legs, or numbness in your legs or feet, you should get a copy of the new book, *The Sciatica Relief Handbook*. The book covers the latest natural, alternative and medical solutions to sciatica. The book reveals how virtually everyone can put an end to sciatica symptoms thanks to new understandings of this problem.

Over 165 million people experience sciatica and lower back discomfort. Many people are needlessly suffering because they are not aware of new ways to put an end to this problem. This book is of vital importance to every person suffering from sciatica or lower back pain.

The book tells you what causes sciatica symptoms, how to alleviate the symptoms and how to prevent and protect yourself from future sciatica and lower back problems. You'll learn about new natural remedies and treatments and find out how and why they work—without unnecessary drugs or surgery.

You'll discover: ● how a simple exercise brings dramatic relief ● specific pressure points that soothe the sciatic nerve ● vital tips to prevent possible serious problems ● what you must know about the mineral potassium ● how certain foods promote healing of the sciatic nerve.

The book explains all about the sciatic nerve, the various ways it may become inflamed and cause pain, how to find out specifically what causes distress (you may be surprised), and what to do and what not to do to prevent flare-ups.

Get all the facts. Put an end to sciatica and lower back pain once and for all. *The Sciatica Relief Handbook* is available for only $14.95, *plus $3 P&H (CA residents add $1.09 sales tax)*. To order, send your name and address with check or money order to United Research Publishers, Dept. 30-22; 132 N. El Camino Real #T; Encinitas CA 92024. For VISA or MasterCard, send card number and expiration date. You may return the book within 90 days for a refund if not completely satisfied.

www.unitedresearchpubs.com

IRRITABLE BOWEL SYNDROME

NATURAL FREEDOM FROM SYMPTOMS

If you suffer from Irritable Bowel Syndrome (IBS) and experience constipation, bloating, diarrhea, gas, stomach cramps, heartburn, pain and discomfort, you should know about a new book, *The Irritable Bowel Syndrome & Gastrointestinal Solutions Handbook*.

This book gives you facts on new up-to-date, all-natural, and alternative ways to stop IBS and gastrointestinal problems. You'll learn all about these new measures and how to beat these problems once and for all—without drugs or surgery.

You'll discover what you can do to avoid Irritable Bowel, colon and digestive problems, what foods promote healing and what to avoid, a safe, natural gel readily available at health food stores that flushes out toxins and clears inflammation, what you should know about peppermint oil and gluten—and why IBS is so often misdiagnosed by doctors. The book reveals simple, natural remedies that are helping thousands overcome IBS every day.

Here's what satisfied readers of the book report: Mrs. Castor said, "after 2 years of searching for relief I ordered your book and finally found relief." Mr. Allen wrote that, thanks to the book, he has been free from IBS symptoms for six months. Mr. Swanson said his wife has been bothered by IBS for years. "She followed your simple tips in the book and is much improved. Our doctor wants a copy."

Many people are putting up with IBS, stomach and digestive problems because they are unaware of new, natural treatments revealed in this book.

Get all the facts. This book is available for only $14.95, *plus $3 P&H (CA residents add $1.09 sales tax)*. To order, send your name and address with a check or money order to: United Research Publishers, Dept. 30-23; 132 N. El Camino Real #T; Encinitas CA 92024. For MasterCard or VISA send card number and expiration date. You may return the book within 90 days for a refund if not completely satisfied.

www.unitedresearchpubs.com

A TUB OF TRUTHS ABOUT ICE CREAM

A tribute to ice cream on the 100th anniversary of the cone.

by Alice Cary

The history of ice cream is a messy one. Although some facts are fixed in time, others are as mixed up as a bowl of chocolate-vanilla swirl. Many nations claim to have invented it, just as various individuals take credit for it. Still, it makes for a chilling drama. So grab a bowl of your favorite flavor or make up a batch with the recipes here, and dig in.

A.D. 54–68 **618–907**

● **For centuries, iced desserts were a** luxury. Roman Emperor Nero is said to have sent his slaves into the mountains to fetch snow to mix with nectar, fruit pulp, and honey, although this widely told tale may be a myth.

—Corbis

The origins of ice cream date back ●— to China's T'ang period (A.D. 618–907), probably as a dish for the country's rulers. The founder of the dynasty, King T'ang of Shang, kept 94 "ice men" on hand to lug ice to the palace. One early treat was made of koumiss (heated, fermented milk) combined with flour and camphor, and cooled.

The Creams That Rise to the Top

America's favorite ice creams include:

1. vanilla
2. chocolate
3. Neapolitan
4. butter pecan
5. chocolate chip

1744   **1782**

—Corbis

Ever hear how Martha Washington left a bowl of sweet cream on the back steps of Mount Vernon one night, and the next morning discovered iced cream? Nice story, but not true.

Nonetheless, George Washington had ice cream at a party hosted by the French minister in Philadelphia in July 1782. Two years later, the future president noted in his ledger that he purchased "a cream machine for ice." George and Martha often served the frozen treat at gatherings, once ordering $200 worth from a local confectioner.

American colonists brought along recipes from Europe. On May 19, 1744, a group of VIPs dined at the home of Maryland Governor Thomas Bladen in Annapolis. The group was negotiating with the Iroquois to buy land west of the Allegheny Mountains. Present was a Scottish colonist named William Black, who in his journal described "a Dessert . . . Among the Rarities of which it was Compos'd, was some fine Ice Cream which, with the Strawberries and Milk, eat most Deliciously." This is the first known written account of ice-cream consumption in the new colonies.

(c o n t i n u e d)

145

Good Reasons to Have Ice Cream for Dinner

- Green-tea, curry, and sea-urchin ice cream can be found in Japanese restaurants.
- Asian ice-cream shops often offer red-bean ice cream.
- Ben & Bill's Chocolate Emporium in Bar Harbor, Maine, serves lobster ice cream.

1790   **1843**   **1850**

In the 1780s, Thomas Jefferson brought a handwritten recipe for vanilla ice cream home from Paris. Dolley Madison, a frequent hostess, often served ice cream. She dished out strawberries with ice cream at the second inaugural festivities of her husband, James, in 1813.

By the late 1790s, ice cream was a popular treat in "pleasure gardens," establishments that first appeared in New York. Vanilla and lemon were the most common flavors; pineapple, strawberry, and raspberry began to appear in 1810. These gardens helped women overcome the then-popular notion that ladies should not eat in public. As ice-cream recipes appeared in American cookbooks, such as *The Universal Receipt Book* of 1814, which featured pineapple ice cream, ladies began making their own. Not everyone loved it, however. People commonly feared that eating cold foods and drinks was unhealthy and bad for digestion.

Until September 9, 1843, ice cream was made by the "pot freezer method," but on this day, the U.S. Patent Office issued a patent to

—Corbis

Nancy M. Johnson of Philadelphia for an "artificial freezer" for ice cream, containing a tub, cylinder, lid, dasher, and crank. Her design inspired many others.

Baltimore dairyman Jacob Fussell saw an opportunity when he realized that he had a sur-plus of cream. To use it up, in the early 1850s he built an ice-cream factory in Seven Valleys, Pennsylvania, and sent his product (packed

—The Maryland Historical Society, Baltimore, Maryland

in ice) by train to Baltimore. Business boomed, with sales spreading to Washington, D.C.; Boston; and New York—making Fussell the father of the wholesale ice-cream industry.

■ The Coromoto, a shop in Merida, Venezuela, has been noted by the *Guinness Book of World Records* for offering hundreds of flavors, including trout, tuna, spaghetti, garlic, champagne, and chili pepper.

1878   1880   1862–1896

● William Clewell of Reading, Pennsylvania, came up with a way to dish up ice cream faster. In 1878, he patented the first mechanical disher, or scoop. It required two hands—one to scoop the ice cream and another to turn a scraper. In the 1890s, the Kingery Company in Ohio sold the first one-handed scoop.

–Charlie Cook

The ice-cream sundae has a check- ● ered past: Buffalo, New York; Evanston, Illinois; Two Rivers, Wisconsin; and Ithaca, New York, all claim to have invented it. Wherever it happened, the new treat first appeared in the 1880s at soda fountains. The name was a

–Corbis

reference to Sunday, because officials across the nation prohibited selling ice-cream sodas on that day of the week. This new sensation of ice cream, syrups, and other toppings may have been concocted as a way to circumvent the restriction. Exactly when the new spelling, sundae, came along isn't known; early versions also included "sundi," "sundhi," and "sundaye."

For years, vanilla was the most popu- ● lar ice-cream flavor in America. After the Civil War, as chocolate candy became popular, the demand for chocolate ice cream spread. Charles Ranhofer, chef at New York City's famed Delmonico's

147

The United States leads the world in ice-cream production (a total of 1.6 billion gallons in 2000), followed by China and Canada.

1920   1927   1938

restaurant from 1862 to 1896, became known for his many ice-cream flavors, including caramel, cinnamon, ginger, and lemon, as well as pumpernickel rye and rice. He molded his asparagus ice cream into the shape of asparagus spears and tied them with ribbon. He also fashioned "potatoes" out of chestnut ice cream rolled in chocolate, with almond slivers for eyes. Ranhofer is often credited with inventing baked Alaska, ice cream covered with meringue and baked, to commemorate the U.S. purchase of Alaska from Russia.

● **In 1920, the Prohibition Act forced** many bar owners to open ice-cream parlors as a way to stay in business. Even Anheuser-Busch and other beermakers switched to making ice cream. As a result, annual American consumption jumped from 260 million gallons in 1920 to 365 million in 1929.

Not only were Americans eating ice ● cream, they were singing about it. In 1927, the famous "Ice Cream" song ("I scream, you scream, we all scream for ice cream!") appeared,

—Corbis

written by Billy Moll, Howard Johnson, and Robert King and performed by Fred Waring's Pennsylvanians. (This Howard Johnson, by the way, was a Tin Pan Alley composer, not the Howard Johnson who founded the restaurant chain.)

In 1938, J. F. "Grandpa" McCullough ● and his son, H. A. McCullough, owners of the Homemade Ice Cream Company in Green River, Illinois, invented the first soft-serve

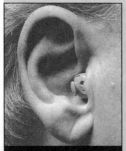
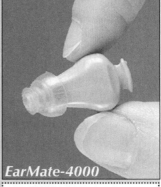
2004   THE OLD FARMER'S ALMANAC   149

1939

1943

ice cream. They later named their product Dairy Queen, because they believed it would prove to be the queen of dairy products.

● **Grocery stores didn't start selling ice** cream until the 1930s—and if you

—Corbis

bought it there, you had to eat it soon. The first dual-compartment, dual-temperature refrigerator with a separate freezer compartment didn't appear until 1939.

By World War II, ice cream had be- ● come so popular that it turned into something of an American sym-

bol. (Mussolini actually banned ice cream in Italy for that very reason.) Ice cream was great for troop

—Corbis

morale, and in 1943, the U.S. Armed Forces were the world's largest manufacturers. Some enterprising U.S. airmen even managed to make ice cream in the rear gunner compartment of an aircraft bomber.

Today, thankfully, **whenever we hanker for ice cream, we need look no further than that wonderful invention—the freezer—in which we can stock any number of sinfully rich cartons. The hardest part is figuring out which flavor to eat.**

(c o n t i n u e d)

How to find the right long-term care policy

Americans are living longer than ever and are now facing the important decision of whether to purchase long-term care insurance. Most people will buy this coverage to protect their assets, preserve their independence and provide quality care.

In general, long-term care protection makes sense for those with assets of at least $100,000 (not including your home and car) and an annual income of at least $35,000.

With over 100 policies on the market — each with different benefits, premiums, exclusions and application requirements — it pays to comparison shop. According to respected *Money Magazine* financial editor Jean Chatzky, "Your best bet is to get quotes from at least three companies." In addition, you should consider a policy with at least a three-year term — the average time people need care.

Look for a daily benefit that would cover the average daily nursing-facility cost in your area. The national average is $140 per day, or over $50,000 per year.* However, in some areas it can run twice as much. Look for an elimination period (the time before your benefits begin) of 90 days. Remember, this is catastrophic coverage. Most people who need the insurance can afford the cost of care for three months. Plus, this approach lowers your cost — in some cases by as much as 30% per year. Equally important, insist on insurers rated "A" or better by A.M. Best and "strong" by Standard & Poor's and Moody's.

If you'd like to receive three quotes with just one call, Long-Term Care Quote will provide them — free of charge. The company which has been recommended in *Consumers Digest, Kiplinger's* and on NBC — will ask for basic information on your age, health and location, then shop 15 top-rated carriers on your behalf. You'll get details and quotes on the three best policies for you and a copy of *The Consumer's Guide to Long-Term Care Insurance*. Plus, no agent will call or visit.

To request your free policy comparisons and personalized quotes, either write to Long-Term Care Quote, 25 South Arizona Place, Suite 560 Chandler, AZ 85225 (please include your date of birth and Special Code #292), visit www.LTCQ.net or call toll-free 1-800-587-3279.

*The Health Insurance Association of America, 2002; Writing agent Robert W. Davis, CA License #0B78024

The Scoop on the Cone

■ In the late 1800s, paper and metal cones were available in France, and edible waffle cones could be had in Germany. Debate rages over several vendors at the 1904 World's Fair in St. Louis, all of whom claim to have invented the ice-cream cone on this side of the Atlantic. Two major contenders are Syrian immigrant Ernest A. Hamwi and Italian immigrant Italo Marchiony. No matter who deserves credit—Hamwi, Marchiony, or another—after the St. Louis

MAKE YOUR OWN OLD-FASHIONED
ICE CREAM

These recipes from the archives of *The Old Farmer's Almanac* predate electric ice-cream makers but can be used with them. If you use an electric ice-cream maker, follow the directions for freezing. For directions for using a hand-crank freezer, go to www.almanac.com and click on Article Links 2004.

—Corbis

Vanilla Ice Cream

4 cups heavy cream
1 cup sugar
1/8 teaspoon salt
1 1/2 teaspoons vanilla extract (or a vanilla pod heated in the cream and then removed)

■ Heat 1 cup of the cream very slowly; do not boil. Stir in sugar and salt until dissolved. Chill. Add remaining 3 cups cream and vanilla. Stir. Freeze. When the mixture is nearly solid, take it out of the freezer and beat it vigorously by hand or with an electric beater (or, for a lighter texture, put it into a blender at top speed) for several minutes. Return it to the freezer until solid.

Makes 1 1/2 quarts.

fair, factories started churning out cones. Not until the late 1940s, however, did the flat-bottom cone appear, when Joseph Shapiro of the Maryland Cup Corporation made it for Dairy Queen bars, so that workers could stand the cones on counters.

Strawberry or Peach Ice Cream

2 cups mashed fruit
1 cup sugar
1/8 teaspoon salt
1 teaspoon vanilla extract
4 cups cream

■ Place fruit into a large bowl; stir in sugar and salt until dissolved. Chill. Add vanilla extract and cream, mix, and freeze. When the mixture is nearly solid, take it out of the freezer and beat it vigorously by hand or with an electric beater (or, for a lighter texture, put it into a blender at top speed) for several minutes. Return it to the freezer until solid.

Makes about 2 quarts.

Alice Cary is a contributing editor at *Biography Magazine.* Her books include biographies of children's authors Jean Craighead George and Katherine Paterson.

DISH IT UP
Sooner or later, we all scream for ice cream! For a recipe for Chocolate Ice Cream and more ice-cream trivia, go to **www.almanac.com** and click on **Article Links 2004.**

Of Dairy Queens and Kings

Men shovel it in, but women are more discriminating when it comes to their ice cream. According to a poll conducted for Dreyer's Grand Ice Cream of Oakland, California:

■ 25% of men consider four scoops of ice cream to be an average serving.

■ 40% of men have seconds.

■ Two scoops are a typical serving for women.

■ 61% of women never have seconds.

■ Women pick through their ice cream to find goodies such as pieces of cookie dough, nuts, or candies.

■ Nearly 50% of men surveyed claim that they never pick out the goodies.

■ 66% of men will eat the last of the ice cream in a carton rather than save it for someone else.

Cool Facts

■ It takes 12 pounds of milk to make just one gallon of ice cream.

■ It takes an average of 50 licks to polish off a single-scoop ice-cream cone.

■ The biggest ice-cream sundae in history was made in Edmonton, Alberta, Canada, in 1988, and weighed over 24 tons.

■ In 1999, residents of Omaha, Nebraska, bought more ice cream per person than residents of any other U.S. city.

■ Children ages 2 to 12 and adults age 45 and over eat the most ice cream per person.

■ More ice cream is sold on Sunday than on any other day of the week.

■ One out of every five ice-cream eaters shares their treat with their dog or cat.

153

Winning Recipes

in the 2003 Recipe Contest

garlic to potatoes, and stir in parsley, basil, salt, pepper, and cheese. Spoon potatoes into a casserole lightly greased with olive oil and place into a preheated 350°F oven. Bake until lightly browned.

Serves 8 to 10.

–Deborah Coberly Goranflo, La Grange, Kentucky

Potatoes

FIRST PRIZE

Italian Potato Torte

3 pounds white potatoes, peeled and cut into pieces
1 1/2 cups milk
1/4 cup (1/2 stick) butter
3 tablespoons olive oil
3 cloves garlic, minced
2 teaspoons dried parsley, crumbled
1 teaspoon dried basil, crumbled
1 teaspoon salt
1/2 teaspoon pepper
1/2 cup grated Asiago cheese

Place potatoes in a large pot with enough water to cover. Bring to a boil over medium-high heat, lower heat, and simmer uncovered until potatoes are tender. Drain potatoes and set aside. In a small saucepan, heat milk and butter over medium heat until milk begins to steam and butter is melted. Add to potatoes and mash with a potato masher. In a small skillet, warm the olive oil over medium heat, just until fragrant. Add garlic and cook until it begins to brown. Add oil and

SECOND PRIZE

Potato Pancakes with Maple Sausage

2 1/2 cups mashed potatoes
1 large 'Granny Smith' apple, peeled, cored, and grated
1/2 pound maple-flavored sausage, browned and crumbled
2 scallions, chopped
2 eggs
1/3 cup flour
1/2 teaspoon salt
1/2 teaspoon ground white pepper
vegetable oil, for frying
6 tablespoons sour cream (optional)

In a large bowl, stir together the first eight ingredients. Heat 1 or 2 tablespoons of oil in a large skillet on medium-low heat. Drop batter into the skillet to make 4-inch pancakes. Brown on both sides, frying for about 5 minutes on each side. Remove from pan and drain on paper towels. Repeat until batter is used up, adding oil to the skillet between batches as needed. Serve immediately, with 1 tablespoon of sour cream on each pancake, if desired. **Serves 6 to 8.**

–Deborah Puette, Lilburn, Georgia

Crispy Potato Quiche

1 package (24 ounces) frozen shredded hash
   browns, thawed
1/3 cup butter, melted
1 cup shredded hot-pepper cheese
1 cup shredded Swiss cheese
1 cup diced cooked ham
1/2 cup half-and-half
2 eggs
1/4 teaspoon seasoned salt

Press thawed hash browns between paper towels to remove moisture. Press the hash browns into a greased 10-inch pie plate, forming a solid crust. Brush crust with melted butter, especially the top edges. Bake at 425°F for 25 minutes, or until golden. Remove and spread cheeses and ham evenly on the crust. Beat half-and-half with eggs and salt; pour over cheese and ham. Bake uncovered at 350°F for 30 to 40 minutes, until a knife inserted into the center comes out clean. **Serves 8.**

–Amy Kerby, Omaha, Nebraska

Editor's note: If frozen hash browns are not available, substitute 4 heaping cups grated raw potatoes, rinsed in cold water and blanched in boiling water. Remove moisture as directed.

Mashed-Potato Candy

3/4 cup mashed potatoes
1 cup pecans, chopped
1 pound powdered sugar
1 package (14 ounces) shredded coconut
1/2 pound semisweet chocolate almond bark,
   melted

Combine the first four ingredients, and chill mixture in refrigerator for 1 hour. Remove from the refrigerator. Spoon out and roll between palms to form small balls. Dip balls into melted chocolate and place on waxed paper to dry. Store in an airtight container.
Makes about 36.

–Jackie Branstetter, Frankford, Missouri

ANNOUNCING

THE 2004 RECIPE CONTEST

Apple Dishes
(anything but pie)

■ An apple a day keeps the doctor away, so show us the many ways we can feast on one (or more). Send us your best recipes using any type and amount of apples as the main ingredient in appetizers, main dishes, salads, side dishes, or desserts, but not pies. (We'll have a pie contest at another time.)

RECIPE AND ESSAY CONTEST RULES

Cash prizes (first prize, $100; second prize, $75; third prize, $50) will be awarded for the best recipes for apple dishes (amateur cooks only, please) and the best original essays on the subject "The Best Decision I Ever Made." All entries become the property of Yankee Publishing Inc., which reserves all rights to the material. The deadline for entries is January 28, 2004. Please type all entries. Label "Essay Contest" or "Recipe Contest" and send to: The Old Farmer's Almanac, P.O. Box 520, Dublin, NH 03444; or send e-mail (subject: Essay Contest or Recipe Contest) to almanac@yankeepub.com. Be sure to include your name and mailing address. Winners will be announced in *The 2005 Old Farmer's Almanac* and posted on our Web site, www.almanac.com.

(See page 186 for the winners in the 2003 Essay Contest.)

Never Say No to
ZUCCHINI

Four ways to use one of the garden's most abundant and underappreciated vegetables.

by Martie Majoros

*F*ew fresh vegetables inspire the reactions that zucchini does. We all love a little, but most of us don't know what to do with a lot. (How many ways can you make zucchini bread?)

The next time you find yourself with more zucchinis than you can handle, whether they're from your own garden or from that of a friend, don't despair. Cook up one of these easy and delicious recipes, kitchen-tested and tasted by the editors of *The Old Farmer's Almanac*. Once you've sampled a few of these dishes, you may find yourself thinking about ways to *increase* next summer's zucchini harvest!

Zucchini Marmalade

This marmalade, with a slight hint of lemon and ginger, will disappear when served with warm scones.

2 pounds zucchini, washed and grated
1 teaspoon grated lemon peel
juice from 1/2 lemon
1 can (13 ounces) crushed pineapple, drained
1 package (1 3/4 ounces) powdered fruit pectin
5 cups sugar
2 tablespoons finely chopped crystallized ginger
melted paraffin, to seal jars

■ Put zucchini into a large kettle and add lemon peel, lemon juice, and pineapple. Bring ingredients to a boil over high heat. Lower heat and continue to simmer, uncovered, until zucchini is tender. Add pectin. Bring to a boil again, and stir in the sugar and ginger. Boil hard for 1 minute, stirring constantly. Remove from heat and skim off foam. Stir for 5 minutes to prevent zucchini from floating. Ladle into sterilized jelly jars, and seal with ¼ inch of paraffin. **Makes 6 pints.**

(c o n t i n u e d)

Growing and Serving Tips

Zucchini likes warm weather, so plant it in a sunny location after the soil has warmed to at least 70°F. Once planted, it requires little attention, needing to be watered only in drought situations. With minimal effort, you will soon be reaping the rewards of an abundant harvest.

Most seed catalogs and nurseries offer several varieties of zucchinis. Keep these ideas in mind as you make your choice:

■

The dark-green 'Black Beauty' is a tried-and-true favorite that's virtually foolproof.

■

If garden space is limited, look for varieties that are suited to container growing. 'Spacemiser' and 'Aristocrat' are prolific producers that grow well in large half-barrel containers.

■

One of the more unusual varieties, deep-yellow 'Gold Rush' zucchini adds a festive touch when grated raw and tossed into a salad.

■

Small globe-shaped varieties, such as 'Roly Poly' or 'Eight Ball', can be used in any zucchini recipe. Having a party? Seed one and use it as a serving bowl, filled with your favorite dip for fresh veggies. Or slice it into rounds or strips for dipping.

Zucchini Sausage Squares

Versatile and hearty, this casserole will claim center stage at any brunch, lunch, or dinner table.

12 ounces bulk pork sausage
3/4 cup finely chopped onion
2 cloves garlic, minced
4 large eggs
2 large zucchinis, grated
1/2 cup Parmesan cheese
1/2 cup bread crumbs
1 teaspoon dried basil
1/2 teaspoon dried oregano
1/4 teaspoon salt
1/8 teaspoon black pepper
1 cup grated sharp Cheddar cheese

■ Preheat oven to 375°F. Sauté sausage, onion, and garlic until sausage is well done. Drain fat. In a medium bowl, beat eggs until frothy. Add the zucchini, Parmesan cheese, bread crumbs, seasonings, and sausage mixture, and stir until blended. Pour into a greased 11x7-inch baking dish, smooth the top, and bake for 25 minutes. Sprinkle Cheddar cheese on top and bake for 15 minutes longer, or until golden. Cut into 1½-inch squares.

Makes 35 squares.

Zucchini Pizza

Here's an all-time favorite adapted from the Moosewood Cookbook. *It's a perfect solution to an overabundance of fresh zucchinis.*

CRUST:
3 to 4 cups coarsely grated zucchini
1 teaspoon salt
2 eggs, beaten
1/3 cup flour
1/2 cup grated mozzarella or
   Cheddar cheese
1/2 cup grated Parmesan or
   Romano cheese
2 tablespoons fresh basil, or
   1 teaspoon dried
salt and freshly ground black pepper,
   to taste

TOPPING:
1/4 to 1/2 cup tomato sauce
your choice of sautéed mushrooms
   or peppers, sliced cooked sausage,
   fresh tomatoes, olives, etc.
1/2 to 1 cup grated cheese (your
   favorite kind)

■ For crust: Put zucchini into a colander, sprinkle with salt, toss, and let sit for 30 minutes. Squeeze out excess moisture with your clean hands. Preheat oven to 350°F. In a large mixing bowl, combine the zucchini, eggs, flour, cheeses, and basil, and season to taste with salt and pepper. Spread the mixture into a lightly oiled 10-inch round or 13x9-inch baking pan. Bake for 20 to 25 minutes, or until the surface is dry and just beginning to brown. Broil for 5 minutes, until top is firm and lightly browned.

Remove from oven and spread with tomato sauce.

(c o n t i n u e d)

-photo: Mike Watson

Arrange your favorite toppings over the sauce, and sprinkle with cheese. Bake for 10 to 15 minutes longer, or until cheese is melted and bubbling.

Serves 8.

Zucchini Brownies

Zucchini adds texture—and nutrition—to this traditional dessert.

1 cup margarine
1/2 cup vegetable oil
1 3/4 cups sugar
2 eggs
1 teaspoon vanilla extract
**1/2 cup milk, with 1 teaspoon lemon
    juice added to sour**
2 1/2 cups flour
1/4 cup cocoa
1/2 teaspoon baking powder
1 teaspoon baking soda
1/2 teaspoon cinnamon
1/2 teaspoon cloves
2 cups shredded zucchini
2/3 cup chocolate chips

■ Preheat oven to 325°F. In a large bowl, cream together the margarine, oil, and sugar. Add the eggs, vanilla, and sour milk, and beat until well blended. In a separate bowl, mix the flour, cocoa, baking powder, baking soda, cinnamon, cloves, and zucchini. Add the dry ingredients to the egg mixture, and stir until well blended. Spread batter into a greased and floured 13x9-inch pan, and sprinkle with chocolate chips. Bake for 40 to 45 minutes.

Makes 20 brownies.

Martie Majoros is a research editor at *The Old Farmer's Almanac*. No matter how small her garden space, she always grows zucchini. She has been known to serve meals featuring zucchini in every course.

160

Save Some for Another Day

■ If you end up with more zucchinis than you can use at one time, prepare some of them for freezing. Choose young squashes with tender skin, and you'll be able to enjoy the fresh-picked flavor long after the season has passed.

To prepare sliced zucchini: Wash and cut into 1/2-inch slices, and blanch in boiling water for 3 minutes. Drain and cool until completely dry. To prepare shredded zucchini: Wash and grate, and blanch for 1 to 2 minutes, or until translucent. Drain and cool.

To freeze, pack measured amounts of prepared zucchini into containers or freezer bags. If using a plastic container, leave about 1/2 inch of space at the top. If using plastic freezer bags, squeeze out the excess air before sealing.

□□

GET GROWING

For more zucchini recipes as well as advice on starting seedlings, preparing your soil, and gardening in containers, go to **www.almanac.com** and click on **Article Links 2004.**

The Juicy Art of Making Wild Grape Jelly

To many people, autumn means cool nights, clear dry days, and leaf peeping.

For some jellymakers, it's also time to search for wild grapes.

by Galen H. McGovern

ild grapes grow almost everywhere in the United States and Canada—almost everywhere that there are folks who like grape jelly. Finding wild grapes, picking them, and making jelly can be a fun project for the whole family.

The grapes are ripe when they achieve a dark-purple or blue color, are still firm, and from a distance don't smell like sweet grape juice. "When you can smell them, they are too ripe," says Betsey Knowles, 74, of Rhode Island, who has been making grape jelly with wild grapes for 65 years.

Grape picking doesn't require much equipment. Knowles uses hand clippers, some baskets to hold the fruit, and a stepladder to reach the high vines. She has only one rule about picking grapes: "Pick as many as you possibly can." She scours the vines at ground level and clips all

162

> Leif Eriksson
>
> named North America
>
> Vinland in A.D. 1000
>
> because of the
>
> abundance of wild grapes
>
> he found here.

that are in reach, randomly sampling them. One day last fall, on a trip to neighboring properties, Knowles harvested two brown grocery bags full.

About 10 percent were unripe, green grapes, which are important to the jelling process. The best jelly grapes are slightly tart; they have the perfect pectin content (pectin is the ingredient that causes the juice of the grapes to jell). Overripe grapes are soft and contain less pectin.

Back at her home with the grapes, she pulls them from the stems, discards the overripe and rotten fruit, and tosses the sticky jewels into a big, flat-bottomed pot. She fills the pot with water to wash the fruit and takes out any floaters (overripe or rotten grapes that were missed earlier). (continued)

How to Recognize a Wild Grape

The difference between wild and cultivated grapes is where you find them: Cultivated grapes are trained to grow on arbors.

Experts estimate that there are from 19 to 29 species of wild grapes, all of the genus *Vitis,* growing in North America, and all are suitable for making jelly. The most prevalent species in North America are *Vitis labrusca* (Alexander grape, black grape, fox grape); *V.riparia* (Bermuda vine, frost grape, June grape); *V. rupestris* (beach grape, bush grape, currant grape); and *V. rotundifolia* (American muscadine, big white grape, black grape). *V. riparia* is the most widely distributed of these. Common names can be confusing because many (for example, beach, bush, canyon, Florida, fox, frost, gulch, mustang, and sugar grapes) refer to two or more different species.

Whatever they're called, all wild grape species are easy to recognize. Look for

■ heart-shaped leaves

■ vines with shaggy bark that blanket shrubs and form canopies over trees

■ round, globular fruits

Once found, watch the grapes carefully until they are ripe. Jellymaking can get competitive among neighbors, so stake out your grapes early. Be aware that in drought years, the sugar content and flavor of grapes is higher and may make for better jelly.

After pouring off the water, she places the pot on the stove to boil, and stirs the grapes occasionally so that they don't burn. When they are slightly soft, she stands on a chair (to get sufficient lever-

Native Americans used wild grapes for food, tonics, and drink.

age), flexes her biceps, and starts crushing the grapes with a potato masher. Finally, she boils the entire batch for 30 minutes, stirring it all the while.

To filter the mixture, Knowles has her husband hold large pieces of quadruple-layered cheesecloth over a bowl while she pours the grape mixture into the cloth. Together they tie the cheesecloth around a broomstick, then suspend the stick between two stools so that the juice can drip into the bowl all night. This stage can not be hurried. "If you squeeze [the cheesecloth], the jelly won't be clear," she says.

The next day, Knowles measures the juice and pours it into a pot. Enamored with its color and smell, she puts it on high heat to boil for five minutes. While it's heating, she measures out an almost equal amount of sugar into a wooden bowl. She puts the sugar into a preheated 250°F oven and stirs it occasionally. Warm sugar "won't be a big shock" to the hot liquid, she explains. She adds the sugar carefully while the juice simmers ("I put in a little less and then taste it"), and heats the batch to boiling again.

A sweet fragrance permeates the house as the mixture boils. Knowles skims foam off the top and every few minutes dribbles juice into small bowls for tasting. After several samples, she adds more sugar.

To determine if the jelly is done, she tests it twice. First, she dips a spoon into the liquid, pulls it out, and holds it sideways. If the jelly sheets and two drops hang together from the side of the spoon, it's done. For the second test, she pours a bit of juice onto a plate and draws her finger across it "to see if the jelly wrinkles." When both tests meet with her approval, she pours the hot liquid into about 20 clean, dry, eight-ounce jars and covers the jelly with a paper-thin layer of hot paraffin. Later, when the jelly is cooled, she seals the jars with a second layer of the wax.

At the end of the day, Knowles's purple-stained shorts are a testament to the frequent required tastings. "Wild grape jelly always tastes *so* good," she says. □ □

Galen H. McGovern, a freelance writer and environmental consultant in Rhode Island, has always been interested in lost traditions involving wild foods.

IT'S JELLY TIME
Betsey Knowles bases her grape jelly loosely on the recipe in the 1930 edition of the *Boston Cooking School Cook Book,* by Fannie Farmer. For a recipe to try, go to **www.almanac.com** and click on **Article Links 2004.**

Enjoy Life the Way It Used to Be–

FREE OF ARTHRITIS PAIN!

(SPECIAL)–A small, central Indiana research company, renowned for its dedication to helping pain sufferers live normal, active lives has developed a special cream that relieves arthritis pain in minutes, even chronic arthritis pain—deep in the joints. The product, which is called **PAIN-BUST-R-II®,** is one of the fastest acting therapeutic formulas ever developed in the fight against arthritis. Immediately upon application, it goes to work by penetrating deep to the areas most affected—the joints themselves, bringing fast relief where relief is needed most. Men and women who have suffered arthritis pain for years are reporting incredible results with this product. Even a single application seems to work remarkably well in relieving pain and bringing comfort to cramped, knotted joints. *PAIN-BUST-R-II® was researched and formulated to be absorbed directly into the joints and muscles—where the pain originates. Long-time arthritis sufferers will be glad to know that this formula will help put an end to agonizing days and sleepless nights. It is highly recommended by users who have resumed daily activities and are enjoying life again.

Read what our users have to say:

"This stuff really works! My knee was cracked on the job, and it's been pure agony to take a step ever since. I tried all the rubs and cortisone shots I could bear. I now use your product everyday–believe it or not, I can walk without being bothered by pain again! A "thank you" just doesn't seem to express how grateful I am. You've changed my life!"
S.J.T., Ga. Age 55

Rina is a brave woman who has been suffering since early 1994 when she had both knees surgically replaced. A simple walk or enjoying a good night's sleep wasn't even an option. She now uses the **PAIN-BUST·R®** formula daily, and she claims her pain is nothing more than an occasional annoyance. She writes: "I feel young and healthy again–thanks for everything you've done for me!"
R.P., Fl. Age 70

100% RISK-FREE OFFER
We Trust You — Send No Money!

TO ORDER: Just write "PAIN BUST-R-11®" on a sheet of paper and send it along with your name, address and the number of tubes you wish to order. We will promptly ship you 1 Large tube for **$9.90**, 2 Large tubes for **$16.80** *(SAVES $3.00)* or 3 Large tubes plus one **FREE** for only **$28.80** *(SAVES $9.90)*. Prices include shipping and handling. We will enclose an invoice, and if for any reason you don't agree that **PAIN BUST-R-II®** relieves pain more effectively than anything you've tried, simply mark "cancel" on the invoice, and there will be no charge to you. You don't even have to bother returning the merchandise. Act quickly–this offer may not be repeated. **CALL NOW! 1-800-451-5773 ask for offer# OFA-04** or Write today to: Continental Quest/Research Corp., 220 W. Carmel Drive, Dept. OFA-04, Carmel, IN 46032
©2003 Continental Quest/Research Corp.

Gestation and Mating Table

	Proper Age for First Mating	Period of Fertility (years)	Number of Females for One Male	Period of Gestation (days)	
				AVERAGE	RANGE
Ewe	90 lb. or 1 yr.	6		147 / 151[8]	142–154
Ram	12–14 mo., well matured	7	50–75[2] / 35–40[3]		
Mare	3 yr.	10–12		336	310–370
Stallion	3 yr.	12–15	40–45[4] / Record 252[5]		
Cow	15–18 mo.[1]	10–14		283	279–290[6] 262–300[7]
Bull	1 yr., well matured	10–12	50[4] / Thousands[5]		
Sow	5–6 mo. or 250 lb.	6		115	110–120
Boar	250–300 lb.	6	50[2] / 35–40[3]		
Doe goat	10 mo. or 85–90 lb.	6		150	145–155
Buck goat	Well matured	5	30		
Bitch	16–18 mo.	8		63	58–67
Male dog	12–16 mo.	8			
She cat	12 mo.	6		63	60–68
Doe rabbit	6 mo.	5–6		31	30–32
Buck rabbit	6 mo.	5–6	30		

[1]Holstein and beef: 750 lb.; Jersey: 500 lb. [2]Hand-mated. [3]Pasture. [4]Natural. [5]Artificial. [6]Beef; 8–10 days shorter for Angus. [7]Dairy. [8]For fine wool breeds.

Maximum Life Spans of Animals in Captivity (years)

Ant (queen)	18+	Chimpanzee	51	Giraffe	36	Kangaroo	30	Quahog	150
Badger	26	Coyote	21+	Goat (domestic)	20	Lion	29	Rabbit	18+
Beaver	15+	Dog (domestic)	29	Goldfish	41	Monarch butterfly	1+	Squirrel, gray	23
Box turtle (Eastern)	138	Dolphin	25	Goose (domestic)	20	Mouse (house)	6	Tiger	26
Camel	35+	Duck (domestic)	23	Gorilla	50+	Mussel		Toad	40
Cat (domestic)	34	Eagle	55	Horse	62	(freshwater)	70–80	Tortoise (Marion's)	152+
Chicken (domestic)	25	Elephant	75	Housefly	17 days	Octopus	2–3	Turkey (domestic)	16

Incubation Periods of Birds and Poultry (days)

Canary	14–15	Goose	30–34	Pheasant	22–24
Chicken	21	Guinea	26–28	Swan	42
Duck	26–32	Parakeet	18–20	Turkey	28

Gestation Periods of Wild Animals (days)

Black bear	210	Otter	270–300	Squirrel, gray	44
Hippo	225–250	Reindeer	210–240	Whale, sperm	480
Moose	240–250	Seal	330	Wolf	60–63

	Estral (estrous) Cycle Including Heat Period		Length of Heat (estrus)		Usual Time of Ovulation	When Cycle Recurs if Not Bred
	AVERAGE	RANGE	AVERAGE	RANGE		
Mare	21 days	10–37 days	5–6 days	2–11 days	24–48 hours before end of estrus	21 days
Sow	21 days	18–24 days	2–3 days	1–5 days	30–36 hours after start of estrus	21 days
Ewe	16½ days	14–19 days	30 hours	24–32 hours	12–24 hours before end of estrus	16½ days
Goat	21 days	18–24 days	2–3 days	1–4 days	Near end of estrus	21 days
Cow	21 days	18–24 days	18 hours	10–24 hours	10–12 hours after end of estrus	21 days
Bitch	24 days		7 days	5–9 days	1–3 days after first acceptance	Pseudo-pregnancy
Cat		15–21 days	3–4 days, if mated	9–10 days, in absence of male	24–56 hours after coitus	Pseudo-pregnancy

Tide Corrections

■ Many factors affect the times and heights of the tides: the coastal configuration, the time of the Moon's southing (crossing the meridian), and the Moon's phase. The High Tide column on the **Left-Hand Calendar Pages 44–70** lists the times of high tide at Commonwealth Pier in Boston Harbor. The heights of some of these tides, reckoned from Mean Lower Low Water, are given on the **Right-Hand Calendar Pages 45–71.** Use this table to calculate the approximate times and heights of high water at the places shown. Apply the time difference to the times of high tide at Boston **(pages 44–70)** and the height difference to the heights at Boston **(pages 45–71).**

Estimations derived from this table are *not* meant to be used for navigation. *The Old Farmer's Almanac* accepts no responsibility for errors or any consequences ensuing from the use of this table.

Predictions for many other stations can be found on our Web site, www.almanac.com/tides/predictions.

Coastal Site	Difference: Time (h. m.)	Height (ft.)
Canada		
Alberton, PE	−5 45**	−7.5
Charlottetown, PE	−0 45**	−3.5
Halifax, NS	−3 23	−4.5
North Sydney, NS	−3 15	−6.5
Saint John, NB	+0 30	+15.0
St. John's, NL	−4 00	−6.5
Yarmouth, NS	−0 40	+3.0
Maine		
Bar Harbor	−0 34	+0.9
Belfast	−0 20	+0.4
Boothbay Harbor	−0 18	−0.8
Chebeague Island	−0 16	−0.6
Eastport	−0 28	+8.4
Kennebunkport	+0 04	−1.0
Machias	−0 28	+2.8
Monhegan Island	−0 25	−0.8
Old Orchard	0 00	−0.8
Portland	−0 12	−0.6
Rockland	−0 28	+0.1
Stonington	−0 30	+0.1
York	−0 09	−1.0

Coastal Site	Difference: Time (h. m.)	Height (ft.)
New Hampshire		
Hampton	+0 02	−1.3
Portsmouth	+0 11	−1.5
Rye Beach	−0 09	−0.9
Massachusetts		
Annisquam	−0 02	−1.1
Beverly Farms	0 00	−0.5
Boston	0 00	0.0
Cape Cod Canal		
East Entrance	−0 01	−0.8
West Entrance	−2 16	−5.9
Chatham Outer Coast	+0 30	−2.8
Inside	+1 54	*0.4
Cohasset	+0 02	−0.07
Cotuit Highlands	+1 15	*0.3
Dennis Port	+1 01	*0.4
Duxbury–Gurnet Point	+0 02	−0.3
Fall River	−3 03	−5.0
Gloucester	−0 03	−0.8
Hingham	+0 07	0.0
Hull	+0 03	−0.2
Hyannis Port	+1 01	*0.3
Magnolia–Manchester	−0 02	−0.7
Marblehead	−0 02	−0.4
Marion	−3 22	−5.4
Monument Beach	−3 08	−5.4
Nahant	−0 01	−0.5
Nantasket	+0 04	−0.1
Nantucket	+0 56	*0.3
Nauset Beach	+0 30	*0.6
New Bedford	−3 24	−5.7
Newburyport	+0 19	−1.8
Oak Bluffs	+0 30	*0.2
Onset–R.R. Bridge	−2 16	−5.9
Plymouth	+0 05	0.0
Provincetown	+0 14	−0.4
Revere Beach	−0 01	−0.3
Rockport	−0 08	−1.0
Salem	0 00	−0.5
Scituate	−0 05	−0.7
Wareham	−3 09	−5.3
Wellfleet	+0 12	+0.5
West Falmouth	−3 10	−5.4
Westport Harbor	−3 22	−6.4
Woods Hole		
Little Harbor	−2 50	*0.2
Oceanographic Institute	−3 07	*0.2
Rhode Island		
Bristol	−3 24	−5.3
Narragansett Pier	−3 42	−6.2

Coastal Site	Difference: Time (h. m.)	Height (ft.)	Coastal Site	Difference: Time (h. m.)	Height (ft.)
Newport	−3 34	−5.9	Hampton Roads	−2 02	−6.9
Point Judith	−3 41	−6.3	Norfolk	−2 06	−6.6
Providence	−3 20	−4.8	Virginia Beach	−4 00	−6.0
Sakonnet	−3 44	−5.6	Yorktown	−2 13	−7.0
Watch Hill	−2 50	−6.8	**North Carolina**		
Connecticut			Cape Fear	−3 55	−5.0
Bridgeport	+0 01	−2.6	Cape Lookout	−4 28	−5.7
Madison	−0 22	−2.3	Currituck	−4 10	−5.8
New Haven	−0 11	−3.2	Hatteras		
New London	−1 54	−6.7	Inlet	−4 03	−7.4
Norwalk	+0 01	−2.2	Kitty Hawk	−4 14	−6.2
Old Lyme			Ocean	−4 26	−6.0
Highway Bridge	−0 30	−6.2	**South Carolina**		
Stamford	+0 01	−2.2	Charleston	−3 22	−4.3
Stonington	−2 27	−6.6	Georgetown	−1 48	*0.36
New York			Hilton Head	−3 22	−2.9
Coney Island	−3 33	−4.9	Myrtle Beach	−3 49	−4.4
Fire Island Light	−2 43	*0.1	St. Helena		
Long Beach	−3 11	−5.7	Harbor Entrance	−3 15	−3.4
Montauk Harbor	−2 19	−7.4	**Georgia**		
New York City–Battery	−2 43	−5.0	Jekyll Island	−3 46	−2.9
Oyster Bay	+0 04	−1.8	St. Simon's Island	−2 50	−2.9
Port Chester	−0 09	−2.2	Savannah Beach		
Port Washington	−0 01	−2.1	River Entrance	−3 14	−5.5
Sag Harbor	−0 55	−6.8	Tybee Light	−3 22	−2.7
Southampton			**Florida**		
Shinnecock Inlet	−4 20	*0.2	Cape Canaveral	−3 59	−6.0
Willets Point	0 00	−2.3	Daytona Beach	−3 28	−5.3
New Jersey			Fort Lauderdale	−2 50	−7.2
Asbury Park	−4 04	−5.3	Fort Pierce Inlet	−3 32	−6.9
Atlantic City	−3 56	−5.5	Jacksonville		
Bay Head–Sea Girt	−4 04	−5.3	Railroad Bridge	−6 55	*0.1
Beach Haven	−1 43	*0.24	Miami Harbor Entrance	−3 18	−7.0
Cape May	−3 28	−5.3	St. Augustine	−2 55	−4.9
Ocean City	−3 06	−5.9			
Sandy Hook	−3 30	−5.0			
Seaside Park	−4 03	−5.4			
Pennsylvania					
Philadelphia	+2 40	−3.5			
Delaware					
Cape Henlopen	−2 48	−5.3			
Rehoboth Beach	−3 37	−5.7			
Wilmington	+1 56	−3.8			
Maryland					
Annapolis	+6 23	−8.5			
Baltimore	+7 59	−8.3			
Cambridge	+5 05	−7.8			
Havre de Grace	+11 21	−7.7			
Point No Point	+2 28	−8.1			
Prince Frederick					
Plum Point	+4 25	−8.5			
Virginia					
Cape Charles	−2 20	−7.0			

*Where the difference in the Height column is so marked, height at Boston should be multiplied by this ratio.

**Varies widely; accurate within only 1½ hours. Consult local tide tables for precise times and heights.

Example: The conversion of the times and heights of the tides at Boston to those at Cape Fear, North Carolina, is given below:

Sample tide calculation July 5, 2004:

High tide at Boston (p. 60)	2:30 P.M.	EDT
Correction for Cape Fear	−3:55 hrs.	
High tide at Cape Fear	10:35 A.M.	EDT
Tide height at Boston (p. 61)	10.3 ft.	
Correction for Cape Fear	−5.0 ft.	
Tide height at Cape Fear	5.3 ft.	

Time Corrections

■ Times of sunrise/sunset and moonrise/moonset, and selected times for transit of the bright stars and for observing the visible planets, are given for Boston on **pages 44–70, 88,** and **94–95.** Use the Key Letter shown to the right of each time on those pages with this table to find the number of minutes, already adjusted for different time zones, that you must add to or subtract from Boston time to get the correct time for your city. (Because of complex calculations for different locales, times may not be precise to the minute.) If your city is not listed, find the city closest to you in latitude and longitude and use those figures. Boston's latitude is 42° 22' and its longitude is 71° 03'. Canadian cities appear at the end of the table. For further information on the use of Key Letters and this table, see **How to Use This Almanac, page 39.**

Time Zone Code: Codes represent *standard time*. Atlantic is –1, Eastern is 0, Central is 1, Mountain is 2, Pacific is 3, Alaska is 4, and Hawaii-Aleutian is 5.

City	North Latitude °	'	West Longitude °	'	Time Zone Code	A (min.)	B (min.)	C (min.)	D (min.)	E (min.)
Aberdeen, SD	45	28	98	29	1	+37	+44	+49	+54	+59
Akron, OH	41	5	81	31	0	+46	+43	+41	+39	+37
Albany, NY	42	39	73	45	0	+ 9	+10	+10	+11	+11
Albert Lea, MN	43	39	93	22	1	+24	+26	+28	+31	+33
Albuquerque, NM	35	5	106	39	2	+45	+32	+22	+11	+ 2
Alexandria, LA	31	18	92	27	1	+58	+40	+26	+ 9	– 3
Allentown–Bethlehem, PA	40	36	75	28	0	+23	+20	+17	+14	+12
Amarillo, TX	35	12	101	50	1	+85	+73	+63	+52	+43
Anchorage, AK	61	10	149	59	4	–46	+27	+71	+122	+171
Asheville, NC	35	36	82	33	0	+67	+55	+46	+35	+27
Atlanta, GA	33	45	84	24	0	+79	+65	+53	+40	+30
Atlantic City, NJ	39	22	74	26	0	+23	+17	+13	+ 8	+ 4
Augusta, GA	33	28	81	58	0	+70	+55	+44	+30	+19
Augusta, ME	44	19	69	46	0	–12	– 8	– 5	– 1	0
Austin, TX	30	16	97	45	1	+82	+62	+47	+29	+15
Bakersfield, CA	35	23	119	1	3	+33	+21	+12	+ 1	– 7
Baltimore, MD	39	17	76	37	0	+32	+26	+22	+17	+13
Bangor, ME	44	48	68	46	0	–18	–13	– 9	– 5	– 1
Barstow, CA	34	54	117	1	3	+27	+14	+ 4	– 7	–16
Baton Rouge, LA	30	27	91	11	1	+55	+36	+21	+ 3	–10
Beaumont, TX	30	5	94	6	1	+67	+48	+32	+14	0
Bellingham, WA	48	45	122	29	3	0	+13	+24	+37	+47
Bemidji, MN	47	28	94	53	1	+14	+26	+34	+44	+52
Berlin, NH	44	28	71	11	0	– 7	– 3	0	+ 3	+ 7
Billings, MT	45	47	108	30	2	+16	+23	+29	+35	+40
Biloxi, MS	30	24	88	53	1	+46	+27	+11	– 5	–19
Binghamton, NY	42	6	75	55	0	+20	+19	+19	+18	+18
Birmingham, AL	33	31	86	49	1	+30	+15	+ 3	–10	–20
Bismarck, ND	46	48	100	47	1	+41	+50	+58	+66	+73
Boise, ID	43	37	116	12	2	+55	+58	+60	+62	+64
Brattleboro, VT	42	51	72	34	0	+ 4	+ 5	+ 5	+ 6	+ 7
Bridgeport, CT	41	11	73	11	0	+12	+10	+ 8	+ 6	+ 4
Brockton, MA	42	5	71	1	0	0	0	0	0	– 1
Brownsville, TX	25	54	97	30	1	+91	+66	+46	+23	+ 5
Buffalo, NY	42	53	78	52	0	+29	+30	+30	+31	+32
Burlington, VT	44	29	73	13	0	0	+ 4	+ 8	+12	+15
Butte, MT	46	1	112	32	2	+31	+39	+45	+52	+57
Cairo, IL	37	0	89	11	1	+29	+20	+12	+ 4	– 2
Camden, NJ	39	57	75	7	0	+24	+19	+16	+12	+ 9
Canton, OH	40	48	81	23	0	+46	+43	+41	+38	+36
Cape May, NJ	38	56	74	56	0	+26	+20	+15	+ 9	+ 5
Carson City–Reno, NV	39	10	119	46	3	+25	+19	+14	+ 9	+ 5

City	North Latitude ° '		West Longitude ° '		Time Zone Code	A (min.)	B (min.)	C (min.)	D (min.)	E (min.)
Casper, WY	42	51	106	19	2	+19	+19	+20	+21	+22
Charleston, SC	32	47	79	56	0	+64	+48	+36	+21	+10
Charleston, WV	38	21	81	38	0	+55	+48	+42	+35	+30
Charlotte, NC	35	14	80	51	0	+61	+49	+39	+28	+19
Charlottesville, VA	38	2	78	30	0	+43	+35	+29	+22	+17
Chattanooga, TN	35	3	85	19	0	+79	+67	+57	+45	+36
Cheboygan, MI	45	39	84	29	0	+40	+47	+53	+59	+64
Cheyenne, WY	41	8	104	49	2	+19	+16	+14	+12	+11
Chicago–Oak Park, IL	41	52	87	38	1	+ 7	+ 6	+ 6	+ 5	+ 4
Cincinnati–Hamilton, OH	39	6	84	31	0	+64	+58	+53	+48	+44
Cleveland–Lakewood, OH	41	30	81	42	0	+45	+43	+42	+40	+39
Columbia, SC	34	0	81	2	0	+65	+51	+40	+27	+17
Columbus, OH	39	57	83	1	0	+55	+51	+47	+43	+40
Cordova, AK	60	33	145	45	4	−55	+13	+55	+103	+149
Corpus Christi, TX	27	48	97	24	1	+86	+64	+46	+25	+ 9
Craig, CO	40	31	107	33	2	+32	+28	+25	+22	+20
Dallas–Fort Worth, TX	32	47	96	48	1	+71	+55	+43	+28	+17
Danville, IL	40	8	87	37	1	+13	+ 9	+ 6	+ 2	0
Danville, VA	36	36	79	23	0	+51	+41	+33	+24	+17
Davenport, IA	41	32	90	35	1	+20	+19	+17	+16	+15
Dayton, OH	39	45	84	10	0	+61	+56	+52	+48	+44
Decatur, AL	34	36	86	59	1	+27	+14	+ 4	− 7	−17
Decatur, IL	39	51	88	57	1	+19	+15	+11	+ 7	+ 4
Denver–Boulder, CO	39	44	104	59	2	+24	+19	+15	+11	+ 7
Des Moines, IA	41	35	93	37	1	+32	+31	+30	+28	+27
Detroit–Dearborn, MI	42	20	83	3	0	+47	+47	+47	+47	+47
Dubuque, IA	42	30	90	41	1	+17	+18	+18	+18	+18
Duluth, MN	46	47	92	6	1	+ 6	+16	+23	+31	+38
Durham, NC	36	0	78	55	0	+51	+40	+31	+21	+13
Eastport, ME	44	54	67	0	0	−26	−20	−16	−11	− 8
Eau Claire, WI	44	49	91	30	1	+12	+17	+21	+25	+29
Elko, NV	40	50	115	46	3	+ 3	0	− 1	− 3	− 5
Ellsworth, ME	44	33	68	25	0	−18	−14	−10	− 6	− 3
El Paso, TX	31	45	106	29	2	+53	+35	+22	+ 6	− 6
Erie, PA	42	7	80	5	0	+36	+36	+35	+35	+35
Eugene, OR	44	3	123	6	3	+21	+24	+27	+30	+33
Fairbanks, AK	64	48	147	51	4	−127	+ 2	+61	+131	+205
Fall River– New Bedford, MA	41	42	71	9	0	+ 2	+ 1	0	0	− 1
Fargo, ND	46	53	96	47	1	+24	+34	+42	+50	+57
Flagstaff, AZ	35	12	111	39	2	+64	+52	+42	+31	+22
Flint, MI	43	1	83	41	0	+47	+49	+50	+51	+52
Fort Myers, FL	26	38	81	52	0	+87	+63	+44	+21	+ 4
Fort Scott, KS	37	50	94	42	1	+49	+41	+34	+27	+21
Fort Smith, AR	35	23	94	25	1	+55	+43	+33	+22	+14
Fort Wayne, IN	41	4	85	9	0	+60	+58	+56	+54	+52
Fresno, CA	36	44	119	47	3	+32	+22	+15	+ 6	0
Gallup, NM	35	32	108	45	2	+52	+40	+31	+20	+11
Galveston, TX	29	18	94	48	1	+72	+52	+35	+16	+ 1
Gary, IN	41	36	87	20	1	+ 7	+ 6	+ 4	+ 3	+ 2
Glasgow, MT	48	12	106	38	2	− 1	+11	+21	+32	+42
Grand Forks, ND	47	55	97	3	1	+21	+33	+43	+53	+62
Grand Island, NE	40	55	98	21	1	+53	+51	+49	+46	+44
Grand Junction, CO	39	4	108	33	2	+40	+34	+29	+24	+20
Great Falls, MT	47	30	111	17	2	+20	+31	+39	+49	+58
Green Bay, WI	44	31	88	0	1	0	+ 3	+ 7	+11	+14
Greensboro, NC	36	4	79	47	0	+54	+43	+35	+25	+17

City	North Latitude °	′	West Longitude °	′	Time Zone Code	A (min.)	B (min.)	C (min.)	D (min.)	E (min.)
Hagerstown, MD	39	39	77	43	0	+35	+30	+26	+22	+18
Harrisburg, PA	40	16	76	53	0	+30	+26	+23	+19	+16
Hartford–New Britain, CT	41	46	72	41	0	+ 8	+ 7	+ 6	+ 5	+ 4
Helena, MT	46	36	112	2	2	+27	+36	+43	+51	+57
Hilo, HI	19	44	155	5	5	+94	+62	+37	+ 7	−15
Honolulu, HI	21	18	157	52	5	+102	+72	+48	+19	− 1
Houston, TX	29	45	95	22	1	+73	+53	+37	+19	+ 5
Indianapolis, IN	39	46	86	10	0	+69	+64	+60	+56	+52
Ironwood, MI	46	27	90	9	1	0	+ 9	+15	+23	+29
Jackson, MI	42	15	84	24	0	+53	+53	+53	+52	+52
Jackson, MS	32	18	90	11	1	+46	+30	+17	+ 1	−10
Jacksonville, FL	30	20	81	40	0	+77	+58	+43	+25	+11
Jefferson City, MO	38	34	92	10	1	+36	+29	+24	+18	+13
Joplin, MO	37	6	94	30	1	+50	+41	+33	+25	+18
Juneau, AK	58	18	134	25	4	−76	−23	+10	+49	+86
Kalamazoo, MI	42	17	85	35	0	+58	+57	+57	+57	+57
Kanab, UT	37	3	112	32	2	+62	+53	+46	+37	+30
Kansas City, MO	39	1	94	20	1	+44	+37	+33	+27	+23
Keene, NH	42	56	72	17	0	+ 2	+ 3	+ 4	+ 5	+ 6
Ketchikan, AK	55	21	131	39	4	−62	−25	0	+29	+56
Knoxville, TN	35	58	83	55	0	+71	+60	+51	+41	+33
Kodiak, AK	57	47	152	24	4	0	+49	+82	+120	+154
LaCrosse, WI	43	48	91	15	1	+15	+18	+20	+22	+25
Lake Charles, LA	30	14	93	13	1	+64	+44	+29	+11	− 2
Lanai City, HI	20	50	156	55	5	+99	+69	+44	+15	− 6
Lancaster, PA	40	2	76	18	0	+28	+24	+20	+17	+13
Lansing, MI	42	44	84	33	0	+52	+53	+53	+54	+54
Las Cruces, NM	32	19	106	47	2	+53	+36	+23	+ 8	− 3
Las Vegas, NV	36	10	115	9	3	+16	+ 4	− 3	−13	−20
Lawrence–Lowell, MA	42	42	71	10	0	0	0	0	0	+ 1
Lewiston, ID	46	25	117	1	3	−12	− 3	+ 2	+10	+17
Lexington–Frankfort, KY	38	3	84	30	0	+67	+59	+53	+46	+41
Liberal, KS	37	3	100	55	1	+76	+66	+59	+51	+44
Lihue, HI	21	59	159	23	5	+107	+77	+54	+26	+ 5
Lincoln, NE	40	49	96	41	1	+47	+44	+42	+39	+37
Little Rock, AR	34	45	92	17	1	+48	+35	+25	+13	+ 4
Los Angeles–Pasadena–Santa Monica, CA	34	3	118	14	3	+34	+20	+ 9	− 3	−13
Louisville, KY	38	15	85	46	0	+72	+64	+58	+52	+46
Macon, GA	32	50	83	38	0	+79	+63	+50	+36	+24
Madison, WI	43	4	89	23	1	+10	+11	+12	+14	+15
Manchester–Concord, NH	42	59	71	28	0	0	0	+ 1	+ 2	+ 3
McAllen, TX	26	12	98	14	1	+93	+69	+49	+26	+ 9
Memphis, TN	35	9	90	3	1	+38	+26	+16	+ 5	− 3
Meridian, MS	32	22	88	42	1	+40	+24	+11	− 4	−15
Miami, FL	25	47	80	12	0	+88	+57	+37	+14	− 3
Miles City, MT	46	25	105	51	2	+ 3	+11	+18	+26	+32
Milwaukee, WI	43	2	87	54	1	+ 4	+ 6	+ 7	+ 8	+ 9
Minneapolis–St. Paul, MN	44	59	93	16	1	+18	+24	+28	+33	+37
Minot, ND	48	14	101	18	1	+36	+50	+59	+71	+81
Moab, UT	38	35	109	33	2	+46	+39	+33	+27	+22
Mobile, AL	30	42	88	3	1	+42	+23	+ 8	− 8	−22
Monroe, LA	32	30	92	7	1	+53	+37	+24	+ 9	− 1
Montgomery, AL	32	23	86	19	1	+31	+14	+ 1	−13	−25
Muncie, IN	40	12	85	23	0	+64	+60	+57	+53	+50
Nashville, TN	36	10	86	47	1	+22	+11	+ 3	− 6	−14
Newark–East Orange, NJ	40	44	74	10	0	+17	+14	+12	+ 9	+ 7

City	North Latitude °	'	West Longitude °	'	Time Zone Code	A (min.)	B (min.)	C (min.)	D (min.)	E (min.)
New Haven, CT 41	18		72	56	0	+11	+ 8	+ 7	+ 5	+ 4
New London, CT 41	22		72	6	0	+ 7	+ 5	+ 4	+ 2	+ 1
New Orleans, LA 29	57		90	4	1	+52	+32	+16	− 1	−15
New York, NY 40	45		74	0	0	+17	+14	+11	+ 9	+ 6
Norfolk, VA 36	51		76	17	0	+38	+28	+21	+12	+ 5
North Platte, NE 41	8		100	46	1	+62	+60	+58	+56	+54
Norwalk–Stamford, CT 41	7		73	22	0	+13	+10	+ 9	+ 7	+ 5
Oakley, KS 39	8		100	51	1	+69	+63	+59	+53	+49
Ogden, UT............... 41	13		111	58	2	+47	+45	+43	+41	+40
Ogdensburg, NY.......... 44	42		75	30	0	+ 8	+13	+17	+21	+25
Oklahoma City, OK 35	28		97	31	1	+67	+55	+46	+35	+26
Omaha, NE 41	16		95	56	1	+43	+40	+39	+37	+36
Orlando, FL.............. 28	32		81	22	0	+80	+59	+42	+22	+ 6
Ortonville, MN 45	19		96	27	1	+30	+36	+40	+46	+51
Oshkosh, WI 44	1		88	33	1	+ 3	+ 6	+ 9	+12	+15
Palm Springs, CA......... 33	49		116	32	3	+28	+13	+ 1	−12	−22
Parkersburg, WV 39	16		81	34	0	+52	+46	+42	+36	+32
Paterson, NJ 40	55		74	10	0	+17	+14	+12	+ 9	+ 7
Pendleton, OR............ 45	40		118	47	3	− 1	+ 4	+10	+16	+21
Pensacola, FL 30	25		87	13	1	+39	+20	+ 5	−12	−26
Peoria, IL................ 40	42		89	36	1	+19	+16	+14	+11	+ 9
Philadelphia–Chester, PA ...39	57		75	9	0	+24	+19	+16	+12	+ 9
Phoenix, AZ 33	27		112	4	2	+71	+56	+44	+30	+20
Pierre, SD 44	22		100	21	1	+49	+53	+56	+60	+63
Pittsburgh–McKeesport, PA 40	26		80	0	0	+42	+38	+35	+32	+29
Pittsfield, MA 42	27		73	15	0	+ 8	+ 8	+ 8	+ 8	+ 8
Pocatello, ID 42	52		112	27	2	+43	+44	+45	+46	+46
Poplar Bluff, MO 36	46		90	24	1	+35	+25	+17	+ 8	+ 1
Portland, ME............. 43	40		70	15	0	− 8	− 5	− 3	− 1	0
Portland, OR 45	31		122	41	3	+14	+20	+25	+31	+36
Portsmouth, NH 43	5		70	45	0	− 4	− 2	− 1	0	0
Presque Isle, ME........... 46	41		68	1	0	−29	−19	−12	− 4	+ 2
Providence, RI 41	50		71	25	0	+ 3	+ 2	+ 1	0	0
Pueblo, CO 38	16		104	37	2	+27	+20	+14	+ 7	+ 2
Raleigh, NC.............. 35	47		78	38	0	+51	+39	+30	+20	+12
Rapid City, SD 44	5		103	14	2	+ 2	+ 5	+ 8	+11	+13
Reading, PA 40	20		75	56	0	+26	+22	+19	+16	+13
Redding, CA 40	35		122	24	3	+31	+27	+25	+22	+19
Richmond, VA 37	32		77	26	0	+41	+32	+25	+17	+11
Roanoke, VA 37	16		79	57	0	+51	+42	+35	+27	+21
Roswell, NM............. 33	24		104	32	2	+41	+26	+14	0	−10
Rutland, VT.............. 43	37		72	58	0	+ 2	+ 5	+ 7	+ 9	+11
Sacramento, CA 38	35		121	30	3	+34	+27	+21	+15	+10
St. Johnsbury, VT.......... 44	25		72	1	0	− 4	0	+ 3	+ 7	+10
St. Joseph, MI 42	5		86	26	0	+61	+61	+60	+60	+59
St. Joseph, MO 39	46		94	50	1	+43	+38	+35	+30	+27
St. Louis, MO 38	37		90	12	1	+28	+21	+16	+10	+ 5
St. Petersburg, FL.......... 27	46		82	39	0	+87	+65	+47	+26	+10
Salem, OR............... 44	57		123	1	3	+17	+23	+27	+31	+35
Salina, KS 38	50		97	37	1	+57	+51	+46	+40	+35
Salisbury, MD............. 38	22		75	36	0	+31	+23	+18	+11	+ 6
Salt Lake City, UT 40	45		111	53	2	+48	+45	+43	+40	+38
San Antonio, TX........... 29	25		98	30	1	+87	+66	+50	+31	+16
San Diego, CA 32	43		117	9	3	+33	+17	+ 4	− 9	−21
San Francisco–Oakland– San Jose, CA 37	47		122	25	3	+40	+31	+25	+18	+12
Santa Fe, NM 35	41		105	56	2	+40	+28	+19	+ 9	0

City	North Latitude °	North Latitude '	West Longitude °	West Longitude '	Time Zone Code	A (min.)	B (min.)	C (min.)	D (min.)	E (min.)
Savannah, GA	32	5	81	6	0	+70	+54	+40	+25	+13
Scranton–Wilkes-Barre, PA	41	25	75	40	0	+21	+19	+18	+16	+15
Seattle–Tacoma– Olympia, WA	47	37	122	20	3	+ 3	+15	+24	+34	+42
Sheridan, WY	44	48	106	58	2	+14	+19	+23	+27	+31
Shreveport, LA	32	31	93	45	1	+60	+44	+31	+16	+ 4
Sioux Falls, SD	43	33	96	44	1	+38	+40	+42	+44	+46
South Bend, IN	41	41	86	15	0	+62	+61	+60	+59	+58
Spartanburg, SC	34	56	81	57	0	+66	+53	+43	+32	+23
Spokane, WA	47	40	117	24	3	−16	− 4	+ 4	+14	+23
Springfield, IL	39	48	89	39	1	+22	+18	+14	+10	+ 6
Springfield–Holyoke, MA	42	6	72	36	0	+ 6	+ 6	+ 6	+ 5	+ 5
Springfield, MO	37	13	93	18	1	+45	+36	+29	+20	+14
Syracuse, NY	43	3	76	9	0	+17	+19	+20	+21	+22
Tallahassee, FL	30	27	84	17	0	+87	+68	+53	+35	+22
Tampa, FL	27	57	82	27	0	+86	+64	+46	+25	+ 9
Terre Haute, IN	39	28	87	24	0	+74	+69	+65	+60	+56
Texarkana, AR	33	26	94	3	1	+59	+44	+32	+18	+ 8
Toledo, OH	41	39	83	33	0	+52	+50	+49	+48	+47
Topeka, KS	39	3	95	40	1	+49	+43	+38	+32	+28
Traverse City, MI	44	46	85	38	0	+49	+54	+57	+62	+65
Trenton, NJ	40	13	74	46	0	+21	+17	+14	+11	+ 8
Trinidad, CO	37	10	104	31	2	+30	+21	+13	+ 5	0
Tucson, AZ	32	13	110	58	2	+70	+53	+40	+24	+12
Tulsa, OK	36	9	95	60	1	+59	+48	+40	+30	+22
Tupelo, MS	34	16	88	34	1	+35	+21	+10	− 2	−11
Vernal, UT	40	27	109	32	2	+40	+36	+33	+30	+28
Walla Walla, WA	46	4	118	20	3	− 5	+ 2	+ 8	+15	+21
Washington, DC	38	54	77	1	0	+35	+28	+23	+18	+13
Waterbury–Meriden, CT	41	33	73	3	0	+10	+ 9	+ 7	+ 6	+ 5
Waterloo, IA	42	30	92	20	1	+24	+24	+24	+25	+25
Wausau, WI	44	58	89	38	1	+ 4	+ 9	+13	+18	+22
West Palm Beach, FL	26	43	80	3	0	+79	+55	+36	+14	− 2
Wichita, KS	37	42	97	20	1	+60	+51	+45	+37	+31
Williston, ND	48	9	103	37	1	+46	+59	+69	+80	+90
Wilmington, DE	39	45	75	33	0	+26	+21	+18	+13	+10
Wilmington, NC	34	14	77	55	0	+52	+38	+27	+15	+ 5
Winchester, VA	39	11	78	10	0	+38	+33	+28	+23	+19
Worcester, MA	42	16	71	48	0	+ 3	+ 2	+ 2	+ 2	+ 2
York, PA	39	58	76	43	0	+30	+26	+22	+18	+15
Youngstown, OH	41	6	80	39	0	+42	40	+38	+36	+34
Yuma, AZ	32	43	114	37	2	+83	+67	+54	+40	+28
CANADA										
Calgary, AB	51	5	114	5	2	+13	+35	+50	+68	+84
Edmonton, AB	53	34	113	25	2	− 3	+26	+47	+72	+93
Halifax, NS	44	38	63	35	−1	+21	+26	+29	+33	+37
Montreal, QC	45	28	73	39	0	− 1	+ 4	+ 9	+15	+20
Ottawa, ON	45	25	75	43	0	+ 6	+13	+18	+23	+28
Peterborough, ON	44	18	78	19	0	+21	+25	+28	+32	+35
Saint John, NB	45	16	66	3	−1	+28	+34	+39	+44	+49
Saskatoon, SK	52	10	106	40	1	+37	+63	+80	+101	+119
Sydney, NS	46	10	60	10	−1	+ 1	+ 9	+15	+23	+28
Thunder Bay, ON	48	27	89	12	0	+47	+61	+71	+83	+93
Toronto, ON	43	39	79	23	0	+28	+30	+32	+35	+37
Vancouver, BC	49	13	123	6	3	0	+15	+26	+40	+52
Winnipeg, MB	49	53	97	10	1	+12	+30	+43	+58	+71

2004   THE OLD FARMER'S ALMANAC   175

Why George Washington NEVER SMILED

BY JOHN MARTALO

George Washington was naturally somber in mood and temperament. During his long military career, he gained a reputation as a firm, no-nonsense leader who maintained a stiff upper lip in public. To many, he never looked very happy and, in fact, never flashed a wide, exuberant grin. Why? His teeth were a mess.

Washington's dental problems began in the mid-1700s, when he was in his early 20s. Frequent episodes of inflamed gums and abscessed teeth were soon followed by yearly tooth extractions, which began at age 24. At that time, specialized saws, files, hammers, chisels, and hand drills were the well-equipped dentist's tools of choice. Unfortunately, those implements, even in the hands of a skilled practitioner, often inflicted more pain on patients than relief. Over the next 30 years, Washington sought help from six dentists and went through several sets of clunky, ill-fitting false teeth. Then he met Dr. John Greenwood.

For the founding father, Greenwood fashioned a set

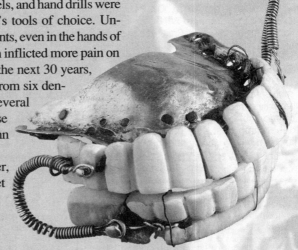

George Washington's dentures, with springs holding the top and bottom plates together.

–The Smithsonian Institution's Division of Science, Medicine, and Society

of upper and lower dentures from hippopotamus teeth that he filed, sanded, and hand-polished. The dentures were held together by two coiled steel springs attached to the back of the dental plates. This was meant to keep the dental work properly aligned and to ensure "horizontal control." In reality, it caused Washington's lips to protrude as though he were puckering up for a kiss, impeded his speech, made eating difficult, and caused such unbearable pain that he sometimes took laudanum, a powerful painkiller.

At age 57, with one natural tooth remaining in his jaw and his presidential inauguration just weeks away, Washington decided to have his lower denture redone. Eight new teeth, said to have been taken from fresh cadavers, were affixed to the president-elect's lower denture and held in place by gold rivets. Etched into the hippopotamus ivory was the inscription "This Was Great Washington's Teeth," along with the name "J. Greenwood." These dentures helped Washington mouth the Oath of Office, though they slipped and clicked as he spoke.

Throughout his life, the commander-in-chief was self-conscious about the way his dentures contorted his face. On December 12, 1798, at age 66, Washington returned the dentures to Greenwood for a refitting. Along with them, he included a letter describing his concerns and the nature of his discomfort. It seems that the springs that provided for horizontal control of the dentures, or "bars," as he referred to them, were so stiff that he had to exert considerable jaw pressure to close his mouth properly. "The principal thing you have to attend to," wrote Washington, "is to let the upper bar fall back from the lower one . . . for I find it is the bars alone, both above and below, that give the lips the pointing and swelling appearance. . . ." Without the necessary adjustment, he wrote, "it will have the effect of forcing the lip out just under the nose."

Greenwood fixed Washington's dentures and charged $15 to do it, but in a letter accompanying their return, the dentist chastised the founding father on his oral hygiene. Greenwood wrote that Washington's teeth were "very black . . . occasioned either by your soaking them in port wine or drinking it." The dentist noted that if the president wanted to drink port after dinner, he should take out his new dentures and put in an older pair, and that if he couldn't be bothered with switching dentures, he would "have to clean them right afterwards with a brush and some chalk dust." In response to Washington's other concern, getting an even shade of tooth color, Greenwood wrote, "If you want your teeth more yellower, soak them in Broth or pot liqueur, but not in tea or Acid."

Though thankful for Dr. Greenwood's efforts, George Washington remained a man of few words—and even fewer smiles—until his death one year later on December 14, 1799. □□

John Martalo has written for *The Rotarian, Ambassador Magazine,* and *Cricket,* among others. His interest in false teeth began several years ago when he found someone's upper denture on top of his mailbox. Today, that denture serves as a paperweight.

SMILE! To visit a dental museum or learn more about George Washington, go to **www.almanac.com** and click on **Article Links 2004.**

HERE'S LOOKING AT YOU!

Everybody reads faces; it's natural. Does a glint in someone's eye mean they're hopeful? Does a scowl suggest that it's not the best day to make a proposal? A personologist takes such ordinary observations one step further. He or she studies the details of the facial features—the forehead, the eyes, the nose, the mouth, the chin—and hair and ears to identify personality characteristics and suitable career avenues.

Personology, a contempory variation of physiognomy, involves actual measurement of, for example, the space between the eyes or the width of the jaw. Each facial feature represents a different personality trait. Sometimes these traits are reflected in a cultural colloquialism: We might say that someone has a strong jaw. In personology, a prominent jaw indicates a tenacious individual.

With practice, anyone can read, analyze, and interpret facial features. Here are some tips to get you started:

THE HISTORY OF FACE READING

Personology dates from the ancient Egyptians and Greeks. Modern interpretations were developed by Edward Vincent Jones, a judge in Los Angeles. He realized that by studying the facial features of people in his courtroom, he could predict their behavior. Beginning in the 1920s and continuing through 1940, Jones developed correlations between the structure of the body and the personality. He painstakingly researched the subject, reviewing the writings of Aristotle, Galen, and Hippocrates, as well as the history of physiognomy (the practice of studying facial features to determine character) and medicine in China dating back nearly 3,000 years.

In the early 1950s, Robert L. Whiteside teamed up with Jones and began to apply statistical methodology to his work. Together, Jones and Whiteside developed theories about body structure and personality, and based on the results of research, they identified 68 personality traits relating to physical characteristics. Continuing research led to the conclusion that all people have the same personality attributes—but in varying degrees.

YOU CAN TELL A LOT ABOUT PEOPLE BY THE LOOK ON THEIR FACE, BUT YOU CAN TELL EVEN MORE IF YOU KNOW HOW TO READ FACES. • BY CELESTE LONGACRE

■ **If a face is wide at the** temples **(1)**, especially when compared with the length of the face, self-confidence is indicated.

Add to this a broad jaw-bone line **(2)** (rather than a pointed chin), and you have an authoritative person, someone who knows what he or she is talking about (or can convince you of it). These features altogether indicate a decisive and commanding individual who may be inclined to take over a conversation with his or her exuberance.

■ **The area above the** eyebrows **(3)** reveals methodicalness. A person who focuses intense concentration on a methodical process and wants things "just so" in most aspects of his or her life will develop a ridge of muscle here.

■ **When the distance** across the eyes from outside corner to outside corner **(4)** is narrow (as opposed to wide) or the chin **(5)** thin or pointy, the person will be one who gains confidence through knowledge. He or she likes to study a subject thoroughly before feeling able to comment upon it.

■ **Tolerance is deter-** mined by the distance between the inner corners of the eyes **(6)**. The wider the space, the more tolerant the person. A person with a wide space between his or her eyes would make an excellent mediator or schoolteacher. A person with less space, and therefore less tolerance (but more precision), would make a good surgeon.

continued

179

EACH FACIAL FEATURE REPRESENTS A DIFFERENT PERSONALITY TRAIT, AND WITH PRACTICE, ANYONE CAN READ, ANALYZE, AND INTERPRET FACES.

■ **The depth of the eyes (7)** indicates serious-mindedness. People with deep-set eyes take life seriously; they like to think things through carefully and may be overly responsible. They are wonderful workers but may need to develop more of a sense of humor in order to participate fully in life's fun.

■ **Irises (8) that are large (com-** pared with the white space of the eye) indicate a person who brings a great deal of emotional expression to words and actions. Expect this individual to be very dramatic.

■ **Prominent cheekbones (9) indi-** cate a person who has a strong need for action and adventure. This type is always on the go; many are flight attendants.

■ **A noticeable bump on the** bridge of the nose **(10)** indicates a skeptic, one who doesn't believe everything he or she hears and seeks proof before accepting new information as fact. In terms of career, this type prefers an administrative or supervisory position.

■ **A flatter or upturned "ski jump"** nose **(11)** indicates a person who accepts new information without proof. These people are caregivers and can be found in careers such as nursing. They are the volunteers of

the world and need to guard against giving too much of themselves away.

■ **The flare of the nostrils (12)** reveals the degree of self-reliance. A lot of flare indicates a self-starter, a person with initiative. An individual with little flare often relies on others and doesn't give him- or herself enough credit for accomplishments and capabilities.

WHAT YOU SEE IS WHAT YOU GET

■ **Thick lips (13) reveal** a person who loves to talk; thin lips **(14)** indicate a person who is direct and wants you to get to the point.

■ **The thickness of a single** shaft of hair **(15)** indicates the degree to which a person insulates him- or herself from noise and the environment. People with coarse hair like extremes: loud music, spicy food, and rigorous play. Those with

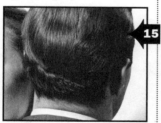

finer hair do not like loud music and prefer more refined entertainment and living conditions.

Thick hair shafts coupled with a ruddy complexion indicate a thick-skinned personality, one that is not sensitive to criticism. Conversely, thin hair shafts coupled with fair skin indicate a sensitive personality.

Let's apply some of these traits to well-known personalities. Senator Hillary Clinton is an interesting study because of her prominent cheekbones. From this, we can tell that she likes to be on the go. Her wide face reveals her natural self-confidence. Her wide-

–AP/Wide World Photos

set eyes indicate that she is tolerant, and her large irises are a sign that she is dramatic. The flare of her nose shows that she is a self-starter.

Comedian Jay Leno is famous for his prominent chin. This indicates a personality that never, ever gives up. He will hang on, perhaps past the point of success. He also has strong cheekbones, a sign that he

–AP/Wide World Photos

likes to be doing something all the time. His wide face and flaring nostrils show self-confidence and the desire to be his own boss. His thin lips indicate that he wants his guests to get to the point rather quickly. A bit of methodicalness is revealed by the area above his eyebrows, a hint that Jay works on his routine until it is just right.

□□

Celeste Longacre, the *Old Farmer's Almanac* astrologer, does face reading as entertainment at small and large gatherings.

A BRIEF HISTORY

I t would be easy to assume that we're in the Golden Age of Napping. Scientists have shown that the performance of mental tasks improves after a one-hour nap. Some companies are setting up "napping rooms" for their employees, who report that they go back to work with greater enthusiasm and increased productivity. The Federal Aviation Administration requires naps for pilots on long flights. Greenwich (Connecticut) High School has an after-school Power-Napping Club, where over-scheduled teens can grab 40 winks before rushing off to extracurricular practices, rehearsals, or lessons. Napping even has its own dedicated Web site (www.napping.com), run by The Napping Company, Inc., which has proclaimed the first Monday after the beginning of Daylight Saving Time (when we all lose an hour's sleep) in April to be National Workplace Napping Day.

Are we suddenly naphappy? Or are we rediscovering ancient wisdom?

The Birth of the
snooze

■ If you take the Bible account of creation as revealed truth, then Adam was the first napper. **The Book of Genesis recounts how the Lord put the first man to sleep before taking one of his ribs to create the first woman.** The *Oxford English Dictionary* (OED), which defines *nap* as "a short sleep," adds that the word was "formerly

–illustrated by Eldon Doty

ZZZZZZZZZZZZZZZZZZZZ

OF NAPPING

Irrefutable proof that periodic dozing does a body good.

BY TIM CLARK

in more dignified use than at present, being frequently employed in renderings of Biblical passages." In fact, the OED cites a passage from the Gospel of St. Matthew that dates back to the year 1647: "They slept but half-asleep, they napped and nodded."

Evolutionists have determined that napping is actually older than sleeping. In a 1967 article in *Scientific American,* sleep researcher Michel Jouvet reports that "early vertebrates slept only lightly, and deep sleep came as a rather late development in animal evolution." **Cats (on whom some of the first scientific sleep research was done) sleep from 13 to 18 hours a day, but half of that is spent in light sleep—the famous "cat nap."**

Even primitive life-forms take naps. Sleep in fruit flies is "eerily similar" to sleep in humans, according to Paul Shaw, sleep researcher at the Neuroscience Institute in La Jolla, California.

How do researchers tell if fruit flies are sleeping? "It is possible to identify elements—such as body position, arousal threshold, muscle activity, and heart rate—that allow us to differentiate rest from sleep . . . in insects [and] also in the scorpion and some crustaceans," Irene Tobler of the University of Zurich related to

ZZZZZZZ

183

ZZZZZZZZZZZZ

www.ScientificAmerican.com in October 2002. "Further back in the evolutionary tree," she added, "the existence of a sleep state has been described . . . in cephalopods [squids and octopi] and aplysia ["sea hair" mollusks]." Even cock-roaches sleep!

The Art of
napping

■ Art historian Carlo Franza points out that there are many famous paintings portraying the custom of the siesta, which is still prevalent in Spain, Italy, and Latin American countries. In 1596, Cara-vaggio painted Mary and Jesus napping during the flight from Egypt, a theme also picked up by Orazio Gentileschi in 1628.

More-secular depictions of napping can be found in Bruegel the Elder's "The Harvest" and "The Land of Cockayne," showing farm-ers flaking out under a tree. The 19th-cen-tury French painter Courbet painted drowsy "Young Ladies on the Banks of the Seine" in 1856, and the pointillist Seurat's famous "A Sunday Afternoon on the Island of La Grande Jatte" shows Parisians stretched out in soporific splendor.

The Dark Side of
napping

■ Sleep scientists caution against tak-ing too long a nap, which can disturb evening sleep. **Napping longer than 30 minutes or so leads to a condition called "sleep inertia," which may leave you groggy** **rather than refreshed.** In addition, many sleep authorities recommend that you take a nap about eight hours after wak-ing up in the morning rather than wait until late afternoon, which can throw off your biological clock and make it dif-ficult to fall asleep at night.

Other consequences can be much worse: In *The Odyssey,* Odysseus falls asleep at the tiller of his ship, allowing his overcurious crewmen to open the bag of winds that blow them all off course within sight of home. Rip Van Winkle takes a nap after overindulging in beer and wakes up 20 years later. And the hero of *Looking Backward,* by Edward Bellamy, falls asleep in 1887 and doesn't awake until 2000.

President Calvin Coolidge took daily afternoon naps of between two and four hours, perhaps because he was depressed over the death of his son. The Mexican

General Santa Anna lost the battle of San Jacinto on April 21, 1836, because he allowed himself and his soldiers to take their customary siesta that afternoon. General Sam Houston and his troops stayed awake, routed their sleepy foes, and won independence for the Republic of Texas.

Napping while driving is a national crisis, second only to alcohol as the leading cause of auto accidents. The National Sleep Foundation's 2002 Sleep in America survey found that more than half of all drivers have experienced drowsiness at the wheel, and 17 percent have actually dozed off; that percentage rises to 22 percent among males between the ages of 18 and 29.

Go Ahead and
nap

■ The weight of scientific evidence, however, continues to pile up on the side of a short midday nap of about half an hour or so. Dr. Robert Springer of the Southwest Regional Sleep Disorder Center in Texas prescribes naps for people who get tired and grumpy in the afternoon. "They seem to have reduced irritability and improved cognitive ability after a 30-minute nap."

Artists, inventors, and political leaders loom large in the history of napping. "Brahms napped at the piano while he composed his famous lullaby," according to Camille and Bill Anthony, proprietors of The Napping Company. **"Napoleon**

napped between battles. Churchill maintained that he had to nap in order to cope with his wartime responsibilities. Geniuses such as Edison and da Vinci napped." As Sir Winston Churchill put it: "Nature had not intended mankind to work from eight in the morning until midnight without that refreshment of blessed oblivion, which, even if it

lasts only 20 minutes, is sufficient to renew all the vital forces."

But that's nothing new. The *Oxford English Dictionary* records this bit of wisdom from the year 1377: "I moste sitte, seyde the segge [sage], or elles shulde I nappe." □□

Tim Clark, author of *A Millennium Primer: Timeless Truths and Delightful Diversions,* has written dozens of articles for *The Old Farmer's Almanac.*

Winning Essays

in the 2003 Essay Contest

My Most Memorable Weather Event

FIRST PRIZE

In the 1930s, my parents and I lived atop a rocky mesa in central New Mexico. We had no electricity, and so no ice or ice cream except when we went to town, and then only if we had money to buy it.

I remember one summer afternoon when big black clouds hid the Sun, and suddenly hail was pouring from the sky. The noise on the tin roof of the cabin was deafening. Soon the hailstorm was over, but the ground was heaped with hailstones. Almost before the hail ended, Dad was out with a shovel and tub. My mother was stirring up something in the kitchen. No matter how much I asked what she was doing, she just told me to wait and see.

Then I saw Dad coming out of the cellar with the ice-cream freezer and I knew! He soon had icy hailstones and salt packed around that freezer, and I was busy turning the crank.

So, far from any freezer or ice house, we had ice cream, and that hailstorm is a wonderful childhood memory.

–Joanne A. Wootan, Fallon, Montana

SECOND PRIZE

When I was a child, one pleasant summer day my mother took me shopping. We walked six blocks to the store. Halfway home, we got caught in heavy rainfall. We didn't have an umbrella, so we ran to the corner where we needed to cross the street. When we crossed over, I thought the rain had miraculously stopped, but I looked and saw that it was still raining on the other side of the street. I also noticed that this opposite side was dry and sunny. My young mind thought this was impossible. I asked my mother why it was raining on one side of the street and dry on the other. She said, "This is nature's way of teaching you that when problems rain into your life, you can get soaked with your troubles or you can cross the street. You will see the rain, but in spite of it, you can choose to walk in the sunshine." From this event, my mother taught me that when faced with problems, we can drown in our sorrows or choose to better face difficulties by approaching them with a sunny, positive attitude.

–Barbara Salpietro, Chicago, Illinois

THIRD PRIZE

In 1979, I attended an Army National Guard Winter Operations Instructor Course at Camp Ripley, Minnesota. Under steady snowfall, our field exercise started by cross-country ski marching, pulling our gear on an ahkio cargo sled. Four miles along toward our field bivouac site, a whiteout engulfed our group. (*Whiteout* means just that: limited visibility caused by blowing snow.)

We slowly shuffled the last miles to camp. Cold and disoriented, we pitched our eight-man tents and climbed inside. With tents up and heaters lit, we rode out the storm.

After three hours, the blizzard subsided and we dug ourselves out. We had pitched the tents away from overhanging trees in what now appeared to be a pasture.

Reentering our tent, we were surprised to see our heater slowly sinking into a pool of water. We grabbed the heater before it was lost. The pool revealed cattails and tall marsh grass beneath us! We were bivouacked on top of one of Minnesota's famous 10,000 lakes.

Realizing our embarrassing mistake, we quickly moved onto frozen ground. Later our evaluator spotted the hole in the ice and asked, grinning, "Which resourceful lieutenant tried to ice fish?"

We all laughed.

–Ken Kelnhofer, Girard, Illinois

HONORABLE MENTION

My husband and I were window-shopping in a nearby city on a blustery, windy day. As we went around the corner of a building, I spied a penny on the sidewalk. When I bent over to pick it up, a playful gust of wind blew my dress up over my back. Trying to fight my dress down, off came my wig. It blew into the middle of the street, and I had to go retrieve it.

My husband, who was standing there laughing at me, said, "Well, look on the bright side. That penny is the first part of a million dollars."

–Joyce Butler, Davis, Oklahoma

ANNOUNCING
THE 2004 ESSAY CONTEST

The Best Decision I Ever Made

■ **Tell us how one decision you made changed your life. It can be a big decision with a significant outcome (like finding a spouse, taking a job, or saving a life) or a seemingly small decision (such as making a wager, taking a different course, or changing your plans) with a surprising outcome. Please describe your experience in 200 words or less.**

See page 155 for contest rules.

Secrets of the Zodiac

Ancient astrologers associated each of the signs with a part of the body over which they believed the sign held some influence. The first sign of the zodiac—Aries—was attributed to the head, with the rest of the signs moving down the body, ending with Pisces at the feet.

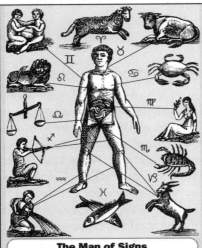

The Man of Signs

♈	Aries, head.........	**ARI**	*Mar. 21–Apr. 20*
♉	Taurus, neck.......	**TAU**	*Apr. 21–May 20*
♊	Gemini, arms.......	**GEM**	*May 21–June 20*
♋	Cancer, breast......	**CAN**	*June 21–July 22*
♌	Leo, heart.........	**LEO**	*July 23–Aug. 22*
♍	Virgo, belly........	**VIR**	*Aug. 23–Sept. 22*
♎	Libra, reins........	**LIB**	*Sept. 23–Oct. 22*
♏	Scorpio, secrets.....	**SCO**	*Oct. 23–Nov. 22*
♐	Sagittarius, thighs...	**SAG**	*Nov. 23–Dec. 21*
♑	Capricorn, knees....	**CAP**	*Dec. 22–Jan. 19*
♒	Aquarius, legs......	**AQU**	*Jan. 20–Feb. 19*
♓	Pisces, feet........	**PSC**	*Feb. 20–Mar. 20*

Astrology and Astronomy

■ Astrology is a tool we use to time events according to the *astrological* placement of the two luminaries (the Sun and the Moon) and eight planets in the 12 signs of the zodiac. Astronomy, on the other hand, is the charting of the *actual* placement of the known planets and constellations, taking into account precession of the equinoxes. As a result, the placement of the planets in the signs of the zodiac is not the same astrologically and astronomically. (The Moon's astronomical place is given in the **Left-Hand Calendar Pages 44–70,** and its astrological place is given in **Gardening by the Moon's Sign, page 189.**)

Modern astrology is a study of synchronicities. The planetary movements do not cause events. Rather, they explain the trajectory, or "flow," that events tend to follow. Because of free will, you can choose to plan a schedule in harmony with the flow, or you can choose to swim against the current.

The dates given in the **Astrological Timetable (page 190)** have been chosen with particular care to the astrological passage of the Moon. However, because other planets also influence us, it's best to take a look at all indicators before seeking advice on major life decisions. An astrologer can study the current relationship of the planets and your own personal birth chart to assist you in the best possible timing for carrying out your plans.

When Mercury Is Retrograde

■ Sometimes when we look out from our perspective here on Earth, the other planets appear to be traveling backward through the zodiac. (All heavenly bodies move forward. An optical illusion makes them seem as if they are moving backward.) We call this *retrograde motion.*

Mercury's retrograde periods, which occur three or four times a year, can cause travel delays and misconstrued communications. Plans have a way of unraveling, too. However, this is an excellent time to research or look into the past. Intuition is high during these periods, and coincidences can be extraordinary.

When Mercury is retrograde, astrologers advise us to keep plans flexible, allow extra time for travel, and avoid signing contracts. It's OK and even useful to look over projects and plans, because we may see them with different eyes at these times. However, our normal system of checks and balances might not be active, so it's best to wait until Mercury is direct again to make any final decisions. In 2004, Mercury will be retrograde from January 1–5, April 6–30, August 10–September 2, and November 30–December 20. *–Celeste Longacre*

Gardening by the Moon's Sign

■ It is important to note that the placement of the planets through the signs of the zodiac is not the same in astrology and astronomy. The *astrological* placement of the Moon, by sign, is given in the table below. (Its *astronomical,* or actual, placement is given in the **Left-Hand Calendar Pages 44–70.**)

For planting, the most-fertile Moon signs are the three water signs: Cancer, Scorpio, and Pisces. Good second choices are Taurus, Virgo, and Capricorn. Weeding and plowing are best done when the Moon occupies Aries, Gemini, Leo, Sagittarius, or Aquarius. Insect pests can also be handled at these times. Transplanting and grafting are best done under a Cancer, Scorpio, or Pisces Moon. Pruning is best done under an Aries, Leo, or Sagittarius Moon, with growth encouraged during waxing (from the day of new to the day of full Moon) and discouraged during waning (from the day after full to the day before new Moon). (For the dates of the Moon's phases, see **pages 44–70.**)

Clean out the garden shed when the Moon occupies Virgo. Fences and permanent beds can be built or mended when Capricorn predominates. Avoid indecision when under the Libra Moon.

Moon's Place in the Astrological Zodiac

	NOV. 2003	DEC. 2003	JAN. 2004	FEB. 2004	MAR. 2004	APR. 2004	MAY 2004	JUNE 2004	JULY 2004	AUG. 2004	SEPT. 2004	OCT. 2004	NOV. 2004	DEC. 2004
1	AQU	PSC	TAU	GEM	CAN	VIR	LIB	SCO	SAG	AQU	ARI	TAU	CAN	LEO
2	AQU	ARI	TAU	CAN	CAN	VIR	LIB	SAG	CAP	PSC	ARI	TAU	CAN	LEO
3	PSC	ARI	GEM	CAN	LEO	VIR	LIB	SAG	CAP	PSC	TAU	GEM	CAN	LEO
4	PSC	ARI	GEM	CAN	LEO	LIB	SCO	CAP	AQU	ARI	TAU	GEM	LEO	VIR
5	ARI	TAU	GEM	LEO	VIR	LIB	SCO	CAP	AQU	ARI	GEM	CAN	LEO	VIR
6	ARI	TAU	CAN	LEO	VIR	SCO	SAG	AQU	PSC	TAU	GEM	CAN	VIR	LIB
7	TAU	GEM	CAN	VIR	VIR	SCO	SAG	AQU	PSC	TAU	GEM	CAN	VIR	LIB
8	TAU	GEM	LEO	VIR	LIB	SAG	CAP	PSC	ARI	TAU	CAN	LEO	VIR	SCO
9	TAU	GEM	LEO	LIB	LIB	SAG	CAP	PSC	ARI	GEM	CAN	LEO	LIB	SCO
10	GEM	CAN	LEO	LIB	SCO	CAP	AQU	ARI	TAU	GEM	LEO	VIR	LIB	SCO
11	GEM	CAN	VIR	LIB	SCO	CAP	AQU	ARI	TAU	CAN	LEO	VIR	SCO	SAG
12	GEM	LEO	VIR	SCO	SAG	AQU	PSC	ARI	TAU	CAN	LEO	LIB	SCO	SAG
13	CAN	LEO	LIB	SCO	SAG	AQU	PSC	TAU	GEM	CAN	VIR	LIB	SAG	CAP
14	CAN	LEO	LIB	SAG	CAP	AQU	ARI	TAU	GEM	LEO	VIR	LIB	SAG	CAP
15	LEO	VIR	SCO	SAG	CAP	PSC	ARI	GEM	CAN	LEO	LIB	SCO	CAP	AQU
16	LEO	VIR	SCO	CAP	AQU	PSC	ARI	GEM	CAN	VIR	LIB	SCO	CAP	AQU
17	VIR	LIB	SCO	CAP	AQU	ARI	TAU	GEM	CAN	VIR	SCO	SAG	AQU	PSC
18	VIR	LIB	SAG	AQU	PSC	ARI	TAU	CAN	LEO	VIR	SCO	SAG	AQU	PSC
19	VIR	SCO	SAG	AQU	PSC	TAU	GEM	CAN	LEO	LIB	SAG	CAP	PSC	ARI
20	LIB	SCO	CAP	PSC	PSC	TAU	GEM	LEO	VIR	LIB	SAG	CAP	PSC	ARI
21	LIB	SAG	CAP	PSC	ARI	TAU	GEM	LEO	VIR	SCO	SAG	AQU	ARI	TAU
22	SCO	SAG	AQU	ARI	ARI	GEM	CAN	LEO	LIB	SCO	CAP	AQU	ARI	TAU
23	SCO	CAP	AQU	ARI	TAU	GEM	CAN	VIR	LIB	SAG	CAP	PSC	ARI	GEM
24	SAG	CAP	PSC	ARI	TAU	CAN	LEO	VIR	LIB	SAG	AQU	PSC	TAU	GEM
25	SAG	AQU	PSC	TAU	GEM	CAN	LEO	LIB	SCO	CAP	AQU	ARI	TAU	GEM
26	CAP	AQU	ARI	TAU	GEM	CAN	LEO	LIB	SCO	CAP	PSC	ARI	GEM	CAN
27	CAP	PSC	ARI	GEM	GEM	LEO	VIR	SCO	SAG	AQU	PSC	ARI	GEM	CAN
28	AQU	PSC	TAU	GEM	CAN	LEO	VIR	SCO	SAG	AQU	ARI	TAU	GEM	LEO
29	AQU	ARI	TAU	GEM	CAN	VIR	LIB	SCO	CAP	PSC	ARI	TAU	CAN	LEO
30	PSC	ARI	TAU	—	LEO	VIR	LIB	SAG	CAP	PSC	TAU	GEM	CAN	LEO
31	—	ARI	GEM	—	LEO	—	SCO	—	AQU	PSC	—	GEM	—	VIR

Astrological Timetable

■ The following month-by-month chart is based on the Moon's sign and shows the most-favorable times each month for certain activities. —*Celeste Longacre*

	JAN.	FEB.	MAR.	APR.	MAY	JUNE	JULY	AUG.	SEPT.	OCT.	NOV.	DEC.
Quit smoking	14, 18, 19	7, 14, 15	9, 13	13, 18	16, 18	11, 15	4, 9	5, 15	2, 11	8, 9	5, 10	2, 7, 29, 30
Begin diet to gain weight	26, 27	6, 23, 24	4, 21	1, 27, 28	3, 25, 30	22, 26	19, 24	20, 28	15, 16, 25	22, 23, 26	18, 22, 23	15, 20
Begin diet to lose weight	14, 18, 19	7, 14, 15	9, 13	13, 18	16, 18	11, 15	4, 9	5, 15	2, 11	8, 9	5, 10	2, 7, 29, 30
Cut hair to discourage growth	14, 15	10, 11	8, 9	15, 16	12, 13	8, 9	10, 11	14, 15	3, 4	1, 2, 13	9, 10	6, 7
Cut hair to encourage growth	1, 2, 29, 30	25, 26	4, 31	4, 27, 28	2, 3, 29, 30	25, 26	23, 24	19, 20	15, 16	23, 24	19, 20	17, 18
Have dental care	12, 13	7, 8	6, 7	2, 3, 30	1, 27, 28	23, 24	20, 21	17, 18	13, 14	10, 11	7, 8	4, 5, 31
End projects	19, 20	18, 19	18, 19	17, 18	17, 18	15, 16	15, 16	15, 16	12, 13	12, 13	10, 11	10, 11
Start projects	22, 23	21, 22	21, 22	20, 21	20, 21	18, 19	18, 19	18, 19	15, 16	15, 16	13, 14	13, 14
Entertain	9, 10	6, 7	3, 4, 31	1, 27, 28	24, 25, 26	21, 22	18, 19	14, 15	10, 11, 12	8, 9	4, 5	1, 2, 29, 30
Go camping	18, 19	14, 15	12, 13	8, 9	6, 7	2, 3, 30	1, 28, 29	23, 24	20, 21	17, 18	13, 14	11, 12
Plant aboveground crops	8, 24, 25	4, 5	1, 2, 28, 29	2, 3, 25, 26	22, 23	1, 28, 29	20, 21, 25, 26	21, 22, 30, 31	26, 27	15, 16, 23, 24	19, 20	17, 18
Plant belowground crops	15, 16	12, 13, 21	10, 11	15, 16	5, 12, 13	8, 9	6, 7, 15, 16	2, 3	8, 9	5, 6	2, 3, 29, 30	9, 10, 27
Destroy pests and weeds	26, 27	23, 24	21, 22	17, 18	14, 15	11, 12	8, 9	4, 5	1, 2, 28, 29	26, 27, 28	22, 23	19, 20
Graft or pollinate	6, 7	3, 4	1, 2, 28, 29	25, 26	22, 23	18, 19	15, 16	12, 13	8, 9	5, 6	2, 3, 29, 30	27, 28
Prune to discourage growth	18, 19	14, 15	12, 13	13, 18	14, 15	11, 12	8, 9	4, 5	8, 9	8, 9	4, 5	1, 2, 29, 30
Prune to encourage growth	26, 27	5, 22, 23	3, 4, 31	1, 27, 28	24, 25	21, 22	18, 19	23, 24	20, 21	17, 18	22, 23	19, 20
Harvest above-ground crops	1, 2, 29, 30	25, 26	23, 24	2, 3, 30	1, 27, 28	23, 24	20, 21	17, 18	22, 23	19, 20	24, 25	21, 22
Harvest below-ground crops	11, 12	7, 8	7, 14, 15	11, 12	17, 18	13, 14	3, 10, 11	7, 8	3, 4, 13	1, 2, 29	7, 8	4, 5
Cut hay	26, 27	23, 24	21, 22	17, 18	14, 15	11, 12	8, 9	4, 5	1, 2, 28, 29	26, 27, 28	22, 23	19, 20
Begin logging	20, 21	16, 17	14, 15	11, 12	8, 9	4, 5	2, 3, 29, 30	25, 26	22, 23	19, 20	16, 17	13, 14
Set posts or pour concrete	20, 21	16, 17	14, 15	10, 11	8, 9	4, 5	2, 3, 29, 30	25, 26	22, 23	19, 20	15, 16	13, 14
Breed	16, 17	12, 13	10, 11	6, 7	4, 5, 31	1, 28, 29	25, 26	21, 22	17, 18	15, 16	11, 12	9, 10
Wean	14, 18	7, 14, 15	9, 17	13, 18	16, 18	11, 15	4, 9	5, 15	2, 11	8, 9	5, 10	2, 7, 29, 30
Castrate animals	22, 23	18, 19	16, 17	13, 14	10, 11	6, 7	4, 5, 31	1, 28, 29	24, 25	21, 22	17, 18	15, 16
Slaughter	15, 16	12, 13	10, 11	6, 7	4, 5, 31	1, 28, 29	25, 26	21, 22	17, 18	15, 16	11, 12	9, 10

The **Old Farmer's**
General Store

40 Mile Electric!

Palmer's one-hand operated, double and single seat 3 wheelers are Gear driven.
Features: – 13 mph – 550 lb capacity – Climbs steepest San Francisco hills

Made in USA ✦ **FREE BROCHURE** ✦ *Since 1973*
Call 800-847-1304
Palmer Industries
P.O. Box 5707ACS · Endicott, NY 13763
ALSO PEDAL TRIKES, HANDCYCLES AND ELECTRIC KITS AND TRIKES
www.palmerind.com

NEW YORK CITY VIDEO
Capturing the sights and sounds of the city. FREE guides, coupons, street maps, phone numbers and contacts for over 70 of the most popular attractions. Video highlights and order form at www.electronictours.net or send $24.95 (check) to Electronic Ed. Tours, 76 North Maple Ave., Suite 116, Ridgewood, NJ 07450

MEN'S WIDE SHOES
EEE-EEEEEE, SIZES 5-13
• High quality
• 200 styles
• FREE catalog

HITCHCOCK SHOES, INC.
Dept. 104 Hingham, MA 02043
1-800-992-WIDE   www.wideshoes.com

(SUN-MAR)
Composting Toilets
Electric & Non-Electric Models

• **No Septic**
• **No Odor**

Free 24 pg. catalog

1-800-461-2461
www.sun-mar.com

Celebrate July 4th & All Events
BIG-BANG® CANNON
GREAT GIFT IDEA!   **$159.⁹⁵**

The only SAFE substitute for fireworks! Cannons produce a loud bang with a realistic flash of light. Patented in 1907. Made of cast iron and sheet metal. Easy loading and firing. Great for display when not in use. Made in the USA to last a lifetime. Available in 3 sizes: 9" cannon, **$69.95 postpaid;** 17" cannon, **$129.95 postpaid;** 25" cannon (shown here) with rapid firing and automatic loading, **$159.95 postpaid.** The larger the cannon the louder the bang! Bangsite® ammo, about 100 shots, **$8.50; 3-pack $20.00.** Spark plugs, 3-pack $2.00. Order via mail, phone or website. Mastercard, Visa, check or money order accepted. Money back guarantee. Send for FREE CATALOG!

The Conestoga Co., Inc., Dept OFA, PO Box 405, Bethlehem, PA 18016
★★ **Call 1-800-987-BANG** ★★
www.bigbangcannons.com

GIFTED PSYCHICS
Experience the difference!

PSYCHIC® SOURCE
WE KNOW

1.888.967.0113
PSYCHICSOURCE.COM
MC2877 ENT. ONLY. 18+

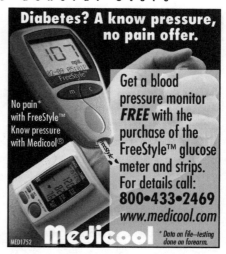
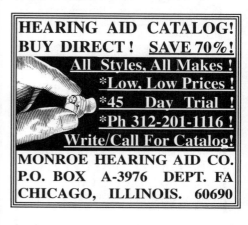

Answers appear on page 203.

Green Thumb Jumble

Your job is to unscramble each group of letters to form a word (or words). Now here's the catch: You need to carry the first letter of each word you unscramble down to the blank space in the next group of letters to become part of that jumble. (Where you've unscrambled two words, carry only the first letter of the first word.) When you're finished, the first letters of the unscrambled words will spell out a possible name for this puzzle when read in order from top to bottom.

1. erneg   saben   (2 words)
2. pasasuar__
3. hedsirs__
4. dit__
5. veine__
6. tinrecan__
7. sevi__
8. codaao__   rete   (2 words)
9. nimroe__   teceltu   (2 words)
10. sii__
11. hinsegl   vy__   (2 words)
12. myth__
13. lelyow   estooma__   (2 words)

–by Betsy Ochester

Mystery Message

Each letter in this cryptic quote stands for another letter in the alphabet. Your job is to crack the code and reveal the message. (If you need a hint, see below.)

"OFKI UVKL HEVJBZTOJH JON XOFKFXJNK VS ENVEBN: HVRN JAKY AE JONZK HBNNCNH, HVRN JAKY AE JONZK YVHNH, FYI HVRN IVY'J JAKY AE FJ FBB."

–Hfr Nuzyt

–by Betsy Ochester

Charades

Three single-syllable words provide the first three answers needed here. The fourth answer is a combination of the first three.

*Among all living things, my **first**
    holds regal sway,*
*And puts my **second** on whene'er
    he goes away,*
*Which helps keep off my **third**,
    produced by solar ray.*
*My **whole**, an island small, holds
    city vast today.*

–from The Old Farmer's Almanac *archives*

Mystery Message hint: H = S.

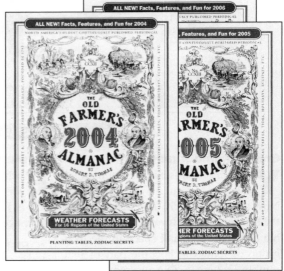

Classified Advertising

ALTERNATIVE ENERGY

YOUR OWN ELECTRIC COMPANY! Diesel generators. Free brochures. Imperial-OFA, 507 Kinsman, Greenville PA 16125. 800-830-0498.

ART

NORMAN ROCKWELL prints, posters. Catalog $4, refundable. Rockwell Gallery Collection, Box 1260F, Huntingdon Valley PA 19006. 215-969-5619. www.rockwellsite.com. E-mail: rockwellsite@snip.net

ASTROLOGY/OCCULT

ASTROLOGY: FREE CATALOG. Books, tapes, tarot, spirituality. 800-500-0453 or 714-255-9218. Church of Light, www.light.org

MRS. KING, spiritual reader, advisor, helps in matters of life where others have failed. Call 912-283-0635.

FREE OCCULT CATALOG! Books, bumper stickers, jewelry, ritual items. AzureGreen, PO Box 48-OFA, Middlefield MA 01243. 413-623-2155. Retail/wholesale. www.azuregreen.com

MISS LISA, astrology reader and advisor. Extraordinary powers. Call for help with all problems. Waycross GA. 912-283-3206.

SKEPTICAL about psychic services? We're also tired of the nonsense. Experience the Difference with Psychic Source. Call 866-945-9562. Web site: www.psychicsource.com Entertainment only, 18+.

MALEENA, GOD-GIFTED. Can reunite lovers. Guaranteed results with all situations. Free mini-reading. 757-549-9090.

WITCH WORKS™. Empowered, moon-cultivated herbal potions, essences. PO Box 1839A, Royal Oak MI 48068-1839. 248-542-3113 or www.witchworks.com

OCCULT CATALOG: complete needs. Herbs, oils, books, incense, etc. $3. Power Products, PO Box 442, Mars Hill NC 28754.

FREE MINI-READINGS. Psychic Diana has the ability to solve all problems. Removes spells and reunites loved ones. Toronto, Ontario; 416-226-5418.

NEW ORLEANS PSYCHIC. Relationship specialist. Guarantees to remove all negative obstacles in two days. 985-652-2969.

POWERFUL SPELLS performed by Gabriella. Specializing in reuniting lovers. Guaranteed in two hours. 504-628-1260.

PSYCHIC SOURCE: a community of over 100 gifted psychic advisors connected by a common desire to provide caring, genuine insight and guidance. Call Psychic Source today, 888-967-0130. www.psychicsource.com Entertainment only, 18+.

FREE LUCKY NUMBERS. Send birth date, self-addressed, stamped envelope. Mystic, Box 2009-R, Jamestown NC 27282.

SPIRITUAL ADVISOR. Help for all problems: relationships, nature, money, jobs. See results in 3 days. Call Dewberry 800-989-1059 or 912-264-3259.

ATTENTION: SISTER LIGHT, Spartanburg, South Carolina. One free reading when you call. I will help in all problems. 864-576-9397.

EUROPEAN PSYCHIC READER and advisor guarantees help with all problems. Call Sylvia for one free reading. 864-583-5776.

DEVELOP PSYCHIC AND OCCULT abilities. Learn by correspondence. Become a psychic, healer, spiritual advisor, counselor, magician, teacher. Metaphysical University, 2110 Artesia Blvd., Admissions B-264, Redondo Beach CA 90278-3014. 310-398-1638. E-mail: mysticadamad@attbi.com

FREE! ONE PERSONALIZED MAGIC spell! Tell us exactly what you need! EKSES, PO Box 9315(B), San Bernardino CA 92427-9315.

SISTER HILLARY solves all impossible problems. Reunites lovers. Predicted over 500 successful marriages. 100% accuracy. Guaranteed results. 512-845-2053.

POWERFUL SPELLS PERFORMED. Alexandria reunites lovers immediately. Reveals future love, finance. One free reading. 423-593-4563.

SISTER MOSES can remove bad luck, sickness, suffering. Restores love, luck, happiness. Guarantees help in 3 days. One free reading. 601-545-8972.

BEEKEEPING EQUIPMENT

ROSSMAN APIARIES. Established 1936 and family-owned. Manufacturers of cypress beehives, protective clothing, honey extracting equipment, honey containers. 800-333-7677. www.gabees.com

BEER & WINE MAKING

FREE ILLUSTRATED CATALOG. Fast service. Since 1967. Kraus, PO Box 7850-YB, Independence MO 64054. www.eckraus.com/offers/fd.asp 800-841-7404.

LEARN THE SECRETS of making great wines naturally using no chemicals. 770-469-8528 or www.atlantamall2000.com/winemaking.htm

BOOKS/PUBLICATIONS/CATALOGS

BECOME A PUBLISHED AUTHOR. Publisher with 80-year tradition. Author's guide to subsidy publishing. 800-695-9599.

FREE BOOKLETS: Life, death, soul, resurrection, pollution crisis, hell, Judgment Day, restitution. Bible Standard (OF), 1156 St. Matthews Rd., Chester Springs PA 19425. www.biblestandard.com

FAMILY FUN. 100-year-old book of children's manners: "Goops and How to Be Them." www.TheGoops.net

END PROBLEMS WITH OTHERS FOREVER! Order two powerful booklets today: "How to Handle Difficult People" and "Your Power to Say NO". $4. Newlife, PO Box 2230-SH, Pine AZ 85544. www.anewlife.org

AMERICA'S BEST CHILDREN'S BOOKS: Beatrix Potter, Americana, farm animals, wildlife, educational. Catalog $5. Storytime, PO Box 203, Dry Run PA 17220.

GRACE LIVINGSTON HILL BOOKS! Free list. We have great L. Walker Arnold books! Call 800-854-8571.

APPLYING FOR DISABILITY? Harassed, discriminated against, or injured at work? Scared? Confused? www.self-protection.info PO Box 3, Roselawn IN 46372 or 219-765-5019.

BUILDING SUPPLIES

HARDWOOD PLANK FLOORING/WAINSCOTING. Premium Vermont hardwood custom milled by our experienced craftsmen. 802-823-7365. www.northeastwoodproducts.com

BUSINESS OPPORTUNITIES

$400 WEEKLY ASSEMBLING PRODUCTS from home. For free information, send SASE to Home Assembly-FA, PO Box 216, New Britain CT 06050-0216.

LET GOVERNMENT GRANTS/LOANS FINANCE your business, to $2,200,000.00. (Web site: www.usgovernmentinformation.com) Free recorded message: 707-448-0270. (KE1)

FREE GRANTS. Home purchase, repair, education, business, $500 to $500,000. 800-306-0873. http://www.capitolpublications.com

EARN $400 TO $700 for 5 to 6 hours' work. Free information. Send stamped envelope to "Off Air DJ," Box 332, Big Bend WI 53103.

RECORD VIDEOTAPES AT HOME! Easy $1,800.00 weekly income. Free start-up information kit. 205-663-9888. CMS Video Dept. 174, 210 Lorna Square, Birmingham AL 35216-5439.

EARN SUBSTANTIAL INCOME locating distressed property. Earn big profits. No experience needed. Complete training provided. Unlimited earnings potential. Free information: 800-331-4555 ext. 7830.

CLOTHING

FREE CARHARTT clothing catalog! Shrock-OFA, 507 Kinsman, Greenville PA 16125. 866-655-2467. "Saving you money $$$."

E-COMMERCE

RED FLANNEL WEBSITE DESIGN. Renovation, design, maintenance, shopping carts. Reasonable rates. Experienced. Service-oriented. Small business specialty. www.redflannelweb.com

EDUCATION/INSTRUCTION

BRITISH INSTITUTE OF HOMEOPATHY. Home-study courses in herbology, clinical nutrition, homeopathy, Bach Flower Remedies, and more. Free prospectus. Call 609-927-5660.

INDEPENDENT STUDY CAREER TRAINING program in Enhanced Medical Assisting with national job placement. 888-354-4325. Web site: www.wholehealtheducation.com

FARM & GARDEN

GREENHOUSES! Beautiful, strong, functional, do-it-yourself hobby/commercial-size kits and accessories. 800-531-GROW (4769). Web site: www.GothicArchGreenhouses.com

NEPTUNE'S HARVEST ORGANIC FERTILIZERS: Extremely effective. Commercially proven. Outperform chemicals. Wholesale/retail/farm. Catalog. 800-259-4769. www.neptunesharvest.com

CANNING SUPPLIES. Extensive selection. Canners, dryers, jars, ingredients, tools, books. Free catalog. 800-776-0575. www.kitchenkrafts.com

POND SUPPLIES. Barley straw and other products. Natural solutions for pond algae. Growers, distributors, wholesale, retail. 315-531-8803. Web site: www.naturalsolutionsetc.com

JACOB SHEEP: Hardy, low maintenance. Excellent for wool, breeding. Resurrection Farm, Massachusetts. E-mail us: healthed@comcast.net

GREENHOUSE TUBING BENDERS. Bend steel tubing into smooth, gracefully curved greenhouse frames in seconds. 903-569-8541. www.lostcreek.net

Classifieds

FOOD & RECIPES

ZUCCHINI, THIRTY RECIPES. $3. H. C. Ward, 645 N. Middle Rd., Newville PA 17241.

PECAN DATE CAKE W/CARAMEL ICING. Scrumptious family recipe! $3.00 and SASE to Susie's Recipes, PO Box 1552, San Marcos TX 78667-1552.

YOU-MAKE-IT. Supplies for cheese to wine, beer to bubblegum, hot sauce and more! www.leeners.com

MAKE YOUR OWN JERKY! Fast, easy, fun! Excellent seasoning for beef, venison, buffalo. 800-647-0996. www.pacificmountainfarms.com

FUND-RAISING

MAKE GOOD MONEY for your school, group, or nonprofit organization selling The Old Farmer's Almanac General Store® products to friends and neighbors. Great products sell themselves! Great prices! Great opportunity! Call today 800-424-6906. The Old Farmer's Almanac Fund-Raising, 220 South Street, Bernardston, MA 01337. www.gbimarketing.com

GARDENING & LANDSCAPING

DEER/CRITTERS BROWSING YOUR GARDEN OR SHRUBS? Stop 'em in their tracks! Cruelty- and chemical-free solution: www.Predator-Products.com

JOHNSON NURSERY. Hardy fruit trees with antique and disease-resistant varieties. Free catalog! 888-276-3187. Ellijay, Georgia. www.johnsonnursery.com

GIFTS

BE LUCKY, BE HAPPY at theluckshop.com. Curios, treasures for your joy, comfort, and fun.

HEALTH & BEAUTY

AUTHENTIC TESTED FORMULAS. Liniments, salves, ointments from Grandma's medicine chest. Alford's, Box 339-OF, Middlesex NC 27557.

OLD-FASHIONED, ALL NATURAL, quality health products since 1868. I recommend them to my patients. www.watkinsonline.com/DrSchultz or call 630-975-0512.

MIRACLE II SOAP. All natural. No chemicals. Cleans, detoxifies, rejuvenates body, soil, and plants! Free booklet. 888-879-7817.

DIABETIC SUPPLIES. Medicare, most insurances (no HMOs) accepted with no cost to those qualified. Free shipping. 800-254-4667.

HEALTH & FITNESS

WEIGHT LOSS. Send $10 and SASE. Farrar's Hypnosis Advantage, Box 210562, Normandy MO 63121.

GENUINE FREQUENCY FOODS™. Revolutionary advancement in quantum nutrition and healing. Free affiliate program. 888-483-2283 ext. 22. (www.NPC.ubiquitousonline.com) Tupperware™ home business opportunities available. 877-2TUPPER. (www.my.tupperware.com/NPC)

SPECIALIZING IN OBESITY, ARTHRITIS. Vitamin herbal products. New natural product Banaba for energy, weight control. Sunshine Vitamin Co., Box 10286, Oakland CA 94610. 510-465-2805. Free brochure.

AMAZING DIABETES TEA used internationally, contains natural insulin, stimulates and detoxifies pancreas. Guaranteed. Toll-free 877-832-9369. www.diabetestea.com

HELP WANTED

EASY WORK! EXCELLENT PAY! Assemble products at home. Call toll-free 800-467-5566 ext. 12627.

INSECT REPELLENT

BUZZ-OFF. Powerful insect repellent. Deet-free. All insects away. $10/4 oz. Lewey's, 176 Amsden Rd., Corrina ME 04928; or 800-leweys-1 (539-3971); or www.4u2buzzoff.com

INVENTORS/INVENTIONS/PATENTS

INVENTIONS/NEW PRODUCTS. ISC, America's leading invention firm, helps submit to companies. Patent services. 1-888-439-IDEA.

LABELS

FULL-COLOR LABELS for soaps, jams, jellies, honey, lotions, creams. Small quantities available. Free samples. 877-901-4989.

MAINE RESORTS

BAR HARBOR AND ACADIA National Park. 153 oceanview rooms. Atlantic-Oakes-by-the-Sea. Open year-round. 800-33-MAINE (62463). Web site: www.barharbor.com

MISCELLANEOUS

JEHOVAH'S WITNESSES, friends, family, discover facts society's hiding. Free, confidential. Box 454, Metaline Falls WA 99153. Web site: www.macgregorministries.org

CASH FOR 78-RPM RECORDS! Send $2 (refundable) for illustrated booklet identifying collectible labels, numbers, with actual prices I pay. Docks, Box 691035(FA), San Antonio TX 78269-1035.

MUSIC/RECORDS/TAPES/CDS

SPIRIT FIDDLE. Old-fashioned fiddle/guitar CDs: Mother's Day Waltz, Blue Jeans and Gingham, Cafe Music. Contact www.spiritfiddle.com or 603-424-0814.

FREE CATALOG. Top-quality vegetable, flower, and herb seeds since 1900. Burrell, Box 150-OFAC, Rock Ford CO 81067.

COMPARE AND SAVE: SEEDS, BULBS, PLANTS, herbs, extracts, supplements, oils, books, horticulture supplies, mycology supplies, and other related items. www.pjtbotanicals.com Catalog $3.00 U.S., $6.00 International. P.J.T. Botanicals, PO Box 49, Bridgewater MA 02324.

VEGETABLE TRANSPLANTS. Quality greenhouse vegetable transplants shipped direct from growers since 1947. Call 229-776-3790; e-mail: plantsbymail@vol.com

SPIRITUAL ADVICE

SPIRITUAL HEALER SOPHIA helps all problems: love, luck, money, health, marriage, and happiness. Free reading. 334-688-1709.

REVEREND GINGER, INDIAN HEALER, works miracles, guaranteed in hours. Specializing in re-uniting the separated. Call 504-463-3358.

SISTER DENISE, spiritual reader, resolves all problems in life. Love, business, marriage, nature, bad luck. Guaranteed results. 678-455-0170.

SPIRITUAL HEALER

EVANGELIST ADAMS, spiritual healer and advisor. Are you suffering with bad luck, love, marriage, sickness, and finances? Immediate results. 770-622-9191.

SISTER NINA, spiritual healer and advisor. Worried, sick, marriage. Have bad luck and evil surroundings? 24-hour results. 770-650-7177.

SISTER DIVINE, spiritual healer, reunites lovers. Solves all matters: love, business, finance. Removes evil spells. Guaranteed results in 24 hours. 251-479-7775.

AFRICAN HEALER. Guarantees to solve all problems. Specializing in spiritual cleanings. Call for Free reading. 866-375-3518.

GIFTED HEALER. Solves all problems, troubles, bad luck, love, life. Removes evil influences, nature problems, brings back lovers to stay, good luck, money. Uncle Doc Shedrickrack, Hwy. 48, 7905 Bluff Rd., Gadsden SC 29052. Call 803-353-0659.

TREES & SHRUBS

CATALOG FREE! Tree seedlings. Wholesale prices. Flickinger's Nursery, Box 245, Sagamore PA 16250. 800-368-7381.

WEATHER VANES

WEATHERVANES AND CUPOLAS. 50% off sale. America's largest selection. Free catalog. Immediate delivery. 800-724-2548. Web site: www.weathervaneandcupola.com

SOMETHING FOR EVERYONE

FREE CATALOG of *Classics Illustrated* comics. 1940s–1970s. Philip Gaudino, 49 Park Ave., Port Washington NY 11050.

PSYCHIC NICOLE BERRY helps with all problems. Reunites lovers. Aura cleansing. 99% accurate. Immediate results. Call 281-987-7360.

The *Old Farmer's Almanac* classified rates: $18.50 per word (15-word minimum per insertion). Payment required with order: MasterCard, Visa, AmEx, and Discover/NOVUS accepted. For *Gardener's Companion* rates, Web classifieds, or additional information, contact Marie Knopp: 203-263-7171; fax 203-263-7174; or e-mail to OFAads@aol.com. Write to: Marie Knopp, Gallagher Group, PO Box 959, Woodbury, CT 06798. **The 2005 Old Farmer's Almanac closing date is May 12, 2004.**

Get the Facts on www.almanac.com

Visit the on-line home of *The Old Farmer's Almanac* for all your information needs. Create your own personal version of the home page, adjusted for your precise location.

- Free electronic newsletter sign-up
- Long-range and five-day weather forecasts
- Gardening information
- Recipes
- Advice
- and lots, lots more

You can even search the classified ads to find just what you're looking for!

Stop by for a visit!

Index to Advertisers

Start every day right: Visit www.almanac.com.

ANSWERS TO

GARDENING Mind-Manglers

from page 195

Green Thumb Jumble

1. green beans
2. asparagus
3. radishes
4. dirt
5. endive
6. nectarine
7. vines
8. avocado tree
9. romaine lettuce
10. iris
11. English ivy
12. thyme
13. yellow tomatoes

First-letter message:
GARDEN VARIETY

Mystery Message

"Hard work spotlights the character of people: Some turn up their sleeves, some turn up their noses, and some don't turn up at all."

–Sam Ewing (American writer, 1921–2001)

Charades

man, hat, tan, Manhattan

ANECDOTES & Pleasantries

A sampling from the hundreds of letters, clippings, and e-mails sent to us by Almanac readers from all over the United States and Canada during the past year.

How and Why Dogs Were Created (CATS, TOO)

Courtesy of W. O., Poultney, Vermont

■ Perhaps you would enjoy reading what the scholars of the Dead Sea Scrolls might have discovered to be an addition to the Book of Genesis. It has been in our family for years and goes like this:

Adam said, "Lord, when I was in the garden, you walked with me everyday. I do not see you anymore and I am lonely. It is difficult for me to remember how much you love me."

God said, "I shall create a companion for you who will always be with you and shall reflect My love for you. His love shall be unconditional; regardless of how selfish, childish, or unlovable you may be, he will accept and love you."

God created an animal for Adam, and it was good. And God said, "Because I

have created this animal to be a reflection of My love for you, his name shall be a reflection of My name, and you will call him dog."

The dog lived with Adam. Adam was comforted. The dog was content and wagged his tail.

Then it came to pass that Adam's guardian angel came to the Lord and said, "Lord, Adam has become filled with pride; he struts and preens and has come to believe that he is worthy of adoration. He has learned from the dog's devotion that he is loved, but he has no humility."

And the Lord said, "I shall create another companion for him who will see him as he is and remind him of his limitations, so that

An Inspiring Example of Human Resourcefulness

A (supposedly) true story, courtesy of I. A., Hancock, New Hampshire

■ Last spring, after stopping for drinks at an illegal bar, a Zimbabwean bus driver found that the 20 mental patients he was supposed to be transporting from Harare to Bulawayo (two cities in this South African country) had escaped. They were nowhere to be found. Not wanting to admit his incompetence, to say nothing of his time at the bar, the driver went to a nearby bus stop and offered everyone waiting there a free ride. He then delivered these passengers to the mental hospital, telling the doctors and nurses that the "patients" were very excitable and prone to rather bizarre fantasies.

The deception wasn't discovered for almost three days.

he knows he is not worthy of adoration and will become humble."

So God created the cat. The cat did not obey Adam, and when he gazed into the cat's eyes, Adam was reminded that he was not the supreme being. He learned humility.

Adam was greatly improved. God was pleased. So was the dog. The cat did not care one way or the other.

How to Bake Four-and-Twenty Blackbirds in a Pie

Courtesy of F. B., Pound Ridge, New York

■ Can you really, as in the old song, have live birds fly out of your freshly baked pie? Sure, according to an old book of recipes titled *The Italian Banquet,* which came out in 1516, 276 years before *The Old Farmer's Almanac* first appeared (1792). Here's how to do it:

Line a deep dish with a sturdy piecrust, and cut a hole "the size of your fist" in the bottom. Fill with flour, heaping it up into a mound, and cover with a top crust. Cut a few slits for ventilation, and bake until the crust is set.

When cool enough to handle, turn the "pie" out of the dish and, through the hole in the bottom, scoop out the flour. To serve, simply pop a few birds up through that hole in the crust, and return the pie to the dish. Voilà! A pie with live birds! How festive! (Incidentally, 24 birds is probably an excessive number. Maybe start with two or three?)

Love-and-Marriage Questions

With answers supplied by various New Jersey elementary-school children, picked at random. Courtesy of F. P., West Caldwell, New Jersey

QUESTION: *How do you decide whom to marry?*
ANSWERS: You got to find somebody who likes the same  stuff. Like, if you like sports, she should like it that you like sports, and she should

keep the chips and dip coming. –*Alan, age 10*

No person really decides before they grow up who they're going to marry. God decides it all way before you, and you only get to find out later who you're stuck with. –*Kirsten, age 10*

QUESTION: *What is the right age to get married?*
ANSWER: Twenty-three is the best age because you've known the person *forever* by then.
–*Camille, age 10*

QUESTION: *How can a stranger tell if two people are married?*
ANSWER: You might have to guess based on whether they seem to be yelling at the same kids. –*Derrick, age 8*

QUESTION: *What would you do on a first date that was turning sour?*
ANSWER: I'd run home and play dead. The next day, I would call all the newspapers and make sure they wrote about me in all the dead columns. –*Craig, age 9*

QUESTION: *When is it OK to kiss someone?*
ANSWERS: When they're rich. –*Pam, age 7*

The law says you have to be 18, so I wouldn't want to mess with that.
–*Curt, age 7*

The rule goes like this: If you kiss someone, then you should marry them and have kids with them. It's the right thing to do.
–*Howard, age 8*

QUESTION: *Is it better to be single or married?*

ANSWER: It's better for girls to be single but not for boys. Boys need someone to clean up after them. –*Anita, age 9*

QUESTION: *How would the world be different if people didn't get married?*
ANSWER: There sure would be a lot of kids to explain, wouldn't there?
–*Kelvin, age 8*

QUESTION: *How would you make a marriage work?*
ANSWER: Tell your wife that she looks pretty even if she looks like a truck.
–*Ricky, age 10*

The Three Worst Puns of 2003
Courtesy of G. P., Nelson, New Hampshire

1 Mahatma Gandhi, as everyone knows, walked barefoot most of the time, which produced an impressive set of calluses on his feet. He also ate very little, which made him rather frail, and with his odd diet, he suffered from bad breath. This made him a—ready?—super callused fragile mystic hexed by halitosis.

2 Two Eskimos sitting in a kayak were chilly, but when they lit a fire in the craft, it sank, proving once again that you can't have your kayak and heat it, too.

3 A group of chess enthusiasts checked into a hotel and were standing in the lobby discussing their recent tournament victories. After about an hour, the manager came out of the office and asked them to disperse. "But why?" they asked, as they moved off. "Because," he said, "I can't stand chess nuts boasting in an open foyer."

> **FACT: It is impossible to lick your elbow.**
> —*courtesy of F. P.,
> West Caldwell, New Jersey*

Two *Additional* Ways to Hypnotize a Chicken

Plus, by popular demand, the reason why anyone would want to do so.

Editor's note: The following suggestions are representative of the many that have steadily trickled in since 1985, when we published an article describing the three principle methods of hypnotizing a chicken: the oscillating-finger method, the sternum-stroke method, and, of course, the old chalk-line method. (If you missed the article, you can find it by searching on our Web site, **www.almanac.com.**)

■ **Lay the chicken on** its side on the ground, move your hand in front of its beak to get its attention, and suddenly draw an arc in the dirt with your finger. It will lie there for several seconds or even a few minutes.

—*S. R., Grand Rapids, Michigan*

■ **Some people may object, but a quick way** to hypnotize a chicken is to lay it on its back, grab a wing, and then spin it. Never fails. —*R.R.S., Waco, Texas*

WHY *WOULD* YOU WANT TO HYPNOTIZE A CHICKEN?

■ **It seems to me that lots of people have no** idea why someone would want to hypnotize a chicken. Well, when I was a youngster, we would hypnotize chickens on the chopping block in order to eliminate the need to have your hand anywhere near the swinging hatchet. —*H. K., via e-mail*

> ## Hey, Maybe Things Aren't So Bad After All
> *Courtesy of R.D.H.,
> Los Angeles, California*
>
> ■ **In 1895, it took perhaps 260 hours of the average American worker's time to amass enough money to buy a one-speed bicycle. Today, an average American worker can buy one of higher quality for less than eight hours of work. In other words, lots of stuff is cheaper today.**

Share Your Anecdotes and Pleasantries

Send your contribution for the 2005 edition of *The Old Farmer's Almanac* by January 30, 2004, to "A & P," The Old Farmer's Almanac, P.O. Box 520, Dublin, NH 03444; or send e-mail to almanac@yankeepub.com (Subject: A & P). □□

2003

January
S	M	T	W	T	F	S
			1	2	3	4
5	6	7	8	9	10	11
12	13	14	15	16	17	18
19	20	21	22	23	24	25
26	27	28	29	30	31	

February
S	M	T	W	T	F	S
						1
2	3	4	5	6	7	8
9	10	11	12	13	14	15
16	17	18	19	20	21	22
23	24	25	26	27	28	

March
S	M	T	W	T	F	S
						1
2	3	4	5	6	7	8
9	10	11	12	13	14	15
16	17	18	19	20	21	22
23	24	25	26	27	28	29
30	31					

April
S	M	T	W	T	F	S
		1	2	3	4	5
6	7	8	9	10	11	12
13	14	15	16	17	18	19
20	21	22	23	24	25	26
27	28	29	30			

May
S	M	T	W	T	F	S
				1	2	3
4	5	6	7	8	9	10
11	12	13	14	15	16	17
18	19	20	21	22	23	24
25	26	27	28	29	30	31

June
S	M	T	W	T	F	S
1	2	3	4	5	6	7
8	9	10	11	12	13	14
15	16	17	18	19	20	21
22	23	24	25	26	27	28
29	30					

July
S	M	T	W	T	F	S
		1	2	3	4	5
6	7	8	9	10	11	12
13	14	15	16	17	18	19
20	21	22	23	24	25	26
27	28	29	30	31		

August
S	M	T	W	T	F	S
					1	2
3	4	5	6	7	8	9
10	11	12	13	14	15	16
17	18	19	20	21	22	23
24	25	26	27	28	29	30
31						

September
S	M	T	W	T	F	S
	1	2	3	4	5	6
7	8	9	10	11	12	13
14	15	16	17	18	19	20
21	22	23	24	25	26	27
28	29	30				

October
S	M	T	W	T	F	S
			1	2	3	4
5	6	7	8	9	10	11
12	13	14	15	16	17	18
19	20	21	22	23	24	25
26	27	28	29	30	31	

November
S	M	T	W	T	F	S
						1
2	3	4	5	6	7	8
9	10	11	12	13	14	15
16	17	18	19	20	21	22
23	24	25	26	27	28	29
30						

December
S	M	T	W	T	F	S
	1	2	3	4	5	6
7	8	9	10	11	12	13
14	15	16	17	18	19	20
21	22	23	24	25	26	27
28	29	30	31			

2004

January
S	M	T	W	T	F	S
				1	2	3
4	5	6	7	8	9	10
11	12	13	14	15	16	17
18	19	20	21	22	23	24
25	26	27	28	29	30	31

February
S	M	T	W	T	F	S
1	2	3	4	5	6	7
8	9	10	11	12	13	14
15	16	17	18	19	20	21
22	23	24	25	26	27	28
29						

March
S	M	T	W	T	F	S
	1	2	3	4	5	6
7	8	9	10	11	12	13
14	15	16	17	18	19	20
21	22	23	24	25	26	27
28	29	30	31			

April
S	M	T	W	T	F	S
				1	2	3
4	5	6	7	8	9	10
11	12	13	14	15	16	17
18	19	20	21	22	23	24
25	26	27	28	29	30	

May
S	M	T	W	T	F	S
						1
2	3	4	5	6	7	8
9	10	11	12	13	14	15
16	17	18	19	20	21	22
23	24	25	26	27	28	29
30	31					

June
S	M	T	W	T	F	S
		1	2	3	4	5
6	7	8	9	10	11	12
13	14	15	16	17	18	19
20	21	22	23	24	25	26
27	28	29	30			

July
S	M	T	W	T	F	S
				1	2	3
4	5	6	7	8	9	10
11	12	13	14	15	16	17
18	19	20	21	22	23	24
25	26	27	28	29	30	31

August
S	M	T	W	T	F	S
1	2	3	4	5	6	7
8	9	10	11	12	13	14
15	16	17	18	19	20	21
22	23	24	25	26	27	28
29	30	31				

September
S	M	T	W	T	F	S
			1	2	3	4
5	6	7	8	9	10	11
12	13	14	15	16	17	18
19	20	21	22	23	24	25
26	27	28	29	30		

October
S	M	T	W	T	F	S
					1	2
3	4	5	6	7	8	9
10	11	12	13	14	15	16
17	18	19	20	21	22	23
24	25	26	27	28	29	30
31						

November
S	M	T	W	T	F	S
	1	2	3	4	5	6
7	8	9	10	11	12	13
14	15	16	17	18	19	20
21	22	23	24	25	26	27
28	29	30				

December
S	M	T	W	T	F	S
			1	2	3	4
5	6	7	8	9	10	11
12	13	14	15	16	17	18
19	20	21	22	23	24	25
26	27	28	29	30	31	

2005

January
S	M	T	W	T	F	S
						1
2	3	4	5	6	7	8
9	10	11	12	13	14	15
16	17	18	19	20	21	22
23	24	25	26	27	28	29
30	31					

February
S	M	T	W	T	F	S
		1	2	3	4	5
6	7	8	9	10	11	12
13	14	15	16	17	18	19
20	21	22	23	24	25	26
27	28					

March
S	M	T	W	T	F	S
		1	2	3	4	5
6	7	8	9	10	11	12
13	14	15	16	17	18	19
20	21	22	23	24	25	26
27	28	29	30	31		

April
S	M	T	W	T	F	S
					1	2
3	4	5	6	7	8	9
10	11	12	13	14	15	16
17	18	19	20	21	22	23
24	25	26	27	28	29	30

May
S	M	T	W	T	F	S
1	2	3	4	5	6	7
8	9	10	11	12	13	14
15	16	17	18	19	20	21
22	23	24	25	26	27	28
29	30	31				

June
S	M	T	W	T	F	S
			1	2	3	4
5	6	7	8	9	10	11
12	13	14	15	16	17	18
19	20	21	22	23	24	25
26	27	28	29	30		

July
S	M	T	W	T	F	S
					1	2
3	4	5	6	7	8	9
10	11	12	13	14	15	16
17	18	19	20	21	22	23
24	25	26	27	28	29	30
31						

August
S	M	T	W	T	F	S
	1	2	3	4	5	6
7	8	9	10	11	12	13
14	15	16	17	18	19	20
21	22	23	24	25	26	27
28	29	30	31			

September
S	M	T	W	T	F	S
				1	2	3
4	5	6	7	8	9	10
11	12	13	14	15	16	17
18	19	20	21	22	23	24
25	26	27	28	29	30	

October
S	M	T	W	T	F	S
						1
2	3	4	5	6	7	8
9	10	11	12	13	14	15
16	17	18	19	20	21	22
23	24	25	26	27	28	29
30	31					

November
S	M	T	W	T	F	S
		1	2	3	4	5
6	7	8	9	10	11	12
13	14	15	16	17	18	19
20	21	22	23	24	25	26
27	28	29	30			

December
S	M	T	W	T	F	S
				1	2	3
4	5	6	7	8	9	10
11	12	13	14	15	16	17
18	19	20	21	22	23	24
25	26	27	28	29	30	31

A Reference Compendium

compiled by Mare-Anne Jarvela

A Table Foretelling the Weather Through All the Lunations of Each Year, or Forever

This table is the result of many years of actual observation and shows what sort of weather will probably follow the Moon's entrance into any of its quarters. For example, the table shows that the week following September 14, 2004, will be very rainy, because the Moon becomes new that day at 12:29 P.M. EDT. (See the **Left-Hand Calendar Pages 44–70** for 2004 Moon phases.)

EDITOR'S NOTE: *Although the data in this table is taken into consideration in the yearlong process of compiling the annual long-range weather forecasts for* The Old Farmer's Almanac, *we rely far more on our projections of solar activity.*

Time of Change	Summer	Winter
Midnight to 2 A.M.	Fair	Hard frost, unless wind is south or west
2 A.M. to 4 A.M.	Cold, with frequent showers	Snow and stormy
4 A.M. to 6 A.M.	Rain	Rain
6 A.M. to 8 A.M.	Wind and rain	Stormy
8 A.M. to 10 A.M.	Changeable	Cold rain if wind is west; snow if east
10 A.M. to noon	Frequent showers	Cold with high winds
Noon to 2 P.M.	Very rainy	Snow or rain
2 P.M. to 4 P.M.	Changeable	Fair and mild
4 P.M. to 6 P.M.	Fair	Fair
6 P.M. to 10 P.M.	Fair if wind is northwest; rain if wind is south or southwest	Fair and frosty if wind is north or northeast; rain or snow if wind is south or southwest
10 P.M. to midnight	Fair	Fair and frosty

This table was created 170 years ago by Dr. Herschell for the Boston Courier; *it first appeared in* The (Old) Farmer's Almanac *in 1834.*

Safe Ice Thickness*

Ice Thickness	Permissible Load	Ice Thickness	Permissible Load
3 inches	Single person on foot	12 inches	Heavy truck (8-ton gross)
4 inches	Group in single file	15 inches	10 tons
7½ inches	Passenger car (2-ton gross)	20 inches	25 tons
8 inches	Light truck (2½-ton gross)	30 inches	70 tons
10 inches	Medium truck (3½-ton gross)	36 inches	110 tons

*Solid, clear blue/black pond and lake ice

■ Slush ice has only half the strength of blue ice.
■ The strength value of river ice is 15 percent less.

Winter Weather Terms

Winter Storm Outlook

■ Issued prior to a winter storm watch. An outlook is issued when forecasters believe that storm conditions are possible, usually 48 to 60 hours before the beginning of a storm.

Winter Storm Watch

■ Indicates the possibility of a winter storm and is issued to provide 12 to 36 hours notice. A watch is announced when the specific timing, location, and path of a storm are undetermined. Be alert to changing weather conditions, and avoid unnecessary travel.

Winter Storm Warning

■ Indicates that a severe winter storm has started or is about to begin. A warning is issued when more than six inches of snow, a significant ice accumulation, a dangerous windchill, or a combination of the three is expected. Anticipated snow accumulation during a winter storm is six or more inches in 24 hours. You should stay indoors during the storm.

Heavy Snow Warning

■ Issued when snow accumulations are expected to approach or exceed six inches in 12 hours but will not be accompanied by significant wind. The warning could also be issued if eight or more inches of snow accumulation is expected in a 24-hour period. During a heavy snow warning, freezing rain and sleet are not expected.

Blizzard Warning

■ Indicates that sustained winds or frequent gusts of 35 miles per hour or greater will occur in combination with considerable falling and/or blowing snow for at least three hours. Visibility will often be reduced to less than ¼ mile.

Whiteout

■ Caused by falling and/or blowing snow that reduces visibility to zero miles—typically only a few feet. Whiteouts are most frequent during blizzards and can occur rapidly, often blinding motorists and creating chain-reaction crashes involving multiple vehicles.

Northeaster

■ Usually produces heavy snow and rain and creates tremendous waves in Atlantic coastal regions, often causing beach erosion and structural damage. Wind gusts associated with these storms can exceed hurricane force in intensity. A northeaster gets its name from the strong, continuous northeasterly ocean winds that blow in over coastal areas ahead of the storm.

Sleet

■ Frozen or partially frozen rain in the form of ice pellets that hit the ground so fast that they bounce and do not stick to it. However, the pellets can accumulate like snow and cause hazardous conditions for pedestrians and motorists.

Freezing Rain

■ Liquid precipitation that turns to ice on contact with a frozen surface to form a smooth ice coating called a glaze.

Ice Storm Warning

■ Issued when freezing rain results in ice accumulations measuring ½ inch thick or more. This can cause trees and utility lines to fall down, causing power outages.

Windchill Advisory

■ Issued when windchill temperatures are expected to be between −20° and −34°F.

Windchill Warning

■ Issued when windchill temperatures are expected to be less than −34°F.

Snowflakes

Snowflakes are made up of six-sided crystals. If you look carefully at the snowflakes during the next snowstorm, you might be able to find some of the crystal types below. The basic shape of a crystal is determined by the temperature at which it forms. Sometimes a snowflake is a combination of more than one type of crystal.

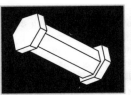

CAPPED COLUMNS
(also called tsuzumi crystals) occur when the temperature is 25°F or less.

NEEDLES
(long and thin but still six-sided crystals) occur when the temperature is 21° to 25°F.

SPATIAL DENDRITES
(irregular and feathery crystals) occur in high-moisture clouds at 3° to 10°F.

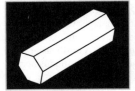

COLUMNS
(dense crystals, act like prisms) occur when the temperature is 25°F or less.

PLATES
(mirror-like crystals) occur under special weather conditions.

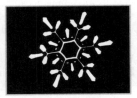

STELLAR CRYSTALS
(beautiful, delicate crystals) occur under special weather conditions.

Weather Phobias

Name of Fear	Object Feared
Ancraophobia	Wind
Anemophobia	Wind
Antlophobia	Floods
Astraphobia	Lightning, thunder
Auroraphobia	Northern lights, southern lights
Brontophobia	Lightning, thunder
Ceraunophobia	Thunder
Cheimatophobia	Cold
Chionophobia	Snow
Cryophobia	Extreme cold, frost, ice
Frigophobia	Cold
Heliophobia	Sun, sunshine

Name of Fear	Object Feared
Homichlophobia	Fog
Hygrophobia	Dampness, moisture
Keraunophobia	Lightning, thunder
Lilapsophobia	Hurricanes, tornadoes
Nebulaphobia	Fog
Nephophobia	Clouds
Ombrophobia	Rain
Pagophobia	Frost, ice
Phengophobia	Daylight, sunshine
Pluviophobia	Rain
Psychrophobia	Cold
Thermophobia	Heat
Tonitrophobia	Thunder

Windchill

As wind speed increases, the air temperature against your body falls. The combination of cold temperature and high wind can create a cooling effect so severe that exposed flesh can freeze. (Inanimate objects, such as cars, do not experience windchill.)

To gauge wind speed: At 10 miles per hour, you can feel wind on your face; at 20, small branches move, and dust or snow is raised; at 30, large branches move and wires whistle; at 40, whole trees bend.

TEMPERATURE (°F)

Calm	35	30	25	20	15	10	5	0	−5	−10	−15	−20	−25	−30	−35
5	31	25	19	13	7	1	−5	−11	−16	−22	−28	−34	−40	−46	−52
10	27	21	15	9	3	−4	−10	−16	−22	−28	−35	−41	−47	−53	−59
15	25	19	13	6	0	−7	−13	−19	−26	−32	−39	−45	−51	−58	−64
20	24	17	11	4	−2	−9	−15	−22	−29	−35	−42	−48	−55	−61	−68
25	23	16	9	3	−4	−11	−17	−24	−31	−37	−44	−51	−58	−64	−71
30	22	15	8	1	−5	−12	−19	−26	−33	−39	−46	−53	−60	−67	−73
35	21	14	7	0	−7	−14	−21	−27	−34	−41	−48	−55	−62	−69	−76
40	20	13	6	−1	−8	−15	−22	−29	−36	−43	−50	−57	−64	−71	−78
45	19	12	5	−2	−9	−16	−23	−30	−37	−44	−51	−58	−65	−72	−79
50	19	12	4	−3	−10	−17	−24	−31	−38	−45	−52	−60	−67	−74	−81
55	18	11	4	−3	−11	−18	−25	−32	−39	−46	−54	−61	−68	−75	−82
60	17	10	3	−4	−11	−19	−26	−33	−40	−48	−55	−62	−69	−76	−84

WIND SPEED (mph)

■ **Frostbite occurs in 15 minutes or less.**

EXAMPLE: When the temperature is 15°F and the wind speed is 30 miles per hour, the windchill, or how cold it feels, is −5°F. For a Celsius version of the Windchill table, visit **www.almanac.com/weathercenter.**   *−courtesy National Weather Service*

Is It Raining, Drizzling, or Misting?

	NUMBER OF DROPS (per sq. ft. per sec.)	DIAMETER OF DROPS (mm)	INTENSITY (in. per hr.)
Cloudburst	113	2.85	4.0
Excessive rain	76	2.4	1.6
Heavy rain	46	2.05	0.6
Moderate rain	46	1.6	0.15
Light rain	26	1.24	0.04
Drizzle	14	0.96	0.01
Mist	2,510	0.1	0.002
Fog	6,264,000	0.01	0.005

Cloud Definitions

High Clouds
(bases starting at an average of 20,000 feet)

CIRRUS: Thin feather-like crystal clouds.
CIRROCUMULUS: Thin clouds that appear as small "cotton patches."
CIRROSTRATUS: Thin white clouds that re-semble veils.

Middle Clouds
(bases starting at about 10,000 feet)

ALTOCUMULUS: Gray or white layer or patches of solid clouds with rounded shapes.
ALTOSTRATUS: Grayish or bluish layer of clouds that can obscure the Sun.

Low Clouds
(bases starting near Earth's surface to 6,500 feet)

STRATUS: Thin, gray sheet-like clouds with low bases; may bring drizzle and snow.
STRATOCUMULUS: Rounded cloud masses that form on top of a layer.

—Weatherstock

NIMBOSTRATUS: Dark, gray shapeless cloud layers containing rain, snow, and ice pellets.

Clouds with Vertical Development
(high clouds that form at almost any altitude and reach up to 14,000 feet)

CUMULUS: Fair-weather clouds with flat bases and dome-shaped tops.
CUMULONIMBUS: Large, dark, vertical clouds with bulging tops that bring showers, thunder, and lightning.

Atlantic Tropical Storm Names for 2004

Alex	Gaston	Matthew	Tomas
Bonnie	Hermine	Nicole	Virginie
Charley	Ivan	Otto	Walter
Danielle	Jeanne	Paula	
Earl	Karl	Richard	
Frances	Lisa	Shary	

East-Pacific Tropical Storm Names for 2004

Agatha	Georgette	Madeline	Tina
Blas	Howard	Newton	Virgil
Celia	Isis	Orlene	Winifred
Darby	Javier	Paine	Xavier
Estelle	Kay	Roslyn	Yolanda
Frank	Lester	Seymour	Zeke

Retired Atlantic Hurricane Names

These storms have been some of the most destructive and costly; as a result, their names have been retired from the six-year rotating hurricane list.

NAME	YEAR RETIRED	NAME	YEAR RETIRED	NAME	YEAR RETIRED
Celia	1970	Alicia	1983	Bob	1991
Agnes	1972	Elena	1985	Andrew	1992
Carmen	1974	Gloria	1985	Opal	1995
Eloise	1975	Gilbert	1988	Roxanne	1995
Anita	1977	Joan	1988	Fran	1996
David	1979	Hugo	1989	Mitch	1998
Frederic	1979	Diana	1990	Floyd	1999
Allen	1980	Klaus	1990	Keith	2000

REFERENCE

International Weather Symbols

Weather Conditions

•	light drizzle
••	steady, light drizzle
⋮	intermittent, moderate drizzle
••	steady, moderate drizzle
⋮	intermittent, heavy drizzle
••	steady, heavy drizzle
•	light rain
••	steady, light rain
⁞	intermittent, moderate rain
••	steady, moderate rain
⁞	intermittent, heavy rain
••	steady, heavy rain
*	light snow
**	steady, light snow
*	intermittent, moderate snow
**	steady, moderate snow
*	intermittent, heavy snow
**	steady, heavy snow
⊽	hail
∿	freezing rain
⊗	sleet
)(	tornado
⸨	dust devil
⟞	dust storm
≡	fog
⌐	thunderstorm
<	lightning
⚡	hurricane

Sky Coverage

○	no clouds
◔	one-tenth covered
◔	two- to three-tenths covered
◑	four-tenths covered
◑	half covered
◕	six-tenths covered
◕	seven- to eight-tenths covered
◕	nine-tenths covered
●	completely overcast

High Clouds
- ⌒ cirrus
- ⌇ cirrocumulus
- ⌇ cirrostratus

Middle Clouds
- ⌣ altocumulus
- ∠ altostratus

Low Clouds
- — stratus
- ⌣ stratocumulus
- ⌿ nimbostratus

Vertically Developed Clouds
- ⌂ cumulus
- ⌂ cumulonimbus

Wind Speed

Symbol	(mph)	(km/h)
◎	calm	calm
	1–2	1–3
	3–8	4–13
	9–14	14–23
	15–20	24–33
	21–25	34–40
	55–60	89–97
	119–123	192–198

Heat Index °F (°C)

TEMPERATURE °F (°C)	RELATIVE HUMIDITY (%)								
	40	45	50	55	60	65	70	75	80
100 (38)	109 (43)	114 (46)	118 (48)	124 (51)	129 (54)	136 (58)			
98 (37)	105 (41)	109 (43)	113 (45)	117 (47)	123 (51)	128 (53)	134 (57)		
96 (36)	101 (38)	104 (40)	108 (42)	112 (44)	116 (47)	121 (49)	126 (52)	132 (56)	
94 (34)	97 (36)	100 (38)	103 (39)	106 (41)	110 (43)	114 (46)	119 (48)	124 (51)	129 (54)
92 (33)	94 (34)	96 (36)	99 (37)	101 (38)	105 (41)	108 (42)	112 (44)	116 (47)	121 (49)
90 (32)	91 (33)	93 (34)	95 (35)	97 (36)	100 (38)	103 (39)	106 (41)	109 (43)	113 (45)
88 (31)	88 (31)	89 (32)	91 (33)	93 (34)	95 (35)	98 (37)	100 (38)	103 (39)	106 (41)
86 (30)	85 (29)	87 (31)	88 (31)	89 (32)	91 (33)	93 (34)	95 (35)	97 (36)	100 (38)
84 (29)	83 (28)	84 (29)	85 (29)	86 (30)	88 (31)	89 (32)	90 (32)	92 (33)	94 (34)
82 (28)	81 (27)	82 (28)	83 (28)	84 (29)	84 (29)	85 (29)	86 (30)	88 (31)	89 (32)
80 (27)	80 (27)	80 (27)	81 (27)	81 (27)	82 (28)	82 (28)	83 (28)	84 (29)	84 (29)

EXAMPLE: When the temperature is 88°F (31°C) and the relative humidity is 60 percent, the heat index, or how hot it feels, is 95°F (35°C).

The UV Index for Measuring Ultraviolet Radiation Risk

The U.S. National Weather Service daily forecasts of ultraviolet levels use these numbers for various exposure levels:

UV Index Number	Exposure Level	Time to Burn	Actions to Take
0, 1, 2	Minimal	60 minutes	Apply SPF 15 sunscreen
3, 4	Low	45 minutes	Apply SPF 15 sunscreen; wear a hat
5, 6	Moderate	30 minutes	Apply SPF 15 sunscreen; wear a hat
7, 8, 9	High	15–25 minutes	Apply SPF 15 to 30 sunscreen; wear a hat and sunglasses
10 or higher	Very high	10 minutes	Apply SPF 30 sunscreen; wear a hat, sunglasses, and protective clothing

"Time to Burn" and "Actions to Take" apply to people with fair skin that sometimes tans but usually burns. People with lighter skin need to be more cautious. People with darker skin may be able to tolerate more exposure.

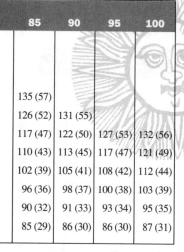

85	90	95	100
135 (57)			
126 (52)	131 (55)		
117 (47)	122 (50)	127 (53)	132 (56)
110 (43)	113 (45)	117 (47)	121 (49)
102 (39)	105 (41)	108 (42)	112 (44)
96 (36)	98 (37)	100 (38)	103 (39)
90 (32)	91 (33)	93 (34)	95 (35)
85 (29)	86 (30)	86 (30)	87 (31)

Richter Scale for Measuring Earthquakes

Magnitude	Possible Effects
1	Detectable only by instruments
2	Barely detectable, even near the epicenter
3	Felt indoors
4	Felt by most people; slight damage
5	Felt by all; minor to moderate damage
6	Moderate destruction
7	Major damage
8	Total and major damage

–devised by American geologist Charles W. Richter in 1935 to measure the magnitude of an earthquake

Temperature Conversion Scale

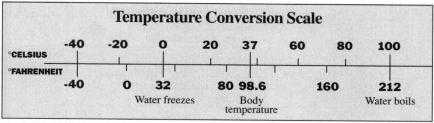

The Volcanic Explosivity Index (VEI) for Measuring Volcanic Eruptions

VEI	Description	Plume Height	Volume	Classification	Frequency
0	Nonexplosive	<100 m	1,000 m³	Hawaiian	Daily
1	Gentle	100–1,000 m	10,000 m³	Hawaiian/Strombolian	Daily
2	Explosive	1–5 km	1,000,000 m³	Strombolian/Vulcanian	Weekly
3	Severe	3–15 km	10,000,000 m³	Vulcanian	Yearly
4	Cataclysmic	10–25 km	100,000,000 m³	Vulcanian/Plinian	10 years
5	Paroxysmal	>25 km	1 km³	Plinian	100 years
6	Colossal	>25 km	10 km³	Plinian/Ultra-Plinian	100 years
7	Supercolossal	>25 km	100 km³	Ultra-Plinian	1,000 years
8	Megacolossal	>25 km	1,000 km³	Ultra-Plinian	10,000 years

REFERENCE

R
E
F
E
R
E
N
C
E

Beaufort Wind Force Scale

"Used Mostly at Sea but of Help to All Who Are Interested in the Weather"

Admiral Beaufort arranged the numbers 0 to 12 to indicate the strength of the wind from calm, force 0, to hurricane, force 12. Here's a scale adapted to land.

Beaufort Force	Description	When You See or Feel This Effect	Wind (mph)	(km/h)
0	Calm	Smoke goes straight up	less than 1	less than 2
1	Light air	Wind direction is shown by smoke drift but not by wind vane	1–3	2–5
2	Light breeze	Wind is felt on the face; leaves rustle; wind vanes move	4–7	6–11
3	Gentle breeze	Leaves and small twigs move steadily; wind extends small flags straight out	8–12	12–19
4	Moderate breeze	Wind raises dust and loose paper; small branches move	13–18	20–29
5	Fresh breeze	Small trees sway; waves form on lakes	19–24	30–39
6	Strong breeze	Large branches move; wires whistle; umbrellas are difficult to use	25–31	40–50
7	Moderate gale	Whole trees are in motion; walking against the wind is difficult	32–38	51–61
8	Fresh gale	Twigs break from trees; walking against the wind is very difficult	39–46	62–74
9	Strong gale	Buildings suffer minimal damage; roof shingles are removed	47–54	75–87
10	Whole gale	Trees are uprooted	55–63	88–101
11	Violent storm	Widespread damage	64–72	102–116
12	Hurricane	Widespread destruction	73+	117+

Fujita Scale (or F Scale) for Measuring Tornadoes

■ This is a system developed by Dr. Theodore Fujita to classify tornadoes based on wind damage. All tornadoes, and most other severe local windstorms, are assigned a single number from this scale according to the most intense damage caused by the storm.

F0 (weak)	40–72 mph, light damage
F1 (weak)	73–112 mph, moderate damage
F2 (strong)	113–157 mph, considerable damage
F3 (strong)	158–206 mph, severe damage
F4 (violent)	207–260 mph, devastating damage
F5 (violent)	261–318 mph (rare), incredible damage

Torro Hailstorm Intensity Scale

INTENSITY	DESCRIPTION OF DAMAGE
H0	True hail of pea size causes no damage
H1	Leaves and flower petals are punctured and torn
H2	Leaves are stripped from trees and plants
H3	Panes of glass are broken; auto bodies are dented
H4	Some house windows are broken; small tree branches are broken off; birds are killed
H5	Many windows are smashed; small animals are injured; large tree branches are broken off
H6	Shingle roofs are breached; metal roofs are scored; wooden window frames are broken away
H7	Roofs are shattered to expose rafters; cars are seriously damaged
H8	Shingle and tiled roofs are destroyed; small tree trunks are split; people are seriously injured
H9	Concrete roofs are broken; large tree trunks are split and knocked down; people are at risk of fatal injuries
H10	Brick houses are damaged; people are at risk of fatal injuries

Weather History

ON JANUARY 23, 1971, the **record-low temperature** in the United States of −79.8°F was reached at Prospect Creek Camp in Alaska.

ON FEBRUARY 8, 1891, winds peaked at 80 miles per hour in what witnesses called **"the worst blizzard ever known"** in Elkton, South Dakota.

ON MARCH 18, 1980, over nine inches of rain caused **severe flooding** in the Catskill Mountains in New York.

ON APRIL 15, 1980, temperatures soared to an early season-high of 110°F in Yuma, Arizona.

ON MAY 5, 1917, Denver, Colorado, set a record for a **May snowstorm** when it received 12 inches.

ON JUNE 16, 1984, a **flash flood** carried 64 cars a quarter-mile in Westby, Wisconsin.

ON JULY 4, 1816, New Englanders had to wear overcoats at midday despite the sunshine, in the so-called **"year without a summer."**

ON AUGUST 9, 1878, a **rare tornado** in Wallingford, Connecticut, killed 34 people.

ON SEPTEMBER 3, 1970, the **largest hailstone** on record fell near Coffeyville, Kansas. The stone was 17.5 inches in circumference.

ON OCTOBER 18, 1930, lake-effect snow fell four feet deep in the suburbs of Buffalo, New York.

ON NOVEMBER 7, 1940, the Tacoma Narrows Bridge (also known as "Galloping Gertie") in Tacoma, Washington, collapsed in **high winds.**

ON DECEMBER 16, 1835, New England experienced its famous **"Cold Wednesday":** The temperature remained steady at −15°F during the day.

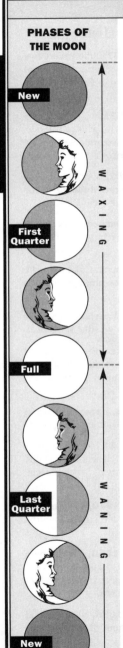

**PHASES OF
THE MOON**

New

WAXING

First
Quarter

Full

Last
Quarter

WANING

New

Origin of Full-Moon Names

Historically, the Native Americans who lived in the area that is now the northern and eastern United States kept track of the seasons by giving a distinctive name to each recurring full Moon. This name was applied to the entire month in which it occurred. These names, and some variations, were used by the Algonquin tribes from New England to Lake Superior.

Name	Month	Variations
Full Wolf Moon	**January**	Full Old Moon
Full Snow Moon	**February**	Full Hunger Moon
Full Worm Moon	**March**	Full Crow Moon Full Crust Moon Full Sugar Moon Full Sap Moon
Full Pink Moon	**April**	Full Sprouting Grass Moon Full Egg Moon Full Fish Moon
Full Flower Moon	**May**	Full Corn Planting Moon Full Milk Moon
Full Strawberry Moon	**June**	Full Rose Moon Full Hot Moon
Full Buck Moon	**July**	Full Thunder Moon Full Hay Moon
Full Sturgeon Moon	**August**	Full Red Moon Full Green Corn Moon
Full Harvest Moon*	**September**	Full Corn Moon Full Barley Moon
Full Hunter's Moon	**October**	Full Travel Moon Full Dying Grass Moon
Full Beaver Moon	**November**	Full Frost Moon
Full Cold Moon	**December**	Full Long Nights Moon

The Harvest Moon is always the full Moon closest to the autumnal equinox. If the Harvest Moon occurs in October, the September full Moon is usually called the Corn Moon.

When Will the Moon Rise Today?

A lunar puzzle involves the timing of moonrise. If you enjoy the out-of-doors and the wonders of nature, you may wish to commit to memory the following gem:

 The new Moon always rises at sunrise

 And the first quarter at noon.

 The full Moon always rises at sunset

 And the last quarter at midnight.

■ Moonrise occurs about 50 minutes later each day.

■ The new Moon is invisible because its illuminated side faces away from Earth, which occurs when the Moon lines up between Earth and the Sun.

■ One or two days after the date of the new Moon, you can see a thin crescent setting just after sunset in the western sky as the lunar cycle continues. (See pages 44–70 for exact moonrise times.)

Origin of Month Names

January Named for the Roman god Janus, protector of gates and doorways. Janus is depicted with two faces, one looking into the past, the other into the future.

February From the Latin word *februa,* "to cleanse." The Roman Februalia was a month of purification and atonement.

March Named for the Roman god of war, Mars. This was the time of year to resume military campaigns that had been interrupted by winter.

April From the Latin word *aperio,* "to open (bud)," because plants begin to grow in this month.

May Named for the Roman goddess Maia, who oversaw the growth of plants. Also from the Latin word *maiores,* "elders," who were celebrated during this month.

June Named for the Roman goddess Juno, patroness of marriage and the well-being of women. Also from the Latin word *juvenis,* "young people."

July Named to honor Roman dictator Julius Caesar (100 B.C.–44 B.C.). In 46 B.C., Julius Caesar made one of his greatest contributions to history: With the help of Sosigenes, he developed the Julian calendar, the precursor to the Gregorian calendar we use today.

August Named to honor the first Roman emperor (and grandnephew of Julius Caesar), Augustus Caesar (63 B.C.–A.D. 14).

September From the Latin word *septem,* "seven," because this had been the seventh month of the early Roman calendar.

October From the Latin word *octo,* "eight," because this had been the eighth month of the early Roman calendar.

November From the Latin word *novem,* "nine," because this had been the ninth month of the early Roman calendar.

December From the Latin word *decem,* "ten," because this had been the tenth month of the early Roman calendar.

Origin of Day Names

The days of the week were named by the Romans with the Latin words for the Sun, the Moon, and the five known planets. These names have survived in European languages, but English names also reflect an Anglo-Saxon influence.

English	Latin	French	Italian	Spanish	Saxon
SUNDAY	Solis (Sun)	dimanche	domenica	domingo	Sun
MONDAY	Lunae (Moon)	lundi	lunedì	lunes	Moon
TUESDAY	Martis (Mars)	mardi	martedì	martes	Tiw (the Anglo-Saxon god of war, the equivalent of the Norse Tyr or the Roman Mars)
WEDNESDAY	Mercurii (Mercury)	mercredi	mercoledì	miércoles	Woden (the Anglo-Saxon equivalent of the Norse Odin or the Roman Mercury)
THURSDAY	Jovis (Jupiter)	jeudi	giovedì	jueves	Thor (the Norse god of thunder, the equivalent of the Roman Jupiter)
FRIDAY	Veneris (Venus)	vendredi	venerdì	viernes	Frigg (the Norse god of love and fertility, the equivalent of the Roman Venus)
SATURDAY	Saturni (Saturn)	samedi	sabato	sábado	Saterne (Saturn, the Roman god of agriculture)

Solar Eclipse Dates (2004–2024)

Date	Regions with Visible Totality
2005 Apr. 8	S. Pacific Ocean
2006 Mar. 29	Africa, Turkey, Russia
2008 Aug. 1	Greenland, Siberia, China
2009 July 22	India, China, S. Pacific Ocean
2010 July 11	S. Pacific Ocean, southern South America
2012 Nov. 13	Australia, S. Pacific Ocean
2013 Nov. 3	Atlantic Ocean, central Africa
2015 Mar. 20	N. Atlantic Ocean, Arctic
2016 Mar. 9	Southeast Asia, N. Pacific Ocean
2017 Aug. 17	United States
2019 July 2	S. Pacific Ocean, South America
2020 Dec. 14	S. Pacific Ocean, South America
2021 Dec. 4	Antarctica
2023 Apr. 20	Indonesia
2024 Apr. 8	Mexico, United States, Canada

How to Find the Day of the Week for Any Given Date

To compute the day of the week for any given date as far back as the mid-18th century, proceed as follows:

■ Add the last two digits of the year to one-quarter of the last two digits (discard any remainder), the day of the month, and the month key from the key box below. Divide the sum by 7; the remainder is the day of the week (1 is Sunday, 2 is Monday, and so on). If there is no remainder, the day is Saturday. If you're searching for a weekday prior to 1900, add 2 to the sum before dividing; prior to 1800, add 4. The formula doesn't work for days prior to 1753. From 2000 to 2099, subtract 1 from the sum before dividing.

Example:
The Dayton Flood was on March 25, 1913.

Last two digits of year:	13
One-quarter of these two digits:	3
Given day of month:	25
Key number for March:	4
Sum:	45

45 ÷ 7 = 6, with a remainder of 3. The flood took place on Tuesday, the third day of the week.

KEY	
January	1
leap year.	0
February	4
leap year	3
March	4
April	0
May	2
June	5
July	0
August	3
September	6
October..........	1
November........	4
December	6

Easter Dates (2004–2008)

■ Christian churches that follow the Gregorian calendar celebrate Easter on the first Sunday after the full Moon that occurs on or just after the vernal equinox.

Year	Easter
2004.....................	April 11
2005...................	March 27
2006.....................	April 16
2007......................	April 8
2008....................	March 23

■ Eastern Orthodox churches follow the Julian calendar.

Year	Easter
2004.....................	April 11
2005	May 1
2006....................	April 23
2007......................	April 8
2008....................	April 27

Triskaidekaphobia Trivia

Here are a few facts about Friday the 13th:

■ Of the 14 possible configurations for the annual calendar (see any perpetual calendar), the occurrence of Friday the 13th is this:

6 of 14 years have one Friday the 13th.
6 of 14 years have two Fridays the 13th.
2 of 14 years have three Fridays the 13th.

■ There is no year without one Friday the 13th, and no year with more than three.

■ There are two Fridays the 13th in 2004. The next year to have three Fridays the 13th is 2009.

■ The reason we say "Fridays the 13th" is that no one can pronounce "Friday the 13ths."

The Animal Signs of the Chinese Zodiac

The animal designations of the Chinese zodiac follow a 12-year cycle and are always used in the same sequence. The Chinese year of 354 days begins three to seven weeks into the western 365-day year, so the animal designation changes at that time, rather than on January 1. See page 42 for the exact date.

RAT
Ambitious and sincere, you can be generous with your money. Compatible with the dragon and the monkey. Your opposite is the horse.

1900	1936	1996
1912	1948	1984
1924	1960	2008
1972		

DRAGON
Robust and passionate, your life is filled with complexity. Compatible with the monkey and the rat. Your opposite is the dog.

1904	1940	1988
1916	1952	2000
1928	1964	2012
1976		

MONKEY
Persuasive, skillful, and intelligent, you strive to excel. Compatible with the dragon and the rat. Your opposite is the tiger.

1908	1944	1992
1920	1956	2004
1932	1968	2016
1980		

OX OR BUFFALO
A leader, you are bright, patient, and cheerful. Compatible with the snake and the rooster. Your opposite is the sheep.

1901	1937	1985
1913	1949	1997
1925	1961	2009
1973		

SNAKE
Strong-willed and intense, you display great wisdom. Compatible with the rooster and the ox. Your opposite is the pig.

1905	1941	1989
1917	1953	2001
1929	1965	2013
1977		

ROOSTER OR COCK
Seeking wisdom and truth, you have a pioneering spirit. Compatible with the snake and the ox. Your opposite is the rabbit.

1909	1945	1993
1921	1957	2005
1933	1969	2017
1981		

TIGER
Forthright and sensitive, you possess great courage. Compatible with the horse and the dog. Your opposite is the monkey.

1902	1938	1986
1914	1950	1998
1926	1962	2010
1974		

HORSE
Physically attractive and popular, you like the company of others. Compatible with the tiger and the dog. Your opposite is the rat.

1906	1942	1990
1918	1954	2002
1930	1966	2014
1978		

DOG
Generous and loyal, you have the ability to work well with others. Compatible with the horse and the tiger. Your opposite is the dragon.

1910	1946	1994
1922	1958	2006
1934	1970	2018
1982		

RABBIT OR HARE
Talented and affectionate, you are a seeker of tranquility. Compatible with the sheep and the pig. Your opposite is the rooster.

1903	1939	1987
1915	1951	1999
1927	1963	2011
1975		

SHEEP OR GOAT
Aesthetic and stylish, you enjoy being a private person. Compatible with the pig and the rabbit. Your opposite is the ox.

1907	1943	1991
1919	1955	2003
1931	1967	2015
1979		

PIG OR BOAR
Gallant and noble, your friends will remain at your side. Compatible with the rabbit and the sheep. Your opposite is the snake.

1911	1947	1995
1923	1959	2007
1935	1971	2019
1983		

Glossary of Almanac Oddities

Many readers have expressed puzzlement over the rather obscure notations that appear on our **Right-Hand Calendar Pages (45–71).** These "oddities" have long been fixtures in the Almanac, and we are pleased to provide some definitions. (Once explained, they may not seem so odd after all!)

–Beth Krommes

Ember Days (Movable)

The Almanac traditionally marks the four periods formerly observed by the Roman Catholic and Anglican churches for prayer, fasting, and the ordination of clergy. These Ember Days are the Wednesdays, Fridays, and Saturdays that follow in succession after (1) the First Sunday in Lent; (2) Whitsunday–Pentecost; (3) the Feast of the Holy Cross, September 14; and (4) the Feast of St. Lucia, December 13. The word *ember* is perhaps a corruption of the Latin *quatuor tempora,* "four times."

Folklore has it that the weather on each of the three days foretells the weather for three successive months; that is, for September's Ember Days, Wednesday forecasts weather for October, Friday for November, and Saturday for December.

Plough Monday (January)

The first Monday after Epiphany and Plough Sunday was so called because it was the day that men returned to their plough, or daily work, at the end of the Christmas holiday. It was customary for farm laborers to draw a plough through the village, soliciting money for a "ploughlight," which was kept burning in the parish church all year. In some areas, the custom of blessing the plough is maintained.

Three Chilly Saints (May)

Mamertus, Pancras, and Gervais were three early Christian saints. Because their feast days, on May 11, 12, and 13, respectively, are traditionally cold, they have come to be known as the Three Chilly Saints. An old French saying goes: "St. Mamertus, St. Pancras, and St. Gervais do not pass without a frost."

Midsummer Day (June 24)

Although it occurs near the summer solstice, to the farmer this day is the midpoint of the growing season, halfway between planting and harvest and an occasion for festivity. The English church considered it a "Quarter Day," one of the four major divisions of the liturgical year. It also marks the feast day of St. John the Baptist.

Cornscateous Air (July)

First used by the old almanac makers, this term signifies warm, damp air. Though it signals ideal climatic conditions for growing corn, it also poses a danger to those affected by asthma, pneumonia, and other respiratory problems.

Dog Days (July–August)

These are the hottest and most unhealthy days of the year. Also known as Canicular Days, the name derives from the Dog Star, Sirius. The traditional timing of Dog Days is the 40 days beginning July 3 and ending August 11, coinciding with the heliacal (at sunrise) rising of Sirius.

Cat Nights Begin (August)

This term harks back to the days when people believed in witches. An old Irish legend says that a witch could turn into a cat and regain herself eight times, but on the ninth time, August 17, she couldn't change back, hence the saying: "A cat has nine lives." Because August is a "yowly" time for cats, this may have prompted the speculation about witches on the prowl in the first place.

Harvest Home (September)

In Europe and Britain, the conclusion of the harvest each autumn was once marked by great festivals of fun, feasting, and thanksgiving known as "Harvest Home." It was also a time to hold elections, pay workers, and collect rents. These festivals usually took place around the time of the autumnal equinox. Certain ethnic groups in this country, particularly the Pennsylvania Dutch, have kept the tradition alive.

St. Luke's Little Summer (October)

A spell of warm weather that occurs about the time of the saint's feast day, October 18, this period is sometimes referred to as Indian summer.

Indian Summer (November)

A period of warm weather following a cold spell or a hard frost, Indian summer can occur between St. Martin's Day (November 11) and November 20. Although there are differing dates for its occurrence, for more than 200 years the Almanac has adhered to the saying "If All Saints' brings out winter, St. Martin's brings out Indian summer." As for the origin of the term, some say it comes from the early Native Americans, who believed that the condition was caused by a warm wind sent from the court of their southwestern god, Cautantowwit.

Halcyon Days (December)

About 14 days of calm weather follows the blustery winds of autumn's end. The ancient Greeks and Romans believed them to occur around the time of the winter solstice, when the halcyon, or kingfisher, was brooding. In a nest floating on the sea, the bird was said to have charmed the wind and waves so that the waters were especially calm during this period.

Beware the Pogonip (December)

The word *pogonip* is a meteorological term used to describe an uncommon occurrence—frozen fog. The word was coined by Native Americans to describe the frozen fogs of fine ice needles that occur in the mountain valleys of the western United States. According to Indian tradition, breathing the fog is injurious to the lungs. □□

Sowing Vegetable Seeds

Sow or plant in cool weather	Beets, broccoli, Brussels sprouts, cabbage, lettuce, onions, parsley, peas, radishes, spinach, Swiss chard, turnips
Sow or plant in warm weather	Beans, carrots, corn, cucumbers, eggplant, melons, okra, peppers, squash, tomatoes
Sow or plant for one crop per season	Corn, eggplant, leeks, melons, peppers, potatoes, spinach (New Zealand), squash, tomatoes
Resow for additional crops	Beans, beets, cabbage, carrots, kohlrabi, lettuce, radishes, rutabagas, spinach, turnips

A Beginner's Vegetable Garden

A good size for a beginner's vegetable garden is 10x16 feet. It should have crops that are easy to grow. A plot this size, planted as suggested below, can feed a family of four for one summer, with a little extra for canning and freezing (or giving away).

Make 11 rows, 10 feet long, with 6 inches between them. Ideally, the rows should run north and south to take full advantage of the Sun. Plant the following:

ROW

1. Zucchini (4 plants)
2. Tomatoes (5 plants, staked)
3. Peppers (6 plants)
4. Cabbage

ROW

5. Bush beans
6. Lettuce
7. Beets
8. Carrots
9. Chard
10. Radishes
11. Marigolds (to discourage rabbits!)

Traditional Planting Times

■ Plant **corn** when elm leaves are the size of a squirrel's ear, when oak leaves are the size of a mouse's ear, when apple blossoms begin to fall, or when the dogwoods are in full bloom.

■ Plant **lettuce, spinach, peas,** and other cool-weather varieties when the lilacs show their first leaves or when daffodils begin to bloom.

■ Plant **tomatoes, early corn,** and **peppers** when dogwoods are in peak bloom or when daylilies start to bloom.

■ Plant **cucumbers** and **squashes** when lilac flowers fade.

■ Plant **perennials** when maple leaves begin to unfurl.

■ Plant **morning glories** when maple trees have full-size leaves.

■ Plant **pansies, snapdragons,** and other hardy annuals after the aspen and chokecherry trees leaf out.

■ Plant **beets** and **carrots** when dandelions are blooming.

Growing Vegetables

Vegetable	Start Seeds Indoors (weeks before last spring frost)	Start Seeds Outdoors (weeks before or after last spring frost)	Minimum Soil Temperature to Germinate (°F)	Cold Hardiness
Beans		Anytime after	48–50	Tender
Beets		4 before to 4 after	39–41	Half-hardy
Broccoli	6–8	4 before	55–75	Hardy
Brussels sprouts	6–8		55–75	Hardy
Cabbage	6–8	Anytime after	38–40	Hardy
Carrots		4–6 before	39–41	Half-hardy
Cauliflower	6–8	4 before	65–75	Half-hardy
Celery	6–8		60–70	Tender
Corn		2 after	46–50	Tender
Cucumbers	3–4	1–2 after	65–70	Very tender
Lettuce	4–6	2–3 after	40–75	Half-hardy
Melons	3–4	2 after	55–60	Very tender
Onion sets		4 before	34–36	Hardy
Parsnips		2–4 before	55–70	Hardy
Peas		4–6 before	34–36	Hardy
Peppers	8–10		70–80	Very tender
Potato tubers		2–4 before	55–70	Half-hardy
Pumpkins	3–4	1 after	55–60	Tender
Radishes		4–6 before	39–41	Hardy
Spinach		4–6 before	55–65	Hardy
Squash, summer	3–4	1 after	55–60	Very tender
Squash, winter	3–4	1 after	55–60	Tender
Tomatoes	6–8		50–55	Tender

When to Fertilize	When to Water
After heavy bloom and set of pods	Regularly, from start of pod to set
At time of planting	Only during drought conditions
Three weeks after transplanting	Only during drought conditions
Three weeks after transplanting	At transplanting
Three weeks after transplanting	Two to three weeks before harvest
Preferably in the fall for the following spring	Only during drought conditions
Three weeks after transplanting	Once, three weeks before harvest
At time of transplanting	Once a week
When eight to ten inches tall, and again when first silk appears	When tassels appear and cobs start to swell
One week after bloom, and again three weeks later	Frequently, especially when fruits form
Two to three weeks after transplanting	Once a week
One week after bloom, and again three weeks later	Once a week
When bulbs begin to swell, and again when plants are one foot tall	Only during drought conditions
One year before planting	Only during drought conditions
After heavy bloom and set of pods	Regularly, from start of pod to set
After first fruit-set	Once a week
At bloom time or time of second hilling	Regularly, when tubers start to form
Just before vines start to run, when plants are about one foot tall	Only during drought conditions
Before spring planting	Once a week
When plants are one-third grown	Once a week
Just before vines start to run, when plants are about one foot tall	Only during drought conditions
Just before vines start to run, when plants are about one foot tall	Only during drought conditions
Two weeks before, and after first picking	Twice a week

R
E
F
E
R
E
N
C
E

Vegetable Gardening in Containers

Lack of yard space is no excuse for not gardening, because many vegetables can be readily grown in containers. In addition to providing five hours or more of full sun, you must give attention to choosing the proper container, using a good soil mix, observing planting and spacing requirements, fertilizing, watering, and selecting appropriate varieties. Here are some suggestions:

Vegetable	Type of Container	Recommended Varieties
Beans, snap	5-gallon window box	Bush 'Blue Lake', Bush 'Romano', 'Tender Crop'
Broccoli	1 plant/5-gallon pot 3 plants/15-gallon tub	'DeCicco', 'Green Comet'
Carrots	5-gallon window box at least 12 inches deep	'Danvers Half Long', 'Short 'n Sweet', 'Tiny Sweet'
Cucumbers	1 plant/1-gallon pot	'Patio Pik', 'Pot Luck', 'Spacemaster'
Eggplant	5-gallon pot	'Black Beauty', 'Ichiban', 'Slim Jim'
Lettuce	5-gallon window box	'Ruby', 'Salad Bowl'
Onions	5-gallon window box	'White Sweet Spanish', 'Yellow Sweet Spanish'
Peppers	1 plant/2-gallon pot 5 plants/15-gallon tub	'Cayenne', 'Long Red', 'Sweet Banana', 'Wonder', 'Yolo'
Radishes	5-gallon window box	'Cherry Belle', 'Icicle'
Tomatoes	Bushel basket	'Early Girl', 'Patio', 'Small Fry', 'Sweet 100', 'Tiny Tim'

TIPS

■ Clay pots are usually more attractive than plastic ones, but plastic pots retain moisture better. To get the best of both, slip a plastic pot into a slightly larger clay pot.

■ Avoid small containers. They often can't store enough water to get through hot days.

■ Add about one inch of coarse gravel in the bottom of the container to improve drainage.

■ Vegetables that can be easily transplanted are best suited for containers. Transplants can be purchased from local nurseries or started at home.

■ Feed container plants at least twice a month with liquid fertilizer, following the instructions on the label.

■ An occasional application of fish emulsion or compost will add trace elements to container soil.

■ Place containers where they will receive maximum sunlight and good ventilation. Watch for and control plant insect pests.

Fertilizer Formulas

Fertilizers are labeled to show the percentages by weight of nitrogen (N), phosphorus (P), and potassium (K). Nitrogen is needed for leaf growth. Phosphorus is associated with root growth and fruit production. Potassium helps the plant fight off diseases. A 100-pound bag of 10-5-10 contains 10 pounds of nitrogen, 5 pounds of phosphorus, and 10 pounds of potassium. The rest is filler.

Manure Guide

Type of Manure	Water Content	PRIMARY NUTRIENTS (pounds per ton)		
		Nitrogen	Phosphorus	Potassium
Cow, horse	60%–80%	12–14	5–9	9–12
Sheep, pig, goat	65%–75%	10–21	7	13–19
Chicken:				
Wet, sticky, and caked	75%	30	20	10
Moist, crumbly to sticky	50%	40	40	20
Crumbly	30%	60	55	30
Dry	15%	90	70	40
Ashed	None	None	135	100

TYPE OF GARDEN	BEST TYPE OF MANURE	BEST TIME TO APPLY
Flowers	Cow, horse	Early spring
Vegetables	Chicken, cow, horse	Fall, spring
Potatoes or root crops	Cow, horse	Fall
Acid-loving plants (blueberries, azaleas, mountain laurels, rhododendrons)	Cow, horse	Early fall or not at all

Soil Fixes

If you have . . .

CLAY SOIL: Add coarse sand (not beach sand) and compost.

SILT SOIL: Add coarse sand (not beach sand) or gravel and compost, or well-rotted horse manure mixed with fresh straw.

SANDY SOIL: Add humus or aged manure, or sawdust with some extra nitrogen. Heavy, clay-rich soil can also be added.

Soil Amendments

To improve soil, add . . .

BARK, GROUND: Made from various tree barks. Improves soil structure.

COMPOST: Excellent conditioner.

LEAF MOLD: Decomposed leaves. Adds nutrients and structure to soil.

LIME: Raises the pH of acidic soil. Helps loosen clay soil.

MANURE: Best if composted. Good conditioner.

SAND: Improves drainage in clay soil.

TOPSOIL: Usually used with another amendment. Replaces existing soil.

pH Preferences of Trees, Shrubs, Vegetables, and Flowers

An accurate soil test will tell you where your pH currently stands and will specify the amount of lime or sulfur that is needed to bring it up or down to the appropriate level. A pH of 6.5 is just about right for most home gardens, since most plants thrive in the 6.0 to 7.0 (slightly acidic to neutral) range. Some plants (blueberries, azaleas) prefer more strongly acidic soil, while a few (ferns, asparagus) do best in soil that is neutral to slightly alkaline. Acidic (sour) soil is counteracted by applying finely ground limestone, and alkaline (sweet) soil is treated with gypsum (calcium sulfate) or ground sulfur.

Common Name	Optimum pH Range	Common Name	Optimum pH Range	Common Name	Optimum pH Range
TREES AND SHRUBS		Spruce	5.0–6.0	Canna	6.0–8.0
Apple	5.0–6.5	Walnut, black	6.0–8.0	Carnation	6.0–7.0
Ash	6.0–7.5	Willow	6.0–8.0	Chrysanthemum	6.0–7.5
Azalea	4.5–6.0			Clematis	5.5–7.0
Basswood	6.0–7.5	**VEGETABLES**		Coleus	6.0–7.0
Beautybush	6.0–7.5	Asparagus	6.0–8.0	Coneflower, purple	5.0–7.5
Birch	5.0–6.5	Bean, pole	6.0–7.5	Cosmos	5.0–8.0
Blackberry	5.0–6.0	Beet	6.0–7.5	Crocus	6.0–8.0
Blueberry	4.0–6.0	Broccoli	6.0–7.0	Daffodil	6.0–6.5
Boxwood	6.0–7.5	Brussels sprout	6.0–7.5	Dahlia	6.0–7.5
Cherry, sour	6.0–7.0	Carrot	5.5–7.0	Daisy, Shasta	6.0–8.0
Chestnut	5.0–6.5	Cauliflower	5.5–7.5	Daylily	6.0–8.0
Crab apple	6.0–7.5	Celery	5.8–7.0	Delphinium	6.0–7.5
Dogwood	5.0–7.0	Chive	6.0–7.0	Foxglove	6.0–7.5
Elder, box	6.0–8.0	Cucumber	5.5–7.0	Geranium	6.0–8.0
Fir, balsam	5.0–6.0	Garlic	5.5–8.0	Gladiolus	5.0–7.0
Fir, Douglas	6.0–7.0	Kale	6.0–7.5	Hibiscus	6.0–8.0
Hemlock	5.0–6.0	Lettuce	6.0–7.0	Hollyhock	6.0–8.0
Hydrangea, blue-flowered	4.0–5.0	Pea, sweet	6.0–7.5	Hyacinth	6.5–7.5
Hydrangea, pink-flowered	6.0–7.0	Pepper, sweet	5.5–7.0	Iris, blue flag	5.0–7.5
		Potato	4.8–6.5	Lily-of-the-valley	4.5–6.0
Juniper	5.0–6.0	Pumpkin	5.5–7.5	Lupine	5.0–6.5
Laurel, mountain	4.5–6.0	Radish	6.0–7.0	Marigold	5.5–7.5
Lemon	6.0–7.5	Spinach	6.0–7.5	Morning glory	6.0–7.5
Lilac	6.0–7.5	Squash, crookneck	6.0–7.5	Narcissus, trumpet	5.5–6.5
Maple, sugar	6.0–7.5	Squash, Hubbard	5.5–7.0	Nasturtium	5.5–7.5
Oak, white	5.0–6.5	Tomato	5.5–7.5	Pansy	5.5–6.5
Orange	6.0–7.5			Peony	6.0–7.5
Peach	6.0–7.0	**FLOWERS**		Petunia	6.0–7.5
Pear	6.0–7.5	Alyssum	6.0–7.5	Phlox, summer	6.0–8.0
Pecan	6.4–8.0	Aster, New England	6.0–8.0	Poppy, oriental	6.0–7.5
Pine, red	5.0–6.0	Baby's breath	6.0–7.0	Rose, hybrid tea	5.5–7.0
Pine, white	4.5–6.0	Bachelor's button	6.0–7.5	Rose, rugosa	6.0–7.0
Plum	6.0–8.0	Bee balm	6.0–7.5	Snapdragon	5.5–7.0
Raspberry, red	5.5–7.0	Begonia	5.5–7.0	Sunflower	6.0–7.5
Rhododendron	4.5–6.0	Black-eyed Susan	5.5–7.0	Tulip	6.0–7.0
		Bleeding heart	6.0–7.5	Zinnia	5.5–7.0

Lawn-Growing Tips

■ Test your soil: The pH balance should be 7.0 or more; 6.2 to 6.7 puts your lawn at risk for fungal diseases. If the pH is too low, correct it with liming, best done in the fall.

■ The best time to apply fertilizer is just before it rains.

■ If you put lime and fertilizer on your lawn, spread half of it as you walk north to south, the other half as you walk east to west to cut down on missed areas.

■ Any feeding of lawns in the fall should be done with a low-nitrogen, slow-acting fertilizer.

■ In areas of your lawn where tree roots compete with the grass, apply some extra fertilizer to benefit both.

■ Moss and sorrel in lawns usually means poor soil, poor aeration or drainage, or excessive acidity.

■ Control weeds by promoting healthy lawn growth with natural fertilizers in spring and early fall.

■ Raise the level of your lawnmower blades during the hot summer days. Taller grass resists drought better than short.

■ You can reduce mowing time by redesigning your lawn, reducing sharp corners and adding sweeping curves.

■ During a drought, let the grass grow longer between mowings, and reduce fertilizer.

■ Water your lawn early in the morning or in the evening.

Herbs to Plant in Lawns

Choose plants that suit your soil and your climate. All these can withstand mowing and considerable foot traffic.

Ajuga or bugleweed *(Ajuga reptans)*

Corsican mint *(Mentha requienii)*

Dwarf cinquefoil *(Potentilla tabernaemontani)*

English pennyroyal *(Mentha pulegium)*

Green Irish moss *(Sagina subulata)*

Pearly everlasting *(Anaphalis margaritacea)*

Roman chamomile *(Chamaemelum nobile)*

Rupturewort *(Herniaria glabra)*

Speedwell *(Veronica officinalis)*

Stonecrop *(Sedum ternatum)*

Sweet violets *(Viola odorata* or *V. tricolor)*

Thyme *(Thymus serpyllum)*

White clover *(Trifolium repens)*

Wild strawberries *(Fragaria virginiana)*

Wintergreen or partridgeberry *(Mitchella repens)*

A Gardener's Worst Phobias

Name of Fear	Object Feared
Alliumphobia	Garlic
Anthophobia	Flowers
Apiphobia	Bees
Arachnophobia	Spiders
Batonophobia	Plants
Bufonophobia	Toads
Dendrophobia	Trees
Entomophobia	Insects
Lachanophobia	Vegetables
Melissophobia	Bees
Mottephobia	Moths
Myrmecophobia	Ants
Ornithophobia	Birds
Ranidaphobia	Frogs
Rupophobia	Dirt
Scoleciphobia	Worms
Spheksophobia	Wasps

REFERENCE

Growing Herbs

Herb	Propagation Method	Start Seeds Indoors (weeks before last spring frost)	Start Seeds Outdoors (weeks before or after last spring frost)	Minimum Soil Temperature to Germinate (°F)	Height (inches)	
Basil	Seeds, transplants	6–8	Anytime after	70	12–24	
Borage	Seeds, division, cuttings	Not recommended	Anytime after	70	12–36	
Chervil	Seeds	Not recommended	3–4 before	55	12–24	
Chives	Seeds, division	8–10	3–4 before	60–70	12–18	
Cilantro/ coriander	Seeds	Not recommended	Anytime after	60	12–36	
Dill	Seeds	Not recommended	4–5 before	60–70	36–48	
Fennel	Seeds	4–6	Anytime after	60–70	48–80	
Lavender, English	Seeds, cuttings	8–12	1–2 before	70–75	18–36	
Lavender, French	Transplants	Not recommended	Not recommended	—	18–36	
Lemon balm	Seeds, division, cuttings	6–10	2–3 before	70	12–24	
Lovage	Seeds, division	6–8	2–3 before	70	36–72	
Oregano	Seeds, division, cuttings	6–10	Anytime after	70	12–24	
Parsley	Seeds	10–12	3–4 before	70	18–24	
Rosemary	Seeds, division, cuttings	8–10	Anytime after	70	48–72	
Sage	Seeds, division, cuttings	6–10	1–2 before	60–70	12–48	
Sorrel	Seeds, division	6–10	2–3 after	60–70	20–48	
Spearmint	Division, cuttings	Not recommended	Not recommended	—	12–24	
Summer savory	Seeds	4–6	Anytime after	60–70	4–15	
Sweet cicely	Seeds, division	6–8	2–3 after	60–70	36–72	
Tarragon, French	Cuttings, transplants	Not recommended	Not recommended	—	24–36	
Thyme, common	Seeds, division, cuttings	6–10	2–3 before	70	2–12	

Spread (inches)	Blooming Season	Uses	Soil	Light*	Growth Type
12	Midsummer	Culinary	Rich, moist	○	Annual
12	Early to midsummer	Culinary	Rich, well-drained, dry	○	Annual, biennial
8	Early to midsummer	Culinary	Rich, moist	◑	Annual, biennial
18	Early summer	Culinary	Rich, moist	○	Perennial
4	Midsummer	Culinary	Light	○◑	Annual
12	Early summer	Culinary	Rich	○	Annual
18	Mid- to late summer	Culinary	Rich	○	Annual
24	Early to late summer	Ornamental, medicinal	Moderately fertile, well-drained	○	Perennial
24	Early to late summer	Ornamental, medicinal	Moderately fertile, well-drained	○	Tender perennial
18	Midsummer to early fall	Culinary, ornamental	Rich, well-drained	○◑	Perennial
36	Early to late summer	Culinary	Fertile, sandy	○◑	Perennial
18	Mid- to late summer	Culinary	Poor	○	Tender perennial
6–8	Mid- to late summer	Culinary	Medium-rich	◑	Biennial
48	Early summer	Culinary	Not too acid	○	Tender perennial
30	Early to late summer	Culinary, ornamental	Well-drained	○	Perennial
12–14	Late spring to early summer	Culinary, medicinal	Rich, organic	○	Perennial
18	Early to midsummer	Culinary, medicinal, ornamental	Rich, moist	◑	Perennial
6	Early summer	Culinary	Medium rich	○	Annual
36	Late spring	Culinary	Moderately fertile, well-drained	○◑	Perennial
12	Late summer	Culinary, medicinal	Well-drained	○◑	Perennial
7–12	Early to midsummer	Culinary	Fertile, well-drained	○◑	Perennial

* ○ = full sun   ◑ = partial shade

Flowers and Herbs That Attract Butterflies

Allium.................... *Allium*
Aster .... *Aster*
Bee balm............... *Monarda*
Butterfly bush......... *Buddleia*
Catmint .... *Nepeta*
Clove pink .... *Dianthus*
Cornflower............. *Centaurea*
Creeping thyme ..... *Thymus serpyllum*
Daylily............... *Hemerocallis*
Dill .... *Anethum graveolens*
False indigo .... *Baptisia*
Fleabane .... *Erigeron*
Floss flower.............. *Ageratum*
Globe thistle .... *Echinops*
Goldenrod................. *Solidago*
Helen's flower .... *Helenium*
Hollyhock.................. *Alcea*
Honeysuckle.............. *Lonicera*
Lavender................ *Lavendula*
Lilac .... *Syringa*
Lupine.................. *Lupinus*
Lychnis .... *Lychnis*

Mallow .... *Malva*
Mealycup sage........ *Salvia farinacea*
Milkweed................. *Asclepias*
Mint .... *Mentha*
Oregano .... *Origanum vulgare*
Pansy........................ *Viola*
Parsley .... *Petroselinum crispum*
Phlox .... *Phlox*
Privet..................... *Ligustrum*
Purple coneflower.. *Echinacea purpurea*
Purple loosestrife .... *Lythrum*
Rock cress................... *Arabis*
Sea holly .... *Eryngium*
Shasta daisy .... *Chrysanthemum*
Snapdragon .... *Antirrhinum*
Stonecrop .... *Sedum*
Sweet alyssum .... *Lobularia*
Sweet marjoram ... *Origanum majorana*
Sweet rocket .... *Hesperis*
Tickseed .... *Coreopsis*
Zinnia .... *Zinnia*

Flowers* That Attract Hummingbirds

Beard tongue .... *Penstemon*
Bee balm.................. *Monarda*
Butterfly bush .... *Buddleia*
Catmint..................... *Nepeta*
Clove pink................. *Dianthus*
Columbine .... *Aquilegia*
Coral bells .... *Heuchera*
Daylily............... *Hemerocallis*
Desert candle .... *Yucca*
Flag iris........................ *Iris*
Flowering tobacco ..... *Nicotiana alata*
Foxglove .... *Digitalis*
Larkspur .... *Delphinium*
Lily .... *Lilium*
Lupine.................... *Lupinus*
Petunia...................... *Petunia*
Pincushion flower.......... *Scabiosa*
Red-hot poker .... *Kniphofia*
Scarlet sage......... *Salvia splendens*
Soapwort................. *Saponaria*
Summer phlox .... *Phlox paniculata*

Trumpet honeysuckle........ *Lonicera sempervirens*
Verbena .... *Verbena*
Weigela................... *Weigela*

* Note: Choose varieties in red and orange shades.

Shrubs and Trees to Plant for the Birds

Bird	Ash	Birch	Blackberry/raspberry	Blueberry	Cedar (red)/juniper	Cherry/plum	Chokeberry	Cotoneaster	Crab apple	Cranberry	Dogwood
Blue jay	F/S	F	F/S	F/S		F	F		F		F/S
Bunting											
Cardinal						F					
Catbird						F			F/S		F/S
Cedar waxwing	F/S	F	F/S	F/S		F		F	F/S	F	
Chickadee	F/S	F		F/S							F/S
Cowbird					F/S						
Crossbill		F/S			F/S						
Duck	F										
Finch	F/S	F	F/S		F/S	F	F	F	F/S		
Flicker					F/S				F/S		F/S
Goldfinch		F				F			F		
Goose											
Grackle			F		F/S						
Grosbeak	F/S		F/S			F	F		F/S	F	F/S
Junco		F					F				F/S
Mockingbird			F/S		F/S	F		F	F/S	F	
Mourning dove		F	F/S								
Nuthatch											
Oriole						F			F		F/S
Pheasant							F				
Pine siskin	F/S	F									
Redpoll		S	F/S		F/S						
Sparrow			F/S	F/S		F				F	F/S
Starling											
Tanager						F					F/S
Thrasher			F/S			F	F	F			
Thrush			F/S		F/S	F				F	F/S
Titmouse		F	F/S						F		
Towhee		F	F/S			F			F	F	
Warbler			F/S		F/S				F		
Woodpecker						F			F/S		F/S

F = FOOD   S = SHELTER

Elderberry	Grape	Hawthorn	Holly	Honeysuckle	Maple	Oak	Pine	Rose	Spruce	Sumac	Viburnum
F/S	F	F/S	F/S	F/S		F	F			F	
F/S											
						F		F/S			
F/S			F/S	F/S					F		
F/S	F	F/S	F/S	F	F/S		F	F	F/S		F
			F/S	F		F	F	F	F/S	F	
									F/S		
						F/S		F/S			
					F/S						
F/S	F		F/S	F	F/S		F/S				
F/S		F/S	F/S			F	F			F	
							F	F	F/S		
									F/S		
							S			S	
F/S				F	F/S		F	F	F/S		F
			F/S				F				
F/S	F		F/S	F/S				F	F/S	F	F
F/S	F		F/S			F	S		F/S		
F/S			F/S			F	F		F/S		
		F/S				F			F/S		
									F/S		
		F/S			F/S		F		F/S		
										F	
F/S	F	F/S		F	F/S		F	S	F/S	F	F
											F
		F/S				S			F/S	F	
F/S	F	F/S	F/S	F		F	F			F	
F/S	F	F/S		F		F		F		F	F
F/S		F/S				F	F				
F/S		F/S	F/S	F		F	F	S		F	F
F/S			F/S		F/S		F			F	
F/S			F/S			F	F		F/S	F	

Food for the Bird Feeder

Bird	Sunflower seeds	Millet (white proso)	Niger (thistle seeds)	Safflower seeds	Corn, cracked	Corn, whole	Peanuts	Peanut butter	Suet	Raisins	Apples	Oranges and grapefruit
Blue jay	✓			✓	✓	✓	✓			✓		
Bunting	✓	✓	✓	✓	✓	✓						
Cardinal	✓	✓		✓	✓					✓	✓	✓
Catbird										✓	✓	✓
Cedar waxwing											✓	✓
Chickadee	✓	✓		✓	✓		✓	✓	✓			
Cowbird		✓										
Crossbill	✓			✓				✓				
Duck		✓			✓	✓						
Finch	✓	✓	✓	✓			✓	✓				✓
Flicker							✓	✓	✓			
Goldfinch	✓		✓									
Goose					✓	✓						
Grackle	✓											
Grosbeak	✓	✓		✓			✓			✓	✓	✓
Junco	✓	✓	✓	✓	✓							
Mockingbird										✓	✓	
Mourning dove	✓	✓		✓	✓	✓	✓					
Nuthatch	✓	✓		✓			✓	✓	✓			
Oriole												✓
Pheasant					✓							
Pine siskin	✓	✓	✓	✓			✓			✓		✓
Redpoll	✓	✓	✓	✓								
Sparrow	✓	✓		✓	✓		✓					
Starling					✓							
Tanager												✓
Thrasher					✓		✓			✓	✓	
Thrush										✓	✓	
Titmouse	✓	✓		✓	✓		✓	✓	✓			
Towhee		✓										
Warbler							✓					✓
Woodpecker							✓	✓	✓			

REFERENCE

Plant Resources

Bulbs

American Daffodil Society
4126 Winfield Rd., Columbus, OH 43220
www.daffodilusa.org

American Dahlia Society
1 Rock Falls Ct., Rockville, MD 20854
www.dahlia.org

American Iris Society
www.irises.org

International Bulb Society (IBS)
www.bulbsociety.org

Netherlands Flower Bulb Information Center
30 Midwood St., Brooklyn, NY 11225
718-693-5400 • www.bulb.com

Ferns

American Fern Society
326 West St. NW, Vienna, VA 22180
http://amerfernsoc.org

The Hardy Fern Foundation
P.O. Box 166, Medina, WA 98039
www.hardyferns.org

Flowers

American Peony Society
www.americanpeonysociety.org

American Rhododendron Society
11 Pinecrest Dr., Fortuna, CA 95540
707-725-3043 • www.rhododendron.org

American Rose Society
P.O. Box 30,000, Shreveport, LA 71130
318-938-5402 • www.ars.org

Hardy Plant Society
Mid-Atlantic Group
1380 Warner Rd., Meadowbrook, PA 19046

International Waterlily and Water Gardening Society
6828 26th St. W., Bradenton, FL 34207
941-756-0880 • www.iwgs.org

Lady Bird Johnson Wildflower Center
4801 La Crosse Ave., Austin, TX 78739
512-292-4200 • www.wildflower.org

Perennial Plant Association
3383 Schirtzinger Rd., Hilliard, OH 43026
614-771-8431 • www.perennialplant.org

Fruits

California Rare Fruit Growers
The Fullerton Arboretum-CSUF
P.O. Box 6850, Fullerton, CA 92834
www.crfg.org

Home Orchard Society
P.O. Box 230192, Tigard, OR 97281
www.wvi.com/~dough/hos/hos1.html

North American Fruit Explorers
1716 Apples Rd., Chapin, IL 62628
www.nafex.org

Herbs

American Herb Association
P.O. Box 1673, Nevada City, CA 95959
530-265-9552 • www.ahaherb.com

The Flower and Herb Exchange
3076 North Winn Rd., Decorah, IA 52101
319-382-5990 • www.seedsavers.org

Herb Research Foundation
1007 Pearl St., Ste. 200, Boulder, CO 80302
800-748-2617 • www.herbs.org

Herb Society of America
9019 Kirtland Chardon Rd., Kirtland, OH 44094
440-256-0514 • www.herbsociety.org

Cooperative Extension Services

Contact your local state cooperative extension Web site to get help with tricky insect problems, best varieties to plant in your area, or general maintenance of your garden.

Alabama
www.aces.edu

Alaska
www.uaf.edu/coop-ext

Arizona
www.ag.arizona.edu/
extension

Arkansas
www.uaex.edu

California
www.ucanr.org

Colorado
www.ext.colostate.edu

Connecticut
www.canr.uconn.edu/ces/
index.html

Delaware
http://ag.udel.edu/
extension

Florida
www.ifas.ufl.edu/
extension/ces.htm

Georgia
www.ces.uga.edu

Hawaii
www2.ctahr.hawaii.edu/
extout/extout.asp

Idaho
www.uidaho.edu/ag/
extension

Illinois
www.extension.uiuc.edu/
welcome.html

Indiana
www.ces.purdue.edu

Iowa
www.exnet.iastate.edu

Kansas
www.oznet.ksu.edu

Kentucky
www.ca.uky.edu

Louisiana
www.lsuagcenter.com/nav/
extension/extension.asp

Maine
www.umext.maine.edu

Maryland
www.agnr.umd.edu/MCE/
index.cfm

Massachusetts
www.umassextension.org

Michigan
www.msue.msu.edu/msue

Minnesota
www.extension.umn.edu

Mississippi
www.msucares.com

Missouri
www.extension.missouri
.edu

Montana
http://extn.msu.montana.edu

Nebraska
http://extension.unl.edu

Nevada
www.unce.unr.edu

New Hampshire
www.ceinfo.unh.edu

New Jersey
www.rce.rutgers.edu

New Mexico
www.cahe.nmsu.edu/ces

New York
www.cce.cornell.edu

North Carolina
www.ces.ncsu.edu

North Dakota
www.ext.nodak.edu

Ohio
www.ag.ohio-state.edu

Oklahoma
www.dasnr.okstate.edu/oces

Oregon
www.osu.orst.edu/extension

Pennsylvania
www.extension.psu.edu

Rhode Island
www.edc.uri.edu

South Carolina
www.clemson.edu/
extension

South Dakota
http://sdces.sdstate.edu

Tennessee
www.utextension.utk.edu

Texas
http://agextension.tamu.edu

Utah
www.extension.usu.edu

Vermont
www.uvm.edu/~uvmext

Virginia
www.ext.vt.edu

Washington
http://ext.wsu.edu

West Virginia
www.wvu.edu/~exten

Wisconsin
www.uwex.edu/ces

Wyoming
www.uwyo.edu/ces/
ceshome.htm

Makeshift Measurers

When you don't have a measuring stick or tape, use what is at hand. To this list, add other items that you always (or nearly always) have handy.

Credit card. . . . . 3⅜" x 2⅛"
Business card (standard) . . . . . . 3½" x 2"
Floor tile . . . . 12" square
Dollar bill . . . . 6⅛" x 2⅝"
Quarter (diameter) . . . . 1"
Penny (diameter) . . . . ¾"
Sheet of paper . . . . 8½" x 11"
(legal size: 8½" x 14")

Your foot/shoe: _____
Your outstretched arms, fingertip
  to fingertip: _____
Your shoelace: _____
Your necktie: _____
Your belt: _____

If you don't have a scale or a measuring spoon handy, try these for size:
A piece of meat the size of your hand or a deck of cards = 3 to 4 ounces.
A piece of meat or cheese the size of a golf ball = about 1 ounce.
From the tip of your smallest finger to the first joint = about 1 teaspoon.
The tip of your thumb = about 1 tablespoon.

The idea of using available materials to measure is not new.
1 foot = the length of a person's foot.
1 yard = the distance from a person's nose to the fingertip of an outstretched arm.
1 acre = the amount of land an ox can plow in a day.

Hand Thermometer for Outdoor Cooking

■ Hold your palm close to where the food will be cooking: over the coals or in front of a reflector oven. Count "one-and-one, two-and-two," and so on (each pair is roughly equivalent to one second), for as many seconds as you can hold your hand still.

Seconds Counted	Heat	Temperature
6–8	Slow	250°–350°F
4–5	Moderate	350°–400°F
2–3	Hot	400°–450°F
1 or less	Very hot	450°–500°F

Miscellaneous Length Measures

ASTRONOMICAL UNIT (A.U.): 93,000,000 miles; the average distance from Earth to the Sun

BOLT: 40 yards; used for measuring cloth

CHAIN: 66 feet; one mile is equal to 80 chains; used in surveying

CUBIT: 18 inches; derived from distance between elbow and tip of middle finger

HAND: 4 inches; derived from the width of the hand

LEAGUE: usually estimated at 3 miles

LIGHT-YEAR: 5,880,000,000,000 miles; the distance light travels in a vacuum in a year at the rate of 186,281.7 miles per second

PICA: ⅙ inch; used in printing for measuring column width, etc.

SPAN: 9 inches; derived from the distance between the end of the thumb and the end of the little finger when both are outstretched

Body Mass Index (BMI) Formula

Here's an easy formula to figure your Body Mass Index (BMI), thought to be a fairly accurate indicator of relative body size. **W** is your weight in pounds and **H** is your height in inches.

$$BMI = \left(\frac{W}{H^2}\right) \times 703$$

■ If the result is 18.5 to 24.9, you are within a healthy weight range.

■ If it's below 18.5, you are too thin.

■ From 25 to 29.9, you are overweight and at increased risk for health problems.

■ At 30 and above, you are considered obese and at a dramatically increased risk

for serious health problems.

There are exceptions to the above, including children, expectant mothers, and the elderly. Very muscular people with a high BMI generally have nothing to worry about, and extreme skinniness is generally a symptom of some other health problem, not the cause.

Tape-Measure Method

■ Here's another way to see if you are dangerously overweight. Measure your waistline. A waist measurement of more than 35 inches in women and more than 40 inches in men, regardless of height, suggests a serious risk of weight-related health problems.

Calorie-Burning Comparisons

If you hustle through your chores to get to the fitness center, relax. You're getting a great workout already. The left-hand column lists "chore" exercises, the middle column shows the number of calories burned per minute per pound of body weight, and the right-hand column lists comparable "recreational" exercises. For example, a 150-pound person forking straw bales burns 9.45 calories per minute, the same workout he or she would get playing basketball.

Chore	Cal/min/lb	Recreational
Chopping with an ax, fast	**0.135**	Skiing, cross country, uphill
Climbing hills, with 44-pound load	**0.066**	Swimming, crawl, fast
Digging trenches	**0.065**	Skiing, cross country, steady walk
Forking straw bales	**0.063**	Basketball
Chopping down trees	**0.060**	Football
Climbing hills, with 9-pound load	**0.058**	Swimming, crawl, slow
Sawing by hand	**0.055**	Skiing, cross country, moderate
Mowing lawns	**0.051**	Horseback riding, trotting
Scrubbing floors	**0.049**	Tennis
Shoveling coal	**0.049**	Aerobic dance, medium
Hoeing	**0.041**	Weight training, circuit training
Stacking firewood	**0.040**	Weight lifting, free weights
Shoveling grain	**0.038**	Golf
Painting houses	**0.035**	Walking, normal pace, asphalt road
Weeding	**0.033**	Table tennis
Shopping for food	**0.028**	Cycling, 5.5 mph
Mopping floors	**0.028**	Fishing
Washing windows	**0.026**	Croquet
Raking	**0.025**	Dancing, ballroom
Driving a tractor	**0.016**	Drawing, standing position

HOW MUCH DO YOU NEED?
Floor Tiles

Before you do anything, make a scale drawing of your room with all measurements clearly marked. Take it with you when you shop for tile flooring. Ask the salespeople to help you calculate your needs for rooms that feature bay windows, unusual jogs and turns, and special patterns or designs in the material.

Ceramic Tile

■ Ceramic tiles for floors and walls come in a range of sizes, from 1x1-inch mosaics up to 12x12-inch (or larger) squares. The most popular size is the 4¼-inch square tile, but there is a trend toward larger tiles (8x8s, 10x10s, 12x12s). Installing these larger tiles can be a challenge because the underlayment must be absolutely even and level.

■ Small 1-inch mosaic tiles are usually joined together in 12x12-inch or 12x24-inch sheets to make them easier to install. You can have a custom pattern made, or you can mix different-colored tiles to create your own mosaic borders, patterns, and pictures.

Sheet Vinyl

■ Sheet vinyl typically comes in 6- and 12-foot widths. If your floor requires two or more pieces, your estimate must include enough overlap to allow you to match the pattern.

Vinyl Tile

■ Vinyl tiles generally

come in 9- and 12-inch squares. To find the number of 12-inch tiles you need, just multiply the length of the room (in feet) by the width (rounding fractions up to the next foot). Add 5 percent extra for cutting and waste. Measure any obstructions (such as appliances and cabinets) that you will not lay tile under, and subtract that square footage from the total.

To calculate the number of 9-inch tiles, divide the room's length (in inches) by 9, then divide the room's width by 9. Multiply those two numbers together to get the number of tiles you need, then add 5 percent extra for cutting and waste.

HOW MUCH DO YOU NEED?
Asphalt Shingles

Asphalt roofing shingles usually have three sections, or "tabs," per shingle and an overall length of 3 feet. The surface area of a roof is measured in "squares" of shingles. One square covers 100 square feet. However, shingles are usually priced per bundle, with 1 square equal to 3 bundles.

■ Calculate the number of bundles you need by measuring the roof's square footage (length multiplied by width). Divide that number by 100 to get the number of squares needed. Multiply the number of squares by 3, and that will be the number of bundles you need to buy.

■ To seal out water, apply an underlayment such as builder's felt (tar paper) before shingling. Builder's felt comes in rolls, and its thickness is gauged in pounds. Typically, a roll of 15-pound felt covers about 400 square feet; a roll of 30-pound felt covers 200 square feet.

HOW MUCH DO YOU NEED?

Wallpaper

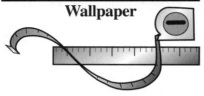

Wallpaper is sold in single, double, and triple rolls. Average coverage for a double roll, for example, is 56 square feet.

■ Measure the length of each wall, add these figures together, and multiply by the height of the walls to get the area (square footage) of the room.

■ Calculate the square footage of each door, window, or other opening in the room. Add these figures together and subtract the total from the area of the room.

■ Take that figure and multiply by 1.15, to account for a waste rate of about 15 percent in your wallpaper project.

■ Divide the coverage figure (from the label) into the total square footage of the room you're papering. Round the answer up to the nearest whole number. This is the number of rolls you need to buy.

■ Save leftover wallpaper rolls, carefully wrapped to keep them clean, or return to the store if unopened.

HOW MUCH DO YOU NEED?

Bricks

How to estimate how many nonmodular standard bricks you need for a project.

■ Multiply the length of the wall in feet by its height in feet, and that by its thickness in feet, and then multiply that result by 20. The answer will be the number of bricks in the wall.

For example, 30 feet (length) × 20 feet (height) × 1 foot (thickness) = 600 × 20 = 12,000 bricks.

HOW MUCH DO YOU NEED?

Exterior Paint

Here's how to estimate the number of gallons needed for one-coat coverage of a home that is 20 feet wide by 40 feet long, has walls that rise 16 feet to the eaves on the 40-foot sides, and has full-width gables on the 20-foot sides rising 10 feet to the peaks.

■ **First, find the area of the walls.**

Add the width to the length:
20 ft. + 40 ft. = 60 ft.

Double it for four sides:
60 ft. × 2 = 120 ft.

Multiply that by the height of the walls:
120 ft. × 16 ft. = 1,920 sq. ft.

The area of the walls is 1,920 square feet.

■ **Next, find the area of the gables.**

Take half the width of one gable at its base:
20 ft. ÷ 2 = 10 ft.

Multiply that by the height of the gable:
10 ft. × 10 ft. = 100 sq. ft.

Multiply that by the number of gables:
100 sq. ft. × 2 = 200 sq. ft.

The area of the gables is 200 square feet.

■ **Add the two figures together for the total area:**
1,920 sq. ft. + 200 sq. ft. = 2,120 sq. ft.

■ **Finally,** divide the total area by the area covered by a gallon of paint (400 square feet) to find the number of gallons needed:
2,120 sq. ft. ÷ 400 sq. ft./gal. = 5.3 gal.

Buy five gallons of paint to start with. The sixth gallon might not be necessary.

—Margo Letourneau

HOW MUCH DO YOU NEED?
Lumber and Nails

The amount of lumber and nails you need will depend on your project, but these guidelines will help you determine quantities of each.

Lumber Width and Thickness (in inches)

Nominal Size	Actual Size DRY OR SEASONED	Nominal Size	Actual Size DRY OR SEASONED
1 x 3	$\frac{3}{4}$ x 2$\frac{1}{2}$	2 x 3	1$\frac{1}{2}$ x 2$\frac{1}{2}$
1 x 4	$\frac{3}{4}$ x 3$\frac{1}{2}$	2 x 4	1$\frac{1}{2}$ x 3$\frac{1}{2}$
1 x 6	$\frac{3}{4}$ x 5$\frac{1}{2}$	2 x 6	1$\frac{1}{2}$ x 5$\frac{1}{2}$
1 x 8	$\frac{3}{4}$ x 7$\frac{1}{4}$	2 x 8	1$\frac{1}{2}$ x 7$\frac{1}{4}$
1 x 10	$\frac{3}{4}$ x 9$\frac{1}{4}$	2 x 10	1$\frac{1}{2}$ x 9$\frac{1}{4}$
1 x 12	$\frac{3}{4}$ x 11$\frac{1}{4}$	2 x 12	1$\frac{1}{2}$ x 11$\frac{1}{4}$

Nail Sizes

The nail on the left is a 5d (penny) finish nail; on the right, 20d common. The numerals below the nail sizes indicate the approximate number of nails per pound.

Lumber Measure in Board Feet

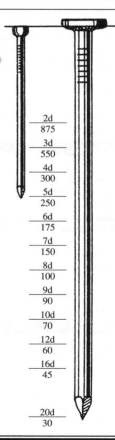

Size in inches	12 ft.	14 ft.	16 ft.	18 ft.	20 ft.
1 x 4	4	4$\frac{2}{3}$	5$\frac{1}{3}$	6	6$\frac{2}{3}$
1 x 6	6	7	8	9	10
1 x 8	8	9$\frac{1}{3}$	10$\frac{2}{3}$	12	13$\frac{1}{3}$
1 x 10	10	11$\frac{2}{3}$	13$\frac{1}{3}$	15	16$\frac{2}{3}$
1 x 12	12	14	16	18	20
2 x 3	6	7	8	9	10
2 x 4	8	9$\frac{1}{3}$	10$\frac{2}{3}$	12	13$\frac{1}{3}$
2 x 6	12	14	16	18	20
2 x 8	16	18$\frac{2}{3}$	21$\frac{1}{3}$	24	26$\frac{2}{3}$
2 x 10	20	23$\frac{1}{3}$	26$\frac{2}{3}$	30	33$\frac{1}{3}$
2 x 12	24	28	32	36	40
4 x 4	16	18$\frac{2}{3}$	21$\frac{1}{3}$	24	26$\frac{2}{3}$
6 x 6	36	42	48	54	60
8 x 8	64	74$\frac{2}{3}$	85$\frac{1}{3}$	96	106$\frac{2}{3}$
10 x 10	100	116$\frac{2}{3}$	133$\frac{1}{3}$	150	166$\frac{2}{3}$
12 x 12	144	168	192	216	240

Nail sizes and number per pound:

Size	per lb.
2d	875
3d	550
4d	300
5d	250
6d	175
7d	150
8d	100
9d	90
10d	70
12d	60
16d	45
20d	30

Table of Measures

Apothecaries'

1 scruple = 20 grains
1 dram = 3 scruples
1 ounce = 8 drams
1 pound = 12 ounces

Avoirdupois

1 ounce = 16 drams
1 pound = 16 ounces
1 hundredweight = 100
  pounds
1 ton = 2,000 pounds
1 long ton = 2,240 pounds

Cubic

1 cubic foot = 1,728 cubic
  inches
1 cubic yard = 27 cubic feet
1 cord = 128 cubic feet
1 U.S. liquid gallon = 4
  quarts = 231 cubic inches
1 Imperial gallon = 1.20 U.S.
  gallons = 0.16 cubic foot
1 board foot = 144 cubic
  inches

Dry

2 pints = 1 quart
4 quarts = 1 gallon
2 gallons = 1 peck
4 pecks = 1 bushel

Liquid

4 gills = 1 pint
2 pints = 1 quart
4 quarts = 1 gallon
63 gallons = 1 hogshead
2 hogsheads = 1 pipe or butt
2 pipes = 1 tun

Linear

1 foot = 12 inches
1 yard = 3 feet
1 rod = 5½ yards
1 mile = 320 rods = 1,760
  yards = 5,280 feet
1 Int. nautical mile =
  6,076.1155 feet

1 knot = 1 nautical mile
  per hour
1 furlong = ⅛ mile = 660 feet
  = 220 yards
1 league = 3 miles = 24
  furlongs
1 fathom = 2 yards = 6 feet
1 chain = 100 links = 22 yards
1 link = 7.92 inches
1 hand = 4 inches
1 span = 9 inches

Square

1 square foot = 144 square
  inches
1 square yard = 9 square feet
1 square rod = 30¼ square
  yards = 272¼ square feet
1 acre = 160 square rods =
  43,560 square feet
1 square mile = 640 acres =
  102,400 square rods
1 square rod = 625 square
  links
1 square chain = 16 square
  rods
1 acre = 10 square chains

Household

120 drops of water =
  1 teaspoon
60 drops thick fluid =
  1 teaspoon
2 teaspoons = 1 dessertspoon
3 teaspoons = 1 tablespoon
16 tablespoons = 1 cup
1 cup = 8 ounces
2 cups = 1 pint
2 pints = 1 quart
4 quarts = 1 gallon
3 tablespoons flour = 1 ounce
2 tablespoons butter = 1 ounce
2 cups granulated sugar =
  1 pound
3¾ cups confectioners' sugar
  = 1 pound
3½ cups wheat flour =
  1 pound

5⅓ cups dry coffee =
  1 pound
6½ cups dry tea = 1 pound
2 cups shortening = 1 pound
1 stick butter = ½ cup
2 cups cornmeal = 1 pound
2¾ cups brown sugar =
  1 pound
2⅜ cups raisins = 1 pound
9 eggs = 1 pound
1 ounce yeast = 1 scant
  tablespoon

Metric

1 inch = 2.54 centimeters
1 centimeter = 0.39 inch
1 meter = 39.37 inches
1 yard = 0.914 meter
1 mile = 1,609.344 meters =
  1.61 kilometers
1 kilometer = 0.62 mile
1 square inch = 6.45 square
  centimeters
1 square yard = 0.84 square
  meter
1 square mile = 2.59 square
  kilometers
1 square kilometer = 0.386
  square mile
1 acre = 0.40 hectare
1 hectare = 2.47 acres
1 cubic yard = 0.76 cubic
  meter
1 cubic meter = 1.31 cubic
  yards
1 liter = 1.057 U.S. liquid
  quarts
1 U.S. liquid quart = 0.946
  liter
1 U.S. liquid gallon = 3.78
  liters
1 gram = 0.035 ounce
1 ounce = 28.349 grams
1 kilogram = 2.2 pounds
1 pound avoirdupois = 0.45
  kilogram

Freezer Storage Time
(freezer temperature 0°F or colder)

Product	Months in Freezer
Fresh meat	
Beef	6 to 12
Lamb	6 to 9
Veal	6 to 9
Pork	3 to 6
Ground beef, veal, lamb	2 to 4
Frankfurters	2
Sausage, fresh pork	2
Ground pork	1 to 2
Ready-to-serve luncheon meats	Not recommended
Poultry	
Chicken or turkey (whole)	6 to 12
Chicken or turkey (parts), Rock Cornish game hens, game birds	6 to 9
Duck, cooked poultry (in gravy), chicken, turkey	6
Goose, squab	4 to 6
Cooked poultry (breaded, fried)	4
Giblets	2 to 3
Cooked poultry (plain meat)	1
Fresh fruits (prepared for freezing)	
All fruits except those listed below	10 to 12
Avocados, bananas	3
Lemons, limes, plantains	Not recommended

Product	Months in Freezer
Fresh vegetables (prepared for freezing)	
Beans, beets, bok choy, broccoli, Brussels sprouts, cabbage, carrots, cauliflower, celery, corn, greens, kohlrabi, leeks, mushrooms, okra, parsnips, peas, peppers, onions, soybeans, spinach, summer squash	10 to 12
Asparagus, rutabagas, turnips	8 to 10
Artichokes, eggplant	6 to 8
Tomatoes (overripe or sliced)	2
Bamboo shoots, cucumbers, endive, lettuce, radishes, watercress	Not recommended
Cheese (except those listed below)	6
Cottage cheese, cream cheese, feta, goat, fresh mozzarella, Neufchâtel, Parmesan, processed cheese (opened)	Not recommended
Dairy products	
Margarine (not diet)	12
Butter	6 to 9
Cream, half-and-half	4
Milk	3
Ice cream	1 to 2
Yogurt	1 to 1½

Freezing Hints

Label foods for easy identification. Write the name of the food, number of servings, and date of freezing on containers or bags.

Freeze foods as quickly as possible by placing them directly against the sides of the freezer.

Arrange freezer into sections for each food category.

For meals, remember that a quart container holds four servings, and a pint container holds two servings.

To prevent sticking, spread the food to be frozen (berries, hamburgers, cookies, etc.) on a cookie sheet and freeze until solid. Then place in plastic bags and freeze.

If power is interrupted, or if the freezer is not operating normally, do not open the freezer door. Food in a loaded freezer will usually stay frozen for two days.

Herb Companions in the Kitchen

Anise. Use in cookies, cakes, fruit fillings, and breads, and with cottage cheese, shellfish, and spaghetti dishes.

Basil. Use in tomato dishes, pesto, sauces, and salad dressings.

Borage. Use leaves in salads; use flowers in soups and stews.

Caraway. Use in rye breads, cheese dips and rarebits, soups, applesauce, salads, coleslaw, and over pork or sauerkraut.

Chervil. Use in soups, salads, sauces, and eggs, and with fish, veal, lamb, and pork.

Chives. Use in vegetable dishes, dressings, casseroles, rice, eggs, cheese dishes, sauces, gravies, and dips.

Dill. Use seeds for pickles and to add aroma and taste to strong vegetables like cauliflower, cabbage, and turnips. Use fresh with seafood and green beans, and in potato dishes, cheese, soups, salads, and sauces.

Fennel. Use in pastries, confectionery, sweet pickles, sausages, tomato dishes, and soups, and to flavor vinegars and oils. Gives warmth and sweetness to curries.

Garlic. Use in tomato dishes, garlic bread, soups, dips, sauces, and marinades, or with meats, poultry, fish, and vegetables.

Lovage. Use in soups, stews, and salad dressings. Goes well with potatoes. The seeds can be used on breads and biscuits.

Marjoram. Use in almost any meat, fish,

dairy, or vegetable dish that isn't sweet. Add near the end of cooking.

Mint. Use in Middle Eastern dishes, salads, jellies, and teas, and with roasted lamb or fish.

Oregano. Use in any tomato dish. Try oregano with summer squash, potatoes, mushroom dishes, and beans, or in a marinade for lamb or game.

Parsley. Use fresh in soups, sauces, and salads. It lessens the need for salt in soups. You can fry parsley and use it as a side dish with meat or fish. It is, of course, the perfect garnish.

Rosemary. Use in tomato dishes, stews, and soups, and with poultry, lamb, and vegetables.

Sage. Use in salads, cheese dishes, stuffings, soups, and pickles, and with beans and peas. Excellent for salt-free cooking.

Summer Savory. Use in soups, stews, and stuffings, and with fish, chicken, green beans, and eggs.

Tarragon. Use with meat, eggs, poultry, and seafood, and in salad dressings, marinades, and sauces.

Thyme. Use in casseroles, stews, soups, and ragouts, and with eggs, potatoes, fish, and green vegetables.

Preserving Herbs

DRYING

■ Pick herbs just before they bloom, while they are still at the peak of their flavor. Harvest them in the late morning after the dew has dried and before the hot afternoon sun draws out their delicate flavors.

■ Gather the herbs in small bunches, and tie the stems together with a rubber band or piece of string.

■ Hang the herbs in a dry, well-ventilated area such as a shed or barn, making sure they are out of direct sunlight. (Basements are often too damp for drying.)

■ Use when the leaves crumble if they are rubbed between your fingers, usually within 10 to 14 days.

■ To dry herbs instantly, place them between four paper towels (two on the bottom and two on the top) in a microwave oven. Set the oven on high for two minutes and check the herbs for dryness. If they are not completely dry, rearrange them and repeat the process. This method is a good way to dry parsley. (Warning: This process requires constant attention. The paper towels in the microwave oven could catch fire.)

FREEZING

■ Strip the leaves off the stems of the herbs, and place the leaves into an airtight freezer bag or a small plastic freezer container. Many herbs freeze well, including chives, dill, fennel, lovage, and tarragon.

■ To make herb ice cubes, purée washed and stemmed herb leaves, such as basil, in a food processor with a small amount of olive oil. Pour the mixture into ice cube trays and freeze. Use in soups, stews, and sauces.

Pan Sizes and Equivalents

In the midst of cooking but without the right pan? You can substitute one size for another, keeping in mind that when you change the pan size, you must sometimes change the cooking time. For example, if a recipe calls for using an 8-inch round cake pan and baking for 25 minutes, and you substitute a 9-inch pan, the cake may bake in only 20 minutes, because the batter forms a thinner layer in the larger pan. (Use a toothpick inserted into the center of the cake to test for doneness. If it comes out clean, the cake has finished baking.) Also, specialty pans such as tube and Bundt pans distribute heat differently; you may not get the same results if you substitute a regular cake pan for a specialty one, even if the volume is the same.

Pan Size	Volume	Substitute
9-inch pie pan	4 cups	■ 8-inch round cake pan
8x4x2½-inch loaf pan	6 cups	■ Three 5x2-inch loaf pans ■ Two 3x1¼-inch muffin tins ■ 12x8x2-inch cake pan
9x5x3-inch loaf pan	8 cups	■ 8x8-inch cake pan ■ 9-inch round cake pan
15x10x1-inch jelly roll pan	10 cups	■ 9x9-inch cake pan ■ Two 8-inch round cake pans ■ 8x3-inch springform pan
10x3-inch Bundt pan	12 cups	■ Two 8x4x2½-inch loaf pans ■ 9x3-inch angel food cake pan ■ 9x3-inch springform pan
13x9x2-inch cake pan	14–15 cups	■ Two 9-inch round cake pans ■ Two 8x8-inch cake pans

■ If you are cooking a casserole and don't have the correct-size dish, here are some baking-pan substitutions. Again, think about the depth of the ingredients in the dish and lengthen or shorten the baking time accordingly.

Casserole Size	Baking-Pan Substitute
1½ quarts	9x5x3-inch loaf pan
2 quarts	8x8-inch cake pan
2½ quarts	9x9-inch cake pan
3 quarts	13x9x2-inch cake pan
4 quarts	14x10x2-inch cake pan

Substitutions for Common Ingredients

ITEM	QUANTITY	SUBSTITUTION
Allspice	1 teaspoon	½ teaspoon cinnamon plus ⅛ teaspoon ground cloves
Arrowroot, as thickener	1½ teaspoons	1 tablespoon flour
Baking powder	1 teaspoon	¼ teaspoon baking soda plus ⅝ teaspoon cream of tartar
Bread crumbs, dry	¼ cup	1 slice bread
Bread crumbs, soft	½ cup	1 slice bread
Buttermilk	1 cup	1 cup plain yogurt
Chocolate, unsweetened	1 ounce	3 tablespoons cocoa plus 1 tablespoon butter or fat
Cracker crumbs	¾ cup	1 cup dry bread crumbs
Cream, heavy	1 cup	¾ cup milk plus ⅓ cup melted butter (this will not whip)
Cream, light	1 cup	⅞ cup milk plus 3 tablespoons melted butter
Cream, sour	1 cup	⅞ cup buttermilk or plain yogurt plus 3 tablespoons melted butter
Cream, whipping	1 cup	⅔ cup well-chilled evaporated milk, whipped; or 1 cup nonfat dry milk powder whipped with 1 cup ice water
Egg	1 whole	2 yolks
Flour, all-purpose	1 cup	1⅛ cups cake flour; or ⅝ cup potato flour; or 1¼ cups rye or coarsely ground whole grain flour; or 1 cup cornmeal
Flour, cake	1 cup	1 cup minus 2 tablespoons sifted all-purpose flour
Flour, self-rising	1 cup	1 cup all-purpose flour plus 1¼ teaspoons baking powder plus ¼ teaspoon salt
Garlic	1 small clove	⅛ teaspoon garlic powder; or ½ teaspoon instant minced garlic
Herbs, dried	½ to 1 teaspoon	1 tablespoon fresh, minced and packed
Honey	1 cup	1¼ cups sugar plus ½ cup liquid
Lemon	1	1 to 3 tablespoons juice plus 1 to 1½ teaspoons grated rind

Vegetable Weights and Measures

Asparagus: 1 pound = 3 cups chopped
Beans (string): 1 pound = 4 cups chopped
Beets: 1 pound (5 medium) = 2½ cups chopped
Broccoli: ½ pound = 6 cups chopped
Cabbage: 1 pound = 4½ cups shredded
Carrots: 1 pound = 3½ cups sliced or grated
Celery: 1 pound = 4 cups chopped
Cucumbers: 1 pound (2 medium) = 4 cups sliced
Eggplant: 1 pound = 4 cups chopped (6 cups raw, cubed = 3 cups cooked)
Garlic: 1 clove = 1 teaspoon chopped
Leeks: 1 pound = 4 cups chopped (2 cups cooked)

Mushrooms: 1 pound = 5 to 6 cups sliced = 2 cups cooked
Onions: 1 pound = 4 cups sliced = 2 cups cooked
Parsnips: 1 pound unpeeled = 1½ cups cooked, puréed
Peas: 1 pound whole = 1 to 1½ cups shelled
Potatoes: 1 pound (3 medium) sliced = 2 cups mashed
Pumpkin: 1 pound = 4 cups chopped = 2 cups cooked and drained
Spinach: 1 pound = ¾ to 1 cup cooked
Squash (summer): 1 pound = 4 cups grated = 2 cups salted and drained
Squash (winter): 2 pounds = 2½ cups cooked, puréed
Sweet potatoes: 1 pound = 4 cups grated = 1 cup cooked, puréed

ITEM	QUANTITY	SUBSTITUTION
Lemon juice	1 teaspoon	½ teaspoon vinegar
Lemon rind, grated	1 teaspoon	½ teaspoon lemon extract
Milk, skim	1 cup	⅓ cup instant nonfat dry milk plus about ¾ cup water
Milk, to sour	1 cup	Add 1 tablespoon vinegar or lemon juice to 1 cup milk minus 1 tablespoon. Stir and let stand 5 minutes.
Milk, whole	1 cup	½ cup evaporated milk plus ½ cup water; **or** 1 cup skim milk plus 2 teaspoons melted butter
Molasses	1 cup	1 cup honey
Mustard, prepared	1 tablespoon	1 teaspoon dry or powdered mustard
Onion, chopped	1 small	1 tablespoon instant minced onion; **or** 1 teaspoon onion powder; **or** ¼ cup frozen chopped onion
Sugar, granulated	1 cup	1 cup firmly packed brown sugar; **or** 1¾ cups confectioners' sugar (do not substitute in baking); **or** 2 cups corn syrup; **or** 1 cup superfine sugar
Tomatoes, canned	1 cup	½ cup tomato sauce plus ½ cup water; **or** 1⅓ cups chopped fresh tomatoes, simmered
Tomato juice	1 cup	½ cup tomato sauce plus ½ cup water plus dash each salt and sugar; **or** ¼ cup tomato paste plus ¾ cup water plus salt and sugar
Tomato ketchup	½ cup	½ cup tomato sauce plus 2 tablespoons sugar, 1 tablespoon vinegar, and ⅛ teaspoon ground cloves
Tomato purée	1 cup	½ cup tomato paste plus ½ cup water
Tomato soup	1 can (10¾ oz.)	1 cup tomato sauce plus ¼ cup water
Vanilla	1-inch bean	1 teaspoon vanilla extract
Yeast	1 cake (⅗ oz.)	1 package active dried yeast (1 scant tablespoon)
Yogurt, plain	1 cup	1 cup buttermilk

Swiss chard: 1 pound = 5 to 6 cups packed leaves = 1 to 1½ cups cooked
Tomatoes: 1 pound (3 or 4 medium) = 1½ cups seeded pulp
Turnips: 1 pound = 4 cups chopped = 2 cups cooked, mashed

Fruit Weights and Measures

Apples: 1 pound (3 or 4 medium) = 3 cups sliced
Bananas: 1 pound (3 or 4 medium) = 1¾ cups mashed
Berries: 1 quart = 3½ cups
Dates: 1 pound = 2½ cups pitted
Lemon: 1 whole = 1 to 3 tablespoons juice; 1 to 1½ teaspoons grated rind
Lime: 1 whole = 1½ to 2 tablespoons juice

Orange: 1 medium = 6 to 8 tablespoons juice; 2 to 3 tablespoons grated rind
Peaches: 1 pound (4 medium) = 3 cups sliced
Pears: 1 pound (4 medium) = 2 cups sliced
Rhubarb: 1 pound = 2 cups cooked
Strawberries: 1 quart = 3 cups sliced

Substitutions for Uncommon Ingredients

ITEM	SUBSTITUTION
Balsamic vinegar, 1 tablespoon	1 tablespoon red wine vinegar plus ½ teaspoon sugar
Bamboo shoots	Asparagus (in fried dishes)
Bergamot	Mint
Chayotes	Yellow summer squash **or** zucchini
Cilantro	Parsley (for color only; flavor cannot be duplicated)
Coconut milk	2½ cups water plus 2 cups shredded, unsweetened coconut. Combine and bring to a boil. Remove from heat; cool. Mix in a blender for 2 minutes; strain. Makes about 2 cups.
Delicata squash	Butternut squash **or** sweet potato
Green mangoes	Sour, green cooking apples
Habanero peppers	5 jalapeño peppers **or** serrano peppers
Italian seasoning	Equal parts basil, marjoram, oregano, rosemary, sage, and thyme
Lemon grass	Lemon zest (zest from 1 lemon equals 2 stalks lemon grass)
Limes or lime juice	Lemons or lemon juice
Lo Mein noodles	Egg noodles
Mascarpone, 1 cup	3 tablespoons heavy cream plus ¾ cup cream cheese plus 4 tablespoons butter
Neufchâtel	Cream cheese **or** Boursin
Palm sugar	Light brown sugar
Rice wine	Pale, dry sherry **or** white vermouth
Red peppers	Equal amount pimientos
Romano cheese	Parmesan cheese
Saffron	Turmeric (for color; flavor is different)
Shallots	Red onions **or** Spanish onions
Shrimp paste	Anchovy paste
Tamarind juice	5 parts ketchup to 1 part vinegar

Can Sizes

CAN NAME	FL. OZ.	CUPS	ML
#10	103.70	12.96	3067
#5	56.00	7.00	1656
#3 cylinder	46.00	5.75	1360
#2.5	28.50	3.56	843
#2	20.00	2.50	591
#303	15.60	1.95	461
#211 cylinder	12.00	1.50	355
#1 picnic	10.50	1.30	311
8 ounces	8.30	1.04	245
6 ounces	5.75	0.72	170

The Party Planner

Cooking for a crowd? These estimates can help you determine how much food you should buy. They're based on "average" servings; adjust quantities upward for big eaters and downward if children are included.

Food	To Serve 25	To Serve 50	To Serve 100
MEATS			
Chicken or turkey breast	12½ pounds	25 pounds	50 pounds
Fish (fillets or steaks)	7½ pounds	15 pounds	30 pounds
Hamburgers	8 to 9 pounds	15 to 18 pounds	30 to 36 pounds
Ham or roast beef	10 pounds	20 pounds	40 pounds
Hot dogs	6 pounds	12½ pounds	25 pounds
Meat loaf	6 pounds	12 pounds	24 pounds
Oysters	1 gallon	2 gallons	4 gallons
Pork	10 pounds	20 pounds	40 pounds
SIDE DISHES			
Baked beans	5 quarts	2½ gallons	5 gallons
Beets	7½ pounds	15 pounds	30 pounds
Cabbage for cole slaw	5 pounds	10 pounds	20 pounds
Carrots	7½ pounds	15 pounds	30 pounds
Lettuce for salad (heads)	5	10	20
Peas (fresh)	12 pounds	25 pounds	50 pounds
Potatoes	9 pounds	18 pounds	36 pounds
Potato salad	3 quarts	1½ gallons	3 gallons
Salad dressing	3 cups	1½ quarts	3 quarts
DESSERTS			
Cakes	2	4	8
Ice cream	1 gallon	2 gallons	4 gallons
Pies	4	9	18
Whipping cream	1 pint	2 pints	4 pints
MISCELLANEOUS			
Bread (loaves)	3	5	10
Butter	¾ pound	1½ pounds	3 pounds
Cheese	¾ pound	1½ pounds	3 pounds
Coffee	¾ pound	1½ pounds	3 pounds
Milk	1½ gallons	3 gallons	6 gallons
Nuts	¾ pound	1½ pounds	3 pounds
Olives	½ pound	1 pound	2 pounds
Pickles	½ quart	1 quart	2 quarts
Rolls	50	100	200
Soup	5 quarts	2½ gallons	5 gallons

The Golden Rule

(It's true in all faiths.)

Brahmanism:
This is the sum of duty: Do naught unto others which would cause you pain if done to you.
Mahabharata 5:1517

Buddhism:
Hurt not others in ways that you yourself would find hurtful.
Udana-Varga 5:18

Christianity:
All things whatsoever ye would that men should do to you, do ye even so to them; for this is the law and the prophets.
Matthew 7:12

Confucianism:
Surely it is the maxim of loving-kindness: Do not unto others what you would not have them do unto you.   *Analects 15:23*

Islam:
No one of you is a believer until he desires for his brother that which he desires for himself.
Sunnah

Judaism:
What is hateful to you, do not to your fellowman. That is the entire Law; all the rest is commentary. *Talmud, Shabbat 31a*

Taoism:
Regard your neighbor's gain as your own gain and your neighbor's loss as your own loss.
T'ai Shang Kan Ying P'ien

Zoroastrianism:
That nature alone is good which refrains from doing unto another whatsoever is not good for itself. *Dadistan-i-dinik 94:5*

—courtesy Elizabeth Pool

Famous Last Words

■ **Waiting, are they? Waiting, are they? Well—let 'em wait.**
(In response to an attending doctor who attempted to comfort him by saying, "General, I fear the angels are waiting for you.")
—Ethan Allen, American Revolutionary general, d. February 12, 1789

■ **A dying man can do nothing easy.**
—Benjamin Franklin, American statesman, d. April 17, 1790

■ **Now I shall go to sleep. Good night.**
—Lord George Byron, British writer, d. April 19, 1824

■ **Is it the Fourth?**
—Thomas Jefferson, 3rd U.S. president, d. July 4, 1826

■ **Thomas Jefferson—still survives . . .**
(Actually, Jefferson had died earlier that same day.)
—John Adams, 2nd U.S. president, d. July 4, 1826

■ **Friends applaud, the comedy is finished.**
—Ludwig van Beethoven, German-Austrian composer, d. March 26, 1827

■ **Moose . . . Indian . . .**
—Henry David Thoreau, American writer, d. May 6, 1862

■ **Go on, get out—last words are for fools who haven't said enough.**
(To his housekeeper, who urged him to tell her his last words so she could write them down for posterity.)
—Karl Marx, German political philosopher, d. March 14, 1883

■ **Is it not meningitis?**
—Louisa M. Alcott, American writer, d. March 6, 1888

■ **How were the receipts today at Madison Square Garden?**
—P. T. Barnum, American entrepreneur, d. April 7, 1891

■ **Turn up the lights, I don't want to go home in the dark.**
—O. Henry (William Sidney Porter), American writer, d. June 4, 1910

■ **Get my swan costume ready.**
—Anna Pavlova, Russian ballerina, d. January 23, 1931

■ **I should never have switched from Scotch to martinis.**
—Humphrey Bogart, American actor, d. January 14, 1957

■ **Is everybody happy? I want everybody to be happy. I know I'm happy.**
—Ethel Barrymore, American actress, d. June 18, 1959

■ **I'm bored with it all.**
(Before slipping into a coma. He died nine days later.)
—Winston Churchill, British statesman, d. January 24, 1965

The Old Farmer's Almanac
GARDENER'S
COMPANION
GARDEN WISDOM FOR ALL SEASONS

THE ORIGINAL: Often Imitated, Never Equaled

THE OLD FARMER'S 2004 ALMANAC

WEATHER FORECASTS

PLANTING TABLES, ZODIAC SECRETS

CONTENTS

—photo: Michael Boys/Corbis

EDITOR'S NOTE

*S*ooner or later, every gardener needs a friend with fresh ideas and reliable planting advice.

The Old Farmer's Almanac Gardener's Companion magazine is that ever-ready friend, and this condensed version is our way of introducing you to it.

Here you'll find tips on growing mums and favorite vegetables, designing a flower garden, keeping your houseplants healthy, and much more.

These are the kind of ideas and how-to help you'll find in each 128-page, full-color issue of the *Gardener's Companion.* Whether you're growing annuals, perennials, fruits, herbs, vegetables, or landscape plants, you'll have more success with advice and hints from our experts.

☞ **Look for the Early Spring edition of *The Old Farmer's Almanac Gardener's Companion*** on your newsstand, at your local supermarket, at garden supply stores, in bookstores, or in any major retail store be-

ginning on **January 20.** Only $3.99, each copy will be polybagged with a **FREE 32-page *Garden Reference and Record Keeper*** that features gardening tips, charts, and specially designed pages to help you keep track of your plantings. **If you can't locate the *Gardener's Companion,* you can purchase a copy directly from us by phone at 800-895-9265, ext. 220, or on our Web site, www.almanac.com.**

Remember: No matter how experienced, every gardener needs a *Companion* once in a while.

GEORGIA ORCUTT
gardening@yankeepub.com

ASK THE OLD FARMER

Questions in search of answers

How and where can I store my begonia tubers? I live in southeastern Alaska, and they are planted at our cabin, where we don't spend the winter. I need to dig them up and bring them down to town, but we live in a condo and I have no place to store them. How about in the trunk of my car in a gunnysack? How cold a temperature can they tolerate? Our garage is not heated.

–Susan Perry

■ They won't survive if they freeze, so you need to find a place to store them indoors. Under the kitchen sink? The back of a closet? Ideally, you should store them at about 50°F. Alternatively, you could pot them up and treat them as houseplants until you can plant them outdoors. They won't bloom, but they will survive.

I have gooseneck gourds in my garden. When can I pick them? The gourds are green, and the vines (which are also green) are starting to die back.

–Angela Whitcomb

■ Pick your gourds when the vines turn brown, and do it before frost hits, or they will get mushy. To keep the gourds from molding, dip them into a bleach solution (1 part bleach to 10 parts water) and then store them in a warm, dry location with good air circulation. They are dry when you can hear the seeds rattle.

SEED SEARCH

■ In the fall 2002 issue of the *Gardener's Companion,* there was a report about stevia, which mentioned growing it from seeds. I have inquired high and low about this plant and have priced it at around $10. I grow many plants from seeds and would love to know where I could purchase stevia seeds, not the plant.

–Val Smatko, Williamston, South Carolina

EDITOR'S NOTE: Fresh or dried, stevia (shown above) is 300 times sweeter than sugar and is catching on as a great alternative. Johnny's Selected Seeds in Winslow, Maine, sells the seeds: A packet of 25 costs $3.50. Call 207-861-3901 or order on-line at www.johnny seeds.com. You can also try our Seed Swap page at www.almanac.com/swap. □□

–photo: Johnny's Selected Seeds

When I saw what Royal Jelly did for me and my son, I started my own company!

For years, Madeline Balletta felt so tired... at times, so exhausted... that she felt unable to properly care for her family. Then, she was introduced to a natural substance called Royal Jelly, and she combined it with a nutritious diet. Amazed by her improvement, she gave Royal Jelly to her young son, Jason. When she saw how Royal Jelly helped to energize his life, she had to share the news with others... and Bee-Alive was born!

If you're interested in feeling better and living a vibrant, healthy lifestyle, I am living testimony that there is a way! For those who knew me way back when, they are amazed at the hectic schedule I now keep. Appearing on radio and TV nationwide, I always extol the benefits of good nutrition and Bee-Alive Royal Jelly. It's a joy to share my knowledge of this remarkable food substance that enhances health and vitality! And at Bee-Alive, we truly care about you. That's why our products cannot be found in any stores. Our toll-free number connects you with your own caring, personal consultant. And our customers... well... they soon become our friends!

Who will benefit from Bee-Alive Royal Jelly?

Tens of thousands of people use Royal Jelly every day. The elderly report being more active, athletes appreciate the competitive edge, as do those people who wish to acquire more physical and mental stamina.

What is Royal Jelly?

Royal Jelly is not honey or pollen. It is actually the food of the Queen Bee, and her long life span is a result of her diet. She lives up to six years on an exclusive diet of Royal Jelly. Worker bees, who eat only honey and pollen, live up to six weeks! And this remarkable substance, so precious and rare, cannot be duplicated in any lab, but comes directly from God's own pharmacy... nature.

Our Royal Jelly is unique.

I believe Bee-Alive is the only company in the U.S. that has pure, non-freeze dried Royal Jelly in capsule form. It's so potent and effective because we keep it as close to nature as possible. And we don't stop there – we stamp an expiration date on every package, guaranteeing you the freshest product possible!

Listen to what this nurse says about Bee-Alive!

"I was so tired that I'd given up hope. After improving my diet and taking Bee-Alive, people now comment on my glowing smile and increased energy. Today, I'm a better nurse, wife, mom and grandma!"

–SHARON GIGL, NURSE, TX

Just as it has improved my life and the lives of thousands of others, I hope it will improve yours, too.

Call Bee-Alive today 1-866-783-6877 and get a FREE GIFT valued at over $30.00 with your first order of Royal Jelly. We're waiting to help you change your life!

Madeline

MADELINE BALLETTA
President & Founder, Bee-Alive, Inc.

P.S. I promise you'll see a difference within 3 months, or I'll happily refund your purchase price.

PLANT AN
*H*eirloom Flower Garden

Get back to the good old days.

by Nancy J. Ondra

W HAT'S EVEN BETTER THAN A GARDEN FILLED with beautiful flowers? A garden full of great stories! When you grow heirloom flowers, you create a living history lesson—an exciting world of people and places, lore and legends. There's no set definition, but in general, an heirloom or antique flower is one that was cultivated at least 50 years ago.

You may decide to plan a single border—or even your whole yard—around the time period when your home was built, or in the style it reflects. Or perhaps you'd enjoy a planting from an era that you find especially interesting, such as a colorful Victorian bedding scheme of cannas and coleuses, a flower-filled English cottage garden, or a medieval garden with medicinal, culinary, and dyeing herbs.

Romance Made Real

■ HEIRLOOM FLOWERS HAVE BEEN GROWN IN MANY different places by many generations of gardeners, and they come with a wealth of fun and fanciful common and variety names, such as kiss-me-over-the-garden-gate, poor-man's weather glass, and ragged robin. Plants that are named after people, like 'Grandpa Ott's' morning glories, 'Nelly Moser' clematis, and 'Madame Isaac Pereire' roses, bring a personal touch to the history lesson. It's fascinating to read up on how

–photos: 1, 4, 7, 9, W. Atlee Burpee & Co.;
2, 6, Select Seeds; 3, 5, 8, Johnny's Selected Seeds

1

2 **3**

9

5   **4**

8   **5**

7

A FOUR-SQUARE DESIGN

This 18x18-foot-square garden contains four separate beds, each approximately 6x6 feet. Each section contains a variety of old-fashioned favorites that will supply you with flowers throughout the growing season. The center three-foot-square diamond can be planted as shown or be used to showcase your own favorites. A gated fence, enclosing the entire garden, lends a traditional feeling to the overall design.

6

these flowers got their names and about the gardeners who grew and cherished them so many years ago.

Old-time plants also have practical benefits for today's gardens. Many heirloom cultivars are taller than their modern counterparts, and their longer stems make them much more useful as cut flowers in arrangements and bouquets. Antique flowers may also have wonderful perfumes that were lost as the plants were bred and selected for bigger or more colorful blooms instead; sweet peas are a perfect example. And because the old-fashioned favorites don't rely on careful crossbreeding by hybridizers, you won't need to buy new seeds each spring; simply save them from your own plants from year to year.

It's Hip to Be Square

■ If you'd like to try an heirloom flower garden and don't have a particular style in mind, a four-square design is a great place to start. This classic pattern fits with a wide range of time periods. A four-square is also simple to lay out, plant, and maintain, because the cross paths make it easy to reach all sides of the beds. You can create a formal effect by using the same plants in each of the squares to emphasize the symmetrical pattern, or make a casual country look by filling the beds with a wide variety of plants. If you leave one square unplanted, you have a perfect spot for a picnic table or for a comfortable garden seat to relax in.

Four-square gardens are traditionally enclosed with some kind of fence or wall, with an entry gate on one side. A picket fence is a classic choice and works well with a wide range of planting styles. Leave it unfinished for a Colonial feel, paint it white for a charming country look, or use your favorite color to give it a personal touch. An arbor makes a wonderful accent for the entry gate and a perfect support for a romantic climbing rose, a fragrant honeysuckle, or a colorful annual vine.

When you combine the easy-care layout of a four-square with your favorite antique flowers, you'll create more than a gorgeous garden: You'll celebrate your link to generations of other gardeners who have gone before you.

Nancy J. Ondra gardens in Pennsylvania. A freelance garden writer and editor, she is the author or co-author of seven books, including *Grasses: Versatile Partners for Uncommon Garden Design* (Storey Books, 2002).

–photos: 10, 15, Select Seeds; 11, 13, 16, W. Atlee Burpee & Co.;
12, 14, 17, Johnny's Selected Seeds

10
11
12
13
14
15
16
17

Modern gardeners with a hankering for historical plants have plenty of resources to turn to. For more inspiration, check these books: Heirloom Flowers, *by Tovah Martin (Fireside, 1999), and* The Southern Heirloom Garden, *by William C. Welch and Greg Grant (Taylor Publishing Company, 1995). For plants and seeds, here are three nurseries that offer extensive selections:*

W. Atlee Burpee & Co.
300 Park Ave.
Warminster, PA 18974
800-888-1447
www.burpee.com
Catalog free.

Johnny's Selected Seeds
955 Benton Ave.
Winslow, ME 04901
207-861-3901
www.johnnyseeds.com
Catalog free.

Select Seeds
180 Stickney Hill Rd.
Union, CT 06076
860-684-9310
www.selectseeds.com
Catalog free.

OFF TO A G

BEANS. Wait until the soil is 60°F before planting bean seeds. When it's warm enough, turn over the soil with a spading fork so that it's nice and loose to a depth of eight inches, and mix in some compost. Plant seeds an inch deep, and as they grow, thin to two inches apart.

CORN. Plant corn seeds one inch deep if the soil is wet, and two inches deep if it isn't. To help seeds germinate, stretch plastic wrap all along the top of the furrow, and anchor it with stones or boards. Remove it as soon as you see plants emerge.

CUCUMBERS. Start cucumber seeds indoors to get a jump on the season. They love bottom heat and temperatures around 70°F. Put planted seeds on top of the refrigerator or perch them atop the water heater to take advantage of extra warmth. When seeds sprout, move plants to a sunny spot.

LETTUCE. Plant a fall crop of lettuce in August to extend your gardening season. Cool down hot soil by moistening the ground and covering it with a bound bale of straw. Let the bale sit for a week, and then remove it and plant a three-foot row of seeds in the cooled soil. Move the bale around as necessary to cool more soil until you've planted as much lettuce as you need.

PEAS. Prepare pea-planting beds in the fall for a head start. Turn over the soil, add manure, and mulch well. When you're ready to plant in the early spring, pull back the mulch and make holes with a dibble, if necessary, to get your seeds into the ground. A blanket of snow won't hurt emerging pea plants, but several days with freezing temperatures could. You can add more seeds later if you discover spaces where some don't germinate.

PEPPERS. Start pepper seeds indoors by planting three in every pot. As soon as the second set of leaves emerges on the seedlings, thin out the weakest one in each pot, leaving the other two. Keep these pairs together and treat them as if they were one plant when you transplant them into your garden.

P L A N T I N G   V E G E T A B L E S .

OOD START

They will help support one another, and the combined foliage helps protect fruits from sunscald.

POTATOES. Plant seed potatoes about a week before your last expected frost date. Put them 12 inches apart in a trench, and cover with four inches of soil. When plant stems are about eight inches high, fill in the trench with more soil, leaving about four inches of the plant exposed.

PUMPKINS. Sow some of your pumpkin seeds a few days before your last expected frost date. Ten days later, when sprouts begin to appear, sow a second row about six inches from the first. If a late killing frost arrives, you can depend on the second crop. If it doesn't, pull out the second planting as if it were weeds.

RADISHES. Mix tiny radish seeds with sand to space them out as you sow them. Be brutal and thin radish seedlings to at least one inch apart as soon as they emerge. This will give you a surprisingly good crop.

TOMATOES. Transplant tomato seedlings into the garden in deep holes, so that the first set of true leaves rests right on the soil surface. Roots will form along the underground stem portion and create a sturdier plant.

SQUASH. Wait until all danger of frost has passed before you plant squash seeds in the garden. Squash plants hate cold weather. Leave a lot of room between plants—it's hard to imagine that they will grow as rampantly as they do. Plant seeds about an inch deep in hills three feet apart and in rows three to five feet apart, so you can get through to harvest them.

SWEET POTATOES. Grow this southern favorite in the north by making a row of bushel baskets, filling them with rich soil, and planting one slip per basket. If an early frost threatens in the fall, simply move the baskets by wheelbarrow to a warmer spot, such as a garage, or bring them in for the night. □ □

22. Have a house in the country
23. Get promoted at work
24. Find a job which is enjoyable and pays well
25. Find true love at last
26. Be madly loved by someone
27. Marry the person I love
28. Attract men
29. Attract women
30. Be on TV
31. Make new friends
32. Solve my financial problems once and for all
33. Be able to stop working with a substantial monthly income

So that's it! Have you chosen your 7 wishes? Then quickly complete the original of the Form below and return it without delay to Maria Duval.

SPECIAL FORM FOR FULFILLING YOUR WISHES

Complete and return as soon as possible (by this evening, if possible) to:
Maria Duval, 11064 Queens Blvd. # 460, Forest Hills, NY 11375-6347

YES, my dear Maria Duval, I accept your offer with pleasure. I would like you to try and realize the 7 Secret Wishes which I have indicated below FOR ME, FREE OF CHARGE.

I understand that I'll never be asked for any money in return for the realization of my 7 Secret Wishes, neither now nor later.

Subject to this condition, please see below the 7 Wishes I'd most like to see coming true in my life:

Indicate here the number corresponding to the 7 Wishes you'd most like to see coming true in your life (no more than 7):

I have chosen wish No. 4, so the amount I'd like to win is: $_____

In a few days' time, you are going to receive a large white envelope containing your secret instructions. Read them carefully, and expect to see some big changes taking place in your life after a few days.

IMPORTANT NOTICE – Answer the following *confidential* questionnaire:

1. Do you have any financial problems? ☐ yes ☐ no
   How much money do you urgently need?
   $_____

2. Are you unlucky (do you feel like you're born under a bad star)? ☐ yes ☐ no

3. Are you working? ☐ yes ☐ no
   Are you retired? ☐ yes ☐ no

4. Are you married or do you have a spouse? ☐ yes ☐ no

5. Are there major problems in your love or family life? ☐ yes ☐ no

6. Do you feel lonely or misunderstood? ☐ yes ☐ no

7. Do you feel as if a spell has been cast on you, like someone has sent bad luck your way? ☐ yes ☐ no

IMPORTANT – Please write below, in a few words, the question that disturbs you the most (IN CAPITALS):

_____
_____
_____

Age: I am ___ years old   Date of birth: _____
Hour of birth: _____/_____ ☐ AM
(if you know it):   Hour   Minute   ☐ PM
Place of Birth: City/ Town: _____
State/Province: _____ Country: _____
I confirm my astrological sign is: _____
(IN CAPITALS) ☐ Ms. ☐ Miss ☐ Mrs. ☐ Mr.
FIRST NAME _____
LAST NAME _____
ADDRESS _____
_____
TOWN/CITY _____ STATE _____
ZIP _____ AQSN
Email address: _____

Mum's
THE WORD

Great choices for cold climates and all-around beauty.

by Evelyn Weibye

N othing salutes the fall season better than chrysanthemums. Their amber, gold, pink, plum, rust, and burnt-red colors brighten sleepy perennial beds and grace porches and centerpieces along with gourds and pumpkins. Southerners enjoy the colorful displays twice yearly, because the equal days and nights of temperate weather that spur mums to bloom arrive in spring and fall. Northerners don't have that luxury, so their golden days of autumn are when gardeners look forward to the vast beauty and variety of chrysanthemums. It's why breeders focus on plants that start blooming in late August and continue into November.

(c o n t i n u e d)

Exotic mums, such as this delicate spider mum, are not grown to be hardy, but are prized for their exquisite form and size.

−Bill Whelan/Index Stock

Why Hardiness Matters

Most chrysanthemum plants purchased at garden centers are hardy, meaning that they are perennials in most climates. However, if these plants are put in the ground from August on, most won't make it through the winter in areas where temperatures dip into the single digits. The reason is that mums planted late in the season are near the flowering stage, and they don't grow roots to sustain the plants through the winter. All the energy is put into blooming. So wait until spring to plant potted mums outdoors. Look for six-packs of them and four-inch pots in the perennials section of your favorite nursery.

Gardeners in northern states and the Canadian provinces, where winter temperatures are often below zero, lose even spring-planted hardy mums to the cold. Mulching helps to preserve root systems, but the bitter cold is too much for many varieties. In response, the University of Minnesota started breeding subzero, extra-hardy mums about 70 years ago. To date, they have developed 76 garden-mum varieties, including their newest, 'Sesqui Centennial Sun'. The university also has developed a special extra-hardy series, My Favorite Perennial Mums, which is marketed commercially by Anthony Tesselaar International to garden centers worldwide. These plants survive temperatures down to −30°F, don't require pinching, and grow to be huge mounds. All hardy and extra-hardy mums do well in temperate and hot climates, too.

–Netherlands Flower Bulb Information Center

'Autumn Red'

'Cherub'

'Angel'

'Autumn Eyes'

(continued)

'Frosty Morn'

'Fantasy'

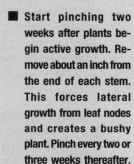

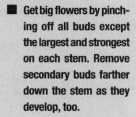

THE SECRETS OF PINCHING

Here's how to keep plants shapely and encourage budding:

■ Start pinching two weeks after plants begin active growth. Remove about an inch from the end of each stem. This forces lateral growth from leaf nodes and creates a bushy plant. Pinch every two or three weeks thereafter.

■ Use July 20 as a good guideline in most of the country for when to stop pinching plants, according to Yoder Brothers, the biggest chrysanthemum producer in North America. In the South, gardeners can pinch up to August 1. Coastal California and Pacific Northwest gardeners should stop earlier, by July 4, the mum grower suggests. After these dates, there is not enough time for new growth to set flower buds.

■ Get big flowers by pinching off all buds except the largest and strongest on each stem. Remove secondary buds farther down the stem as they develop, too.

GROWING TIPS

■ Don't cut back dead foliage on plants in the fall. A University of Iowa study found that unpruned plants survive winter better. For more protection, add four to six inches of mulch after the ground has frozen.

■ Feed mums a steady diet of a balanced fertilizer, as they are heavy feeders. To produce big flowers, switch to a high-nitrogen food after buds have set. If flower size is not a concern, stop feeding plants after August 15.

■ Divide plants every spring a couple weeks after the last killing frost, setting divisions 18 to 24 inches apart. Chrysanthemums seldom produce as good a flower quality in the second year as they did in the first because roots become too crowded.

■ Plant mums in a dark area of the garden, or shade them every night from light sources such as street and security lights. Bloom time is determined by day length (12 hours or less), and buds start forming then. Plants that receive light at night will be slow to bud.

Nonhardy Mums

Potted mums from the florist or grocery store and exotics like the huge football chrysanthemums, delicate spiders, and quills don't survive cold winters and are best grown in greenhouses. They are not bred to be hardy; it's their form, color, and size that are prized. Exhibition types, too, are tender. They have been raised to have long stems and huge flowers and are generally sold as cut flowers or exotic potted plants. If your winter is warm, these plants will probably survive in the garden. Otherwise, it's best to start with fresh plants every spring. Several mail-order nurseries specialize in these types, and starter plants can be ordered for less than $2 each.

(c o n t i n u e d)

–King's Mums

'Purple Lucky Time'

Are you losing your hair?
There's good news...

Clinically proven hair restoration system is so effective, it is awarded U.S. patent!

See dramatic results in your first month of use!

Powerful New Formula Stops Hair Loss _and_ Re-Grows New Hair!

It is commonly known that the major cause of hair loss is due to the buildup of the "bad hormone" Dihydrotestosterone (DHT). Clinical trials prove that when used together, the powerful ingredients in Prolific™ prevent the buildup of DHT, stopping your hair loss and allowing your follicles to strengthen and reproduce strong healthy hairs. We are proud to announce that after years of clinical research and testing, Prolific's™ scientifically advanced formula is now available to the general public. This highly effective formula is so advanced it has even been awarded a U.S. patent number. (Reference U.S. Patent number 5,972,345)

Stop worrying about your hair loss, Do something about it!

If you fear that your thinning hair will eventually leave you bald or you are tired of watching your hairline recede, you can stop worrying! Get Prolific™ and take action. This patented formula will stop your hair from falling out and even grow back the hair you've lost, guaranteed! Now for a limited time you can try Prolific™ absolutely risk-free for 90 days. Call now for more information and be sure to mention offer #903.

Works great for both men and women!

Gentlemen and Ladies...We are proud to say that Prolific™ is specially formulated to work for both men and women and is now available to you without a prescription. Don't wait any longer. Prolific™ is safe, highly effective and best of all it only takes a few seconds a day to use.

Now you can try Prolific™ absolutely risk-free!

You don't have to live with thinning hair! Now you can try Prolific™ absolutely risk-free for 90 days! Put this revolutionary formula to work for you. Take action and call now! Get back your youthful hairline with ease and confidence! Call now, toll-free 1-800-519-7871, offer #903. Get Prolific™ and get ready to look younger and feel great!

Get back your thick, healthy hair _and keep it!_

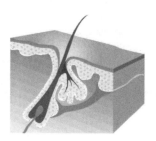

Call now for your 90-day risk-free trial
1-800-519-7871 Offer #903

MUMS FOR COLD CLIMATES

'Lemonsota'

'Betty Lou'

'Grape Glow'

–photos: Mums from Minnesota

'Apricot Alexis'

–King's Mums

Saving a Mum

If winters are too cold for a favorite, or you didn't plant them early enough, chrysanthemums can overwinter in the basement or a dark, cold closet. Pot up plants after the first frost in the fall, including as much root system as possible. Water well and place in an area where it is totally dark and the temperature ranges between 32° and 50°F. The plants will hibernate for the winter if you keep their roots damp. Check pots weekly. In the spring, gradually accli-mate plants to light, and set them out in the garden after the last killing frost.

Mail-Order Sources

Evelyn Weibye is a freelance writer who has grown mums for years in the Midwest.

ALL ABOUT HOUSEPLANTS

How to keep an indoor garden at its best.

by Doreen G. Howard

Houseplants are hot. Perhaps it's our nostalgia for everything '70s, including the earth tones and masses of potted plants that defined interior decorating of that decade. Or maybe it's the natural progression to the indoors of container plants that are this millennium's new flower gardens.

Houseplants never went out of fashion for me. My college dorm room was a jungle of green fronds, vines, and tendrils. In the many homes I've occupied as an adult, I've always been greeted by towering palms and ivy cascades. Potted primroses bloomed brightly above the kitchen sink in the dead of winter. In fact, I've rented trucks to move plants in my 25-year migration from California eastward,

and north from the Texas Gulf Coast to the Canadian border. Along the way, I've learned quite a few things about houseplants. The best hints, gleaned from experience, follow.

Bring Home a Healthy Plant

Some houseplants are destined to die, because they arrive at your home with incurable problems. They can even infect other plants.

■ **Pass up plants with foliage that is yellowed** or limp or has soft, discolored spots. All are indications of disease or root damage. Also, leave behind plants with tiny dots on their leaf undersides, which indicate insect infestations.

■ **Avoid plants that look like they have been** pruned. Store personnel may have cut off diseased or damaged parts.

■ **Slip the plant out of its pot to inspect the** roots, if possible. If they are dark brown, black, or mushy, the plant has been overwatered and probably will die. Look for whitish, plump, firm roots.

■ **Seek plants with new shoots, buds, and** leaves. This is a sign of active growth and health. Vivid hues are signs of health on colored foliage plants. Pick a small plant over a lanky, overgrown one. (c o n t i n u e d)

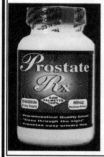

What's Wrong with My Houseplants?

	SYMPTOM	CAUSE	CURE
	Long, pale leaves; small new leaves	Not enough light; too much nitrogen	Give plant more light; reduce fertilizer frequency
	Leaves curl under or have yellow or brown spots	Too much light	Move plant away from light source, or shade plant with blinds or sheer curtain
	Mushy stems; lower leaves curl and wilt	Too much water	Water only when soil is dry to touch; make sure drain hole is not clogged
	Leaf tips are brown and leaves wilt	Not enough water	Soak pot for 20 minutes and let drain; water when soil is dry to touch
	Leaf edges are crinkly and brown	Lack of humidity	Mist leaves, or place on tray of moist pebbles
	Lower leaves turn pale and drop off	Lack of fertilizer	Fertilize plant regularly during growing season
	Leaves turn yellow or curl and wilt	Too much heat	Move plant to cooler spot in house; be sure plant is not close to heat vent or on top of TV
	Plant wilts between waterings; roots growing out of drainage hole	Pot too small	Repot plant into a container one size larger

–courtesy Hermann Engelmann

–illustrated by Kathleen McKeehen

(continued)

Pots and Soil

Pay attention to your houseplants as they grow. Don't be afraid to move them to larger pots.

■ **Repot plants before they become** pot-bound. If water runs through pots rapidly and growth has slowed down or stopped (except when it does so naturally in winter), chances are that they need a bigger pot.

■ **Do not increase the container size** when repotting in the fall, but stay with the same-size pot. Growth slows or stops in reduced winter light, and the extra soil in a larger container will retain more water, which can cause root rot.

■ **Repot your purchases with any** commercial potting mix. Or use a specialty mix formulated for cactuses (good for succulents and bromeliads, too) or African violets. Most growers use the lightest-weight potting media they can find to save on shipping costs. The mix is not the best for maintaining a healthy plant.

Ongoing Care and Feeding

Keep an eye on your houseplants as you go through your day. Watch for signs that they need water or fertilizer.

■ **Determine if a plant needs watering** by this easy method: Push your index finger into the soil up to the second joint. If your fingertip detects dry soil, water the plant.

■ **Use room-temperature water. If** water is too chilly, it can shock the root system. Also, if your household water is run through a water softener, use bottled water for plants. Salts in treated water build up rapidly in the soil and affect plant health adversely.

■ **Put a thermometer among the plants** to monitor temperature conditions. Plants need a five- to ten-degree drop in temperature at night so that they can build new tissues from the food they manufacture during the day. The ideal range is from 75°F during the day to 60°F at night. A sunny window can reach 90°F even on a winter day. Use a small fan to cool the area, or move plants a few feet away from the glass.

■ **Clean plant leaves once a month** so that their surface openings (stomata) stay open and exchange oxygen and CO_2 efficiently. A soft cloth (an old T-shirt works great) moistened with warm water does the job well. Don't use "leaf shine" or "luster" products; they clog stomata and attract dust.

■ **Stop fertilizing during winter months** when light is less intense and plants create reduced amounts of new tissue. Don't feed plants from October 1 until Valentine's Day. Start again with weekly doses of water-soluble fertilizer. Use fertilizer at half strength for the first two weeks, and then resume full-strength feeding on a weekly basis until late September. ☐☐

Doreen G. Howard lives with banana plants, Norfolk pines, bromeliads, and orchids in her Wisconsin home.

The Science *of* Appearances

Successful farmers in the old days were adept at watching natural indicators to know when to plant their seeds. This science of appearances, called phenology, has given rise to a few planting "rules." See if these hold true in your own backyard.

Insect Watch

Mexican bean beetle larvae appear when foxglove flowers open.

Grasshopper eggs hatch when lilacs bloom.

Planting Time

■ Plant **corn** when elm leaves are the size of a squirrel's ear, when oak leaves are the size of a mouse's ear, when apple blossoms begin to fall, or when the dogwoods are in full bloom.

■ Plant **lettuce, spinach, peas,** and other cool-weather varieties when the lilacs show their first leaves or when daffodils begin to bloom.

■ Plant **cucumbers** and **squashes** when lilac flowers fade.

■ Plant **tomatoes, early corn,** and **peppers** when flowering dogwood is in peak bloom or when daylilies start to bloom.

■ Plant **perennials** when maple leaves begin to unfurl.

■ Plant **morning glories** when maple trees have full-size leaves.

■ Plant **pansies, snap-dragons,** and other hardy annuals after the aspen and chokecherry trees leaf out.

■ Plant **beets** and **carrots** when dandelions are blooming.

Expect crabgrass seed to germinate when forsythias are in bloom.

Make This the Beginning of Your Best Garden Ever!

I f you enjoyed this sample, you'll love the 128-page, full-color Early Spring *Gardener's Companion*.

STILL ONLY $3.99!

IN EVERY ISSUE: • gardening advice for beginners • easy-to-follow planting and growing tips • news from experts on flowers, vegetables, and landscaping.

PLUS, the Early Spring issue features great articles on: • the best roses for small spaces • vegetable tips • success with mints • choosing shrubs • growing the best apples

BONUS:

This issue also includes a **FREE** 32-page *Old Farmer's Almanac Garden Reference and Record Keeper*, just in time for you to start planning your beds and borders.

Look for the **Early Spring** issue of *The Old Farmer's Almanac Gardener's Companion* on your newsstand, in your local supermarket, in garden-supply stores, in bookstores, or in any major retail store beginning on January 20. You can also purchase a copy directly from us by phone at **800-895-9265**, ext. 220, or at our Web site, **www.almanac.com**. $1.95 will be added to cover our costs for postage and handling ($5.94 total).

Fund-Raising with The Old Farmer's Almanac General Store

T he **Old Farmer's Almanac** has created an exciting fund-raising program that offers your nonprofit group a great profit percentage and a chance to enjoy some of New England's finest products. This exclusive program offers gift items that are unique, of the highest quality, and in a range of prices that fits all budgets.

- *The Old Farmer's Almanac* and YANKEE Magazine
- Stonewall Kitchen® Jams
- Organic Trail Mix and Cereal Bars
- Badger® Balms
- Droll Yankees® Bird Feeders
- Yankee Candles®
- Vermont Gold Grilling Sauces

Contact **GBI Marketing,** exclusive distributors of **The Old Farmer's Almanac General Store Fund-Raising Program,** at **1-800-424-6906,** or visit our Web site at **www.gbimarketing.com** or The Old Farmer's Almanac Web site at **www.almanac.com** for more information. Available **only** in the continental United States.